PROFESSIONAL EDUCATION SERVICES, LP
The Professional's Choice for Quality CPE

8303 Sierra College Blvd., Suite 146
Roseville, CA 95661

Order: 1-800-998-5024
Customer Service: 1-800-990-2731
Fax: (916) 791-4099

THE
PORTABLE MBA

The Portable MBA Series

THE
PORTABLE MBA

Third Edition

Robert F. Bruner
Mark R. Eaker
R. Edward Freeman
Robert E. Spekman
Elizabeth Olmsted Teisberg

John Wiley & Sons, Inc.
New York • Chichester • Weinheim • Brisbane • Singapore • Toronto

To our children,
Who bring joy to our lives and balance to our work.

Jonathan Edward Bruner
Alexander Williamson Bruner

Noah Hamilton Eaker
Adam Samuel Eaker

Benjamin Wellen Freeman
Emma Wellen Freeman
Molly Wellen Freeman

Marit Rachael Spekman
Alyssa Haynes Spekman

Thomas Olmsted Teisberg
Tyler Olmsted Teisberg

This text is printed on acid-free paper.

Copyright © 1998 by Robert F. Bruner, Mark R. Eaker, R. Edward Freeman,
Robert E. Spekman and Elizabeth Olmsted Teisberg.
Published by John Wiley & Sons, Inc.

Library of Congress Cataloging-in-Publication Data:

The portable MBA / Robert F. Bruner . . . [et al.]. — 3rd ed.
     p.   cm. — (The Portable MBA series)
    Includes index.
    ISBN 0-471-18093-9 (alk. paper)
    1. Industrial management. I. Bruner, Robert F. II. Series.
HD31.E795 1998   97-17566
  658—dc21   CIP

Printed in the United States of America

10 9 8 7 6 5 4 3 2

CONTENTS

PART II: THE FUNCTIONS OF BUSINESS

PART III: NEW HORIZONS

PREFACE

As we begin this new edition of *The Portable MBA*, it makes sense to declare at the outset that all of the authors are faculty at the Darden Graduate School of Business Administration at the University of Virginia. This statement is important because it truly sets the tone of the book. There are three characteristics that distinguish the Darden School, and these characteristics are basic to the premise upon which this new edition was conceived and written.

First, Darden has as its dual mission the education of MBA students and practicing managers. One of the hallmarks of the Darden School is its dedication to student-centered learning and our faculty's willingness to devote a great deal of time and energy to thinking about curriculum and its relevance to practicing managers. Among our criteria in designing the MBA curriculum are relevance and the need to develop in our students the ability to make credible business decisions based on the facts at hand. It is in this same spirit we set out to revise *The Portable MBA*.

Second, our faculty are not housed in functional departments; instead, we take the perspective of the general manager and view problems from an integrated, enterprise level of analysis. Our objective is to help students appreciate the impact of a single functional unit's decision on the rest of the organization. We emphasize throughout this new edition the need for cross-functional thinking and the problems inherent in a *functional silo* approach to business decision making. We believe that such cross-functional thinking is pervasive throughout this edition. Business functions, such as finance and marketing, are couched within a broader context and are tied to enterprise problems/opportunities. To treat each discipline in isolation is to mask the true "business of business."

Third, we approached this project with the same spirit of teamwork we try to instill in our students. As a case method school, we believe that teamwork and shared problem solving lead not only to better answers, but this approach helps to better prepare our MBAs for the challenges that lie ahead after graduation. One goal was to create a forum in which we could learn from each other and bring the functional expertise we all have into a tighter, more integrated enterprise perspective.

The team of authors share another common bond in that we created a unique executive experience, the Darden Partnerships Program (DPP), which has graduated several hundred senior middle managers. DPP is a consortium program composed of 10 noncompeting companies that attempt to understand better business transformation and the changes required to lead in these turbulent times. DPP is driven by our desire to create a unique learning experience—it is this same motivation that drives this edition of *The Portable MBA*.

Chapter 14, "Leading from the Middle," is one outcome of our commitment to DPP and our interest in understanding more about business transformation. Through both our consulting and MBA and executive teaching and our case writing and scholarly research we are struck by the profound changes affecting corporations independent of their type of business. For example, telecommunications, electric utilities, steel, and banking all share similar concerns regarding how they will compete in today's turbulent world. It is simple to say that the rate of change is faster than we've witnessed in the past and that old tried-and-true rules are less likely to apply. This statement is not very useful unless we also provide a framework through which individuals can better manage change and orchestrate the appropriate organizational response. *The Portable MBA* is our attempt to provide such a framework.

As you read the chapters that follow, keep in mind that at the core of this book lie three related principles that served as guides throughout the development of this book: relevance, an integration of functional thinking, and an enterprise-wide perspective. Chapters 1 and 2 introduce the book, discussing the common themes that underlie our approach and addressing the challenges facing managers as we enter the twenty-first century. Chapters 3 through 6 discuss some of the underlying concepts that cross functional lines and responsibility and provide a foundation and guide for functional problem solving. Note, for example, that we treat an understanding of business ethics on par with an understanding of economics. Chapters 7 through 13 address each of the functional areas, ranging from accounting to operations. Technology is viewed as an enabler of strategy rather than as an opportunity to discuss recent changes in information technology per se. In addition, strategy is presented as a vehicle to more overtly show the need to link functional views into an enterprise perspective.

The final section of the book can be considered capstone material that highlights the challenges facing the twenty-first century manager. Global trade and understanding international investment is key to business survival. Capital knows no national boundaries and flows freely to deserving investments, which changes the face of competition in virtually every market. To compete effectively no doubt requires funds, but also in a number of cases requires a partner. Product life cycles are getting shorter; development is too costly; access to markets and technology require both speed and acumen that often lie outside of one firm's competencies. Knowledge of and facility with the tools of alliance formation and management are essential business skills. Finally, over the last decade or so, corporations have been downsized and reengineered to reduce costs and improve processes. Middle managers have felt the brunt of these changes in the social contract with their employers. Leading from the middle offers a new paradigm for managing in periods of turbulence and rapid change.

We have not provided a formula for managing the challenges that lie ahead. To do so would be a risky proposition, as there is no one right path to success. We have, however, provided insight into the management tools, concepts, and frameworks with which you can better understand the scope and significance of the business opportunities that lie ahead. Good luck, and may you live in interesting times!

PART I

What Is Business About?

In Chapter 1, "What Is Business?," we cover the basics, beginning with a brief introduction to the nature of business, its scope, and the premises upon which the remaining chapters are built. Chapter 2, "The Future," deals with planning for the future and assumes that change is constant. Scenario planning is offered as one tool for managing change, as it provides a framework for managers to plan for and anticipate the effects of future events. Chapters 3 ("Managing People") and 4 ("Business Ethics") emphasize the fact that business is truly about managing people and stress the importance of dealing with all constituents and stakeholders in an honest and fair manner. When all is said and done, a business is as successful as its people are; they are its greatest asset. Business ethics is viewed as an essential ingredient in understanding the role of business in society as well as the relationship between the firm and its employees. Changes in the "social contract" do not give managers a license to treat people in any way other than fairly and ethically. Chapters 5 ("Making Decisions Rigorously") and 6 ("Understanding Economics") discuss fundamental tools and concepts. Statistical analysis and the ability to assess risk and make an informed decision in the absence of full information are essential managerial skills. In most decision-making situations, managers either have incomplete information or cannot afford the cost of complete information. In either case, they do not often have the luxury of collecting additional data—and managerial action must be taken. Chapter 6 discusses the language of business, the lexicon by which we understand the costs, revenues, fund flows, external economic conditions, governmental policy, and other details of financial markets that are the vital signs used to manage a business. Taken together, this section serves as the foundation for this new edition of *The Portable MBA*.

The structure for this new edition has been improved and updated to provide a solid foundation for managing change into the next century. Chapter 1 introduces the themes that frame the book. Chapter 2 adds form to the book's structure by stressing the importance of planning for the future. Chapter 3 emphasizes the contributions of employees, who are an essential ingredient in the planning process. Chapter 4, which is new to this edition, affirms that ethical business behavior is a key principle for all business activity. Chapters 5 and 6 provide analytical rigor to the book's structure by introducing the key building blocks of how to manage under conditions of uncertainty and how to understand economic principles that guide all business decisions.

1 WHAT IS BUSINESS?

In 1989 Drucker[1] talked about sharp transformations or divides that signal fundamental changes in the basic structure of society. The same theme was developed by Piore and Sabel in their book, *The Second Industrial Divide*.[2] The authors trace the development of those processes and key transformations in business that have had profound effects on society. They begin their discussions with the creation of guilds, go on to describe the industrial revolution, and end with a delineation of business activity during the first half of the twentieth century. These authors pay homage to *The Wealth of Nations* by Adam Smith as they develop the various transformations that have led to the postmodern industrial era.

It would be easy, and almost obligatory, to proceed down the same path as these authors have described and provide a similar review of business history. However, instead of serving the same wine in a new bottle, we will introduce new, exciting, dominant themes that are occurring in the rapidly changing business world of today. Our goal in this chapter is to briefly set a context for the remainder of the book and to draw attention to the challenges that face managers as they prepare to enter a new century.

These dominant themes are related, and they lay a foundation for understanding what is going on in today's business environment. By delineating these themes, we show that "business as usual" is a bankrupt concept. A number of fundamental changes are occurring that impact business and the larger society of which it is a part. These changes are reflected in the following themes. One theme is the new competition, in which a new business paradigm affects the very soul of the business enterprise. The second theme is based on a shift to a knowledge-based society and the rise of the intelligent enterprise.[3] The third and final theme refers to the rise of cooperation among firms that now compete as constellations of companies. These ecosystems[4] of firms are as strong as their weakest partner. They vie for resources and customers against other competing constellations of firms. These ecosystems redefine how managers should think about competition and competitive forces. We believe that these themes set the tone for many of the issues raised in this book. And, more important, these themes reflect basic changes in how business will be discussed and transacted into the next century.

THE NEW COMPETITION

At the core of the new competition[5] is the belief that continuous improvement will be driven by the entrepreneurial firm. Based on the Schumpeterian notion of creative destruction, these firms offer a new approach to business production and processes. Benetton, for example, is a collection of collaboratively linked smaller firms that manufacture, design, and market a line of stylish clothing based on a model first developed centuries ago by Italian lace producers. Benetton, the name most people recognize, is mainly a marketing and distribution company that relies on its alliances and cooperative relationships to design and manufacture under its label. There are many other examples of networks of companies that form virtual corporations with the sole intention of challenging the dominant paradigm by which business conducts itself. During the 1980s and 1990s a number of industries have converged and been redefined. Recognizable names like Nike, FedEx, Nucor, Calyx & Corolla, and Dell have emerged as change agents in their respective industries.

The new competition is based on four dimensions and is driven by a proactive approach to strategy whereby the competitive landscape is not taken as a given, but rather is subject to reinterpretation. Managers strive to invent the world in which they choose to compete, often by changing the rules of the game. These four dimensions are: (1) the firm, (2) the production chain, (3) the sector, and (4) the government.

The Firm

The *firm* is here defined as an entrepreneurial company, which is in contrast to the firm as portrayed by Chandler and others[6] who view the firm as a bureaucratic hierarchy. Here, the firm strives to maintain continuous improvements in support of its strategic goals. Innovation comes as a result of marginal gains in production, processes, and organization. Innovation is seen as part of the learning process, which lies at the core of the firm's values and culture. While a centralized research and development facility can engage in sea-change levels of innovation, the entrepreneurial firm survives by its ability to induce workers at all levels to participate in small, incremental attempts at continuous improvement. There is no question that inventions derived from work at Bell Labs have changed the course of history. Yet AT&T's bureaucratic structure has strained the firm's ability to sustain a competitive edge in a number of markets. To be sure, MCI's competitive spirit and entrepreneurial culture has caused senior management at AT&T many a sleepless night! Is MCI's *friends and family*™ campaign on par with the invention of the transistor? Certainly not—but MCI's relentless attempts to create innovative marketing programs has caused AT&T to lose important and costly market share in the residential long-distance market.

The Production Chain

The notion of the production chain is similar to the value chain concept in which each discrete phase of value-adding activity is traced from the acquisition of raw material to its sale and after-sale service. The traditional model presumes that these activities are all performed internally in the firm. Under the new competition, it is quite likely that firms will partner to perform value-adding activities and that through cooperation one firm can better leverage the unique skills and competencies of another firm.

In an attempt to be more price competitive, IBM has shifted some PC manufacturing responsibility downstream to its distributors. Inacom Corp., an IBM distributor, customizes the IBM PC, reduces IBM's costs, and maintains the corporate relationship. While still not as efficient as Dell, IBM has used this new value chain to market 60% of its commercial PC line. Inacom uses Skyway, a Union Pacific subsidiary, to handle its logistics as it attempts to reduce its inventory levels through more information-intensive exchanges with its outsourced logistics provider. Suddenly, we have a production chain that relies on the shared mutual goals of interdependent firms that establish a set of shared working norms. This new configuration can easily be contrasted to the vertically integrated IBM of the "big iron" days. To be sure, terms like *outsourcing* and *value chain analysis* have entered the lexicon of today's managers in a way unimagined five or ten years ago.

The Sector

The previous discussion suggests the existence of a network of firms that transcend the single firm. Now the interfirm cooperative relationships become the appropriate level of analysis. Alliances and partnerships become key success factors in a large number of industries. The business sector becomes the focal point of discussion, and interfirm relationships driven by cooperative interests become the meaningful competitive metric. A more traditional model might view such cooperative actions as cartel-like behavior. Such an interpretation would suggest that cooperation is anticompetitive and serves to stifle innovation. Under the new competition, the opposite is true, because these new organizational linkages often give rise to heightened competition and are the result of new and innovative thinking. Milliken, for example, sits at the hub of a number of interfirm networks whose immediate goal is to improve the inventory levels of the apparel industry through economic order levels and other types of just-in-time systems. This cooperation from the mill to the fabricator, retailer, and consumer removes unnecessary costs from the entire channel of distribution.

The Government

At a deeper level, the Milliken example represents a change in government policy regarding the interpretation of antitrust behavior. By focusing on a different level of analysis, concern now shifts to international trade: At stake is the survival of the U.S. textile industry as it attempts to compete against lower-cost Asian imports. Similar stories can be told about the horizontal alliances among global airlines, ocean shipping, and the various research consortia that exist in the semiconductor, specialized metals, and multimedia industries. In short, when the new competition is taken to a global context, firms do not have the luxury of a go-it-alone strategy and are likely to be severely disadvantaged if they try to do so. As we'll discuss elsewhere in the book, capital and knowledge know no company or national boundaries. Access to national resources is not sufficient to ensure success. The only sustainable means of production is knowledge! The rise of the Internet, for instance, has made information widely available in real time. Drucker[7] suggests that the function of the business enterprise is to make knowledge productive.

THE INTELLIGENT ENTERPRISE

The notion of the intelligent enterprise has a profound impact on the definition of business. Our goal is not to argue that the U.S. economy has shifted away from its manufacturing base and become a service economy. Rather, our intent is to show how a number of Quinn's points serve to reshape managers' thinking. Many of the points raised here are consistent with the new competition.

Basic Restructuring of the Economy

Basic power relationships have shifted away from those who produce to those who control information. Whether we examine Toys 'Я' Us, Wal-Mart, or Boeing, it is clear that all are driven by a need to compete through reduced cycle time. For retailers, the issue is how to reduce inventory levels so they can be responsive to changing customer tastes. To be sure, Wal-Mart tracks consumer taste along with its distribution costs with equal concern. For Boeing, the question is how to develop, FAA-certify, and sell a new generation of aircraft in the fastest possible manner without sacrificing quality and safety. For all three companies, sharing information with their partners contributes to competitive success. These linking technologies permit real-time information access and sharing that have restructured the economy. It is important to recognize that the 777 went from concept to production without the different stages of development and prototypes witnessed with the production of the 757 or the 767. Again, the airframe industry is being redefined as Boeing's constellation of firms compete against AirBus and its consortium of Pan-European aerospace companies.

Different Organizational Strategies

The notion that organization follows strategy must be complemented by the second adage that structure follows technology. Organizations have become flatter as a result of technology, and the concept of mass production as the only way to achieve low costs has become passé. In later chapters we espouse the merits of mass customization. To be sure, this new paradigm has changed the face of business forever! Again, these different structures and strategies are knowledge-based and depend on information exchanges both among function units within the firm and among different organizations. In short, command-and-control administrative systems are not effective with these new organizational forms. In addition, the strategies that emerge allow innovative relationships with customers and competitors. These new strategies are driven, in part, by the role of middle managers, as we discuss in Chapter 14, "Leading from the Middle."

Management Challenges

More and more, the distinction between manufacturing and service is fading as the two become more intertwined. The issue becomes one of understanding the full value chain, recognizing unique competencies, and identifying the skills

essential for competitive advantage. In many instances, core competencies center on an ability to use and manipulate knowledge. In addition, it is possible that
this knowledge is not resident in the firm and must be leveraged from its partners. In the health care arena, for example, a number of key business strategies
are involved in accessing information about patients for the purpose of improving total disease management. It was not long ago that drug companies fought
for market share by drug category. Now the rules have changed, information is
key, and the total cost of managing a disease is of paramount concern. A primary
challenge becomes knowing what investments need to be made in infrastructure
and people to accomplish your goals. As stated earlier, both capital and information know no boundaries—if not managed wisely, these factors of production are
fungible and move across both firm and national boundaries. A key goal for
today's senior executives is to enable managers to encourage and develop their
knowledge workers. Related to these managerial challenges are regulatory concerns affecting the nature and scope of competition, the protection of intellectual property, and global trade policies.

UNDERSTANDING BUSINESS ECOSYSTEMS

Moore[8] uses the biological metaphor of looking at business relationships as an
ecosystem to examine a new paradigm for understanding competition and the
effects of competitive forces. Rather than focus on downsizing and cost reduction as the default response to a hostile business environment, managers should
attempt to create market opportunities. These opportunities often come through
innovation and a new way of viewing the marketplace—seeing the market from
the perspective of those who can change the competitive terrain. Often, change
comes by working more closely with customers and suppliers to jointly create the
future. Even the term *industry* might be obsolete in that it presumes an easily
delineated business area in which a fixed set of firms compete. You need only
look to the convergence of voice, data, and video technologies to appreciate the
difficulty in defining the scope of competition in this burgeoning industry. Partners compete with partners in one part of the market and cooperate in other
parts; ventures are started and disbanded at a moment's notice; the technology
changes daily. There is an element of complexity reflected here that is unparalleled in recent business history. Survival is based on an ability to transform and
adapt to new business conditions—similar to evolution in the biological arena.

The business ecosystem evolves from conversations with suppliers and customers and is not limited to more traditional analyses that compare competitors
head-to-head regarding their skills and competencies. The objective here is to

cast a wide intellectual net and see where it is possible to change the rules of engagement and to develop a sustainable value proposition at the same time.

IMPLICATIONS

As we reach the end of the century, it is clear that the criteria that defined business in the early part of the century are less relevant. We have in the present generation of managers witnessed changes in how firms are managed and how they are defined. Terms like *economic value added* (EVA), *brand equity,* and the *lifetime value of a customer* have changed the metric by which firms are evaluated. Exhibit 1.1 compares the market value of both Bethlehem Steel and Nucor. You can infer from this exhibit that Wall Street's perception of the value inherent in integrated steel mills has decreased over time. In the early part of this century, vertical integration was a sign of market strength and dominance. Chrysler has, in effect, become an assembler and marketer of automobiles, while of the Big Three, GM is still the most vertically integrated. Chrysler, on a percentage basis, has in recent years shown higher profit levels than GM.

Not long ago, banks looked to their number of branches as an indication of market share. Now the battle cry is "banking anywhere, anytime, any way." Docutel, Intuit, Mondex, CyberCash, and a host of other firms have changed the face of retail banking forever. Using PC banking and the Internet, these burgeoning nonfinancial institutions have challenged the likes of Citibank and NationsBank for a share of the purse. Our point is that old rules no longer apply.

EXHIBIT 1.1   Comparison of Bethlehem Steel and Nucor.

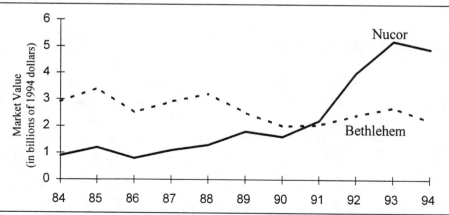

Source: Reprinted with permission of Harvard Business School Press. From CDI Value Growth Database, cited in Slywotzky, *Value Migration* (Boston: HBS Press, 1996), p. 9. Copyright © 1996 by the President and Fellows of Harvard College; all rights reserved.

The manager of the twenty-first century must be prepared to challenge the status quo.

The role of business has changed dramatically, and the transformations that point to fundamental changes in the basic structure of society alluded to at the beginning of this chapter are likely to occur more frequently. Andy Grove,[9] CEO of Intel, confirms this view and speaks of *inflection points* that cut to the heart of the business, threatening its existence. Inflection points reflect those moments that changes in the nature of competition, technology, or the marketplace present profound opportunities/threats for a firm's future survival. The role of senior management will be to set the vision that ultimately transforms the business. However, it is often the middle manager who will need to anticipate this change, who appreciates its potential impact, and who is charged with implementing a response to this change. Success often hinges on execution—achievement of goals is truly in the details! The chapters that follow move with facility between questions of strategy and problems of implementation. All the chapters combine to prepare you for the challenges that face managers in the twenty-first century. Our journey takes a number of turns and twists. Some chapters focus on the traditional functional business disciplines such as marketing and operations. Others address the details of accounting, quantitative analysis, and net present value. Still other chapters soar into the stratosphere of the corporate environment by dealing with the business policy level as we address issues germane to strategy and the management of alliances. These issues stand side by side with a discussion of the effects of empowerment, the stresses associated with the changing social contract, the need to incorporate business ethics as an essential part of management's thinking, and the challenges inherent in leading from the middle.

FOR FURTHER READING

Michael Best, *The New Competition* (Cambridge, MA: Harvard University Press, 1990).

Francis Gouillart and James Kelly, *Transforming the Organization* (New York: McGraw-Hill, 1995).

James Moore, *The Death of Competition* (New York: Harper Business, 1996).

James Brian Quinn, *The Intelligent Enterprise* (New York: The Free Press, 1992).

Michael Yoshino and U.S. Rangan, *Strategic Alliances* (Cambridge, MA: Harvard Business School Press, 1995).

2 THE FUTURE

The future ain't what it used to be.
—Yogi Berra

So much of managing is about events that will occur in the future. Observers often view business success as the result of either luck or superior prediction skills. Without a doubt, luck does play a role, but few managers spend much time gazing into a crystal ball. The sense of most managers is that instead of trying to predict the future, it is more important to be prepared to respond to a variety of possible futures. In some sense, the key is to keep your options open and to know when to adjust or change course to respond to events that are different from what was anticipated. Although we might not know what the business environment and technology will be like in ten years or even five, we do know what they will be like tomorrow. In other words, the future unfolds; it does not appear out of thin air. Accordingly, we do not need to know exactly how we will manage in the year 2010, but we do need to realize that it will be different from how we manage today and that we can prepare for the uncertainty.

On the home page of the Institute for the Future, one of the many think tanks devoted exclusively to challenges and problems that corporations, societies, and nations are expected to encounter in the future, is a phrase spoken more than 2,500 years ago by Heracleitus, which never seemed more true than it does today: "Nothing endures but change." The very fact that we use the term *home page* and assume you are cognizant of its meaning demonstrates this concept of enduring change. Three years ago, only a minuscule percentage of the populace would have known that it refers to the World Wide Web, an entirely new medium that is revolutionizing communication.

As the millennium approaches, more and more experts, many dubbed *futurists,* have been debating, presenting, and analyzing future scenarios. Conferences, publications, and organizations have sprung up with the intention of solving problems that are expected to transpire in the future. The burgeoning futurist industry would no doubt take issue with Albert Einstein's comment, "I never think about the future. It comes soon enough."[1] These organizations and experts have flourished based on their perceived ability to predict the future.

A recent survey of the advisory boards of the American Management Association asked its members what their greatest concerns were as they looked to the twenty-first century. The most frequently expressed concern was change. (Exhibit 2.1 reports the responses.) In other words, senior managers recognize that knowledge requirements, management practices, and the markets in which they operate will be different, if not unrecognizable.

Despite the American Management Association survey results, the well-known management scholars Gary Hamel and C. K. Prahalad, authors of *Competing for the Future,* believe that very little time is spent by managers planning for the future. They ascribe to the 40-30-20 rule. According to this rule, "40 percent of senior executive time is spent looking outward, and of this time about 30 percent is spent peering three or more years into the future. And of the time spent looking forward, no more than 20 percent is spent attempting to build a collective view of the future (the other 80 percent is spent looking at the future of the manager's particular business). Thus, on the average, senior management is devoting only 2.4 percent of its energy to building a corporate perspective on

EXHIBIT 2.1   Managerial concerns of the twenty-first century.

Issue	Percent of Respondents
Change	21%
Finding and developing skilled employees	14%
Creating and managing growth	12%
Controlling costs	8%
Managing productivity	8%
Pricing pressures	7%
Dealing with regulations	6%
Keeping up with technology	4%
Other	20%

the future."[2] Hamel and Prahalad think that senior management should in fact be allocating 20% to 50% of its time contemplating the future, and during this time they must be willing to develop and adapt their perspectives.

Hamel and Prahalad state that the goal for senior management is to see the future before it arrives—and to see it before anyone else does. They believe that the future can be found in the "intersection of changes in technology, lifestyles, regulation, demographics and geopolitics." CNN, with its 24-hour cable news coverage, is cited as an example of management seeing the future based on changes in lifestyle, technology, and regulation. In order to compete for the future, management needs to gain foresight based on these trends and be able to completely reconceive and revamp the structure of the corporation and the nature of the industry.

Often the future is seen by those perceived by the rest of us as contrarians, like CNN's Ted Turner. Turner has been instrumental in creating the future in much the same way as does Sony (led by visionary Akio Morita)—by telling consumers what products they want as opposed to just selling them what they ask for. The Japanese are known for planning on the horizon. Hitachi, Sony, and Fuji are developing products slated to be marketed not only 10 years hence, but 25 years in the future. Now that is future planning.

On the other hand, Ian Smith, the managing director of Monitor, a consultancy actively studying the next century, believes that companies should stop thinking in terms of strategic planning and shift to strategic thought: "Ten-year plans are not a good enough prediction of how the competitive environment works. However good your ten-year plan is, it's going to be irrelevant if the Japanese come in next week with a better product . . . CNN, Rupert Murdoch and those guys don't do ten-year plans."[3] The company of the next century is not concentrating on 10-year plans, but on 25-year plans and beyond.

The Royal Society of Arts completed a study on "tomorrow's company" and concluded, based on analyses of dozens of blue-chip companies, that there are three different types of business. "There are those which anticipate change, those which react to change, and those which ignore change. The first will flourish. The second will struggle to survive. And the third will not survive."[4] Clearly, anticipating change is one of the keys to survival, but creating change is the key to success.

As we outlined in the previous chapter, the world has become less stable and more prone to change. Organizational structures have changed, reflecting this overall instability—and have responded with a flatter, more decentralized organization capable of adapting to change more quickly than in a hierarchical, top-down control system. Tom Peters envisions a structure that he calls a "blueberry organization"—very flat, no headquarters, and all the blueberries are graded equally.[5] The blueberry organization Peters most often refers to is VeriFone, the booming U.S. company that makes equipment for credit-card authorization. According to Peters, this virtual company is constantly reinventing itself and could be the company of tomorrow.

It is very important to grasp that entire industries can be obliterated in a relatively short period of time. Austrian economist Joseph Schumpeter had this in mind when he described *creative destructionism,* which in simple terms postulates that it is impossible to create something completely and utterly new without significantly changing or destroying the old. Industry winners succeed at the expense of losers. An often-used example is the demise of the buggy whip due to the rise of the automobile. In the late 1800s, even the best buggy whip manufacturer was doomed by the invention of the automobile. According to Paul Saffo, a director at the Institute for the Future, "The lesson of the buggy whip is, in a period of change, everybody has to be attuned to the whispering through the trees. If you wait for the gale, it's too late. It is not what becomes obsolete, but how soon you can tell."[6]

In anticipation of change, one tool that is widely used to help firms prepare is *scenario planning,* a process whereby alternative scenarios are developed to describe the key forces or factors that will drive the industry or business environment in which the firm operates. Managers use these scenarios to prepare for or anticipate developments and to evaluate how the future is unfolding. They have a set of scripts, and by observing what actually occurs they get a measure of which script is most likely to be relevant. This process allows the managers and their firms to adjust to events.

This process was developed by Shell Oil in the 1960s. At that time there was plenty of oil, and its price was $3.00 per barrel. No one at Shell or in the industry predicted the oil crisis created by the shortage of the 1970s, but because Shell's scenarios included the possibility of a reduction in the supply of oil, the company was better prepared than other oil companies when it occurred. Although Shell did not have contingency plans, it had considered options. As the events leading up to the crisis unfolded, Shell was more agile than its competitors and, as a result, could minimize the impact on its operations (i.e., the agility allowed Shell to react more quickly).

Later in this chapter we will discuss scenario planning in more detail and develop a set of scenarios. Those scenarios will be based on very general macroeconomic themes as opposed to industry-specific or firm-related forces. In this way we will get some experience with the process of scenario planning without constraining ourselves to a particular industry. Before we do this scenario planning, however, we want to look at a cautionary tale of misreading the future. Later we'll examine some trends that might influence the scenarios we develop.

THE MILLENNIUM PROBLEM

As the world awaits the beginning of the twenty-first century with hopes of peace, economic prosperity, and increasing freedom across much of the earth, two digits are causing a problem that knowledgeable people believe will cost the world $1 trillion. The so-called millennium problem in computers is an object lesson for all of us as we consider the future.

The problem arose in the 1960s when one of the foremost concerns of software developers was memory. To save space, programmers shortened dates by eliminating the first two digits of the year, and the 19 became implicit. Thus 1947 became 47 and 1972 became 72. This seemed innocuous enough, but as the millennium approaches, these two digits have become a time bomb. When the clock strikes 12 on December 31, 2000, these computer programs will assume that the years have a 20 prefix. A 1947 date of birth will become 2047, and instead of being 53 years old an individual born in that year will be considered nonexistent for another 47 years. Individuals born in 1947 who die in 2005 will have passed away 42 years before they were born! Pensions, interest payments on loans, insurance premiums, eligibility for federal or state benefits, and much more will be jeopardized as computers attempt to calculate starting dates, years of credit, and so forth. The solution is an end-of-century frenzy to rewrite computer codes in essentially every program at banks, insurance companies, brokerage houses, and government agencies. How could this have happened, and what does it say about how firms prepare for the future?

It happened because people overestimated the value of memory and computational time and underestimated the value and difficulty of software development. Due to technological advances, there are now laptop computers that are far more powerful than 1960s mainframes, and saving two digits of code by ignoring the century prefix is unnecessary. At the same time, many of the programs in use today are variations of programs written 25 or 30 years ago. Embedded in these programs are the quirks and economies of software development based on old hardware. When these programs were written, it was assumed that their useful lives would not extend to the end of the century. In fact, the programs have outlived their developers, so that those attempting to correct the problem are not the original creators. This has added to the difficulty. In response, consulting firms have been established just to address the millennium problem and to try to develop innovative solutions. A couple of these firms have gone public, with market values in the hundreds of millions of dollars, reflecting the lure of capturing some of the trillion dollars to be spent on correcting the problem.

It is not possible to *foretell* the future. It is possible and essential to *consider* the future or, more accurately, futures. Managers need to think broadly about the forces that will influence their firms and industries. As strategies are formulated, investments made, and products designed, management must predict their appropriateness in a world that might be very different from today's. Changes in the workforce, technology, and markets will all have a significant impact on how firms are organized and on the policies and procedures they implement. Because the future cannot be predicted with certainty, management must be prepared to adapt its strategies and plans when the future unfolds differently than anticipated. Successful firms are not necessarily those that guessed right, but those that are agile enough to thrive in many different futures.

The millennium problem is a unique one in both the scope of its impact and the simplicity of its origin. It is a real-life example of chaos theory, where a butterfly flapping its wings in Malaysia causes an earthquake in California. Seemingly minor decisions or events can have major consequences, yet those consequences can be mitigated if we adjust as events unfold and the shape of the future becomes more apparent.

ELEMENTS OF DEVELOPING SCENARIOS

There is no precise way to develop scenarios, but there are a number of guidelines that are helpful. Following them keeps the process from going astray. Scenario planning is neither blue-sky guesswork nor statistical forecasting. It is a process that provides structure for thinking about the future and is used by many organizations, including Global Business Network (GBN). Scenario planning entails considering different possibilities that a firm might confront in the future. Peter Schwartz of GBN has provided a list of steps to assist those who are developing scenarios.[7] Exhibit 2.2 summarizes these scenarios. GBN developed scenarios for AT&T, its

---

EXHIBIT 2.2   Steps to developing scenarios.

1. Identify the focal issue or decision.
2. Key forces in the local environment.
3. Driving forces.
4. Rank by importance and uncertainty.
5. Selecting scenario logic.
6. Fleshing out the scenarios.
7. Implications.
8. Selection of leading indicators and signposts.

Source: From *The Art of the Long View* by Peter Schwartz. Copyright © 1991 by Peter Schwartz. Used by permission of Doubleday, a division of Bantam Doubleday Dell Publishing Group, Inc.

first client, that predicted the possibilities of the cellular telephone boom and pre-sented Nissan with scenarios of coping with the then-outrageous possibility of the yen falling below 100—it actually ending up falling to an all-time low of 79.

One: Identify the Focal Issue or Decision

According to Schwartz, good scenarios begin inside and then move outside toward the environment. A firm needs to identify key decisions or focal issues that will have an impact on how it does business. Schwartz gives the example of automobile companies being concerned with energy prices. Decisions such as the type of engine model design are dependent on energy prices. Should the company invest in a new engine plant to produce fuel-efficient engines or use those funds in other ways? Companies' scenarios should, therefore, contribute to their understanding of energy prices and the factors that will influence them. A transportation company would also be interested in energy prices, and aspects of its scenarios might be very similar to those of the automobile firms. A financial services company, however, would be much less affected by energy prices and would benefit more from scenarios projecting different regulatory structures or alternative policies for funding pensions. Valuable information for the financial services company to know would be whether companies are offering defined benefits plans or defined contributions. The former would be serviced by insti-tutional brokers, whereas the latter would more nearly reflect a retail nature. The 1997 merger of Morgan Stanley and Dean Witter is consistent with Morgan believing that the retail approach will become more important in the future.

Two: Key Forces in the Local Environment

This step involves the major factors that will influence the success or failure of the decision. It is a list of how customers, suppliers, competitors, employees, and other stakeholders will react. Do we know that high energy prices will lead cus-tomers to want fuel-efficient cars? Does it follow that the availability of tax-deferred savings plans will lead individuals to invest in them? What alternatives might arise in the form of substitutes? Could energy prices rise so much that mass transportation would expand? These are considerations that will mean suc-cess or failure for the decision, and the scenario must include them.

Three: Driving Forces

These are the trends that will influence the key factors or forces in the local envi-ronment. Driving forces are big, broad, macroenvironmental trends or themes.

Driving forces involve economic, political, social, and technological developments. Schwartz believes that this stage of scenario planning is the most research-intensive part of the process. It is also one of the most difficult. At this point it is necessary to stretch the analysis to consider not just the obvious or inevitable, but also the unlikely and improbable.

Demographic trends are relatively inevitable; therefore financial services companies know that the population will be graying and that individuals will live longer. This means that pensions will need to last longer. Or does it? Perhaps retirement ages, which have been declining for the past 50 years, will reverse. Health trends have not only extended life expectancy, but have kept people more active as they age. If people wait until they are 70 or 75 to retire, that will dramatically impact pension requirements, savings patterns, and investment strategies. As financial services firms think about the future, they need to consider whether the existing trend will continue or will reverse. Moreover, they need to assess the various political and social forces that would lead to the reversal. For example, what legislation would be necessary to bring about the change and what social changes would have to occur to get people to extend their working lives?

Although the example is about pension funding and financial services, it is interesting to think of other businesses that would be affected by similar forces. Retirement communities, resort and travel firms, and health maintenance organizations would all face dramatic changes if people worked until age 75.

Four: Rank by Importance and Uncertainty

This is really an issue of focus. After a large number of factors have been identified, they should be ranked or sorted on the basis of importance and uncertainty. This differentiates the scenarios and makes them useful for individual firms. Using one of our examples, the aging population is inevitable and will be present in every scenario. However, changes in retirement age will have much more importance for some firms than for others. Automobile manufacturers might be affected primarily internally, whereas financial services firms will need to address changes in retirement age both internally and externally.

Five: Selecting Scenario Logic

With the key drivers identified and ranked, it is possible to separate out specific scenarios according to combinations of the drivers or forces. These combinations need to have a reasonable logic about them. The dimensions upon which the combinations are formed mirror the key drivers. For example, the automobile company might view energy prices and the degree of trade protectionism as the drivers. We can then think of a 2 × 2 matrix that has high and low energy prices on one axis and high and low protectionism on the other. This gives us four scenarios: high prices and high protectionism, high prices and low protectionism, low prices and high protectionism, and low prices and low protectionism (see Exhibit 2.3).

The more driving forces and key trends we can identify, the more scenarios we will have. The rankings that come out of step four are a means of reducing the scenarios to a manageable number. In addition, we want to evaluate the combinations for consistency and eliminate any that would not make sense.

Six: Fleshing Out the Scenarios

The driving forces form the logic of the scenarios, but they need to be extended or embellished by understanding the trends identified in steps two and three. This allows us to understand the various events that would lead a driving force to become a reality. For example, high energy prices could be the result of inflation and a general level of higher prices, or they could result from a political crisis involving oil exporting countries. We would need to understand how macroeconomic policy is made and what actions would lead to higher inflation. Also, we would have to evaluate the politics of the Middle East or the extent of transformation in Russia to be able to see how events in these countries might affect oil supplies and prices.

These causal chains need to be specific enough for us to see their impact on the driving forces. Since each scenario is the result of several different chains, we

EXHIBIT 2.3   Trade policy and energy price scenarios.

H	High Prices Low Protection	High Prices High Protection
ENERGY PRICES		
L	Low Prices Low Protection	Low Prices High Protection

L   H

PROTECTIONISM

need to link them together. They compose a narrative by which the scenarios are identified and we are informed.

Seven: Implications

With scenarios in hand it is now possible to return to the focal decision or issue and ask how that decision fares under each scenario. It is not just a matter of success or failure. The analysis of implications should reveal weaknesses in decisions or plans. These might be shored up by altering strategies. In addition, we can determine under how many scenarios a given decision is viable. If there are four scenarios and the decision is effective under each one, then the choice is easy. However, if the decision works only under one of several scenarios, then it is more problematic. Certainly in the latter case a firm might not want to make a "bet the company" type of investment.

Eight: Selection of Leading Indicators and Signposts

We began this section by suggesting that it was not about predicting the future, but about anticipating it. The scenarios help us formulate and evaluate strategies. They prepare us in advance to react to the future that unfolds. We need to identify signposts or leading indicators to alert us to the unfolding of a particular scenario.

The earlier we become aware of events and an impending scenario, the better we can prepare and take advantage of it. When Congress starts to debate changing the retirement age to 75, then everyone is informed. We want to get information or clues earlier. It is important to be imaginative to find what some researchers have referred to as *unobtrusive measures*. With regard to changing retirement patterns, you might look at individual company policies as precursors of public policy. An analysis of temporary-work firms might be a guide. If the scenarios have been built with care and sufficient detail, then the indicators will become evident, if not obvious.

Scenarios are a road map to the future and to the twenty-first century. Those of us who paid attention to the 1996 presidential elections heard about building the bridge to the next century. It is the managers who will have to cross that bridge. It is our road maps that will allow us to navigate through the uncharted territory. Theodore Gordon, founder of The Futures Group and a former rocket scientist, believes that there will be a new corporate focus on decision making in uncertainty. In order to facilitate this decision making, managers will employ new tools along with old tools. Gordon believes that successful management will become more dependent on inspired intuition than on carefully developed strategies.

MACROTRENDS

To develop a set of scenarios at this point would require us to have a specific industry and situation in mind, consistent with step one of the previous section. Rather than do this, we will develop three different macroenvironments that could be the foundation for many different scenarios.

These three environments begin with an extrapolation of the most important recent trends. We call this first scenario one of *cooperation*. The second scenario is an optimistic one in which the current trends accelerate with generally favorable outcomes, and it is marked by *coordination*. The third scenario, that of *national autarchy,* is one in which the current trends are reversed due to a negative political and social reaction to the liberalization policies of the last half of the twentieth century.

Scenario One: Cooperation

In the current scenario, we observe a continuation of several themes dominated by moderate governments on both the right and the left in which a change of political parties in democracies and newly democratic countries would not precipitate a dramatic change in policies. In Europe that would be represented by a continuing commitment to the economic community and expansion of its membership and the transformation and enlargement of NATO to include former East Bloc countries.

European countries would eliminate many of the inefficient regulations now contributing to high unemployment and the lack of innovation among European firms. In this scenario, we would observe a slow reversal or decline in unemployment rates in Europe. Inefficient firms would be acquired by more successful companies, and there would be a consolidation within industries on a Pan-European basis.

The role of national governments on the issues of labor policy, social welfare, tax policy, and monetary policy would converge toward a European standard. A more competitive Europe would become more supportive of similar transformations elsewhere in the world.

More Latin American countries will follow the Chilean model of market liberalization, privatization, and responsible economic policy. Trade among these countries and between this region and others will become freer and more diverse. Countries that have liberalized will experience rising incomes, and their populations will enjoy improved standards of living. These countries will not only be hosts to successful foreign multinationals from the developed world, but some of their companies will emerge as transnational corporations. Their ability to compete globally will have been enhanced and tested by their need to succeed in their own markets.

In Asia, where economic development has preceded the process in Latin America, the shift will be more subtle. The quasi-capitalist systems in the Asian tiger countries will evolve into a system with less government involvement and more reliance on private markets, particularly for capital.

This scenario is one in which world growth in GDP will be relatively evenly distributed and will be in the 3% to 4% range. It is a world of moderate inflation, stable employment, and strong national cooperation despite the continued importance of the European Community and the regional agreements such as NAFTA, ASEAN, and MERCOSUR. The primary decision maker and engine for change will be at the national level and not multilateral.

Scenario Two: Coordination

This is in contrast to the second scenario of coordination, in which multilateral organizations come to dominate global economic policy. In this scenario, the benefits of liberalization, deregulation, and democratization are so great that governments, with the support of their populations, accelerate the pace of change. Europe moves successfully to a single currency and to a single economic policy.

This single economic policy provides for rapid economic growth, declining rates of unemployment, and near zero inflation. Europe benefits from having strong global companies that are willing and able to compete without government interference or protection. Trade barriers of all types have been eliminated. The World Trade Organization has been made superfluous because almost all countries of the world now adhere to the free trade doctrines of Adam Smith.

Although Europe has set the tone for these developments, the United States and Japan are equal participants. They have set aside any ethnocentric predispositions so that they may participate in the new global economic order.

Free trade, free movement of capital, free mobility of people, and the free exchange of ideas are the hallmarks of this economic world. In this scenario, not only have the Asian and Latin American countries participated, but in addition the nations of Africa and the sub-Asian continent have also benefited. The enthusiastic participation of so many countries has been made possible by the dramatic expansion of the world's economies. GDP is growing in excess of 5% per year, inflation is close to zero, and unemployment is at record lows. This has allowed even the most impoverished and least-skilled members of society to improve their standards of living and to acquire a positive outlook.

Under either of the first two scenarios, an immediate consequence of these trends for business is that competition will grow increasingly intense, and as a result it is more important for companies to be agile and responsive to changing market conditions. Companies will need to think more globally (see Chapter 16, "International Business") and in terms of forming strategic alliances (see Chapter 15, "Strategic Alliances") in an increasingly competitive market and world. A major part of this responsiveness is for firms to develop new products and to control costs. This requires a more knowledgeable and skilled workforce (see Chapter 14, "Leading from the Middle").

The twenty-first century will not belong to a handful of countries. With the explosive emerging markets, competition will come from countries that in 1997 are not yet forces in today's industries. Some countries will compete on the basis of low labor costs, but for the United States and other developed countries, it will be incumbent to compete on the basis of knowledge. George Gilder, in his book *Microcosm,* talks about Silicon Valley and its development based upon sand and knowledge. In the nineteenth century, the steel industry developed on the basis of availability and proximity of raw materials such as coal, iron, and water. But industries of the future can be located anywhere in the world where there exists freedom of ideas and capital. The raw materials of the twenty-first century will be knowledge, entrepreneurship, and the freedom to act.

Scenario Three: National Autarchy

The widespread sharing in the benefits of economic growth stand in stark contrast to the uneven income distribution present in the third scenario, that of national autarchy. This scenario is characterized by a return to xenophobic policies. It is generated by the failure of the liberalization policies of the last half of the twentieth century. Growth rates slow rather than increase. Many countries experience no growth at all, or even prolonged recession. In these countries, unemployment rises significantly, especially among the young and marginally skilled. Social and political reactions to the harsh economic realities focus on foreign competition and the role of multilateral organizations. Countries retreat from their involvement in worldwide and regional economic associations. In an effort to protect jobs, governments find new ways to erect trade barriers and to restrict competition. This scenario is a return to the economic environment of the 1930s.

The political parties are extreme on both the right and left. Right-wing or extremely conservative parties continue to advocate less regulation and free markets, but only behind high national barriers. On the left, socialist parties reemerge to reverse the market liberalization policies of the twentieth century.

Their solution to high unemployment is to embark on a new round of government regulations, subsidization, and nationalization of major industries.

In their effort to address the problem of unemployment, governments resort to expansive monetary policy and large fiscal deficits. As a result, inflation rises, reaching 15% to 20% in many countries.

In Europe all efforts to achieve a common currency and economic policy are abandoned. Although the EC continues to exist, it is a mere shadow of its former self. In Latin America the results are even more extreme. The discontent and malaise created by the lack of economic progress opens the door for a new generation of military dictatorships. All attempts at regional cooperation are discontinued, and national budgets are directed more toward the armed forces than to educating the workforce.

Asia continues to experience a higher than average rate of growth, but at the expense of personal liberty and consumption. Strong government and business alliances force sacrifices on the part of the working man and woman. Economic growth comes not so much from technological advances and new knowledge, but from longer hours and harder work from the population. In some countries, incipient labor strife is stopped by military action.

Globally, GDP is barely positive and economies are beset by frequent boom and bust periods. Inflation is high, as is unemployment, and in individual countries the distribution of income has widened, leaving a shrinking elite of haves and a growing mass of have-nots.

Although the three scenarios are sweeping and broad, they do give an indication of the thought process that is necessary to generate the macroenvironment that scenario planning requires. In full-blown, scenario-planning activities, even more extensive analysis is necessary in order to explore cultural, social, technological, and economic themes.

FOR FURTHER READING

Peter F. Drucker, *Managing for the Future: The 1990s and Beyond* (New York: Plume, 1993).

Peter F. Drucker, *Post-Capitalist Society* (New York: HarperCollins, 1994).

Peter Swartz, *The Art of the Long View* (New York: Doubleday Currency, 1991).

3 MANAGING PEOPLE

INTRODUCTION

John was a difficult employee for Heather, a director of marketing at a major service company. He constantly undermined her with other employees. He often sent e-mail that was critical of her decisions to Heather's boss and to others in his informal network. John was a longtime employee who managed a group of technical experts in marketing research. The group had been left alone for several years before Heather was given responsibility for it in a reorganization. John had applied for Heather's position and been turned down. While the group often did good work, it almost never met its deadlines and had a reputation within the company for surly service. Heather found John to be moody, often depressed, cynical, and not firmly committed to the production of world-class service that was the firm's mission. She knew that she needed to turn this group around, but she was uncertain how to proceed.

Heather has to contend with at least four levels of analysis. The first is to understand John and what makes him tick. The second level is to understand the set of relationships surrounding herself and John, particularly the authority relationship. The third level is that of small-group dynamics, working together to accomplish definite tasks. The final level is the organization as a whole: its culture, processes, and ways of doing things that affect her and John and their relationship and the small group in which they work.

Understanding Heather's problems on these multiple levels points us to the so-called soft side of management: people. Understanding and managing people is the most crucial task that managers face. And, given the changes that the next century is going to bring, its importance is increasing at a rapid pace.

As companies restructure, reorganize, and reengineer, they all too often use the same old models, assumptions, and theories about what makes people tick. And, ironically, it was these old models that led to the need to transform the company in the first place. Without a deep and sophisticated understanding of people in organizations, all transformation paths lead to a dead end.

The purpose of this chapter is to begin the process of developing a set of concepts for understanding why people behave the way that they do in an organizational setting. Such a process is open-ended and ongoing. People are complex, and their behavior is not easily predictable. Today's managers must develop a sophisticated understanding of people, an understanding that is always open to question and revision.

We'll begin by reviewing business history since the industrial revolution to see how our current thinking evolved. In particular, we shall argue that in today's world we must broaden the concept of human beings in organizations along a number of dimensions and levels. Next we'll look at the individual and relationship levels and suggest that we need to understand basic human psychology to be effective managers. After that we'll discuss the small-group level by reviewing research on group dynamics. Then we'll analyze the macro-organizational level and develop some criteria for effective organizational design, paying special attention to the challenge of learning in organizations. Finally, we will suggest some practical principles for managing people.

A BRIEF TOUR THROUGH BUSINESS HISTORY

Since the start of the industrial revolution, the emergence of modern management has meant a concern with people.[1] Traditionally we have thought of the manager's job as one of planning what to do, organizing the resources to accomplish the plans, leading people in the accomplishment of the plans, and checking (or controlling) to make sure that the work was properly done. Many introductory management textbooks are organized in this manner.

To better carry out these tasks, early management theorists proposed to build a "science of management." The hallmark of the industrial revolution was the division of labor and specialization so that factories could be built on a large scale. A worker would specialize in a particular task instead of producing the entire product as in the craft approach. Henry Ford's assembly line exemplifies the benefits and difficulties of this idea.

The scientific approach to management is generally attributed to Frederick Winslow Taylor, who performed some studies at Bethlehem Steel Works in the early part of the century. Taylor believed that workers' contribution to the production process could be scientifically studied and improved. Traditionally, workers carried pig iron for eight hours straight, with production dropping off as they became tired. Taylor proved that it was possible to design the pig iron–carrying process so that workers could do more work and get less tired. For example, by building rest cycles into the process, the worker would be able to sustain heavier loads over longer periods of time. Taylor studied the processes and workers and designed rules such as "Carry for 15 minutes, rest for 5."

By breaking down jobs into component parts, Taylor could reassemble the process in a way that allowed for more productivity. Workers who were more productive could be paid at differential rates, again maximizing overall efficiency. Such time-and-motion studies are still the hallmark of companies that are concerned with maximum efficiency, such as United Parcel Service.

Of course, many companies misused these time-and-motion studies to increase the productivity of workers without paying them more. The annals of business history are full of examples of exploitation of workers, and while such exploitation is often associated with scientific management and Taylorism, it is important to keep in mind that Taylor himself believed his methods would improve the lot of workers.

The underlying view of human beings that is implicit in Taylorism is that we can treat human input into the production process as just another machine. Time-and-motion studies can be used to fine-tune the machine, since we can predict when the "human machine" needs maintenance, rest, more fuel, and the like. Once again, such a mechanistic view is still in use in many companies today, because the assumptions that underlie Taylor's view are deeply embedded in our normal way of thinking about business. The very idea of efficient mass production, still an important business concept, can easily lapse into a kind of crude Taylorism.

A different way of thinking about the role of humans in business emerged from thinkers such as Mary Parker Follet, Elton Mayo, and Fritz Roethlisberger. The so-called human relations approach adopted a very different idea of people in the workplace. In a famous set of experiments known as the Hawthorne experiments, researchers began to alter a number of conditions under which workers operated. Pay concepts were changed, workers were given some choice over when they worked and when they rested, work hours were altered, and other changes were introduced. As expected, these changes had the effect of boosting productivity, but the productivity increases did not last. The researchers concluded that productivity increased simply because the workers had been singled out for special attention and because they believed that managers actually cared about them (why else would they be singled out?).

The *Hawthorne effect* says that if you pay attention to workers and show concern for their well-being, then they will respond with increased productivity. And the researchers discovered that it doesn't much matter how you show that concern.

The human relations approach says that we are complex social creatures, not machines. A complicated network of human beliefs fits into a complicated social scheme to produce behavior that has social consequences and feeds back into the social structure from whence it came.

Abraham Maslow gave us one way to understand the complexity of people by positing that we have different needs and, furthermore, that these needs could be arrayed into a hierarchy of importance. The now famous Maslow's hierarchy of needs is depicted as a pyramid, with physical needs such as food, air, water, and safety at the bottom of the pyramid and our more conceptual needs for self-esteem, respect from others, and self-actualization appearing at the top. Maslow's idea was that lower-order needs must be met before higher-order ones could be addressed. A hungry person cares about food, not self-actualization and meaningful work.

In a now famous book, *The Human Side of Enterprise,* Douglas MacGregor articulated the early views of people in the workplace as a paradox that he called *Theory X and Theory Y management.*[2] Theory X assumes that people basically do not want to work. To get them to work the manager has to coerce, cajole, give orders, threaten sanctions, and in general strike fear into the workers' hearts.

Theory Y assumes that people want to work, that they want to excel and do a good job, that they want to use their creative and intellectual abilities in the workplace.

MacGregor's paradox is as follows. Suppose that people are really motivated in terms of Theory Y. Think of the cost of using the mistaken theory X. MacGregor believed that most companies, and certainly most ideas about management, implicitly assumed theory X, therefore incurring a tremendous opportunity cost. If companies and theories about management could be designed more in tune with theory Y, then both productivity and the happiness of workers would increase.

One theorist who did precisely this was W. Edwards Deming, the father of Total Quality Management.[3] Deming studied factories during World War II, especially those with women workers, and discovered that those people closest to the work knew the most about how that work should be organized. Furthermore, if they had some training in modern statistics they could design processes that both lowered overall costs and increased the quality of the final products. While such wisdom is standard business practice today, in the late 1940s Deming's advice was rejected everywhere he went except Japan. In Japan today, a prestigious award for quality is called the Deming Prize, and the application of Deming's principles is one reason that Japanese companies have made a substantial mark on the business world from the 1970s onward.

While Deming articulated many principles, one in particular is relevant to our present discussion. Deming believed that fear had no value in the workplace. Only by driving fear out of the workplace would workers really be free to suggest improvements that are the hallmark of Total Quality Management.

It is important to understand the evolution of management thinking from Taylor and the human relations school to Deming and MacGregor. Each theorist makes important assumptions about the nature of human beings and what we are capable of accomplishing in the workplace. So, too, does each manager in an organization make assumptions about human beings. A deeper analysis of these assumptions will help to build a more useful model of human beings in organizational settings.

THE ROLE OF INDIVIDUALS AND RELATIONSHIPS

The Problem of Motivation

Corporations are made up of individuals, and, as we saw in the previous section, there are many different models or ideas of individual human beings and what makes them tick. The problem of understanding how to get people to act in the interest of the organization is often called the *problem of motivation.* And a lot of energy is expended in most organizations trying to understand how to motivate people. Two relevant theories for understanding the problem of motivation are *needs theory* and *equity theory.*

Clay Alderfer built upon Maslow's hierarchy of needs to develop a more modern and useful version of needs theory called ERG theory.[4] ERG is an acronym based on the three kinds of needs in the theory. *Existence* needs are close to Maslow's physical needs and include our desire for adequate physical comforts. *Relatedness* needs include our need to affiliate with others and to have interpersonal relationships. *Growth* needs refer to our desire to be creative, to express ourselves through our work, and to be productive. Alderfer's view is that these three sets of needs can motivate people differently from situation to situation. It is not a simple matter of moving up the hierarchy from physical needs to self-actualization. If growth-level needs are not being met, then people will revert to having relatedness needs met. Alderfer also tells us that multiple needs may operate at the same time, complicating the understanding of what individuals actually need in the workplace.

To see how ERG theory might help us to understand individuals in companies, consider a situation where an employee is having difficulty getting along with a work group. In short, that employee's relatedness needs are not being met, and he or she may well have difficulty with the interpersonal skills that are necessary to fulfill those needs.

Consider a company that needs to restructure. One policy to motivate employees would be to create an atmosphere of uncertainty around who will be laid off and what criteria will be used to decide who will stay. Employees would be motivated by their existence needs to act to preserve their jobs at all costs. Conversely, a company like Motorola appeals to the existence of growth needs by offering retraining and education rather than layoffs.

Needs are important to understand, but *equity theory* says that there is more to motivation than just meeting needs. Equity theory postulates that how workers perceive the basic fairness of the system of rewards directly affects their own motivation. Fairness is judged either by comparisons with other people or by comparisons with some other standard (such as "more than 40 hours deserves some extra compensation"). Equity is identified as the "ratio of an individual's inputs (such as level of effort on the job) to outcomes (such as pay) as compared with a similar ratio for a relevant 'other.' "[5]

Equity theory depends on the idea that work is a social environment and that any understanding of human nature must take into account the fact that we are social creatures, always engaging in relationships with others. Reorganizing or redesigning jobs may not improve productivity if there is a perceived inequity. The managerial task is to focus on perceived fairness and to communicate about the distribution of rewards as related to efforts.

The problem of motivation is, according to equity theory, largely about reducing and eliminating perceived inequities in the workplace. Sources of inequities are diverse: from job assignments and compensation to processes like performance appraisal and promotion. Equity theory tells managers to pay attention to the underlying dynamic processes and the behavior that results from these processes in addition to the set of needs that employees have.

The Authority Relationship

Equity theory focuses us on the relational aspects of organizations, and no relationship is more important than the authority relationship. Authority and its related concept, power, come in many different flavors. Some authority or power can be coercive, such as the authority that issues from the person or group with weapons trained on others. Other authority is legitimate in the sense that it is derived from consensual social processes about which there is little question. Elected officials are the paradigm case of legitimate authority, though there are many others.

Corporations work in large part because there is respect for the authority relationship. For the most part, when the boss says to do X, the subordinate actually does X. Authority is obeyed or at least accepted. In a world of stability, the dominant idea is that managers know better than workers, senior managers know better than middle managers, CEOs know better than senior managers, and a trail of legitimate authority is passed down the hierarchy. If everyone obeys authority then the organization will run smoothly. However, there is another side to this reliance on obedience to authority.

In a famous set of experiments carried out at Yale University, Professor Stanley Milgram decided to find out why people obeyed authority.[6] He devised a set of experiments designed to put subjects into a situation that had great consequences, but in which they would have to directly disobey instructions in order to prevent the consequences. The subject was introduced to another alleged subject who was in reality an actor. Both were told that the experiments were about the effect of punishment on learning. One would be the teacher and the other learner, and when the learner made mistakes in repeating word pairs, the teacher was to administer an electric shock. The subject was always the teacher and the actor/accomplice was always the learner. As the experiment proceeded, the teacher was required to deliver increasingly severe shocks. The idea was to see when the teacher would disobey and refuse to administer the shocks. The accomplice was in another room, playing a tape of standardized responses that included blood-curdling screams at certain shock levels. Steps were taken to ensure that the subject believed that the accomplice was actually in pain.

Milgram and other psychologists had predicted that few subjects would continue the experiment all the way to the end and deliver 450 volts to the victim. Yet over 50% of the subjects did so. Were these subjects evil? Were they sadistic? Milgram argued that the structure of the authority relationship was the issue. The experimenter was in the room with the subject and gently prodded the subject to continue, even when he or she resisted. Hence, given that the subject believed the experimenter to be a legitimate authority, there was a predisposition, built into the situation, to obey that authority.

Milgram opined that such a situational predisposition to obey is learned when we are small children obeying our parents. Such blind obedience leads to accepting authority even when it is illegitimate—such as the Nazi death camps.

When questioned at the Nuremberg trials, Eichman responded that he was only doing his job, only doing what he was told to do.

From the Milgram studies and others like it, we can conclude that the forces surrounding authority relationships are strong indeed. Most people in most organizations do what they do most of the time because they are told to do so by those perceived to be legitimate authorities. The good news is that the authority relationship leads to the smooth working of organizations. The bad news is that in an environment where we need to try new behaviors and new ideas, where we need *innovation* and *disobedience,* we are unlikely to get either unless managers specifically encourage them.

The Gender Relationship

More than ever before, men and women are working together in today's corporations. The rise of women in managerial ranks in Western countries is rapidly being followed around the world. Yet many have argued that there is a *glass ceiling* that seems to prevent women from reaching the very top managerial levels. As of 1997, there were only two women CEOs at Fortune 500 companies.

The rise of women in business has led many people to analyze the role of gender in the structure of work and to suggest that we need to pay more attention to the way that gender influences behavior. Gender issues in the workplace include expressions of sexuality, family benefits such as child care, maternity and paternity leave, dual-career families, and sexual harassment.

Deborah Tannen has suggested that gender influences the way that we communicate with each other.[7] For instance women often view what is said in terms of *intimacy,* because they see "a world of connection where individuals negotiate complex networks of friendship, minimize differences, try to reach consensus, and avoid the appearance of superiority, which would highlight differences."[8] Men, on the other hand, sometimes interpret conversations in terms of *independence,* because in a world concerned with status, "a primary means of establishing status is to tell others what to do, and taking orders is a marker of low status."[9] The difficulties that can arise from this difference alone are remarkable. Consider how a group of men and women working together might misunderstand each other. Requests for meetings and conversations may well get misinterpreted along the intimacy-independence dimension. Tannen goes to great lengths to say that she is not generalizing about all men and all women, but that communication is in fact gender-related and we need to be aware of it if we are to truly understand what we are saying to one another.

Judith Rossener has suggested that women lead differently from men.[10] Women are more likely to rely on charisma and personal power than on positional power conferred by title or status. Women are more likely to try to transform the interests of others into common goals than to appeal to their self-interest. Women are more participatory and go to greater lengths to include others. Rossener's conclusion is not that women's style is better than men's, but that we need to expand our definition of effective leadership so as to allow more people to utilize their strengths.

The New Psychological Contract

The changes in business—the need for a deeper analysis of human behavior as socially constructed around issues such as authority and gender—and the increased intensity and rate of change has led to a new understanding of the fundamental employment relationship. Traditionally, we could think of the employment relationship as a kind of implicit contract—a psychological contract, according to Chris Argyris—whereby the expectations of the company and the expectations of the individual were in harmony.[11] If these expectations got out of balance, then the contract would be perceived to be broken and would need renegotiation.

Traditionally the contract went as follows: Work hard, perform well, and the company will take care of you. Employee loyalty to the company will be rewarded with continued employment—virtually for a lifetime. With the advent of global competitiveness, restructuring, and reengineering, this contract has changed.[12] In a penetrating analysis, Charles Heckscher has suggested that the traditional concept of loyalty has outlived its usefulness for most employees and that it needs to be redefined.[13] Heckscher proposes that loyalty be redefined around working toward a common purpose, with both company and employee taking some responsibility for contributing to that purpose. Others have proposed a new psychological contract that focuses on employability rather than employment. Such a concept argues that the company's role is to ensure that the employee is employable (can find another job) if the work done for the company is no longer necessary. This idea has far-reaching implications, from the portability of benefits to the protection of trade secrets.

GROUPS AND TEAMS

One change that is sweeping the corporate landscape is the emergence of teams as the basic unit that produces work. Management theory has long paid attention to groups and the group process, but the basic unit of analysis has usually been thought of as the individual. That is changing rapidly as business moves to respond to the new competitive realities. However, before we examine this new emphasis on teams we need to review the basic structure of groups and group processes.

Many years ago a management thinker named B. W. Tuckman identified five separate phases of group development: *forming, storming, norming, performing,* and *adjourning.*[14] This idea has become entrenched in management literature and is an important starting point for understanding the group process.

Initially, when a group forms, members test out what kinds of behavior are acceptable and set up working rules (both formal and informal rules) as the members get to know each other's styles and expectations. As the group becomes more comfortable with one another, conflict inevitably sets in—especially with respect to individuals becoming subservient to the group. As individuals assert their personalities and styles, they often conflict with each other and the initial working rules of the group. In short, there is a battle for control of the group. This "stormy" period lasts until group members can agree on some norms to solve the conflicts. If the group is to function well, then all members of the group, not just the "stormy" personalities, must agree to the norms.

Hopefully a group can move through these first three stages quickly, and by paying deft attention to process concerns as well as task concerns a well-facilitated group can get on with the performing aspect of group work. The group can begin to work positively together as a whole, dividing tasks and sharing ideas to do the real work of the group. When its work is over, the group moves on to adjournment, but this is not as simple as it appears. Often, in adjournment, group members engage in a battle for who gets credit individually for what the group has done, especially if the group is operating in a corporate culture that rewards individual contributions and not group contributions. During this phase group members search for closure.

While every group does not go through all stages of this process, it can be a useful heuristic for understanding why many groups fail to perform. They have not gone through the initial processes necessary to create a cohesive group; thus there is little commitment to the tasks at hand.

While the difference between groups and teams may well be semantic, the idea of "team" focuses on a common effort: namely, winning. Some companies have gone so far as to create what *Fortune* called "superteams" or "high-performance teams."[15] These teams are often cross-functional and are drawn together to solve a particular thorny problem or to reengineer a business process. For the most part, superteams are self-managing and are related to a very old idea of "autonomous work groups" that grew out of theorist Eric Trist's work with coal miners in Britain in the 1950s.[16] The idea is that if the team accepts the responsibility of leading itself, it is more likely to commit to the person or persons who are chosen or who emerge as leaders. Leadership can be shared, and the team can be more participatory.

In a groundbreaking book, *The Wisdom of Teams,* Katzenbach and Smith highlight four key lessons from their study of teams in many companies.[17]

1. "Significant performance challenges energize teams regardless of where they are in an organization."[18] The idea that teams are only about feeling good about each other, creating "warm and fuzzy" feelings, and so forth, is fallacious. Focusing on performance is what makes teams work, and the leader's job is to clearly identify performance challenges.

2. "Organizational leaders can foster team performance best by building a strong performance ethic rather than by establishing a team-promoting environment alone."[19] Teams for teams' sake doesn't work in the eyes of Katzenbach and Smith. While a supportive environment is a good thing to have in a company, it must be oriented toward performance.

3. "Biases toward individualism exist but need not get in the way of team performance."[20] Teams are not committees. Individuals can contribute to teams; indeed, in effective teams, individuals must use all of their individual talents to meet the team's challenge. Katzenbach and Smith propose that we view individuals and teams not as antitheses, but rather that we come to view them as complementary, both necessary for organizational success.

4. "Discipline—both within the team and across the organization—creates the conditions for team performance."[21] Teams are formed to engage in the work of the organization—creating value for customers, shareholders, employees, suppliers, and communities. By relentlessly focusing on the need to create value, organizational leaders can help create the performance ethic that high-performance teams need.

While building a culture of performance is a good way to focus teams on tasks, we know that in every organization there are going to be conflicts between groups inside the organization, as well as conflicts between organizational groups and external stakeholders. Such intergroup conflict can be both healthy and destructive to the organization, so it is important to know how to understand these conflicts and what to do about them. Exhibit 3.1 shows two dimensions, cooperativeness and assertiveness, and five resulting styles for handling conflicts.[22]

Some groups are adept at *avoiding* conflict by being both uncooperative and unassertive. Others adopt a *competing* mode of conflict resolution by being assertive and uncooperative, advancing their own agendas at the expense of other groups. Some groups adopt an *accommodating* style by being unassertive

EXHIBIT 3.1   Two-dimensional model of ways to handle conflict.

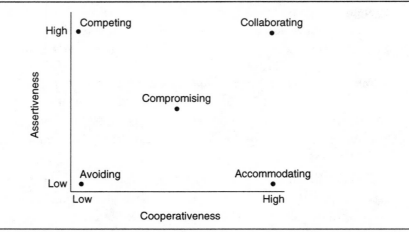

Source: Adapted from T. Ruble and K. Thomas, "Support for a Two-Dimensional Model of Conflict Behavior," *Organizational Behavior and Human Performance*, vol. 16, 1976, p. 145.

and cooperative, often giving in to another group at their own expense. Others find a *compromising* posture that tries to strike a middle ground between high and low cooperativeness and assertiveness, searching for middle-ground solutions whereby both groups have to give in a little. Finally, groups can adopt a *collaborating* style where they work assertively yet cooperatively to find solutions that satisfy all parties involved.

THE ORGANIZATIONAL LEVEL

Traditionally we have thought of management as, in part, choosing the right organizational design or the right organizational structure to fit the strategic direction of a business. Given the fast-paced business environment of today, managers are better off thinking about two related issues: *managing change* and *organizational learning*. By focusing on change and learning, managers can create structures and processes, which may well be quite temporary, to match fast-shifting business conditions.

Managing Change

Professor John Kotter of Harvard Business School has suggested that we can understand how to lead and manage change through the eight-stage process depicted in Exhibit 3.2.

EXHIBIT 3.2   The eight-stage process of creating major change.

1. Establish a Sense of Urgency

- Examining the market and competitive realities
- Identifying and discussing crises, potential crises, or major opportunities

2. Creating the Guiding Coalition

- Putting together a group with enough power to lead the change
- Getting the group to work together like a team

3. Developing a Vision and Strategy

- Creating a vision to help direct the change effort
- Developing strategies for achieving that vision

4. Communicating the Change Vision

- Using every vehicle possible to constantly communicate the new vision and strategies
- Having the guiding coalition role model the behavior expected of employees

5. Empowering Broad-Based Action

- Getting rid of obstacles
- Changing systems or structures that undermine the change vision
- Encouraging risk taking and nontraditional ideas, activities, and actions

6. Generating Short-Term Wins

- Planning for visible improvements in performance, or "wins"
- Creating those wins
- Visibly recognizing and rewarding people who made the wins possible

7. Consolidating Gains and Producing More Change

- Using increased credibility to change all systems, structures, and policies that don't fit together and don't fit the transformation vision
- Hiring, promoting, and developing people who can implement the change vision
- Reinvigorating the process with new projects, themes, and change agents

8. Anchoring New Approaches in the Culture

- Creating better performance through customer- and productivity-oriented behavior, more and better leadership, and more effective management
- Articulating the connections between new behaviors and organizational success
- Developing means to ensure leadership development and succession

Source: Reprinted with permission of Harvard Business Review. Copyright © 1997 by the President and Fellows of Harvard College; all rights reserved. Adapted from John P. Kotter, "Why Transformation Efforts Fail," *Harvard Business Review,* March–April 1995, p. 61.

Of particular importance is the first stage of creating a sense of urgency. General Motors has long been under attack by Toyota and other global competitors, but during the decade of the 1980s GM was posting great earnings. It was difficult to create a sense of urgency for change when profits were high. It was only after a record restructuring loss of many billions of dollars that GM finally began to feel the urgency to change.

At General Electric, CEO Jack Welch has developed a clear vision of being either first or second in every business in which GE competes and of creating a boundaryless organization. Such a vision moves the change process forward.

Grand and glorious change programs have often foundered on the shoals of the everyday processes in organizations. Change requires paying attention to little details and learning to walk before running. Kotter emphasizes the importance of small, early wins that build confidence and momentum for change.

Organizational Learning

In summarizing much of this chapter about managing people, we could say that if organizations are to adapt to the changes in the business environment they must pay attention to how they learn and how they generate and use knowledge to create value for customers and other stakeholders. In a pathbreaking book called *The Fifth Discipline,* MIT professor Peter Senge has suggested that there are five disciplines related to understanding and increasing organizational learning: (1) systems thinking, (2) personal mastery, (3) mental models, (4) shared vision, and (5) team learning.[23]

Systems thinking is complicated, but basically it is an analysis of how things fit together and reinforce each other. Systems thinking does not proceed by analyzing the parts of an issue, but by looking outward and uncovering the larger system in which the issue is contained. For example, suppose that you have a problem employee who is not very productive, is often late, and is even abusive to others. A traditional method of dealing with the problem would be to break down that employee's job-related behavior and try to address what is wrong. A system's perspective would try to determine which system is causing the employee's behavior. For instance, the family system may well be driving the employee's behavior at work. Yet another example might focus on a service problem with a customer. Rather than addressing the service problem directly, we might look at how the service problem came about and discover that, since our compensation system favors new accounts, the salespeople are paying no attention to account retention. Senge suggests that there are recognizable patterns in the systems that we have in place in business and that we need to turn our predilection for analysis to the system as a whole.

Personal mastery recognizes that people make up organizations and that without investment in people's capabilities, organizations are unlikely to succeed. The discipline of personal mastery explores how personal values and corporate goals can be made to fit together. One exercise that many executives have found useful is to engage in a personal vision statement. Such a statement is a picture of a future that you want to bring about. You then work backward from that envisioned future to create the day-to-day conditions for it to be realized.

Mental models refer to the shared set of assumptions and frameworks that we use to conceptualize business. Shell Oil has spent a great deal of time and effort developing alternative sets of assumptions that may affect its business. Such scenario planning forces managers to consider what they would do if the world changed along a number of dimensions. For a long time, the mental model that most U.S. companies had of their executives was a white male. As the workforce has become more diverse, that implicit mental model and the processes and systems derived from it have had to change.

Shared vision is the discipline that focuses on coming to understand the purposes and values that we have in common. In today's business world we need to see the manager's job as one of creating and sustaining common purpose. We need to work from a common set of values that allows us to create value for customer and shared meaning for ourselves through our work. At Merck there is a shared vision of producing medicine that heals the sick. The commitment to that vision is so strong that it results in a continual stream of innovation. Managers' jobs at Merck entail continually reinforcing and reinterpreting the shared vision for all employees.

Team learning refers to many of the ideas in the previous section. If more and more companies are moving toward teams as a basic unit of analysis, then we need to immerse ourselves in the understanding of team process: both what it is and how to improve it. This discipline is becoming increasingly important for effective managers.

SOME PRACTICAL PRINCIPLES

While managing people is too complex to reduce to a formula or a model, we have found the following principles to be a useful heuristic against which we can begin to build a more complex and individualized conception of how to manage people.

1. *Communication with employees is central to the effective manager's job.* This ought to go without saying, but some managers insist on communicat-

ing only by formal means and insist on withholding as much information as possible. We can understand needs and perceived equity only by immersing ourselves in the social life of the organization. As Tannen argued, communication is complicated and gender-based, and we need to work on hearing other voices.

2. *Effective managers also have needs and also perceive equities and inequities.*   What works to motivate employees also works to motivate managers. Many successful organizations simply start with some theory Y assumptions like "People really can be great and want to win." They don't differentiate between levels of employees in terms of their motivation. They drive a sense of ownership and egalitarianism about the company throughout the organization with the result that the company can become a means to meeting the needs of all employees in a fair and evenhanded manner. At Johnsonville Sausage, CEO Ralph Stayer explicitly adopts this philosophy of the organization as a mere means.

3. *Effective managers foster an environment that celebrates need fulfillment and fairness, and one that openly addresses inequities.*   Negotiations with labor unions are often an elaborate ritual. Managers need to address the perceptions of fairness created by issues such as opening new plants in other countries, trade agreements, and contracting out part of the production process to nonunion employees.

4. *Effective managers choose to obey authority rather than blindly follow it, and they encourage the same attitude in their subordinates, even to the point of encouraging disobedience.*   At a meeting in the early 1980s to celebrate unparalleled success in Motorola's history, one sales manager stood up and amidst the celebration began to complain about quality. In many companies such an act of speaking out or acting up or disloyalty would have been career suicide. At Motorola, it was the beginning of their famed quality approach called *six-sigma quality.* Motorola encourages such acts of free speech and has benefited greatly from it.

5. *Effective managers are willing to engage in conversations about diversity. They foster an environment where everyone can fulfill their potential and seek to address issues such as gender, race, sexual orientation, ethnicity, age, and language.*   At Inland Steel, a number of African-American employees were frustrated and thinking of leaving the firm. They worked together and found someone to be a champion of starting a conversation about diversity. As a result, the company was singled out for a national award for its attention to creating a supportive and diverse workplace.

6. *Effective managers understand how groups and teams work, and they focus on creating a culture of performance through teamwork.*   At Saturn, teams are the order of the day. By paying attention to cross-functional teams and giving those teams the power to lead themselves, Saturn has been able to break out of the functional silos that prevented General Motors from competing with Toyota in the small-car market.

7. *Effective managers are change leaders.*   Today managers are not expected to administer—to follow bureaucratic and systematic processes that mean business as usual. Managers are expected to lead change—to propose ways to make the organization more competitive and more effective and then to marshal the resources to bring about that change.

8. *Effective managers build the intellectual capital of themselves and their subordinates by focusing on learning.*   Motorola, GE, and countless others have focused on learning and on learning how to learn in order to prepare their employees to act in a new business environment. Motorola found that it had to teach some employees how to read. At GE, education sessions with CEO Jack Welch took on legendary significance, as Welch debated a number of propositions about the future of GE with employees at all levels.

Managing people is complex, and you will develop your own methods and skills. There is a story about a lion keeper in the Dublin zoo named Mr. Flood who was quite adept at breeding lions in captivity (which is difficult).[24] When asked his secret, Mr. Flood replied, "Understanding lions." When asked how he did that, he responded, "Every lion is different." So it is with managing people. In striving to develop a deep understanding of human nature and what makes people tick, we need not lose sight of the individual uniqueness that sets us apart.

FOR FURTHER READING

In addition to the books that are referenced in this chapter there are a number of books that focus on managing people.

James A. Belasco and Ralph C. Stayer, *Flight of the Buffalo* (New York: Warner Books, 1993) is a comprehensive guide to empowerment and treating employees as more fully human. This very readable book is full of lessons from life by Belasco, a world famous consultant, and Stayer, CEO of Johnsonville Sausage, an employee-run company.

Peter Drucker, *Management: Tasks, Responsibilities, and Practices* (New York: Harper, 1973) is a classic that keeps getting better with time. Drucker knows more about people and managing people than most of us will know in a lifetime.

Abraham Zaleznik, *Executive's Guide to Motivating People* (Chicago: Bonus Books, 1990) is an attempt to use psychoanalytic theory to understand and analyze people in organizations. It takes as axiomatic the view that human beings are complex creatures and that simple explanations for their behavior in organizations will not work.

4 BUSINESS ETHICS

INTRODUCTION

It is not unusual to open any day's edition of a major newspaper or to turn on the television news anywhere in the world and be greeted by something like one or more of the following:

- Exxon involved in major oil spill off the coast of Alaska.
- Financial scandals in Italy and Japan rock markets.
- Indonesian business accused of trying to buy influence in U.S. presidential election.
- Avis and Texaco accused of having racist corporate cultures.
- Workers in shoe manufacturers said to have unsafe working conditions.

Each of these issues and countless others that bombard us on a daily basis raise questions in our minds about the relationship between business and ethics. The purpose of this chapter is to explore this connection along a number of dimensions. We will examine some criteria for determining what makes a business issue an ethical one as well. Along the way we'll look at some common myths about the role of ethics in business. We will examine the basic moral reasoning tools as they are applied to business, and we shall pay particular attention to the role of values and principles. Then we'll examine a way of understanding business so that ethical issues are endogenous to the way that we think about our companies. We shall argue that this method, which we call *stakeholder capitalism,* is in keeping with Adam Smith's ideas about business several hundred years ago. Finally, we shall explore some difficult ethical challenges for business in today's business environment.

WHAT CONSTITUTES AN ETHICAL ISSUE?

Andrea is negotiating a difficult contract with a supplier. The supplier is responsible for a key manufacturing component for Andrea's company and has driven a hard bargain around terms, conditions, and price. After a tough day of negotiating in a hotel conference room, the supplier team leaves with the deal not yet consummated. After they have left, Andrea notices that a folder has fallen down under the table. She picks up the folder, glances at the inside, and immediately recognizes that it contains what appears to be very important information about the supplier's costs. What should she do? Should she read the folder?[1]

Does Andrea have an ethical issue? Granted there is no large, front-page headline issue at stake, but what Andrea does will potentially have large effects on others. There are several arguments to the effect that Andrea needs to see this issue in ethical terms.

The first argument is that the folder is not Andrea's property, and therefore she should not read the folder or use it in any way. Suppose that Andrea had found a wallet under the table instead of the folder. Common morality requires that she should return the wallet without using the contents to her own advantage. The folder case is an ethical issue because it involves making decisions about the legitimate uses of private property. Does Andrea have the right to use other people's property without their permission?

The second argument is about fairness. According to this position, Andrea would be taking unfair advantage of her suppliers by reading this information. She would know something that they don't intend for her to know, and she would not have earned the right to that knowledge. Andrea would not be negotiating from a "level playing field," and that would be unfair. An alternative to this position is to see business as a game or institution with its own set of rules: "All's fair in love and war and business" suggests that in a negotiation, you can use whatever tactic is available—from bluffing to getting information nefariously. Note that even in this interpretation, Andrea still has an ethical issue about fairness. The difference in the two interpretations is not the lack of an ethical issue in one, but a disagreement about defining fairness.

A third argument involves the consequences of Andrea's action. Will the relationship with the supplier be sustainable? Will others think that Andrea is not a woman of good character? Will using the information lead to a better or worse outcome for Andrea's company? The supplier company? Andrea has an ethical problem because of the consequences that are possible.

Each of these arguments goes a long way in helping us to identify ethical issues. Ethical issues are usually concerned with (1) rights and duties, (2) principles such as fairness, or (3) harms and benefits. Ethics concerns how we ought to live our lives. It is about how we reason together regarding the effects of our actions on others. We always have an alternative to entering such a conversation—that alternative is violence and coercion. However, we can think of ethics as the substitution of reason for violence as we try to figure out how we can survive and flourish together in spite of our differences.

There are usually two levels of ethical issues. The first is the personal level, and our example of the folder is a good illustration. Andrea must figure out what she believes is the right thing to do, what fits with the way that she is trying to live her life and with her own principles and values. However, ethics doesn't end there. Because others are affected by Andrea's decision, their own interests, indeed the way they are trying to live their lives, are also important. Ethical issues almost always appear at the personal and interpersonal (or social) levels simultaneously.

It is a mistake to think that ethics are only personal. The standard test, "Well, I have to live with myself if I do this," is a good start, but what that test misses is that others have to live with you, too. Being true to your own beliefs— being authentic—is a good starting point for a conversation with others, but it is only a starting point.

The view that each person is the sole arbiter for right and wrong is called *ethical relativism,* and it prevents us from reasoning together. If the only criterion for the correctness of a particular action is your personal belief, then we don't need to reason about ethics. We just need to check whether a person truly acted on his or her beliefs. Furthermore, if a person or a group of people is trying to solve a difficult ethical issue, it is just a waste of time, because the real measure of correctness, according to ethical relativism, would be personal beliefs.[2]

Needless to say ethical relativism is a thoroughly discredited view, but it does contain a grain of truth. For the most part, individuals make ethical decisions. Individuals are the locus of decision making. In an individualist culture it would be natural to give individual a great deal of autonomy. Such *individualism,* the view that individuals know their interests best and should be left free to pursue them, is different from relativism. You can easily think of ethical rules agreed to by individuals in order to smooth the way for them to pursue their interests.

Almost all major issues that managers face have an ethical component. However, to read the business press or to examine business books, you would think that ethical issues are the exception rather than the rule.

Tell someone that you are worried about business ethics and you'll likely as not get a response like "I didn't know that business had any" or "Isn't that an oxymoron like jumbo shrimp." Our common idea of *business* has evolved into the belief that *business* and *ethics* are somehow separate—that managers can think about business without thinking about ethics and vice versa.[3] Such a separation leads to a natural tendency for us to think of business as morally suspect and to joke about business ethics. However, if the arguments in this book are correct—that business is the dominant institution for creating value in today's world—then business must be part and parcel of the very best way that humans can live. We must intertwine business and ethics in a very fundamental way.

It is impossible to determine just how business became separated from ethics in history. If we go back to Adam Smith, we find no such separation. In addition to his famous book on business and capitalism, *The Wealth of Nations*, Adam Smith also wrote *The Theory of Moral Sentiments*, a book about our ethical obligations to one another. It is clear that Smith believed that business and commerce worked well only if people took seriously their obligations and, in particular, their sense of justice.[4]

The early capitalists in the United States, the so-called robber barons, clearly separated business from ethics, but brought back their social responsibility through philanthropy.[5] Andrew Carnegie, in *The Gospel of Wealth*, outlined two principles for businesspeople. The *charity principle* suggested that more fortunate people in society should help those who are less fortunate by contributing to organizations designed to offer assistance. The *stewardship principle,* from the Bible, viewed the wealthy as holding their property in trust for society, with the obligation to use it for any legitimate societal purpose. Acting on these principles, Carnegie and U.S. Steel had an active program of social philanthropy. Over time, these principles became increasingly accepted, as did the idea that power implies the responsibility to use it for at least some common good.

A more modern version of these two principles could be called the *principle of social responsibility*—the view that business has an obligation to act in the interests of society. This principle has been invoked to justify many different business actions, from giving to the arts to rebuilding neighborhoods to contributions to political figures. The idea is that business must see itself as a citizen in the community and do what it can to make the community a better place.

If business did not act in a socially responsible way, many executives realize that government would regulate and force such action. Indeed, one explanation of the extensive regulatory regimes in countries around the world is that business has failed to act in a way that fulfills its social responsibility.

The chief counterview of business as a socially responsible entity was promulgated by Chicago economist Milton Friedman, who is usually identified with the view that the only ethical obligation of a business is to maximize profits. This is sometimes interpreted to mean that capitalism is an "anything goes" system without morality or humanity. What Friedman actually said is a bit different.

Friedman recognized that business creates and allocates wealth in society. He suggested that, within certain rules and constraints, the system of shareholder capitalism could efficiently create and allocate such wealth only if managers focused on managerial tasks—efficiently managing the business. Of course, Friedman knew, as did Adam Smith, that the anything-goes philosophy couldn't work, and Friedman believed that profits could be maximized within the constraints of law and ethical custom. In particular, Friedman knew that if people did not tell the truth most of the time, and if they tried to mislead others about the attributes of products and services, that business would not work very well. Capitalism as an anything-goes system is neither Friedman's idea nor a very sound one.

While there are hundreds of articles written to counter Friedman's view, the best suggestion is to think more deeply about ethics in business. What are some ways of understanding ethical rules and custom? How can we analyze ethics and business together? In short, we need to critically examine the tools that we have for ethical or moral reasoning.

THE TOOLS OF MORAL REASONING

The language of ethics is very rich. We teach our children about values, rights, duties, principles, and the like, and there is no reason to believe that these processes are not relevant to business life.

Values

Much of our thinking about ethical issues in business is based on our *values*. Values represent our desires and can be either good in themselves, *intrinsic values,* or a means to other ends, *instrumental values*. Values provide a framework that serves as both the reasons for and the causes of many of our actions. It is relatively important to know whether a value is intrinsic and worth pursuing for its own sake or instrumental and likely to lead to or be an indicator of something more important.

Some business thinkers (for example, Peter Drucker) have argued that a common mistake that managers make is to make profit an intrinsic value to be pursued in its own right. Drucker suggests that organizations are far more interesting when profit is an instrumental value, pursued for the sake of some other values.

Merck and Co., a U.S.-based pharmaceutical company, is a good example. First of all, Merck has had a tradition of being very profitable for many years. Yet profit is an instrumental value. At Merck the intrinsic value is to help the sick. In the words of George Merck, "We try never to forget that medicine is for the people. It is not for the profits. The profits follow, and if we have remembered that they have never failed to appear. The better we have remembered it, the larger they have been." Being highly profitable allows Merck to pursue other, more important values.[6]

Obviously, individuals have values that determine in part their behavior. Not so obviously, companies also have values. Often these appear to be business-related values such as "customer service," "quality," and "teamwork," but often there are more straightforwardly ethical values such as "respect" and "integrity."

Values serve as an important tool in reasoning about ethical issues in business. There is often a conflict among competing values. For instance, if a company values both customer service and respect, there are certain kinds of behavior expected of its employees to meet customer service requirements. Many companies, such as Johnson and Johnson, try to capture values in a statement or code. Exhibit 4.1 is Johnson and Johnson's corporate values statement or credo.

Values can help an organization and its members clarify what is important in the organization. Values serve to raise interesting and important questions and to reveal difficult trade-offs. It is a mistake to see corporate values statements as mere "warm and fuzzy" statements that make everyone feel good. Rather they are statements of what an organization stands for—its main purpose for existence.

Oftentimes corporate values and individual values can conflict. Many times the statements of the values don't conflict, but the interpretations that bosses and employees put on the values vary widely. If values statements are to be effective in organizations in empowering employees to work for the organizational purpose, then there must be some means to question the values and, more important, to question processes, systems, and behaviors that appear not to be aligned with the values.

EXHIBIT 4.1   Johnson & Johnson's Credo.

Our Credo

We believe our first responsibility is to the doctors, nurses and patients,
to mothers and fathers and all others who use our products and services.
In meeting their needs everything we do must be of high quality.
We must constantly strive to reduce our costs
in order to maintain reasonable prices.
Customers' orders must be serviced promptly and accurately.
Our suppliers and distributors must have an opportunity
to make a fair profit.

We are responsible to our employees,
the men and women who work with us throughout the world.
Everyone must be considered as an individual.
We must respect their dignity and recognize their merit.
They must have a sense of security in their jobs.
Compensation must be fair and adequate,
and working conditions clean, orderly and safe.
We must be mindful of ways to help our employees fulfill
their family responsibilities.
Employees must feel free to make suggestions and complaints.
There must be equal opportunity for employment, development
and advancement for those qualified.
We must provide competent management,
and their actions must be just and ethical.

We are responsible to the communities in which we live and work
and to the world community as well.
We must be good citizens — support good works and charities
and bear our fair share of taxes.
We must encourage civic improvements and better health and education.
We must maintain in good order
the property we are privileged to use,
protecting the environment and natural resources.

Our final responsibility is to our stockholders.
Business must make a sound profit.
We must experiment with new ideas.
Research must be carried on, innovative programs developed
and mistakes paid for.
New equipment must be purchased, new facilities provided
and new products launched.
Reserves must be created to provide for adverse times.
When we operate according to these principles,
the stockholders should realize a fair return.

Johnson & Johnson

Source: Courtesy of Johnson & Johnson.

Rights, Duties, and Responsibilities

Values form the background against which other moral notions can be applied.
Some values are so important and pervasive that they are picked out for special
acclaim in the form of rights.[7] Because we value freedom and autonomy so
much, we define *rights* as a sphere of autonomy in which everyone can act
equally. The right to free speech is a right that everyone has, not just a few. The
rights to life, liberty, and the pursuit of happiness are broad categories of per-

missible actions. However, rarely are rights absolute. The scope of any individual's rights are limited by the rights of others. It is often said that my right to swing my fist ends at the beginning of your nose.

While there is much talk of rights in our society, there is little talk of a correlative concept—*duties*. Duties are obligations that we incur to take specific steps, or to refrain from taking specific steps, that are connected with the rights of others. For example, if Jack has the right not to be killed, then everyone has the correlative duty not to kill Jack. If Jill has the right to a living wage, then someone (a government, a community, a company) has the obligation/duty to provide or guarantee that wage. Rights without duties are not very useful. And duties without rights are not worth the trouble.

A third idea helps to tie together these abstract notions, and that is *responsibility*. Responsibility is a set of behaviors that we should engage in if a system of rights and duties is to be stable and useful. For instance, while Jack may have the right to free speech, it would be unwise and irresponsible to use that right in a way that constantly harmed others. Indeed, if Jack and others did such a thing, it would undermine the very nature of civil society that gives rise to the rights in the first place. In this sense, responsibility involves the judicious exercising of a set of rights.

Rights, duties, and responsibilities play an important role in analyzing ethical issues in business. What rights do customers have vis-à-vis product performance and safety? What duties do companies have regarding employees? What rights do employees have in terms of basic political freedoms? What does it mean to be a responsible company? A responsible manager? A responsible employee?

Consequences

One of the most critical concepts in ethics is quite familiar to all modes of business analysis—the idea that actions have *consequences*. Most business theories and models assume that all consequences of a business decision can be measured in economic terms and quantified, or at least specified in enough detail to allow a cost-benefit analysis. With ethical issues the consequences are not always so simple.

Consider an issue such as *insider trading*—buying and selling securities on the basis of material, nonpublic information—a practice that is illegal in the United States. The decision to trade on such information clearly allocates harms and benefits in a certain way. The insider is benefited at the expense of the person on the other side of the trade who is harmed. However, there is a more subtle consequence here. If insider trading were prevalent, then public confidence in the market could well be undermined. It is not clear how to value this consequence economically, but it must be taken into account in a thorough analysis of the ethics of insider trading.

Business ethics issues often focus on harms that have been created by business activity. Too often, benefits are ignored. And, we shall argue, business as an institution creates a lot of good things. Computer technology, new life-prolonging drugs, and systems for the spread of knowledge are but a few of the inventions that have made our lives better. If we blame businesses for the harm they create, then we should also give them credit for the good they create. Understanding both harms and benefits of business issues is critical to a balanced view of business ethics.

Principles and Rules

Over time, we have developed a number of generalizations from the judgments that we make about right and wrong. These generalizations are based on our values, our assignment of rights and duties, and our experience with consequences to be desired and those to be avoided. We capture these generalizations in the form of moral rules or principles.[8]

For most ethical problems we have devised a set of rules or principles on which there is widespread agreement. *Common morality* is the set of principles that determine how we live most of the time. Promise keeping, mutual aid, respect for persons, respect for property, and so forth are usually uncontroversial principles that cover a host of daily situations. We learn these principles as children, and they are reinforced in most of our social institutions.

Business is no exception here. Businesspeople keep their promises most of the time, treat others with respect and dignity, and help each other when they can do so at little additional cost. Furthermore, when we find someone not living by these common principles, we call his or her character into question. Business consultant Stephen Covey has gone so far as to suggest that we come to view the idea of leadership as living by moral principles and advocating the same in others.[9]

However, moral dilemmas arise for common morality in several instances. First, new technology makes us unsure of how a principle applies. For instance, we might agree on the right to privacy and the corresponding duty to respect the privacy of others, and we might formulate a principle such as "Unless there is an emergency, you shouldn't interfere in the private affairs of another." (The "unless" clause covers the cases where you could save someone's life by interfering, for example.) Normally, we would agree that personal mail, desk files, and so on are the private affairs of a person. However, the new computer technology may change this definition. E-mail, voice mail, electronic files, Lotus notes, and the Web may force us to rethink the applicability of this principle. There are sure to be a number of meaty dilemmas that get raised.

Principles can also be questioned when we encounter a society or a culture that does things differently or applies the same principle in a different manner. For instance, in many cultures the principle of freedom of the press is not understood in as far-reaching a manner as it is in the United States. We need more conversation and more reasoning to figure out how our principles may or may not apply in those situations.

A third challenge to principles and common morality may come from new groups being empowered in society. Indeed, in today's business world, the empowerment of women and minorities in the workforce has forced a rethinking of the biases that may be present in the workplace. The very idea of respect may be interpreted differently along gender roles. We don't need a new principle, but we do need a new conversation about its interpretation and applicability.

Parallel Cases

When we are faced with a difficult ethical dilemma, one in which principles conflict, where there are uncertain consequences and where values and rights don't clearly help us to find an answer, we need to turn to parallel cases. We need to look for cases that we are clear about and to extrapolate reasoning from those cases to ones that are similar but less clear.

Consider the case of the H.B. Fuller Co., maker of a glue called Resistol. This glue was being abused by young children in Honduras, who were called *Resistoleros*. A parallel case would be someone driving a car while intoxicated. The car is not being used in a manner for which it is intended, and if there is a crash we could hardly blame the car manufacturer. At the other end of the spectrum we find Johnson and Johnson's response to the deaths of Extra Strength Tylenol users that were caused by product tampering. J&J was not to blame, yet the company took the product off the market until it could introduce a tamper-resistant package. H.B. Fuller weighed such parallels and others to find a course consistent with its corporate values and the ethical expectations of both Honduras and the United States. In fact the company undertook an extensive program of education and social service to try to help those who had been affected and to prevent others from misusing the product. Eventually this meant addressing the formulation of the product itself in an ongoing manner.[10]

A Different Voice

Carol Gilligan has argued that the reliance on rights and principles in ethics represents only one point of view. She and others have suggested an alternative mode of reasoning called *the ethic of care* or *the ethic of connection.*

The idea is that rights and principles assume that people are separate from each other, that there is a kind of distance between them, and when that distance is closed, then there is interference. Rights and principles serve as rules for permissible boundary crossings. These rules are supposed to apply in all cases, with no exceptions for particular relationships. Gilligan suggests that such a view assumes a model of the self as separate and disconnected from others—an autonomous self that is threatened by connection.

The ethic of care, on the other hand, starts from different assumptions. It sees the self as first and foremost connected to others. There is no autonomous self completely apart from a set of relationships with others. Imagine the self as the center of a network of important relationships. In this view, ethics begins by caring about those with whom we have formed relationships. Moral problems arise because we have conflicting responsibilities to care, and we should solve those problems by focusing on the situational and individual contexts in which we find them.

While the ethic of care may seem abstract for business, the idea of stakeholders tries to capture at least one part of that ethic—the notion that business shouldn't be seen as completely autonomous but, rather, connected to an important set of relationships that define the very process of value creation. By seeing business in these terms we can more easily integrate the tools of moral reasoning, values, rights, duties, responsibilities, principles, and common morality into the very foundations of business so that the term *business ethics* becomes redundant rather than contradictory.

A METHOD FOR UNDERSTANDING CAPITALISM IN ETHICAL TERMS

One way to connect business and ethics is to begin by understanding that businesses can affect more than just shareholders.[11] Indeed, customers, suppliers, employees, communities, and shareholders are all affected in major ways by businesses. These groups have come to be known as the *stakeholders* in the firm. The stakeholder concept tries to set forth exactly who is affected by a business and to map the set of relationships that comprises the value-creation enterprise.

The concept of stakeholders was developed in the 1960s through the work of management theorists Eric Rhenman, Igor Ansoff, Russell Ackoff, and their students. The idea is connected to a very old tradition that sees business as an integral part of society rather than as an institution that is separate and purely economic in nature. Identifying and analyzing stakeholders was originally a simple way to acknowledge the existence of multiple constituencies in the corporation. The main insight was that executives must pay some strategic attention to those groups who were important to the success of the corporation.[12]

As the pace of change accelerated in business, these thinkers and others began to advocate more interaction with stakeholders so that they would have some sense of participation in the day-to-day affairs of the corporation. We had the emergence of consumer advisory panels, quality circles, just-in-time inventory teams, community advisory groups, and so on, all designed to get the corporation more in touch with the key relationships that affected its future. During the 1980s, the idea of "stakeholder management" was articulated as a method for systematically taking into account the interests of "those groups which can affect and are affected by the corporation."

As discussed previously, we have recently seen the emergence of a strong movement concerned with business ethics. Much of the business ethics movement has been in response to perceived corporate excesses such as oil spills, financial scandals, business-government collusion, and celebrated cases of whistle-blowing. But a small number of thinkers began to ask questions about the very purpose of the corporation. Should the corporation serve those who own shares of stock, or should it serve those who are affected by its actions? The choice was laid bare: Corporations can be made to serve stockholders or they can be made to serve stakeholders.

Most thoughtful executives know that this choice between stockholders and stakeholders is a false one. Corporations must be profitable at rates determined by global capital markets. No longer can executives ignore the fact that capital flows freely across borders and that rates of return are more complicated than indicated by internally generated financial hurdle rates and payback schemata. Business today is truly global.

Most thoughtful executives also know that great companies are not built by obsessive attention to shareholder value. Great companies arise in part out of a shared sense of purpose among employees and management. This sense of purpose must be important enough for individuals to expend their own human capital to create and deliver products and services that customers are willing to pay for. We need only return to the wisdom of Peter Drucker and W. Edwards Deming to see the importance of meaning and purpose and the destructiveness of fear and alienation in corporate life.

Management thinkers such as Tom Peters, Charles Handy, Jim Collins, and Jerry Poras have produced countless examples of how employees, customers, and suppliers work together to create something that none of them can create alone. And capital is necessary to sustain this process of value creation. From Cadbury to Volvo, Nordstrom to Hewlett-Packard, executives are constantly engaged in intense stakeholder relationships.

In this view, the interests of stockholders and stakeholders are very often in alignment rather than in conflict. Stockholders are a key stakeholder group whose support must be sustained in the same way that customer, supplier, and employee support must be garnered. The issue is one of balancing the interests of these groups, not favoring one at the expense of the others. Furthermore, in a relatively free political system, when executives ignore the interests of one group of stakeholders systematically over time, these stakeholders will use the political process to force regulation or legislation to protect themselves. Witness the emergence of "stakeholder rights" in the United States in the form of labor legislation, consumer protection legislation, environmental (community) protection legislation, even shareholder protection legislation.

Quite simply, there are many ways to manage a successful company. Management styles of Daimler Benz will be different from those of Volvo. Procter & Gamble's methods will differ from Unilever's. However, all will involve the intense interaction of employees—management and nonmanagement alike—with critical stakeholders. The more that stakeholders participate in the decisions that affect them, be they product design decisions or employment contract decisions, the greater the likelihood that they will be committed to the future of the corporate enterprise.

Contrast this commonsense view of the workings of business with the traditional business ideology that we outlined earlier: separating business from ethics, proclaiming that it is amoral, that business ethics is an oxymoron, and that business exists to do only what shareholders require. In this old philosophy, business is seen as warfare, and executives are the lonely soldiers on the battlefield of global markets, playing "shoot 'em up" with competitors. This myth of the primacy of the shareholder and its view of business as "cowboy capitalism" leads to a profound public mistrust and misunderstanding of the basic processes that make companies successful. We need a new story—one that elevates business to the higher moral ground—and one that smacks of common sense and reality in today's business world.

Stakeholder capitalism, properly formulated, is just the new story that we need. Stakeholder capitalism is based on four principles (see Exhibit 4.2), each of which is important to remember if we are to craft a capitalism that will serve us in the next century.

EXHIBIT 4.2   Four principles of values-based capitalism or stakeholder capitalism.

---

1. **The principle of stakeholder cooperation**
   Value is created because stakeholders can jointly satisfy their needs and desires.

   (Capitalism works because entrepreneurs and managers put together and sustain deals with stakeholders, rather than becoming agents of the owners of capital.)

2. **The principle of complexity**
   Human beings are complex creatures, capable of acting on multidimensional values, some of which are selfish, some of which are altruistic, and many of which are jointly created and shared with others.

   (Capitalism works because of this complexity rather than in spite of it.)

3. **The principle of continuous creation**
   Cooperating with stakeholders and motivated by values, people continuously create new sources of value.

   (Capitalism works because the creative force is primarily continuous rather than primarily destructive.)

4. **The principle of emergent competition**
   In a relatively free and democratic society, people can create alternatives for stakeholders.

   (Capitalism works because competition emerges out of the cooperation among stakeholders, rather than being based on some primal urge of competition.)

First of all, the *principle of stakeholder cooperation* says that value is created because stakeholders can jointly satisfy their needs and desires. Business is not a zero-sum game. Capitalism works because entrepreneurs and managers put together and sustain deals or relationships among customers, suppliers, employees, financiers, and communities. The support of each group is vital to the success of the endeavor. This is the cooperative commonsense part of business that every executive knows, but the myth of primacy of the shareholder tells us that some stakeholders are more important than others. Try building a great company without the support of all stakeholders. It simply cannot be sustained.

Second, the *principle of complexity* claims that human beings are complex creatures capable of actions based on many different values. We are not just economic maximizers. Sometimes we are selfish and sometimes we are altruistic. Many of our values are jointly determined and shared. Capitalism works because of this complexity rather than in spite of it.

Third, the *principle of continuous creation* says that business as an institution is a source of the creation of value. Cooperating with stakeholders and motivated by values, businesspeople continuously create new sources of value. This creative force of humans is the engine of capitalism. The beauty of the modern corporate form is that it can be made to be continuous rather than destructive. One creation doesn't have to destroy another; rather, there is a continuous cycle of value creation that raises the well-being of everyone. People come together to create something, be it a new computer program, a new level of service, a way to heal the sick, or simply greater harmony.

Finally, the *principle of emergent competition* says that competition emerges from a relatively free and democratic society and therefore stakeholders have options. Competition emerges out of the cooperation among stakeholders rather than being based on the primal urge to defeat the other person. Competition is important in stakeholder capitalism, but it is not the primary force. It is in its ability to manage the tension created by simultaneous cooperation and competition that stakeholder capitalism distinguishes itself.

Stakeholder capitalism takes a firm ethical stand: that human beings are required to be at the center of any process of value creation, that common decency and fairness are not to be set aside in the name of playing the game of business, that we should demand the best behavior of business, and that we should enact a story about business that celebrates its triumphs, admonishes its failures, and fully partakes of the moral discourse in society as a routine matter.

Stakeholder capitalism is no panacea. It simply allows the possibility that business may become a fully human institution. There will always be businesspeople who try to take advantage of others, just as there are corrupt government officials, clergy, and professors. Stakeholder capitalism bases our understanding and expectations of business, not on the worst that we can do, but on the best. It sets a high moral standard, recognizes the commonsense, practical world of global business today, and asks managers to get on with the task of creating value for all stakeholders.

ETHICAL CHALLENGES TO BUSINESS

In the global business environment of today there are a host of ethical issues that managers must learn to deal with. The first group of issues could be called *cross-cultural issues* and is the result of encountering different ways of doing business around the world—in other words, a different set of assumptions about people and their motivations. For instance, one typical cross-cultural issue is bribery. In some countries, such as the United States, bribery paid to officials is not an acceptable social practice (and is illegal), while in other countries, making payments to facilitate officials' complying with a request is standard practice. Gift giving, entertainment of purchasing and marketing executives, showing favoritism to relatives or to relatives of important clients are all issues that are dealt with differently all over the world. There are vast global differences in employment practices with respect to women and minority groups, minimum wages, and working conditions. Executives need to address these issues in sophisticated ways that can coherently justify corporate policy.

Thomas Donaldson has suggested a heuristic for solving such issues.[13] Suppose that a particular practice, say petty bribery, is not permitted in the home country but is permitted in the host country. Donaldson claims that executives should ask two questions. First, is engaging in the practice a necessary condition for doing business in the host country? If it is not, then the company should not engage in the practice; since it is not ethically permitted in the home country, the company already has a good reason not to engage in it. Second, does the practice violate any important human rights as defined by international treaties that home and host country have both signed? Even in cases where a practice is necessary to do business, companies should not violate important human rights. We might argue that small payments to customs officials to expedite orders are in fact necessary in some countries, but violate no important human rights. Donaldson would distinguish such a case from engaging in unsafe working practices and conditions that would indeed violate basic human rights.

A second group of ethical issues could be called *competitiveness issues*. Issues such as restructuring and reengineering, the new social contract with employees, aligning individual and corporate values, outsourcing of work, contract/temporary employees, offshore moves of production, and many more are all ethical issues that are present in the current business environment. To address these issues with "I'm only doing what is best for the business" does not excuse the manager from making ethical justifications. We have suggested that these issues can best be addressed in a stakeholder framework, but regardless, with the information technology available today, they must be addressed in a way that stands the *publicity test:* Can our solution to this problem face the light of day? What happens when what we did is printed in the newspaper? Increasingly, competitiveness issues are public, especially for large multinational companies. Solving issues differently in different countries is a strategy that is increasingly indefensible.

Often the choice is offered between "when in Rome do as the Romans do" and "when in Rome do as we do in Charlottesville." The latter doesn't respect the Romans and leads to a moral imperialism that is increasingly irrelevant. The former doesn't respect our own values and leads to moral relativism and situational ethics that are alien to the moral point of view. Perhaps we should offer an alternative: "When in Rome do as we and the Romans can agree upon." Such a directive places a premium on learning and sharing in an open conversation about the connection between business and ethics.

A final group of ethical issues in business could be called *everyday issues.* Honest performance appraisal and objective setting, openness in communication, employee empowerment, dealing with customer complaints, treating suppliers fairly, representing corporate performance honestly, dealing with troubled employees, family and work issues, sexual harassment, the glass ceiling, racism in hiring and promotion decisions, and affirmative action are but a few of the ethical issues that companies must address on a daily basis. While there are a host of complex issues, the following questions can be used to guide an ethical analysis:

1. Who are the stakeholders? Who is affected by this issue and how? What does each party have at stake?
2. What are the most important values of each stakeholder? How is each stakeholder harmed or benefited by options that might be considered?
3. What rights and duties are at issue?
4. What principles and rules are relevant?
5. What are some relevant parallel cases?
6. What should we do?

These questions offer no more than an analytical start to asking questions about ethics in business. The role of ethics in business is likely to increase, as is the complexity of the issues involved. Today's effective executive must have a keen ability to sense and address issues in both business and ethical terms.

FOR FURTHER READING

Business Ethics Quarterly is the source for many scholarly articles, book reviews, and new ideas about business ethics.

The Dictionary of Business Ethics, edited by Patricia H. Werhane and R. Edward Freeman, Blackwell's Publishing Inc., 1997, is a comprehensive guide to topics in business ethics written by the leading thinkers in business ethics from around the world.

The Ruffin Series in Business Ethics, published by Oxford University Press, currently contains 13 volumes of the latest ideas, theories, and concepts about the connection of ethics to business.

5 MAKING DECISIONS RIGOROUSLY: THE USE OF QUANTITATIVE METHODS

Conventional wisdom applauds the intuitive genius, the manager who decides important questions successfully by the seat of the pants. But the best decisions are made rigorously, on the basis of facts (not opinions) and with the help of tools that clarify the economic reality of alternative choices. For the most part, these tools are recent inventions, having gained popularity in the last 50 years. They help illuminate the costs and benefits of alternatives and generally sharpen the way the modern manager approaches problems. This chapter will focus on the four most important tools in decision analysis and then illustrate their use in the analysis of a complex problem. The four tools are as follows:

- *Influence diagrams.* An influence diagram maps the interrelationships among elements of a decision.

- *Decision trees.* A decision tree is simply a way of laying out in graphical form the choices that confront a manager, the events that follow thereafter, and the time sequence whereby choices and outcomes occur. The power of this tool is that it clarifies the *structure* of a problem.

- *Statistics and probability.* Probability is the chance that something will occur. Statistics help describe the probability. Statistics and estimates of probability help clarify the *impact of uncertainty* on today's decision.

- *Discounting and the time value of money.* Discounting helps estimate the *value today* of a cash flow arriving in the future. This technique helps the decision maker understand the consequences today of cash flows that may be distant in time.

Combined, these tools do not necessarily provide all the right answers to complicated problems. However, they can help the manager avoid big errors. Howard Raiffa[1] has offered four classic categories of errors:

1. Rejecting a good idea.
2. Accepting a bad idea.
3. Solving the wrong problem.
4. Solving the right problem too late.

If you sense any of these looming in your decision environment, the tools described here might help you.

INFLUENCE DIAGRAMS

Influence diagrams map systems of cause and effect. These diagrams show what causes are involved, how they are linked, and how they affect outcomes. Such diagrams can clarify tangled analytical problems, form a useful foundation for spreadsheet modeling, and help uncover key points of sensitivity and leverage for tackling the problem.

An influence diagram draws on four elements:

□ = a decision node, a point at which the manager must make a choice. These are choices controlled by the decision maker.

○ = an intermediate quantity, something influenced by the decision and affecting the outcome.

○ = an outcome or performance node.

→ = a linkage between nodes that indicates a direction of influence both in substance and time.

To illustrate the use of influence diagrams, consider the decision a pharmaceutical company faces when it must decide whether to invest in a new drug research and development program. The influence diagram at its simplest is shown in Exhibit 5.1.

Upon careful reflection, you conclude that the decision to invest and the ability to earn a profit are influenced by other factors:

- *Investment* is influenced by strategy (should we offer this new line of drug?), organization (do we have the human capital necessary to mount this R&D program?), and returns (how big and certain are the profits?)

EXHIBIT 5.1   Simplistic relationship between R&D and profit.

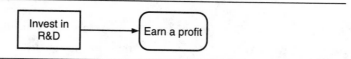

- *Profit* is influenced by costs and revenues, both which are influenced by the success rate of the R&D program.

Reflecting on this richer set of influences, the diagram of the investment decision would become more elaborate, as shown in Exhibit 5.2, which is more useful to the decision maker than the simple version. It shows how the profitability of the R&D program depends on several factors (revenues, costs, and success rate). In addition, it shows a *feedback loop*—the investment decision affects intermediate factors that affect profits, which in turn affects the investment decision. Finally, the diagram shows that the investment decision depends not only on expected profits, but also on considerations of strategy and organizational capacity. As a manager, you might gain insights from this diagram that involve the refinement of investment analysis and also help you set an agenda for decision making and action taking. The diagram suggests that in the course of assessing the R&D investment program, you will need to incorporate a range of departments or expertise in strategy, organization, finance, marketing, production, and so on.

In short, the influence diagram is a useful tool for mapping trails of cause and effect. Knowing these trails can help you address the right questions, at the proper time, and at appropriate depth.

EXHIBIT 5.2   A richer model of the relationship between R&D and profit.

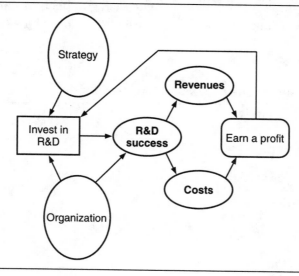

DECISION TREES

A decision tree diagrams a decision problem. It is similar in some ways to an influence diagram, but it can give much more insight on discrete decision alternatives. Each tree is composed of just three basic elements:

□ = a decision node, a point at which the manager must make a choice. These are choices controlled by the decision maker.

○ = an event node, a point at which a result occurs. These are choices controlled by chance.

→ = a linkage between decisions and events.

The simplest decision is a choice with two alternatives: yes or no, go/no-go. Like a fork in a road, the choice of one precludes the other. In diagram terms, a simple decision is shown in Exhibit 5.3.

Sometimes, simply identifying the basic choice in a decision is a vast improvement in a manager's thinking. Even the simplest, most basic choices have *consequences*. One possible consequence is that a choice opens or forecloses other choices down the road. For instance, if you decide to change the oil in your car, you must then decide which brand of oil to use, and how and where to dispose of the old oil.

A second possible consequence is that a choice may trigger an event. For instance, to enter your competitor's home territory may elicit a strategic response from the competitor. To drill for oil will trigger a finding of oil or no oil.

These consequences complicate the simplest decisions. Fortunately, the consequences can be modeled along with the simple decision. Where careful judgment is required in modeling the sequencing of decisions and their consequences is in laying out the *correct sequence* of decisions and events.

EXHIBIT 5.3   The simple "go/no-go" decision.

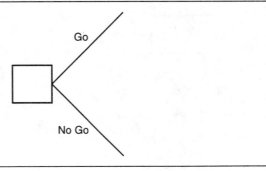

For example, consider J. Paul Getty's famous formula for getting rich: "Rise early. Work hard. Find oil." How would you model the decision to follow his advice? First, suppose that you choose between rising early or sleeping late—this is our simple choice with two alternatives. Second, suppose you choose between working hard or taking it easy (another simple choice). Third, suppose that you decide to get out of bed, *then* you decide whether to work hard—this sequence should be reflected in the design of our tree. Next we have "find oil": Is this a decision or an event? To some people, "find oil" means to look for it. But simply looking for oil does not make you rich, as many broke prospectors will agree. Remember that Getty was telling us how to get rich. By "find oil" he must have meant to actually discover its presence. Finding oil is an event, not a decision. It must come *after* "rise early" and "work hard." A final consideration: Is it possible to find oil without working hard? Perhaps, but it's not very likely. For the sake of completeness, let's suppose that if you sleep late and take it easy, no oil will be found. The diagram helps explain why "find oil" was the last element in J. Paul Getty's formula. It is a consequence of long days and hard work. To model the decision to follow J. Paul Getty's advice entails a series of decision and event forks. The outcome or event of finding oil is represented in the diagram with an event node, ○. The choices of when to rise and how hard to work are represented by decision nodes, □. A representation of the decision is shown in Exhibit 5.4. Reading the tree in reverse (from right to left) helps the decision maker see which

EXHIBIT 5.4   A decision-tree modeling: "Rise early, work hard, find oil."

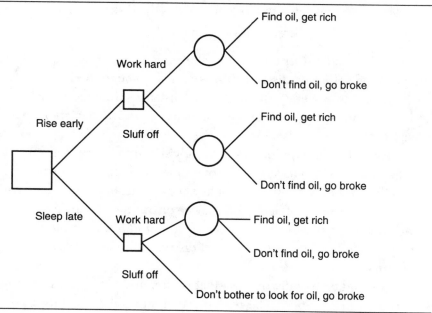

paths lead to good outcomes and which paths lead to bad ones. The tree clarifies the structure of the problem of getting rich.

PROBABILITY AND STATISTICS

Simply structuring a problem in the form of a decision tree is rarely sufficient to help managers make decisions. One main reason is that the outcomes at the event nodes are usually *uncertain*. (The other main reason has to do with the time value of money, which is covered in the next section.) We express the uncertainty associated with events in terms of *probabilities,* the number of times out of 100 that the event is likely to occur. For instance, weather forecasters express the uncertainty about rain tomorrow as a percent chance. Oil prospectors study geological data to estimate the percent chance of finding oil in a certain location. Medical doctors estimate a percent chance of a patient's recovery given a certain kind of treatment.

Underlying every expression of probability is an implicit or explicit *probability distribution.* A probability distribution describes the chances of a range of different outcomes occurring. Distributions can be described by *statistics,* which measure central tendency and dispersion. Measures of central tendency are statistics such as the following:

- *Mean* (or *average*) is the sum of the observations divided by the number of observations.
- *Median* is that value that exactly divides the distribution in half.
- *Mode* is the most frequent value in the distribution.

The dispersion of a distribution (i.e., the spread or narrowness) is described by the *range* (which is the distance from the high value to the low value), the *variance* (which is the average of the squared distances from individual observations and the mean of the distribution), and the *standard deviation* (which is the square root of the variance).

Probability distributions are relatively straightforward to graph: At the simplest, we can use bar charts like the one shown in Exhibit 5.5, which displays the probability of drawing any of four suits out of a deck of well-shuffled cards. Each suit has a 25% chance of being drawn. The distribution of chances is level or uniform—this particular distribution is called a *uniform distribution.* Exhibit 5.5 illustrates one very important point of distributions: *The probabilities of all discrete outcomes always sum to 100%.*

A second type of distribution that is often used in business management is the *triangle distribution.* The triangle is based on three points assessed by an

EXHIBIT 5.5   Probability distribution of drawing cards by suits.

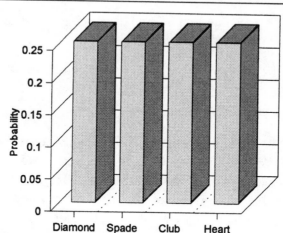

analyst: a minimum outcome, a maximum outcome, and a best guess. The result-ing distribution forms a triangle, hence its name (see Exhibit 5.6).

Many occurrences in science and society can be described by the well-known bell-shaped curve, or *normal distribution.* A common mistake of many managers is to assume that the normal distribution describes all phenomena (it does not). Indeed, the uniform and triangle distributions, along with a wide variety of others, may do a better job of describing the world than the normal distribution. But the normal distribution has a number of interesting features. First, it is symmetric around the middle. Second, the middle, or *central tendency,* of the distribution is equally well described by the mean, median, and mode. For a normal distribution,

EXHIBIT 5.6   Triangle distribution.

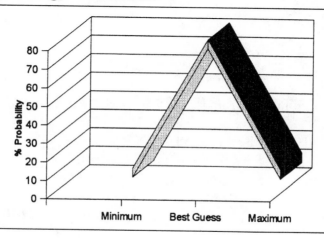

$$\text{Mean} = \text{median} = \text{mode}$$

Third, the standard deviation of a normal distribution instantly reveals the following:

- 68% of the observations lie within ± one standard deviation.
- 95% lie within ± two standard deviations.
- Over 99% lie within ± three standard deviations.

Exhibit 5.7 gives information on the frequency distributions of annual returns on various kinds of investments from 1926 to 1994. Many researchers suspect that if we had more data, the distributions would smooth out to conform to the well-known bell-shaped curve, or normal distribution. To illustrate this concept of spread, Exhibit 5.7 shows that the annual rates of return on U.S. Treasury Bills have a very tight or narrow distribution, with a standard deviation of 3.3%—thus, in 68 percent of the years, U.S. Treasury Bills have yielded a return within ±3.3 percentage points of the mean return of 3.7%. In contrast, the returns on small stocks have a very wide distribution, with a standard deviation of 34.6%—in 68% of the years, small stocks have yielded a return in the range from −17.2% to +52.0%.[2] The key idea here is that *standard deviation measures uncertainty*—the narrower the spread, the more certain the return; the wider the spread, the less certain the return.

The fourth and final important characteristic of normal distributions is that they can be completely described by two statistics: the mean and standard deviation. If you have these two numbers, then you can use *normal tables* to determine the probability of occurrence. For instance, suppose that you wish to determine the likelihood that your investment in small stocks will earn a rate of return of at least 25%. Also, you assume that the distribution of returns in the future is the same as in the past. Using the mean (0.174) and standard deviation (0.346) of the distribution of historical returns, you compute a Z value with this formula:

$$Z = \frac{(\text{target return} - \text{average return})}{(\text{standard deviation of returns})} = \frac{(0.25 - 0.174)}{0.346} = 0.22$$

Z measures the number of standard deviations away from the mean that your target return is. Looking up the value 0.22 in the normal table reveals a probability of about 41% that the return will be 25% or more.[3]

The whole point of learning something about probability and statistics is to sharpen your managerial decision making. Recall that the shortcoming of using decision trees alone is that they don't describe uncertainty very precisely. Here is where probabilities help: You can use them to estimate *expected values of out-*

EXHIBIT 5.7   Stock returns by type from 1926 to 1994.

Series	Geometric mean	Arithmetic mean	Standard deviation	Distribution
Large company stocks	10.2%	12.2%	20.3%	
Small company stocks°	12.2	17.4	34.6	
Long-term corporate bonds	5.4	5.7	8.4	
Long-term government bonds	4.8	5.2	8.8	
Intermediate-term government bonds	5.1	5.2	5.7	
U.S. Treasury bills	3.7	3.7	3.3	
Inflation	3.1	3.2	4.6	

                                                           −90%   0%   90%

°The 1933 Small Company Stock Total Return was 142.9 percent.
Source: © Computed using data from *Stocks, Bonds, Bills & Inflation 1995 Yearbook*™, Ibbotson Associates, Chicago (annually updates work by Roger G. Ibbotson and Rex Sinquefield). Used with permission. All rights reserved.

comes. An expected value is just the average of the possible outcomes of an event node weighted by the probabilities of those outcomes. You must understand that the expected value is just the average of an uncertain outcome across many trials—you cannot be sure of receiving exactly that amount in any particular attempt to illustrate the calculation of expected value. Suppose that the probability of finding oil is only 2%, and therefore the probability of *not* finding oil is 98 percent (1.00 − 0.02). If you find oil, suppose you will earn a profit of $10 million by selling the oil rights to a big oil company. If you don't find oil, suppose you must eat the costs of exploration, $200,000. The expected value of the outcome (find/don't find oil) is the average of the economic outcomes, weighted by their probabilities (see Exhibit 5.8).

Such calculations provide the expected values to be inserted into the decision tree. Let's illustrate this further with the J. Paul Getty decision tree. Suppose the probability of finding oil is affected by how hard you work and how

EXHIBIT 5.8   Calculation of the probability-weighted expected value of finding oil.

	Find Oil	Don't Find Oil
Profit/loss	$10,000,000	–$200,000
Probability	0.10	0.90
Profit/loss × probability	$1,000,000	–$180,000
Expected value of outcome	$1,000,000 – 180,000 = $820,000	

EXHIBIT 5.9   Expected values associated with decisions about rising early and working hard.

	Long Day (Rise Early)	Short Day (Sleep In)
Work hard	p (find oil) = 10% p (don't find) = 90% Expected value = (0.1 × $10m) + (0.9 × –0.2) = $820,000	p (find oil) = 5% p (don't find) = 95% Expected value = (0.05 × $10m) + (0.95 × –0.2) = $310,000
Sluff off	p (find oil) = 1% p (don't find) = 99% Expected value = (0.01 × $10) + (0.99 × –0.2) = –$98,000	p (find oil) = 0% p (don't find) = 100% Expected value = –$20,000

long a day you put in (see Exhibit 5.9). Inserting the probabilities and outcome values into the decision tree yields expected values for events (see Exhibit 5.10).

This decision tree, augmented with probabilities and expected values, begins to yield findings that will help us make decisions. For instance, if we rise early and work hard, the expected value is $820,000—this dominates all other paths, and if you want to get rich this is the path to follow. However, the tree suggests that if you can't muster the energy to both rise early *and* work hard, then sleeping late and working hard will result in a better return than rising early and doing a mediocre job—to the tune of about $408,000 better. In short, casting the outcomes of decision tree branches into terms of expected monetary values helps us rank, compare, and choose the best path.

TIME VALUE OF MONEY

The final ingredient in our analysis of decisions is to account for time in our valuation of economic outcomes. Time is money. Our intuition tells us this is true because a dollar we receive today could be invested for the next year to return the dollar plus some added value. Thus, receiving a dollar today is worth more than receiving a dollar one year from now.

EXHIBIT 5.10   The decision tree with expected values (k stands for thousands, "mil." stands for millions, p stands for probability, EV stands for expected value).

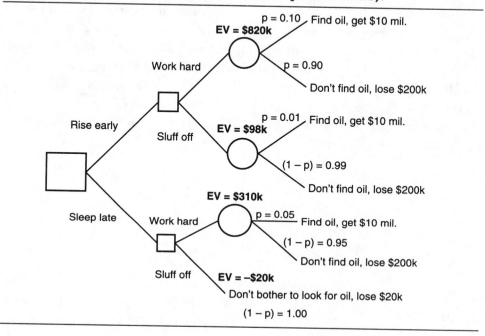

Compounding Estimates Future Values

To find out what a dollar invested today would be worth one year from now (i.e., to find the future value or FV), consider that at the end of the year we will receive the dollar back, plus a profit or return. This return can be calculated by multiplying r, the interest rate if we invest in bonds or a required equity return if we invest in stocks, times our invested amount. At the end of the year, we will receive back $(1 + r)$ times our initial investment.

This logic can be extended to more than one year. Over two years, we receive $(1 + r)$ times the investment at the end of the first year—*and then turn right around and reinvest it at the same rate for the second year.* This means that at the end of two years, we have a future value worth our investment times $(1 + r)$ times $(1 + r)$. The pattern continues for three years and longer. Fortunately, the use of exponents simplifies what could otherwise become a lengthy equation. The following equations show the future value of $1 invested today at the rate of return r.

$$\text{FV, year 1} = \$1.00 \times (1 + r) = \$1(1 + r)$$
$$\text{FV, year 2} = \$1.00 \times (1 + r) \times (1 + r) = \$1(1 + r)^2$$
$$\text{FV, year 3} = \$1.00 \times (1 + r) \times (1 + r)(1 + r) = \$1(1 + r)^3$$

Discounting Estimates Present Values

Of more interest to most decision makers is today's value of some future value. Because of the hidden opportunity cost in virtually all investments you make, it is necessary to recognize the time value of money. Instead of just waiting for the future value to arrive, perhaps there is an alternative course of action that would give us some *present value* that, if invested, would yield a future value larger than the one we foresee. Only by discounting all future values to the present can we truly compare them on the same apples-to-apples basis of time.

Arithmetically, the process of discounting is just the reverse of compounding—we divide the future value by the compound interest factor:

$$\text{PV of year 1 FV} = \frac{\$1.00}{(1+r)} = \frac{\$1.00}{(1+r)}$$

$$\text{PV of year 2 FV} = \frac{\$1.00}{(1+r)(1+r)} = \frac{\$1.00}{(1+r)^2}$$

$$\text{PV of year 3 FV} = \frac{\$1.00}{(1+r)(1+r)(1+r)} = \frac{\$1.00}{(1+r)^3}$$

Let's return to the decision tree about J. Paul Getty's advice and consider how applying present values would affect things. Suppose that the costs of searching for oil are incurred immediately. If we strike oil, any cost incurred is immediately refunded, and any revenues from the sale of oil reserves are realized in two years (customers take their time paying). To recognize this timing difference, we need to convert all expected values into expected present values. The final assumption we need is the discount rate,[4] which is 20% (oil wildcatters have highly attractive alternative investments).

Exhibit 5.11 shows that when we take into account the time value of money, the payoffs in today's terms are much less than originally thought. This is because the benefit of the future gain of $10 million must be discounted over the two years, whereas the loss must be absorbed immediately. Thus, the discounting process gives us new information with which to evaluate the decision (see Exhibit 5.12).

The revised decision tree shows no change in the dominance of one route over another—the best path to getting rich is to rise early and work hard. But *now* we are reasonably more confident that we are making an apples-to-apples comparison of the attractiveness of the alternative paths to riches.

EXHIBIT 5.11   Expected present values associated with decisions about rising early and working hard.

	Long Day (Rise Early)	Short Day (Sleep In)
Work hard	p (find oil) = 10% p (don't find) = 90% Expected value = $820,000 Expected present value = $(0.1 \times \$10m/(1.2)^2) + (0.9 \times -0.2) =$ $514,444	p (find oil) = 5% p (don't find) = 95% Expected value = $310,000 Expected present value = $(.05 \times \$10m/(1.2)^2) + (0.95 \times -0.2) =$ $157,222
Sluff off	p(find oil) = 1% p(don't find) = 99% Expected value = −$88,000 Expected present value = $(0.01 \times \$10/(1.2)^2) + (0.99 \times -0.2) =$ −$128,555	p(find oil) = 0% p(don't find) = 100% Expected value = −$20,000 Expected present value = −$20,000

EXHIBIT 5.12   The decision tree with expected present values (k stands for thousands, "mil." stands for millions, p stands for probability, EV stands for expected value).

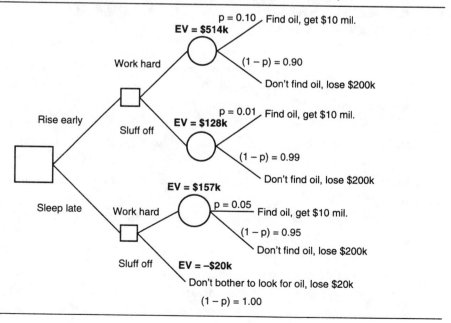

THE PROS AND CONS OF DECISION ANALYSIS

Deciding to use techniques such as those described here is not a straightforward decision.[5] You must weigh the potential benefits and costs of going to the trouble to use these techniques. Plainly, these techniques can motivate a more rational and holistic view of decisions. The clarity produced by these techniques can help communication about the alternatives as well as stimulate careful gathering of good information. However, the approach needs probabilities and outcomes that can be quantified. It is costly in time and talent to work up a decision tree analysis. What happens if such quantification is impossible? The more you guess about probabilities, discount rates, and outcomes, the less powerful are the expected present monetary values in helping you make decisions. As the saying goes, "Garbage in, garbage out."[6] Finally, the results may mean different things to different people; the methods ignore these. For instance, a fully blown decision tree analysis may dictate the location of a large toxic waste dump—but if that location is your backyard, you will feel differently about the recommendation than if you are a decision maker hundreds of miles away. Plainly, different decision makers with different sets of objectives might filter the results of a decision analysis in different ways.

CASE STUDY: TAKEOVER STRATEGY TOWARD CONRAIL CORPORATION

In early October 1996, CSX Corporation was putting the finishing touches on its plan to acquire Conrail Corporation, thus creating the largest railroad in the eastern United States. Conrail had been created by the U.S. government in the early 1970s out of the remains of several bankrupt railroads, most notably Penn Central. By the early 1980s, Conrail had established a record of financial health. The Reagan administration sought to sell Conrail to Norfolk Southern Corporation, but Congress and the management of Conrail itself insisted on a public offering of securities through an initial public offering. Conrail became an independent, publicly held corporation in 1986. Norfolk Southern had continued to pursue an acquisition of Conrail over the years, most recently (September 1996) secretly offering to buy Conrail's shares for $101 apiece (the shares had been trading at around $70). However, Conrail's management decided to sell the firm to CSX Corporation, Norfolk Southern's archrival, in the belief that the resulting firm would be healthier and more competitive. Conrail and CSX believed that combining the two firms would result in synergies and operating benefits worth $550 million annually.

John Snow, the CEO of CSX, had negotiated many of the terms of the acquisition of Conrail. All that remained was to agree on a price. Given Norfolk Southern's keen interest in acquiring Conrail, Snow knew that the price and other terms of acquisition would have a big influence on whether Norfolk Southern actively entered the bidding for Conrail. While Conrail had agreed to a number of defensive measures[7] aimed at preserving Conrail for CSX, nothing could prevent Norfolk Southern from trying to acquire Conrail for itself.

Suppose that John Snow weighed two competing bidding strategies:[8]

- *Open with a low bid.*   Opening with an offer to pay a low price would result in a high net present value of the acquisition to CSX, but it would also encourage Norfolk to enter the bidding. Let us suppose that with a low bid, there was a 95% chance that Norfolk would contest the acquisition and a 5% chance that it would not.

- *Open with a high bid.*   Opening with an offer to pay a lot of money would lower the net present value of the acquisition to CSX, but it would also tend to discourage Norfolk from entering the bidding. Let us suppose that with a high bid, there was a 60% chance that Norfolk would contest the acquisition and a 40% chance that it would not.

Analysts believed that if Norfolk Southern contested the acquisition, three outcomes might occur:

- *Auction is triggered.*   Under one scenario, CSX and Norfolk would get into a bidding contest, either declared officially by the directors of Conrail, or de facto as the two firms sought to outbid each other. Though CSX was larger than Norfolk, analysts believed that Norfolk had deeper pockets of cash and unused debt capacity with which to finance an acquisition. Therefore, the guess was that Norfolk would win an auction process. CSX would be left with the breakup fee of $300 million and profits on Conrail shares it owned of $500 million, for a total NPV of $800 million under the "bid high" strategy. Under the "bid low" strategy, the fees and profits would total only $400 million.

- *Defenses work: CSX stonewalls Norfolk and buys Conrail.*   The elaborate defenses on the deal stood a fair chance of protecting CSX's chance to buy Conrail, no matter what Norfolk offered. Unfortunately, because of the high initial-bid price, the NPV of this outcome would be only $200 million. With a low initial-bid price, the NPV would be $1 billion.

- *Government intervenes.*   In the public interest, the Surface Transportation Board of the U.S. government could overrule any proposed acquisition and dictate virtually any outcome. Analysts believed that rather than favor one buyer over another, the STB would divide Conrail between the two suitors. Under the high-bid strategy, suppose that the NPV of this outcome to CSX would be $900 million; under the low-bid strategy, the NPV would be $1 billion.

Suppose that the probability of an auction was 40 percent, of defenses working was 40 percent, and of government intervention was 20 percent. If Norfolk Southern did not contest the acquisition, the NPV of the high-bid strategy would be $1 billion; the low-bid NPV would be $1.5 billion.

Exhibit 5.13 presents the decision tree, probabilities, and expected monetary values of this problem. The analysis reveals that a high-bid strategy has a larger expected monetary value ($832 million) than does the low-bid strategy ($797 million). The tree shows why: The benefit of deterring Norfolk Southern from entering the bidding is significant—the expected monetary values (EMVs) of the no-contest cases are much higher than the EMVs of the contested cases. Strictly on the basis of this initial quantitative analysis, John Snow would be advised to open with a high bid for Conrail.

To go one step further, you can vary the assumed probabilities in order to test the sensitivity of the recommendation to variations in the assumptions. Exhibit 5.14 shows an example of such a sensitivity table (shaded cells indicate values from the "base case" scenario presented in the decision tree).

The exhibit shows that the EMV of each strategy is quite sensitive to variations in the probability of Norfolk entering the bidding. The more probable is Norfolk's entry, the lower is CSX's EMV. The shaded areas show the results for the base-case analysis in Exhibit 5.13. If there is any underestimate of probabilities of Norfolk entering the bidding, then the low-bid strategy would almost surely dominate.

The Conrail analysis raises a final consideration regarding the presence of a thinking, rational competitor. The decision tree implicitly assumes a benign (or at least indifferent) Norfolk Southern. If the possibility exists that Norfolk Southern might try to prevent CSX from acquiring Conrail at almost all costs, then the scheme of decisions and events could become considerably more complicated (and the stakes considerably higher). In such a world, CSX would need to approach the problem *strategically* (i.e., like a chess player thinking about many possible moves and countermoves). The subfield of decision analysis that addresses problems like these is called *game theory*. Unfortunately, it is beyond the scope of this introduction, but to pique your interest, it is worth pointing out

EXHIBIT 5.13 Full decision tree, Conrail case.

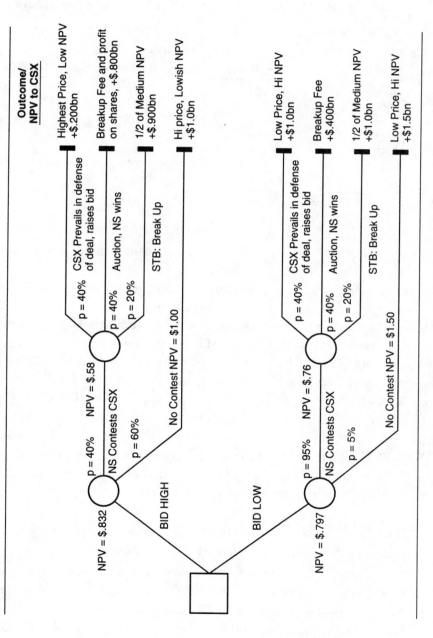

		Outcome/ NPV to CSX

NPV = $.832

BID HIGH

p = 40%   NPV = $.58
NS Contests CSX

p = 60%
No Contest NPV = $1.00

p = 40%   CSX Prevails in defense of deal, raises bid — Highest Price, Low NPV +$.200bn

p = 40%   Auction, NS wins — Breakup Fee and profit on shares, +$.800bn

p = 20%   STB: Break Up — 1/2 of Medium NPV +$.900bn

Hi price, Lowish NPV +$1.0bn

BID LOW

NPV = $.797

p = 95%   NPV = $.76
NS Contests CSX

p = 5%
No Contest NPV = $1.50

p = 40%   CSX Prevails in defense of deal, raises bid — Low Price, Hi NPV +$1.0bn

p = 40%   Auction, NS wins — Breakup Fee +$.400bn

p = 20%   STB: Break Up — 1/2 of Medium NPV +$1.0bn

Low Price, Hi NPV +$1.5bn

EXHIBIT 5.14   Expected monetary values to CSX of attempt to acquire Conrail broken down by type of bidding strategy, and probability of Norfolk Southern entering the bidding.

Bid-Low Strategy		Bid-High Strategy	
Probability of Norfolk entering the bidding	EMV ($ millions)	Probability of Norfolk entering the bidding	EMV ($ millions)
100%	760	60%	748
95%	797	55%	769
90%	834	50%	790
85%	871	45%	811
80%	908	40%	832
75%	945	35%	853
70%	982	30%	874

Note: Shading indicates results depicted in Exhibit 5.13.

that game theory can model one well-known adverse phenomenon in takeovers: the prisoner's dilemma (where both competitors likely lose).

On October 15, 1996, CSX announced terms of merger with Conrail. Norfolk Southern responded on October 26 with an unsolicited offer that was materially higher. CSX raised its bid; Norfolk raised even higher. Eventually, the U.S. Surface Transportation Board let it be known that it favored an amicable division of Conrail between CSX and Norfolk. Norfolk and CSX eventually agreed that CSX would purchase Conrail and then sell half of Conrail's assets to Norfolk. On March 9, 1997, Conrail approved a takeover by CSX for $10.5 billion, 60% higher than Conrail's stock price just before the bidding began. As part of the deal, Norfolk was to acquire about half of Conrail from CSX. CSX's share price rose at the announcement of the outcome.

This example of CSX's bidding for Conrail illustrates a number of insights about making decisions rigorously with quantitative methods:

- Disciplined thinking begins with disciplined analysis. Make decisions on faith, hope, and clarity; the greatest of these is clarity.

- There are no right answers. Our objective should be, however, to avoid the "wrong" answers caused by thinking that is muddled about systems of cause and effect, uncertainty, and time value of money.

- Quantitative methods can help highlight key bets that might otherwise be only implicit in your thinking. Major failures in business seldom result from many small miscalculations, but rather from a few sizable errors. Quantitative tools can help highlight the things that *really* have to go well in order for the project to succeed.

FOR FURTHER READING

Samuel E. Bodily, *Modern Decision Making: A Guide to Modeling with Decision Support Systems* (New York: McGraw-Hill, 1985).

Howard Raiffa, *Decision Analysis: Introductory Lectures on Choices under Uncertainty* (Reading, MA, Addison-Wesley Publishing Company, 1970).

Richard H. Thaler, *The Winner's Curse: Paradoxes and Anomalies of Economic Life* (Princeton, NJ, Princeton University Press, 1992).

6 UNDERSTANDING ECONOMICS

Practical men who believe themselves to be quite exempt from any intellectual influences are usually the slaves of some defunct economist. Madmen in authority who hear voices in the air are distilling their frenzy from some academic scribbler of a few years back.
— John Maynard Keynes

Keynes was an economist who certainly would not have underestimated his own influence on practical people and those in authority. In fact, he probably considered all those who did not seek out and listen to his advice to be mad. Although Keynes recognized his own importance during his lifetime, even he might be surprised by the continuing controversy and enduring influence of his ideas. It is not unreasonable to assert that, since his death in 1946, Keynes's theories about macroeconomics and the policies that have been based on them have been at the center of the debate regarding the role of government in the management of domestic economic policies and the global economic system.

To understand issues such as balanced budgets, Federal Reserve policies, and how interest rates are determined requires some knowledge of Keynesian economics and its philosophical counterpoint, monetarism. At times, the theories underlying the conduct of economic policy are grounded in arcane mathematics and highly stylized assumptions, yet the essential points can be presented in an accessible manner. It is important to keep the following points in mind as you proceed through the chapter. First, economics can be extremely useful in understanding what is going on in the financial markets, in industry, or in the efforts of a firm trying to enhance its value to shareholders. The second point is that there are substantial differences of opinion regarding many economic issues. However, while disagreements exist on precisely how policies affect outcomes, we should not dismiss the use of the frameworks to refine our economic forecasts and improve our decision making. Think of it as a map that directs us to the correct neighborhood even if it neglects to provide the specific address. Finally, as Keynes pointed out in the opening quote, many of our ideas, policies, and actions stem from the theories of economists, perhaps largely unknown and now defunct.

Economics is usually divided into two areas: microeconomics and macroeconomics. *Macroeconomics* looks at the economy as a whole, providing answers, or at least insights, into how rapidly an economy grows, the rates of inflation and unemployment, the factors that determine the level of interest rates, and the establishment of the exchange rate. *Microeconomics* is more concerned with individual household, firm, or industry issues. For example, how is the price of a product determined, what influences the profit of a firm, and how do individuals allocate their limited budgets among almost unlimited wants, needs, and choices? Although these questions will not be addressed specifically here, a framework will be developed that relates to many of these questions as well as other important issues.

Microeconomics is a good starting point because its basic framework of supply and demand will be used to introduce the macroeconomic issues. In addition, emphasis will be placed on markets and how they function. The basic principles of markets reside on the microeconomics side of the discipline, thus making this the logical place to begin.

MICROECONOMICS

Microeconomics is frequently about choices. How much does my firm produce? At what price do we sell it? What quantity will we sell? These decisions are not made in a vacuum. They are affected by literally hundreds and thousands of factors that can be reduced to a handful of key determinants. In addition, these determinants or factors often interact with one another. For example, the pricing decision is affected by factors affecting the cost of production, the quantity that consumers are willing and able to buy, and the availability of alternative or substitute products. To deal with all of these factors and their interactions, economists since Alfred Marshall, the nineteenth-century British economist, have used the framework or tool of supply and demand analysis.

SUPPLY AND DEMAND

Supply and demand graphs, tables, and equations summarize those factors or forces in a market that determine the price and quantity of a particular good, product, or service. Exhibit 6.1 is a representative graph containing a supply curve and a demand curve. Before looking at the details of the factors that influence the shape and position of the curves, let us first examine the conclusions that can be drawn from them by learning what those conclusions are and by what means these conclusions are determined. While this may initially appear a bit mechanical, we will flesh out the details later.

The intersection of the two curves reflects the interaction of all the forces in the market for that product. In our example, assume the product is a six-pack of beer. The price of a six-pack of beer is $3.75, and the quantity produced and sold is 4 million units (remember, this is the whole market for beer, so this is probably too small a number). This combination of price and quantity represents the market-clearing equilibrium (point E_1 on Exhibit 6.1). These terms are important. Equilibrium implies that there are no forces leading to a change in price or quantity. As long as all the factors stay as they are, brewers will continue

EXHIBIT 6.1   Supply and demand for beer.

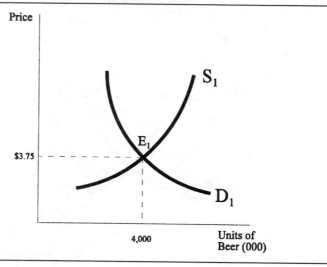

to produce 4 million six-packs and consumers will buy them at $3.75 each. It is the market-clearing point because all of the six-packs that are produced are sold, and everyone willing and able to pay $3.75 for a six-pack gets one.

What would happen if producers attempted to set a price different from the equilibrium, say $4.00 (see Exhibit 6.2)? At that price, brewers want to sell more than 4 million units. They are getting a higher price per six-pack so they produce a higher quantity: 4.25 million. At that higher price, however, consumers will buy less than 4 million six-packs; in fact, they will buy only 3.75 million. What happens to the difference between 4.25 million and 3.75 million? The market does not clear; brewers will find themselves with unwanted inventories. As the inventories build up, brewers will cut their production and their prices. Brewers reduce production because they have too much in stock; they cut their prices in order to sell off the excess. As the price falls, the quantity bought will increase, and eventually the market will clear. At what price? We know that already: $3.75 per unit is the equilibrium price.

What happens if something occurs to disturb the equilibrium as represented by the shift in the demand curve shown in Exhibit 6.3?

The outward movement of the demand curve implies that consumers are now willing and able to buy more six-packs at any and every price that brewers might charge. A number of things could lead to the shift: higher income levels, leading consumers to buy more of everything; an increase in the price of wine and spirits, leading consumers to substitute beer for these products; or a decrease in the price of pizza, leading consumers to eat more pizza and, of

EXHIBIT 6.2   A temporary disequilibrium.

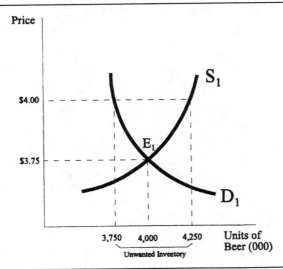

EXHIBIT 6.3   A shift in demand.

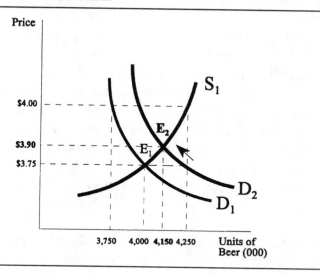

course, drink more beer. At the point in time when demand changes, brewers are still producing 4 million six-packs and selling them at $3.75 apiece, but now consumers want 4.25 million six-packs. Brewers experience a decrease in their inventories, and some consumers are unable to get all they are willing and able to buy. This signals the brewers to do two things: Increase prices and increase production. As prices rise, some of the additional demand for beer from consumers at the old price disappears, and eventually the quantity of beer produced and consumed becomes equal again. The market thus arrives at a new equilibrium, with a price of $3.90 per six-pack and production of 4.15 million units. Notice that this new equilibrium has a higher price and quantity than the original equilibrium because it was caused by an increase in demand. It is a change in equilibrium because demand changed, unlike the temporary changes brought about by the failed efforts of producers to raise prices and output in the face of no changes in the fundamental factors driving the market.

What is it that determines the shape and position of the demand and supply curves? We have already alluded to several of the most important factors:

1. The income level of consumers.
2. The price of substitute goods or products.
3. The price of complementary goods or products.
4. Tastes, style, and fashion.

In general, as income, the price of substitute goods, and tastes (preferences) increase, the demand increases and the curve will be farther to the right, because there is a positive relationship between the demand for a good and those three factors. Regarding complementary goods, the relationship is reversed. As the price of a complement rises, the demand falls. In the previous example, pizza was a complement to beer, because when the price of pizza fell, the demand for beer increased. Had pizza prices risen, beer demand would have fallen.

The supply curve is equally intuitive; it is related to the cost of production. For firms in many industries, the cost of producing an additional unit increases at some point. That is, if it costs a brewer $3.00 to make the millionth six-pack, the millionth and one costs $3.02. Economists refer to the incremental cost of producing a unit of output as its *marginal cost*. Because the marginal cost increases as output increases, suppliers are willing and able to produce more only if they get higher prices. This leads to the upward-sloping supply curve.

What factors determine the shape and position of the curve? Those that affect costs. The prices and availability of labor and materials are the key components. Therefore, if hops and yeast prices rise, then brewers will be willing to produce a given quantity only if the prices they receive also rise. A more subtle factor that affects the supply curve is the opportunity cost of using resources to produce a particular good. The opportunity cost is the next-best available use of those resources. What happens if the resources needed to brew beer could also be used to produce soft drinks and the price of soft drinks rises? Brewers will look at their alternatives and switch to the soft-drink industry, because the higher prices in this latter market represent greater profit opportunities. This would shift the beer supply curve upward to the left and reduce the quantity of beer produced. Beer prices would rise (see Exhibit 6.4).

Although we have simplified this process enormously, the framework outlined here is a very powerful tool. It is an analytical tool that allows decision makers to quickly evaluate the impact of changes that occur in the marketplace. This framework can be used by policymakers to assess the effect of changes in regulation, taxes, subsidies, and tariffs. Moreover, this process is an important philosophical concept. What has been outlined here in terms of the price mechanism and how it reacts to changes in supply and demand is what Adam Smith called "the invisible hand" in his classic book *The Wealth of Nations,* published in 1776. Resource allocation is determined in a market system by reactions to and changes in prices.

An Industry Example

To be a little more concrete about demand and supply, let's examine an important policy change and how it led to major changes in an industry. The industry or product in this discussion pertains to the long-distance telephone service

EXHIBIT 6.4   A shift in supply.

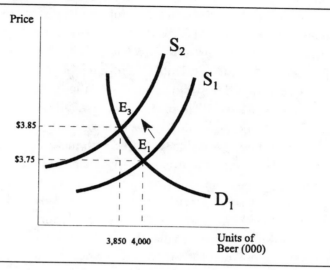

industry, and the policy change involving this industry was the decision to open long-distance service to competition and to deregulate prices.

Prior to January 1, 1984, the only long-distance provider in the United States was AT&T. No other company could even offer to sell long-distance services. AT&T had a monopoly. It was the sole company in the industry.

Being a monopolist and left to its own devices, AT&T would have set a very high price for long-distance service, one that maximized its profits. To determine that price, AT&T would have estimated its marginal cost and marginal revenue and delivered that quantity of service at which the two were equal. We have already defined marginal cost. *Marginal revenue* is the change in a firm's revenues brought about by selling one more unit. Usually selling another unit means lowering prices. Thus, the marginal revenue is the net effect of selling the last unit and getting lower prices on all of the preceding ones. As long as marginal revenue is greater than marginal cost, it is worth it to the firm to produce and sell that last unit.

As a monopolist, AT&T had a lot of power in the marketplace. A company acquires or achieves this power by developing products or services that no one else can match. Intel is not a monopolist, but it comes close to being one in the microprocessor market. Intel has achieved such a dominant position that it sets the prices for the whole industry. As a result, this firm has profit margins in excess of 60%. Intel got there by developing superior technology and by skillful marketing. So much of the software that people want to use in their PCs is based on the Intel processors that no other firm can develop a position to fight them. Other firms have to compete aggressively on price; hence, they have lower profits and less ability to develop new products. Intel uses its profits to stay ahead of the competition.

Unlike Intel, however, AT&T did not win its monopoly power by superior performance. The government gave AT&T its monopoly because it viewed a single supplier as socially efficient. Until recently, telephone service required wires or lines. It was considered wasteful to build multiple-line systems and, moreover, once a company had a network in place, it could manipulate prices to keep other competitors out. The cost of building a system was so great that anyone attracted to the industry by the high profits would have to make a significant investment to enter the market. Since the existing provider already had made the investment, it could cut prices temporarily to discourage or damage new competitors. Situations like long-distance service were considered natural monopolies. The solution was to allow them to exist, but as regulated monopolies.

Regulators limited the profit that the monopolist could earn by establishing prices that were below the profit-maximizing price. In the case of long-distance service, the regulator was the Federal Communications Commission. The FCC tried to establish a price that was consistent with allowing AT&T shareholders a fair return on investment—a return that reflected the risk to the shareholders. Under this arrangement, long-distance prices were relatively stable. Changes needed to be approved by the regulator and were brought about either by AT&T demonstrating a change in its costs, which caused its supply curve to shift, or a change in the required or fair return demanded by the shareholders.

All of this changed dramatically when long-distance service was deregulated. In a complicated settlement, the entire telecommunications industry was suddenly restructured. The major factor leading to this change was the development of new technology, which allowed for alternative means of signal transmission. Satellites, microwave, and other technologies meant that land-based transmission could be bypassed, opening long-distance service to competition.

As companies made the investments necessary to enter the market, a number of things changed. First, prices and profits fell. The new competition forced AT&T to cut its prices as it attempted to hold onto market share. As prices fell, the amount of long-distance usage increased dramatically. Using supply and demand graphs, the new competition brought about an increase in supply (an outward shift of the curve). The new equilibrium was at a lower price and an increased quantity. However, the changes did not stop there. The competitors, including AT&T, began to offer better and expanded services. Also, because there was competition, the firms in the industry aggressively pursued new technology and lower costs. As costs fell, the supply curves moved out even farther, prices fell, and the rate usage increased (see Exhibit 6.5). Thus, by 1997, there were hundreds of providers of long-distance services, and the price per minute was

EXHIBIT 6.5   The impact of deregulation.

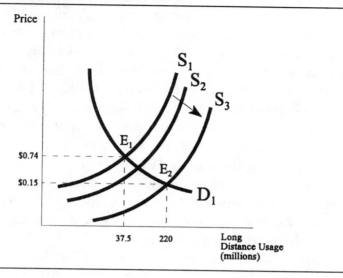

approximately 15¢. At that price, the quantity demanded was 220 million, in comparison with a price of $.74 and quantity of 37.5 million prior to deregulation.

There are a number of lessons that can be learned from the AT&T case and the related supply and demand analysis. When a firm is able to gain competitive advantages, it can increase prices and profits. In fact, a measure of its competitive advantage is the level of profit margin compared with those earned by firms in more competitive industries. When prices are held at high levels because of regulation or monopoly power, then the quantity produced is lower than in more competitive industries. High profits attract competition. To maintain these profits, the monopolist or near monopolist must have some means of keeping new competitors out of the industry. The barrier to entry might be that the industry is regulated (e.g., AT&T) or that the technological lead of the dominant firm (e.g., Intel) is too great to overcome. There are many other possible barriers, but the point here is that firms strive to keep competition out because of the ability to earn superior returns, and the lure of these same returns makes maintaining a competitive advantage difficult.

MACROECONOMICS

Whereas microeconomics is about individual and company decisions, macroeconomics is about the aggregate state of the economy. When people ask about the state of the economy or the stock market, they generally have in mind macroeconomic issues. Macroeconomics is about unemployment, inflation, growth, inter-est rates, and the policies governments pursue to influence them. Because the impact of policies ultimately depends upon the behavior of individuals and firms, macroeconomics cannot ignore microeconomic analysis. This is particularly true when someone is trying to develop models for the economy. We will not be doing that here. Instead, we will focus on the key macroeconomic relationships and the two primary policy instruments: fiscal policy and monetary policy.

To begin with, what goes on in the economy can be represented with a sup-ply and demand graph very similar to those used in the microeconomics section. Exhibit 6.6 is such a graph. Notice that we have appended an A to the D and S to note that we are now dealing with aggregate demand and supply. The term *aggre-gate* refers to all of the goods and services produced in the economy during a period of time. The more common phrase is the *gross domestic product* (GDP). The price in this case is some price index that is representative of the millions of good and services produced in the economy; the GDP deflator is the broadest. The aggregate demand and supply curves are generally determined by the same factors as individual demand and supply, although we need to interpret them in a broader way. Notice that the supply curve becomes almost vertical at some level, Q_F. This point represents the absolute highest possible level of production in the economy, when all of the resources are fully employed.

Two crucial questions are implicit in the construction of the AD and AS curves in Exhibit 6.6. Is it possible to have an equilibrium at some level of GDP other than full employment, and is it possible to have inflation at a level of GDP below full employment? In simplistic terms, these questions characterize the

EXHIBIT 6.6   Aggregate demand and aggregate supply.

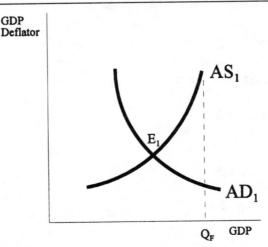

debate between Keynesians and monetarists. The first question in particular is the one that Keynes addressed in his book, *The General Theory of Employment, Interest and Money,* published in 1936. Before turning to these questions and related ideas, we first need to introduce national income accounting and examine in more detail the concept of GDP.

NATIONAL INCOME ACCOUNTING

To understand the relationship between aggregate demand and aggregate supply and to be able to better evaluate economic policy, economists began to develop the concept of *national income accounting* in the 1920s. This concept attempts to measure the output or production of the economy, how that output is allocated among different uses, and what decisions are made about the income the output generates. The key to analyzing and using the national income accounts is to understand that they are based on an identity or a relationship that is by definition true. This identity connotes that the total output, what we have called GDP, is equal to the total income, which in turn is equal to the total allocation of income among the various forms of expenditure and savings:

Output = income = expenditure

This might appear to be vague at first glance, but once the discussion has been expanded it will become clearer. Output has already been defined as the total value of goods and services produced in an economy during some period of time or GDP. Since the value of something equals its cost plus the profit margin, and the cost and profits represent someone's income, then GDP can be measured from an income or an output perspective. Moreover, since the recipients of the income can either spend that income, save it, or pay taxes, the total income must then equal GDP. And finally, if we look at the various types of expenditures in the economy, they must total the output or GDP as well. Therefore, the national income identity can be worked with in the following form:

$$GDP = C + I + G + (X - M) = C + T + S$$

where

C = household *consumption*
I = business *investment*
G = *government* spending
X = *exports*
M = *imports*
T = *taxes*
S = *savings*

Aside from some estimation issues, there is nothing controversial about these relationships. Every economist, regardless of his or her policy views, accepts these relationships. Exhibit 6.7 provides the actual numbers for the United States for 1995. The controversy among economists is whether or not the level that exists is basically the full employment level and what impact, if any, government policies can have on GDP.

The argument in support of the economy finding itself at or near full employment as an equilibrium is similar to the adjustment process described in the microeconomics section. Start by assuming that the economy is below its full employment level. Resources are idle. Plants are running below capacity. Workers are unemployed and raw materials are abundant. The unemployed workers begin to despair of getting a job, so they become willing to work for less. With excess capacity and raw materials available, manufacturing costs drop. As wages and other costs drop, manufacturers are willing to produce more (the supply curve shifts outward); however, they need to lower prices to sell the expanded output. That is fine with the manufacturers, because costs have fallen. As prices fall, households, businesses, and government are all willing and able to buy more, so the quantity demanded increases. When does this stop? At full employment! At that level of output, there are no excess resources or pressures for wages and prices to fall.

For those who believe in the power of markets, this example is an elegant and convincing story. And there is no question that this situation has some empirical validity. When there is excess capacity, prices do fall, or at least rise at a slower rate. However, in general, the evidence is pretty overwhelming that the economy can and does operate at levels below full employment for sustained periods of time. Exhibit 6.8 shows the employment rate for the United States since the end of World War II. It is apparent that unemployment varies quite a bit and is quite high during recessions.

The counterstory begins with the view that prices and wages, although softer during weak economic periods, seldom actually fall enough to keep the economy

EXHIBIT 6.7   1995 GDP (in billions of dollars).

Consumption	$4,924.9
Business investment	$1,065.3
Government spending	$1,358.2
Exports	$807.4
Imports	$902.0
Taxes	$1,177.1
Savings	$1,151.8
Total GDP	**$7,253.8**

Source: Economic Report of the President, 1996.

EXHIBIT 6.8   U.S. unemployment rates, 1947–1995.

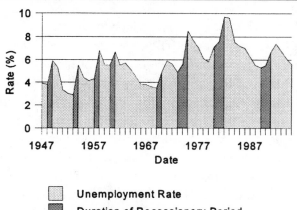

Unemployment Rate

Duration of Recessionary Period

Source: Economic Report of the President, 1996.

at full employment. The reason the economy is below full employment is that demand is insufficient to sustain the higher rate of GDP. Households have lower income because people are unemployed and they spend less. Businesses that already have excess capacity reduce their investment in capital equipment. These reductions lead aggregate demand to shift to the left or downward and the economy stagnates. In the 1920s in Europe and 1930s in the United States, the downward spiral reached dramatic proportions as the unemployment rate exceeded 20%. Although prices, wages, and interest rates fell to very low levels, there was so little demand that businesses did not even invest at a rate equal to depreciation; thus they had no incentive to increase production. Many people feared for the future of democracy and capitalism because these type of economic conditions contributed to the rise of fascism and communism. Among those most concerned was John Maynard Keynes, who not only identified insufficient demand as the primary problem of the Great Depression, but offered a policy to combat it.

Keynes argued that steps needed to be taken to stimulate the economy. There was a need for the government to intervene in such a way as to increase aggregate demand through expansionary fiscal and monetary policy. For reasons beyond the scope of this book, Keynes advocated fiscal policy. However, the major contribution he made was that government should and could do something to keep the economy closer to full employment. After the war, this view became the dominant one among economists and policymakers. Governments have tried to maintain stable economies by utilizing fiscal and monetary policy to manage aggregate demand.

FISCAL POLICY

Fiscal policy refers to the use of government expenditures and taxation to influence the level of aggregate demand. The government's activities have both direct and indirect effects on demand. As the government spends money on programs such as defense, education, highways, or space exploration, it is buying goods and services. This shifts aggregate demand upward and to the right, which raises prices and the level of output. In order to meet the new, higher level of quantity demanded, firms need to expand production by offering more overtime or hiring new workers. Either way, wages increase, and the additional income allows households to increase their spending. This represents an increase in C, or consumption. At some point, firms will find themselves short on capacity, so they will buy more manufacturing equipment and build new plants. The increase in C and I leads to an outward shift in aggregate demand that is more than the initial shift brought about by the increase in G, government spending. The total change in output that occurs is a multiple of the initial change in demand, and when economists speak of fiscal policy, they speak of this multiplier effect.

Fiscal policy is about both government expenditures and tax collections. A similar stimulus to the economy could have been brought about by the government reducing taxes instead of increasing its expenditures. As the government reduced taxes, households and businesses would have more disposable income, some of which they would choose to spend. This spending shifts aggregate demand outward and sets into action the round of income and spending increases described above.

There are a number of programs and policies that have caused fiscal policy to be countercyclical. When the economy is slowing, fiscal policy becomes more expansionary; when the economy is growing rapidly, fiscal policy turns contractionary. These countercyclical effects are referred to as *automatic stabilizers*. What are they, and how do they work? Basically, automatic stabilizers take effect because some government expenditures and tax revenues are directly related to the level of income in the economy.

The two key places where automatic stabilizers occur are the entitlement programs and the progressive tax system. Entitlements are programs that provide some form of government payment based on an individual's income. As incomes rise, fewer people are eligible for the payments, and government expenditures fall. A progressive tax system causes tax collections to rise as incomes rise. As long as the tax schedule is progressive, collections rise at an increasing rate. The impact of the automatic stabilizers is to decrease government expenditures and increase tax collections when incomes rise. This puts a brake on the economy to keep it from overheating. Conversely, when the economy is slowing or enters a recession, incomes fall, government spending increases, tax collections decline, and the economy receives the necessary stimulus.

Fiscal policy, whether discretionary or automatic, cannot by itself keep the economy on an even keel. It takes time for the effects of fiscal policy to be felt, and often other issues such as political concerns keep it from being implemented in a timely fashion. The other half of the policy tool kit is monetary policy, which often can be implemented more quickly because it is more independent of the political arena.

MONETARY POLICY

The conduct of monetary policy is determined by the Federal Reserve system, which is the central bank of the United States and consists of two major parts: the Board of Governors and the Federal Reserve Banks, of which there are twelve. The Board of Governors has seven members who are appointed by the President of the United States. Each of the banks has an administrative, policy, and research staff headed by a president who is appointed by the Board of Governors. The seven members of the board and five of the twelve presidents, serving on a rotating basis, make up what is called the Federal Open Market Committee (FOMC). It is this group that determines monetary policy.

How does monetary policy work? This is not such an easy question to answer. Monetary policy is the source of considerable disagreement among economists (you are probably getting the idea that economists are a contentious group). To simplify discussion of this topic, points of dispute will be ignored here, and instead, the focus will be put on the basics. Like fiscal policy, monetary policy has its impact through its ability to affect aggregate demand. Monetary policy does this through two routes: changing the level of interest rates in the economy and altering the availability of credit. The former leads to more or less demand for funds and influences the amount of consumption and investment. The latter makes banks more or less willing to make loans and also influences the amount of consumption and investment. When the economy is too strong and showing signs of inflation, the Federal Reserve tries to raise interest rates and contract credit. If the economy is below full employment, the Federal Reserve wants to lower rates and expand credit.

To see how this happens, assume that the FOMC detects signs that inflation is accelerating. These signals might be that wages are increasing more rapidly than productivity, that commodity prices are rising, or that manufacturing plants are operating near capacity. The members of the committee feel that they should act so they instruct their operating arm, the Open Market Desk at the New York Federal Reserve Bank, to pursue contractionary policies. The committee might even specify quantitative targets for their policies; however, what they basically want is for the open-market desk to raise interest rates and slow the growth of the money supply.

The open-market desk accomplishes this by entering the securities market and selling U.S. Treasury bonds. In order to sell the securities, the open-market desk will offer them at a lower price than it had previously demanded. The lower price on a bond causes its yield or interest rate to rise. As banks buy the bonds from the Federal Reserve, their ability to make loans is simultaneously reduced. The Federal Reserve actions drain liquidity from the banking system. Banks go along with these actions and buy the bonds because the interest rate on them is higher. Banks reallocate their funds from loans to government bonds. As the banks reduce their loan volume, the level of deposits decreases. This, in turn, reduces the money supply.

With interest rates higher, loans less available, and the money supply smaller, aggregate demand will fall. The higher interest rates will lead consumers to put off purchases of durables like homes, automobiles, and appliances. Firms will invest less because the higher rates make fewer projects pass the net present value hurdle rate. Banks are restrictive in making loans, so credit is not available for discretionary purposes. All of these changes shift the aggregate demand curve to the left, slowing the economy and easing the inflationary pressures.

If the Federal Reserve wanted to stimulate the economy by increasing aggregate demand, it would lower interest rates and increase the money supply. The appropriate open-market operation would be to buy bonds, raising their price and expanding the reserves in the banking system.

INTEREST RATES

An important element of the macroeconomy is the level of interest rates. As pointed out earlier, monetary policy works in part through its influence on rates. In addition, because so many business and personal decisions are influenced by interest rates, these rates receive a great deal of attention. Interest rates are the price of credit. They are what we pay when we borrow and receive when we lend. The general level of interest rates in the economy is determined by the supply and demand for credit and the level of inflation. The specific rate an individual or firm pays depends on the general level plus a premium for credit riskiness of the borrower.

The famous economist Irving Fisher was the first to recognize the importance of inflation in the determination of interest rates. He distinguished between nominal rates and real rates, where the nominal rate includes expected inflation.

$$\text{Nominal rate} = \text{real rate} + \text{expected inflation}$$

The nominal rate is the interest rate we observe in the market or see in the press. The real rate has to be estimated or measured with hindsight, but the key is to realize that interest rates rise when inflation rises. Countries experiencing the highest rates of inflation also have the highest interest rates.

Real rates tend to be influenced by the demand for credit. During periods of economic expansion, more people want to borrow because profit opportunities are plentiful. As a consequence, higher interest rates tend to occur during rapid growth periods, and lower rates occur during recessions.

BALANCE OF PAYMENTS

The earlier discussions of national income accounting and economic policymaking were couched almost entirely in domestic terms. That is not as big a gap as it might at first appear. Most nations' economies are still largely domestic. For the United States, only about 23% of the GDP consists of exports and imports. At the same time, this number has been growing, and more companies are doing business overseas, either as importers or exporters or by investing in foreign operations. As a result, it is important to understand the fundamentals of international economics.

The balance of payments is a statistical record of all the cross-border transactions engaged in by the residents of a country—an importer who brings wine or olive oil into the United States, an exporter who distributes movies overseas, a tourist who travels in China, and an investor who buys Brazilian equities—all are engaging in cross-border transactions that show up in the balance of payments.

The range of transactions is broad. Therefore a number of measures or definitions of the balance of payments exist. We are going to focus on one measure of the balance of payments: the current account balance. This current account balance measures all the transactions involving goods and services and unilateral transfers or foreign aid. Using the same notation from the national income accounts, the current account balance is as follows:

$$X - M = \text{GDP} - (C + I + G)$$

An intuitive way to think about the relationship is as follows:

Current account = total production − total expenditure

Countries such as the United States that have a current account deficit have expenditures greater than production. How does a country consume more than it produces? It borrows some of the output from other countries. That is exactly what a current account deficit represents, the borrowing of output beyond the level of a country's current production. The borrowing country gives the lending country a claim on its future output. When a country is described as a debtor country, this means that it is running a current account deficit in financial assets. Surplus countries are those that save. They consume less than they produce and acquire financial assets in exchange for their surplus production.

There are numerous factors that influence whether a country runs a current account deficit or surplus. Many of these factors are related to macroeconomic policies that influence the levels of output, consumption, investment, and government spending. As an economy grows more rapidly than its trading partners, its consumption increases. Generally, this leads imports to grow more rapidly than exports, resulting in a deficit. A country with a higher inflation rate than its trading partners will see its goods become less desirable; this will also result in a deficit. Policies that are implemented to correct the deficit are actually policies designed to influence the levels of aggregate demand (expenditure) and aggregate supply (output).

To conclude this section, it is important to note that a current account deficit is not necessarily bad. At various times, it is desirable for countries to borrow in order to consume more than they produce. The key question is what type of consumption or expenditure is taking place. If the borrowing is to build infrastructure and expand manufacturing capabilities, then the deficit is positive. The country's future output will grow, allowing it to repay the financial claims and improve its overall standard of living. If the borrowed consumption is not invested or does not create future production, then the country will have to default on its claims or experience a decline in its standard of living.

FOR FURTHER READING

Rudiger Dormbusch and Stanley Fischer, *Macroeconomics,* 6th ed. (New York: McGraw-Hill, 1993).

Economic Report of the President, Government Printing Office.

Jack Hirshleifer and Amihai Glazer, *Price Theory and Applications* (Englewood Cliffs, NJ: Prentice Hall, 1992).

Paul Krugman, *The Age of Diminished Expectations: U.S. Economic Policy of the 1990s* (Cambridge, MA: MIT Press, 1994).

Lawrence Ritter and William Silber, *Principles of Money, Banking and Financial Markets,* 8th ed. (New York: Basic Books, 1993).

PART II
The Functions of Business

Part I served as the foundation for this book. Part II addresses the seven functions of business, often referred to as the *core bases of knowledge* for an MBA curriculum: "Marketing Management" (Chapter 7), "Operations Management" (Chapter 8), "Innovation and Technology Management" (Chapter 9), "Accounting" (Chapter 10), "Finance" (Chapter 11), "Human Resource Management" (Chapter 12), and "Strategy" (Chapter 13). In most MBA curricula, each topic is taken in isolation and examined as though a manager can affect one business function without impacting other functions. Perhaps in theory this is true. However, we take a general management perspective that managers cannot affect policy or make decisions in one area of business without impacting other areas. It is in the spirit of business function integration that we present these seven chapters. Chapter 7 addresses the area of marketing and builds on the premise that marketing's goal is to create value for customers. Chapter 8 focuses on operations strategy from the perspective of the enterprise, not just from the more internally focused inventory or logistics planning process. Chapter 9 goes beyond the more traditional information technology (IT) view and presents a broader view of technology and the innovation process. Chapter 10 addresses issues germane to managerial accounting, going beyond just "debits and credits." Taken together with Chapter 11, the goal is to understand how firms create value and to better appreciate the impact of managerial decisions on the firm's financial health. Chapter 12 addresses the challenges of managing people and creating an environment in which workers can prosper and contribute in a very positive manner to a firm's mission and objectives. Chapter 13 discusses elements of strategy and presents a framework to assist in setting the future direction of the enterprise.

7 MARKETING MANAGEMENT: LEVERAGING CUSTOMER VALUE

Imagine dialing an 800 number to order flowers from a catalog for a special occasion. A dozen long-stemmed roses are delivered within two days, each rose individually fed from a bulb filled with water to provide nourishment during shipment to your home or office. Ruth Owades's mail-order business, Calyx & Corolla shipped 2.5 million catalogs in 1995. Her concept was to provide a valuable service that allowed the customer to see the flower arrangement before ordering and to eliminate the cumbersome distribution system that resulted in 10 days passing from the time the flowers were picked to the time they were purchased. Through a set of alliances with FedEx and independent growers, Calyx & Corolla is able to provide customer value by both eliminating the element of surprise (because the buyer knows what kind of assortment to expect) and reducing the transit time from grower to consumer (thereby increasing both the freshness and the life of the flowers). In addition, through its direct consumer contact and enabling technology, Calyx adds value by building a database of its better customers' preferences and special dates—to remind you, for example, that a certain birthday is next week and that you ordered the Golden Glow Bouquet last year.

The Calyx & Corolla (C&C) example is quite appropriate for the beginning of this chapter because it symbolizes a number of trends[1] appearing on the marketing horizon that are presenting challenges for today's managers. First, Calyx & Corolla challenged the status quo, asking why flowers have to travel through such a cumbersome distribution system. Like Dell Computers, C&C looked for new ways to add value and improve quality. Second, C&C is built on repeat business and works very hard to retain its base of customers. Ms. Owades understands the value of customer loyalty and can demonstrate the costs associated with customer turnover and generating new business as opposed to retaining existing business. Third, the entire business proposition for C&C is built on an alliance between a set of hand-picked growers, Calyx, and FedEx, providing logistical support and technical expertise. Fourth, the entire network represents a win-win value chain where each part works seamlessly to provide value to the customer. While functional specialization exists, the Calyx system attempts to remove those barriers and obstacles that prohibit the flow of information through the entire process. Finally, C&C serves to illustrate the importance of services to the field of marketing, because the United States is truly becoming a services economy. Even the giant manufacturer, GE, announced recently that by the year 2000, only 32% of its revenue would come from its manufacturing operations.[2]

Throughout this text you will hear about empowerment, business process redesign, total quality, and other remedies for business problems. It is true that all of these are key to business success and that each taken alone is not sufficient. It is equally valid to say that each of these remedies has been billed as a business panacea and that managers sit in fear of the next big fix. There is a great deal of evidence that a new business paradigm is needed in today's business environment. The marketing concept is at the core of this new paradigm. Efforts by corporations across all disciplines should work together in creating value for customers.[3]

THE MARKETING CONCEPT

Bandag is a major tire retreading company that brings a high level of innovation to its industry. In addition to providing specialty composite materials in its retreads in response to different road conditions and travel patterns, Bandag offers an added element of high technology. By embedding a computer chip in the tire, trained field technicians can monitor the tire's performance, calculate wear and tear, and determine balance, thereby providing an important set of value-added services to fleet managers. With this information, fleet managers can better gauge the total cost of tire purchases, which can run into the millions of dollars per year for large fleets of trucks. With this value-added service, Bandag acknowledges that the fleet manager is interested in far more than replacement tires at a low cost. Value in use is derived through information and a tracking system that provides important savings through added tire life and reduced fuel cost.

In the 1960s the field of marketing came to embrace the concept that its objective was to provide products and services that meet the needs and wants of customers. Such a position was quite a departure from a sales or production orientation that was firm-centered, simply providing to the customer what was produced. Drucker felt that marketing was so basic to the purpose of the firm that it must permeate each functional unit and be central to the culture of the organization. He stated, "[Marketing] encompasses the entire business. It is the whole business seen from the point of view of its final result, that is, from the customer's point of view. . . . Because it is its purpose to create a customer, any enterprise has two—and only two—basic functions: marketing and innovation."[4]

Bandag is a company that understands the needs of its customer (i.e., the fleet manager) and attempts to provide value that exceeds the cost of replacement tires. Certainly Bandag could compete as a low-cost producer of retreads; however, it has chosen to provide value that provides a differential advantage. Through its technology, field service, marketing, and production, Bandag has changed the nature of competition such that tire life and fuel savings become part of the calculation for fleet purchases. The company even works with its distributors and certifies their technicians, who can become Bandag Certified Craftsmen.

This singular focus on the customer and the importance of all units working together in support of customer value is succinctly stated at Motorola: There are two kinds of people who work at Motorola—people who serve customers and people who serve people who serve customers. Interestingly, Motorola also invests heavily in its employees, viewing education as central to its business. The notion of value is not something produced in the factory—it is delivered in the marketplace through each customer interaction. Ian Carlsson, CEO of SAS, refers to these customer interactions as "moments of truth." Each customer interaction presents an opportunity to better meet the needs of future customers. A great deal of effort goes into training personnel to raise the probability of a positive outcome. At Nordstrom's, the focus on customer satisfaction and the importance of creating value for the customer has created a cultlike culture. Employees are likely to self-select into the system and discover early on whether they are comfortable.[5] That is, people who do not buy in to the Nordstrom way of thinking are less likely to seek employment. Employees who do not fit into the company culture typically do not survive. A marketing culture that places customer value as the number one priority must be pervasive throughout the organization.

Thus, the marketing concept can be expanded to encompass the objective of achieving superior customer value and to emphasize the importance of making this concern central to the processes that guide the strategy of the total enterprise. Several points implicit in our redefinition of the marketing concept are key to our understanding of marketing strategy. These points are the framework for the remainder of this chapter:

- Marketing strategy's role in corporate strategy.
- The importance of customer selection.
- Marketing activity must pervade the organization.
- Customer value creation and the role of employees.
- Value creation through alliances and partnerships.

MARKETING STRATEGY'S ROLE IN CORPORATE STRATEGY

If you take the view that corporate strategy must be forward-thinking in order to position the firm to compete in the future, you'll understand that this strategy must search for the markets of tomorrow.[6] It is not enough to excel today. Efforts must be directed to developing those core competencies that will determine success in the future. As FedEx and UPS compete for share of today's overnight delivery of packages and documents, they must address emerging Internet capabilities and the possible effects this phenomenon will have on the timely shipment of documents. Corporate strategy provides the road map by which managers plan the journey to the future and decide what mechanisms need to be in place to achieve that future state.

To some degree, this effort requires bifocal vision[7]—an ability to both serve the market today and to develop new markets. Bifocal vision allows companies to invest in current markets and customers while simultaneously developing resources to successfully face tomorrow's opportunities. For example, the face of retail banking is changing daily, and the role of the branch bank is being redefined. No longer is brick and mortar essential to market share, as consolidation has led to a reduction in the number of branch offices nationwide. Not only has ATM use increased in recent years, but now you can bank by phone or through your home computer. In the last two years alone, banks have flocked to the Internet to understand the implications for future strategy. Now the major money-center banks look at Netscape and Microsoft as key competitors and are partnering with each other and small start-up companies like CyberCash and Mondex to provide alternative banking products and services.

The primary responsibility of marketing is to provide insight into the needs of current customers and competitors and to scan the relevant business environment for future opportunities. The general management role of marketing is to interpret this environment and to make decisions regarding which key customers to serve, which competitors to challenge, and what bundle of product or service attributes to assemble for the marketplace. While tensions often exist between marketing and other functional units, this information must be integrated with other functional decisions. In essence, marketing and its role as customer advocate must be core to the values of the firm and central to its strategy formulation and execution.

Recent research[8] has attempted to better understand how a marketing orientation affects a company's performance. The results seem to suggest that a marketing orientation matters and that company profits are improved. Equally important, however, is interpreting what a marketing orientation is, which will help define marketing's role in the planning process. Consistent with our previous discussion, a marketing orientation consists of the following:

- *Customer focus:* Understanding customer needs, creation of value, and the importance of customer satisfaction.
- *Competitor focus:* Looking for competitive advantage, responding to competitive moves, and monitoring competitive behavior.
- *Interfunctional coordination:* Achieving functional integration, sharing information across functions, and having all functions contribute to customer value.
- *Future profit orientation:* Managing the business for future profits, not just sales.

Marketing strategy exists at three levels. At the corporate level, marketing provides invaluable input for future opportunities. Marketing provides insight into the question of what business we are in. More important, marketing addresses the question of what business we *should* we be in. At the business level, marketing strategy combines with other functional strategies to bring products and services to the marketplace that, hopefully, achieve a sustainable competitive advantage. On one level, PepsiCo competes with Coca-Cola for global dominance of the soft-drink market. PepsiCo relies to some extent on its restaurant businesses to provide a captive retail outlet to support its market share goals. On another level, Pizza Hut competes for "share of the stomach" in the market for meals prepared away from the home. On a third level, marketing strategy includes planning marketing programs and implementing and controlling the actual marketing effort. Simply stated, segments must be chosen and targeted, offerings must be positioned, products and channels of distribution must be developed, and a consistent marketing communications plan must be executed.

THE IMPORTANCE OF CUSTOMER SELECTION

In recent years the number of people working out of their homes has risen. The number of home workers has expanded at a rate of over 10% a year since 1988. Due to, among other things, corporate downsizing and a movement to virtual offices and environmental air-quality concerns, it is likely that the number of home workers will continue to grow well into the twenty-first century. It would be an error to treat this growing market as a unified whole. In fact, many of the Regional Bell Operating Companies (RBOCs) have attempted to better understand the nature of this market. There appear to be four major segments: *self-employed*—those whose work at home is a primary source of income; *moonlighter*—those who hold a corporate job but engage in some contract work away from the office; and two *corporate* segments—those who either telecommute (i.e., conduct most of their work from home) or bring home additional work in the evenings and weekends. The data seem to suggest that the use of advanced telecommunications and computing equipment differs across segments as do the benefits sought from using this equipment. Moreover, self-employed and moonlighters are more difficult to reach than are corporate home workers, who can be identified through their companies. The questions facing many of the RBOCs are how to prioritize among these segments, how to develop products and services that meet their individual and collective needs, and how to plan and implement tailored marketing programs that provide value to the chosen segment(s) of customers. What is clear is that one strategy will not work for the entire work-at-home market.

The PIMS data are very clear: Firms that segment their markets have higher returns than those that do not.[9] Fundamental to all marketing strategy is the recognition that there often exist groups of customers who differ from other groups of customers on any one of a number of key dimensions. For instance, in the work-at-home market, self-employed and moonlighters might be more value-driven and seek products and services that offer a strong price and performance relationship, while corporate users might be less price-sensitive because they are less likely to own their equipment and might desire better service and technical support. To the extent that marketers can understand and meet the needs of these different segments, they are able reap higher returns, although the costs associated with segmentation exceed those of a mass marketer who does not attempt to differentiate among classes or groups of customers. Closely linked to the segmentation process are targeting and positioning, which are the sine qua non of marketing strategy.

There are two basic approaches to the marketplace, as as shown in Exhibit 7.1. Companies can approach the market as though all consumers are the same and as though differences in products, or product offerings, are not meaningful to these people. The legendary remark made by Henry Ford is an illustration of

EXHIBIT 7.1   Alternative approaches to the marketplace.

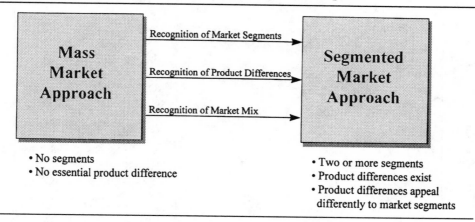

this approach: "Customers can have any color car they want as long as it is black." Interestingly, a number of health care delivery programs instituted at the federal level during the 1970s failed to acknowledge that differences exist between customer groups. Their primary desire was not to exclude anybody, so they developed very general programs. The problem with this thinking is that those who were most in need of federal assistance were the hardest to reach through traditional middle-class channels. On the other hand, customer differences occur because measurable and important differences exist between sets of customers. Both FedEx and UPS differentiate customers by their degree of time urgency— offering, at different rates, a number of options for the delivery of overnight or second-day packages and documents. Similarly, airline prices discriminate, or segment, travelers by their sense of urgency and ability to plan ahead. With enough notice, you can arrange to fly from Washington, D.C., to Los Angeles for fares as low as $450. Those who travel at the last minute and have not been able to prearrange a longer stay in Los Angeles will pay in excess of $1,200.00 for the same economy seat.

What Is Market Segmentation?

Market segmentation is the process whereby companies recognize that differences exist between two or more customer groups and that these groups will respond differently to offerings made available in the marketplace. Differences might exist in the price/performance ratio associated with the product, as is seen in Exhibit 7.2. Or differences might exist in the channel through which the product is sold. One channel might offer superior service and technical assistance,

EXHIBIT 7.2   Price/performance barriers.

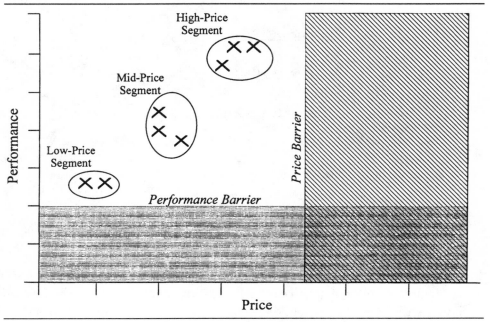

while another channel might carry the product with no service but at a more competitive price. Today's PC marketplace typifies the range of options available. A consumer can buy a PC at Sam's Club or from a value-added reseller (VAR) who supplements the basic "box" with customized software for specific applications, training, and on-site repair and technical assistance. Both Hewlett-Packard and Compac sell through both channels and are thus able to attract different segments of the marketplace.

A customer-focused segmentation strategy involves a six-step process, as is shown in Exhibit 7.3. Firms tend to segment markets for several reasons. Among these are the following:

- Segmentation allows a firm the ability to match the product or service to the most suitable customer. Marriott, for example, has in its portfolio of hotel chains a number of choices for different customer groups. Residence Inn by Marriott is designed for the business traveler who is on an extended stay away from home, while the Ritz Carlton (a recent acquisition) is recognized worldwide as a fine luxury hotel.

- Segmentation provides an opportunity for a company to develop alternative channels of distribution to reach different kinds of customers in a more cost-efficient manner. Motorola is experimenting with club stores as a

EXHIBIT 7.3   A customer-focused segmentation strategy involves a six-step process.

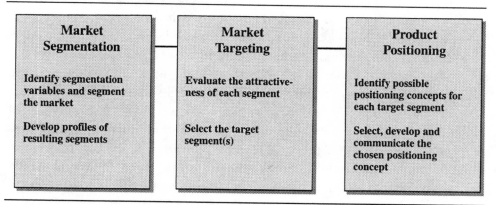

Market Segmentation	Market Targeting	Product Positioning
Identify segmentation variables and segment the market	Evaluate the attractiveness of each segment	Identify possible positioning concepts for each target segment
Develop profiles of resulting segments	Select the target segment(s)	Select, develop and communicate the chosen positioning concept

viable outlet for its least-sophisticated mobile radios in order to reach the low end of the marketplace.

- There might exist a segment of the market that is now being neglected. Segmentation affords an opportunity for the firm to develop strategies to reach this part of the marketplace. For example, Charles Schwab discount brokers reached out to a segment of investors who objected to relatively high brokerage fees for transactions where no advice was given or needed. Based on the success of this marketing strategy, a number of discount brokerage houses have sprung up; now investors can trade over the Internet.

- Rather than attempting to compete in a larger market, a firm might decide to select one segment on which to focus its entire marketing efforts. This narrower market might be defined as a small group of consumers within what appears to be a larger segment. For example, Paccar competes quite favorably against Ford in the long-haul truck business by concentrating its energies on the high-end, customized part of the truck-buying market. Although Ford enjoys a more favorable cost structure by virtue of its volume, Paccar's Kenworth and Peterbilt brands have a higher market share in the high end of the independent-trucker market. Paccar has decided to focus its efforts to unrelentingly serve a niche of the market. Again, the PIMS[10] data suggest that high market-share niche marketers enjoy high returns on their investment.

Why Is Segmentation Important?

Higher returns accrue to firms that segment their markets; however, this is not reason enough to do so. From a corporate or marketing strategy perspective, the *analytical process* of segmentation is important. By analytical, we mean the process whereby companies attempt to define viable, sustainable, and profitable customer groups. From an analytical perspective, the process of segmentation helps define the customer universe because it provides a richness to an understanding of customer groups. Industrial buyers are not just found in large and small firms or across different SIC classifications. Buyers can be adversarial in nature or collaborative; they can be risk-averse or risk-seeking; they can be leaders or laggards. Such descriptions allow marketing managers additional insight so they can better formulate and implement marketing programs that address the needs of these different potential market segments. The ability to thoroughly define a customer universe also provides an opportunity to track changes in buying behavior over time. For instance, in early-growth markets, buyers might require high levels of service and training as part of the product offering to achieve differentiation in the marketplace. It is easy to recall the days when IBM's reputation was enough to ensure a serious consideration by any data processing manager because "no one was ever fired for buying IBM." Now, chief information officers debate whether it is appropriate to outsource their data processing functions. IBM might still be calling on the same set of customers; however, over time, the decision rules have changed as they relate to information technology. IBM finds itself competing with the likes of EDS and Anderson Consulting rather than Digital and NCR.

Through a segmentation process, a better understanding of a company's own competitive position is gained—and how its products and services are perceived in the marketplace. Such an analysis provides a better understanding of areas of opportunity as well as areas of vulnerability. In the airline industry, Southwest Air has grown to be a significant presence in the short-haul market and has never lost sight of its target market. While American, United, and Southwest all serve the business user, each does so differently. It is important for United and American to understand where these differences lie, because neither United nor American enjoy the cost advantages of Southwest, and therefore they find it difficult to compete on that basis. United had to spin off a United shuttle service to handle traffic between Los Angeles and San Francisco. While comfort and first-class service are always nice, most business travelers between the two cities were more interested in frequent flights and lower fares. Business travelers on longer flights from Los Angeles to New York or Washington are more likely to be attracted to the type of business-class comfort people have come to expect on international flights. Such an analysis helps managers to appreciate the dynamics within the industry. Therefore, it is not simply enough to describe the customer universe and devise a number of cute descriptors for different segments. A company must ask what the impact will be on strategic decisions and on the allocation of resources.

Thus, from a *planning perspective,* segmentation provides a basis for the more precise setting of marketing objectives and strategy. Managers no longer attempt to increase their market share in the work-at-home market. They make an informed decision to focus on the corporate user rather than the moonlighter because one might be easier to reach than the other—or one manager can develop better programs to meet the needs of one versus the other. Or, by offering work-at-home products and services, the RBOC is able to position itself as a full-line, one-stop, telecommunications provider in the minds of its large corporate customers. In addition, companies face competition on the segment level. Battles are fought segment by segment, with market shares (and hopefully profits) going to the winner. Dell and Compac both compete in the PC market, but their strategies and success in the corporate client-server market is different from the more basic PC home-use market. Also, while the threat posed by Packard Bell is large in the home market, it is virtually nonexistent in the corporate market.

It should be clear that a rigorous segmentation exercise helps guide marketing plan development, marketing mix changes, product development efforts, and the allocation of resources. For example, Exhibit 7.4 suggests that certain marketing-mix elements are easier to change than others as companies attempt to meet the needs of different segments. The decision to change markets or segments can be significant and pose great risk to a firm. Management must understand that these decisions often carry longtime horizons. Again, FedEx was in the overnight package business for 10 years before UPS entered the market. Today, both companies have been transformed by serving the urgent-package segment and providing complete logistics services to other segments of the market. At the other extreme, price changes can be made on the spot and, barring any antitrust considerations,[11] can serve more as a tactical weapon. As would be expected, both new-product decisions and channel decisions hold reasonably longer-term consideration. New-product decisions are affected by both market and technological uncertainty. For example, in late 1996 Bell Atlantic announced in excess of $200 million in losses incurred in seeking new video and network applications as part of its strategic foray into technology convergence. Similarly, NYNEX, AT&T, and others have, after many years of struggling, closed their retail phone stores because they never achieved the expected returns. Often, manufacturers will stay with existing distributors after market shifts have rendered these channels less useful—simply because the resistance to change is too great.

EXHIBIT 7.4   Marketing momentum.

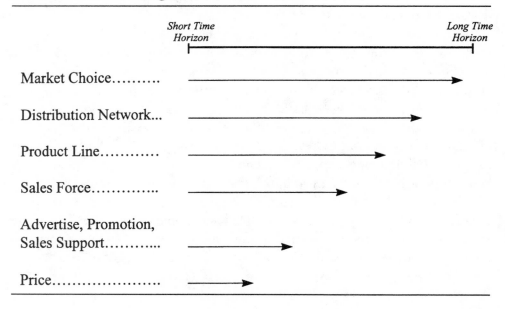

Segmentation in the Industrial Marketplace

Industrial companies sometimes segment their markets by business operations, using internal activities as a way to differentiate among different kinds of customers. Unfortunately, this segmentation approach is internally focused. This approach also does not permit a full picture of the customer's buying behavior and how it changes over time or how the customer makes decisions and what affects the customer decision-making processes—nor does it provide a complete appreciation of the competitive landscape. For example, Exhibit 7.5 illustrates how a business might segment according to its operations.

While the preceding approach to segmentation is not necessarily wrong, and it does depict what many companies actually do, it has several inherent weaknesses. First, this approach is internally focused and may not reflect accurately the differences that exist in the marketplace. Second, segments overlap and cannot be bounded easily given that product functionality can be substituted at certain ranges of performance (e.g., one channel might serve multiple segments). Third, such an internally focused approach oversimplifies the segmentation process and fails to fully capture the factors that drive buyer behavior and the buyer's decision-making process. We would complement the business-operations approach with a segmentation approach that is customer-based and is derived

EXHIBIT 7.5   Segmenting by operations.

Product segmentation	Centrex versus PBX Mini versus micro versus midi "Boxes" versus "systems"	Focuses mainly on product lines or product offerings from firm. The problem is the differences in segments might not be clean and might overlap.
Price segmentation	Sale versus lease Bundled versus unbundled	Focuses mainly on pricing options from company. Might reflect an element of buyer risk taking but is superficial.
Distribution segmentation	OEM versus end users versus VAR	Illustrates more how the firm decides to go to market than it reflects the differences in buyer behavior and segment requirements.
Service segmentation	Systems selling—solutions selling Product only services extra on demand	Reflects firm's willingness to provide value-added services that capture aspects of buyer behavior or preferences.
Promotional segmentation	Deal-prone buyers Discounts, extended dating	Reflects different pricing options that firm might use. Company can infer level of price sensitivity but system does not easily allow trade-off analysis.

from factors that more accurately describe the industrial marketplace. You will note that factors range from more macro-, industry-level variables to more micro-, individual characteristics. Practically speaking, as companies attempt to measure more microlevel variables, the cost of marketing research goes up significantly because it becomes impossible to rely on secondary data. Exhibit 7.6 summarizes the range of segmentation bases as well as the kind of information gained and how a manager might use that information in the formulation of a marketing program to address the needs of a particular segment.

Exhibit 7.6 paints a different picture of the industrial buying process and provides the marketer with a much richer interpretation of the buying process from which to develop a comprehensive marketing strategy for a segment, or even an account within a segment. Macrovariables are often easily ascertained and can often be found in trade and government publications. While the SIC code is useful, its applicability is often limited to questions of how big the market is and what the market potential is for a particular product by SIC segment. This SIC data is less useful in helping understand the decision-making processes of a particular segment to be. At the other extreme, individual and decision-making-unit characteristics bring to life the political realities of the buying process and shed light on the complex interplay between organizational

EXHIBIT 7.6 Different approaches to segmenting the business marketplace.

Type of business, SIC class	SIC classes 3500, 2500, manufacturing versus wholesale	Might suggest application or functionality; different industries or businesses might make different demands from the same piece of equipment.
Firm demographics (size, number as of plants, sales)	Large versus small Regional versus multinational Strong corporate versus decentralized operations	Might suggest application and use of product as well as other concerns such as productivity or control. Could help understand where decision-making authority lies and the role of centralized purchasing.
Type of buying situation	New purchase Modified rebuy Straight rebuy	The type of buying situation directly affects the manner in which information is sought and how it is processed and used. It affects also the decision-making style and the decision-making participants.
Approach to decision making	Adversarial versus collaborative Decision calculus used	By understanding the approach taken to decision making, the marketer appreciates better the decision criteria that are important and how they might be weighted in the decision process.
Characteristics of the buying decision-making unit (DMU)	Composition Stage in the process Decision-making rules used	Typically, industrial buying decisions are multiperson in nature, with different degrees of influence held by different people at different stages. It is a political process.
Characteristics of the individual	Demographics Organizational role Psychographics Buying criteria used	Ultimately, people make buying decisions; organizations do not. It is useful to understand what drives people to do things.

members, each having a personal agenda as well as a stake in the decision outcome. While SIC code or company demographics might be adequate for certain buying decisions, it would appear that—as the decision becomes more complex and more expensive, and as the selling cycle becomes longer—more information is required beyond the typical macrosegmentation variables. Bombardier, a North American supplier of subway and railcars, must carry its segmentation processes down to the individual level, given the complex interplay of politics involved in a local government's decision to purchase subway cars. This multiyear process entails a number of constituents and, as a result, is probably much more complex than is CSX's decision to buy a comparable number of railcars.

Final Comments on Segmentation

Once segments have been developed, they must be prioritized and resources must be allocated. Furthermore, a value proposition must be developed for each targeted segment. This value proposition addresses how the company intends to meet the needs of the targeted segment(s) as well as placing the firm in a defensible "perceptual" posture vis-à-vis its competitors. Both BASF and its "we don't make it, we make it better," and Siemens and its "that was then, this is now," campaigns are intended to create unique perceptual positions in the minds of their customers and are also intended to contribute to enhanced differential advantage. Despite more than a decade since the breakup of the Bell System, there is still confusion about who provides local service and what role AT&T plays. The question arises of whether AT&T can leverage its perception of being seen as "the phone company" once competition is permitted in the local loop.

A final point relates to measuring the outcome of a successful segmentation strategy. Accessing the correct segments and effectively reaching targeted customers are important. Exhibit 7.7 summarizes the steps used to develop a segmentation plan. Note that managers must determine whether these segments are profitable. At the very least, they should know what the expense-to-revenue ratio is. It would be better to know the contribution margin per segment dollar invested. The problem is that such information is difficult to capture, because most accounting systems are not market-friendly. They probably capture information at either the SBU, product line, or product level and cannot easily reflect the fact that products are typically sold across market segments. Movements to adopt activity based on costing are a step in the right direction. Companies that are truly market-facing attempt to capture such information on a segment-by-segment basis. However, such reporting systems are costly to build and are difficult to implement. Thus, if a manager is going to take the time to develop a strong segmentation plan, it would be useful to know what the bottom-line implications are.

MARKETING ACTIVITY MUST PERVADE THE ORGANIZATION

Several years ago, managers at Du Pont were concerned about their perceived degree of dependence upon their largest customer. During the discussion, the question was asked, "Should this customer choose not to buy from us any more, how long would it take for our sales to disappear?" Such a concern seemed quite

EXHIBIT 7.7 Steps in the segmentation process.

1. Make the segmentation plan generalizable. Don't limit it to a particular product.
2. Group customers on the basis of similarities or differences.
3. Describe the groups (segments) accurately and thoroughly.
4. Utilize a sequential segmentation scheme so that the most important descriptors are used first and become a condition for future segmentation.
5. Develop competitive positions for each segment.
6. Make sure the development and the execution of segmentation plans are compatible.
7. Evaluate revenue-to-expense ratios for each segment to ensure profitability.

plausible, because many of the products sold to this customer were commodity-like products (e.g., nylon). After much analysis of the nature of the relationship between the two firms and the number of "touch points" existing between the two firms, it became clear that Du Pont was less *dependent* than the two firms were *interdependent*. It also became clear that there would be a six-year time lag from the time the decision was made to buy from a Du Pont competitor to the point where Du Pont was no longer involved in any aspect of the customer's business!

This example illustrates that while some at Du Pont might argue that part of the close linkage between Du Pont and its customer could be attributed to the "oval" (the Du Pont logo and the equity built up in the brand), a more meaningful explanation lies in the fact that customer interaction is not relegated only to the marketing department. Customer care is a concern for the total enterprise and must be the responsibility of all functions of the company that interact with the customer.

A number of barriers exist that limit a firm's ability to spread customer responsibility across the entire enterprise. The primary hurdle is that many companies are organized by independent functional silos. Each function has its own reporting hierarchy, and interaction typically occurs when task forces are assigned to solve a business problem. Frequently, when one area fails to talk to another, it establishes metrics for success that not only are internally focused, but often conflict with success criteria found in other areas. One of the most apparent areas of conflict that illustrates this point is between operations, manufacturing, and marketing. Operations would be pleased to run its factories at the lowest possible per-unit costs, which translates to few model changes, long production runs, and standard order sizes. To meet the demands of different segments and customers, marketers would prefer to have shorter production runs, many models from which to select, and very flexible order sizes and cycles. To be sure, these postures represent extreme positions; the world of mass production is less tenable in a highly competitive global economy. In other words, customers can afford to be demanding, because competitors are ready and willing to meet their varied tastes and preferences with precision and with minimal time delay.

Mass customization,[12] made possible by advances in information technology, allows firms to meet customers' varied product and service requirements at low cost, with short time delays and with an ability to engage in breakthrough and continuous innovation. Panasonic, a large bicycle manufacturer, can custom-build literally thousands of varieties of bicycles to fit the buyer's size, weight, and riding style. Panasonic found that customers did not believe their bike was custom-made because they received it from the factory too quickly! By delaying shipment and slowing down delivery to the customer, Panasonic was able to achieve the level of credibility required to compete in the customized bike business.

A shift to mass customization demands that the enterprise undergo a basic transformation in how it thinks. This transformation must be communicated throughout the company. The primary shift occurs when the primary stakeholder of the company is the customer and this person or company has unique needs and requirements that must be met. Equally as important is the tenet that such a transformation does not dismiss the need to focus on cost reduction and efficiency in meeting that customer's needs. To this end, each function of the organization must determine how its activities fit in the company's value chain. Motorola, for example, totally reengineered its pager production processes so that it is now able to produce on a single automated production line every model of its Bandit pager with zero setup time and by holding only 45 minutes' worth of inventory. Clearly, this feat could not have been accomplished if only the marketing and manufacturing areas cooperated. The need for integration among functions extended to the far corners of the firm, including R&D, procurement, and its relationship with Motorola's vendor base. This business transformation was a response to the Japanese, who have entered the U.S. market with competitively priced pagers.

Mass customization is only one example of business processes whereby marketing must be integrated with other business activities to share in the responsibilities involved in meeting customer needs. A second obvious linkage is the relationship between marketing and R&D. The traditional conflict between basic and applied research is often cited as the primary source of discord between these two areas. Despite its many successes, Xerox is often cited as a company whose superior technological development (e.g., the mouse- and icon-based point and click, the fax machine) could not be commercialized because of its weak ties between technology and marketing. Booz Allen and others[13] have long advocated and empirically demonstrated that higher levels of marketplace acceptance of new products can, in part, be attributed to close and formal linkages between marketing and R&D. One study shows that when functions interact in a sequential manner as the product moves through the development process, only 1 of 60 ideas results in commercial success. When functions interact in parallel, multifunction teams, the success rate for new ideas increases to 1 in 7. By working with key customers, it is also possible to improve the hit rate, since they often have insight that the firm lacks. This insight is leveraged when the company uses a multidisciplinary team to visit customers.

Suppliers are a good source of information about both the marketplace and competitive behavior. Suppliers are also a key source of innovation and should be courted as such. Traditionally, procurement managers were not market-facing at all, viewing each purchase as an opportunity to challenge the stated price and to gain a better price. More recently, procurement has engaged in reverse marketing[14] whereby, working with marketing and other areas, procurement transforms itself into a manager of external resources whose responsibility is to leverage the expertise and skills of the company's supply base. While lower costs are always a concern, the primary motivation is to work with the supply base to achieve higher levels of customer satisfaction. Recent proclamations of the value gained through either integrated supply chain management or outsourcing are extensions of this thinking. Cost reduction, therefore, becomes a benefit gained through a willful attempt to work with the supply base to improve customer value. Part of Compac's success is directly attributable to its relationships with its suppliers, notably Intel.

CUSTOMER VALUE CREATION AND THE ROLE OF EMPLOYEES

In the U.S. Navy, the Bravo Zulu flags indicate a job well done. At FedEx, the Bravo Zulu award is given for performance above and beyond in support of delivering customer value. One FedEx courier recently won the award for delivering his packages on foot after his van died.

It probably is not an overstatement to say that the word *FedEx* has entered the English language to mean guaranteed overnight delivery. To be sure, FedEx has been a success story, although it is not entirely clear how the company will continue to fair in its competitive battle with UPS. In part, the FedEx success has been based on innovation and a willingness to take risks. To a larger extent, however, its success is a function of its people and their willingness to do what it takes to meet the customers' requirements. FedEx works very hard at inspiring its employees because it is aware that they are a key resource and are an essential ingredient in the company's success formula. Marketing-oriented companies are successful because they have empowered employees who can act on behalf of the company to satisfy customer requirements. The stories about Nordstrom employees are legendary. They behave professionally because they are trained to preform their jobs; continuous learning is one of the obligations the company has to its employees. Also, marketing-oriented companies have a supporting infrastructure that enables employees to perform their tasks in an innovative and customer-responsive manner. While L.L. Bean is widely recognized for its product quality and customer service, few people realize that its customer service representatives who answer the phone may well be working from their homes. Working with NYNEX, L.L. Bean developed smart terminals, using ISDN lines to equip their home workers with state-of-the-art technology. For the customer, the interface is seamless. Customers never know that the voice at the other end of the phone is not in the large wooden facility located in downtown Freeport, Maine.

Bain and Company demonstrates that good customers are not enough and that loyal employees play heavily in gaining higher profits with a loyal customer base.[15] By investing in employees, companies enjoy less turnover, have to train fewer new employees, and can use funds to increase the efficiency of their workers. These efforts result in the desire to satisfy customers by creating increased value. FedEx's many reward programs are externally focused and are intended to improve value to the customer. Marriott is piloting a program where it spends time with its less-skilled workforce, providing English language classes, help with child care, immigration, and the like—with the express purpose of decreasing turnover and absenteeism. While many of these employees are not frontline people, they are mission-critical to Marriott's ability to provide a high level of service in order to remain competitive.

This begs the question of how we can espouse loyalty in an era of downsizing and corporate restructuring. What about the new social contract? We address these questions specifically in Chapter 14, "Leading from the Middle." Nonetheless, loyalty has been redefined and is no longer taken as lifetime employment. The more important question here is how employee loyalty enhances customer value. Loyalty has been shown to directly affect customer retention and new-customer volume. Across the entire spectrum of professional service, the loss of a key employee (be it an attorney, a physician, or a hair dresser) often results in the loss of existing business, because people take clients with them. As word spreads of customer defection, new-customer volume falls. The cost of gaining a new customer far exceeds the cost of retaining an existing one. In financial services, higher customer retention rates correlate with greater market share. Exhibit 7.8 demonstrates why long-term employees create value.

The notion of customer value being created through employees touches again on the core beliefs of the organization and is related to the notion of managing through values. In everything management does, it must convey the message that the customer is key and that all systems point to, and that structures exist to support, the idea of creating customer value. All sights must be focused outward on customers and competitors to create internally an innovative and responsive organization. This culture of customer orientation cannot exist in a highly structured organization where functional roles are narrowly defined and limited in scope. Employees must understand the role they play in bringing value to customers and must bring their hearts and minds to the job each and every day.

VALUE CREATION THROUGH ALLIANCES AND PARTNERSHIPS

At the start of the chapter we spoke about Calyx & Corolla and how, through a network of partnerships, C&C provides the seamless delivery of flowers from

EXHIBIT 7.8   Costs associated with customer loyalty.

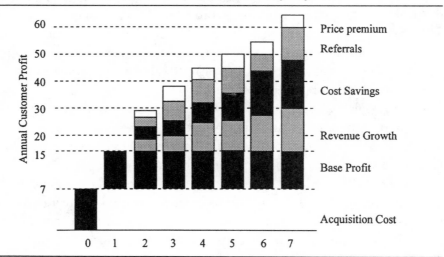

grower to final customer in one-fourth the time of traditional channels. This symbolizes the new competition, where firms realize that they do not have, or cannot develop internally, the competencies needed to compete in world markets. Either market access is unattainable, technology unaffordable, resources unavailable, or other barriers exist that prohibit a single firm from competing alone. Partnerships and alliances become important and, in fact, become essential for many firms to deliver value to customers. Both Sun Microsystems and Hewlett-Packard are dependent on third-party distributors to provide tailored applications for certain key niche markets. Certainly, both could develop software applications. However, limited windows of opportunity do not provide the requisite time for this to occur. Even the massive IBM finds itself engaged in a number of alliances as it attempts to deal with the WinTel, the Internet, and the plethora of information technologies.

The corporate model of the 1970s and 1980s, where growth and acquisitions were the ticket to corporate success, is no longer valid. The burden of cost of such a model has proven to be too great, and the nimbleness needed to compete in an ever changing world is too precious to be saddled by slow, bureaucratic organizations. Many marketing-focused organizations have found that they can only compete effectively and provide superior customer value in partnership with other firms. Whether we examine comarketing arrangements in the airline and pharmaceutical industries or value-added distribution in the computer and manufacturing sector, it is clear that networks of firms are competing with other networks of firms for global markets. AT&T and its world partners compete with Global One (Sprint, French Telecom, and Deutsche Telecom), and British Telecom-MCI and its affiliations compete for domination of the worldwide long-distance business.

As the marketing concept must pervade the firm, it must also pervade the partnership or the alliance and all its members. It should be apparent that an interdependent network of cooperating firms is as strong as its weakest member. The challenge becomes one of developing a marketing orientation among a loosely aligned group of firms so that no one firm has direct control and upon whom all can depend. While it might be difficult to develop a customer-focused orientation within a single firm, it is even more so across firms. Corporate cultures often are not the same, company objectives might not always coincide, and a number of other factors might inhibit such a culture change. Despite these challenges, many firms do not have a choice and must partner if they are to deliver value to the customer. Webster[16] suggests that the alliance leader, the firm at the core of the network, must make the marketing concept a core value of the alliance. Not only do functional and organizational barriers have to fall, but alliance leaders must educate their partners to appreciate that mutual gain results only when all members of the alliance embrace the marketing concept and come to recognize the importance of creating superior customer value.

FOR FURTHER READING

David Aaker, *Managing Brand Equity* (New York: Free Press, 1991).

George Day, *Analysis for Strategic Market Decisions* (St. Paul: West Publications, 1986).

Bradley Gale, *Managing Customer Value* (New York: Free Press, 1994).

Philip Kotler, *Marketing Management: Analysis, Planning and Control* (NJ: Prentice Hall, 1996).

Frederick Reichheld, *The Loyalty Effect* (Cambridge: HBS Press, 1996).

Adrian Slywotzky, *Value Migration* (Cambridge: HBS Press, 1996).

Louis W. Stern, Adel El-Ansary, and James Brown, *Management in Marketing Channels* (NJ: Prentice Hall, 1989).

Michael Treacy and Fred Wiersema, *The Discipline of Market Leaders* (Reading, MA: Addison Wesley, 1995).

Frederick Webster Jr., *Market-Driven Management* (New York: Wiley 1994).

Fred Wiersema, *Customer Intimacy* (Santa Monica: Knowledge Exchange, 1996).

OPERATIONS MANAGEMENT: IMPLEMENTING AND ENABLING STRATEGY

8

OPERATIONS MANAGEMENT IS THE IMPLEMENTATION OF BUSINESS STRATEGY

Operations management[1] is the implementation of the firm's business strategy. Operations are the processes by which the firm creates and delivers value to customers. These processes embody the firm's capabilities, which determine its future options. Key capabilities—that is, the activities and processes the firm does better than its competitors—critically affect how successfully the firm competes and how effectively it improves and renews itself. Thus, operations management not only enables the delivery of value to current customers, but it also determines the firm's abilities to serve future customers. Excellence in operations creates strategic opportunities by freeing resources for new uses, as illustrated in Exhibit 8.1, or by building new capabilities, as illustrated in Exhibit 8.2.

An operations manager oversees the organization's processes that transform inputs into outputs of greater value. This includes service operations as well as manufacturing, and it includes processes such as project management, improvement programs, and training. An operations manager may be concerned with manufacturing, new products, research, technology, procurement, distribution, and customer service.

EXHIBIT 8.1   New strategic choices: the winner's dilemma.

In 1993, Raychem Corporation's Interconnection Systems Division faced the winner's dilemma of how to grow. Only three years earlier, Raychem had considered selling or closing the division. Given the division's dramatic turnaround, however, the corporation was ready to expand its investment in the business. Operating income had rebounded from −$3.5 million in 1990 to $6 million in 1993, despite a $2 million decrease in revenue. Revenue per employee had increased 44%, and inventory turns had more than doubled.

In 1990, the situation seemed almost hopeless. "[Because] we were always running around trying to find orders and get them finished and shipped, we never had time to think about the future," commented one manager. Of the 285 employees, half were directly involved in assembly and parts manufacturing, while the other half performed supervisory, support, and development roles.

A new operations manager initiated a change to a cellular manufacturing process based on work teams. The new system enabled a 33% reduction in employees serving overhead functions. Replacing the old batch-based operation, a just-in-time (JIT) flow process was established within the firm and then with vendors. Inventory at the division dropped by $7 million over the next several years. With the new cost structure, Raychem could consider entering markets in which it could not previously compete profitably. By focusing on process improvement and operational excellence, the division was not only able to regain its profitability, but able to create significant strategic opportunities for the future.

Source: Clayton Christensen, "Raychem Corporation Interconnection Systems Division," Harvard Business School Case #9-694-063, 1994.

It is the job of the operations manager to ensure that the firm achieves and maintains a position on the frontier of best practice and to push the frontier forward by continuous improvement or by developing and implementing new approaches to the firm's processes. (See Exhibit 8.3.) Improving operational effectiveness may take many forms, such as enhancing quality in products or

EXHIBIT 8.2   Investing to build future capabilities: Hitachi-Seiki.

In 1952, Hitachi-Seiki, a small Japanese manufacturer of machine tools, set the ambitious goal of developing the capabilities to become a world leader in computerized automation. To build its knowledge base, the company performed basic research about automated production, hired electrical engineers, and set up a new engineering discipline, "mechatronics." The first two projects, although financial failures, taught the company critical lessons about taking a systems approach to develop a flexible manufacturing process. By the mid-1980s the company had become one of the world's leading suppliers of computer-controlled equipment that could perform variable sequencing of machine tasks. By setting long-term goals to build future capabilities, the company was able to leverage the lessons and skills developed over time to design a world-class flexible manufacturing system.

Source: Robert H. Hayes, and Gary P. Pisano, "Beyond World-Class: The New Manufacturing Strategy," *Harvard Business Review,* January–February 1994, pp. 77–86.

**EXHIBIT 8.3   The productivity frontier defines the state of best practice.
Firms operating below the frontier (B) have higher costs
than competitors, or deliver less value to customers, or
both. Firms operating on the frontier (A) offer value to
customers that competitors cannot match at a lower cost.
The challenge is to improve operational effectiveness and
move the frontier outward, enabling even more value to be
delivered with the same (or lower) costs.**

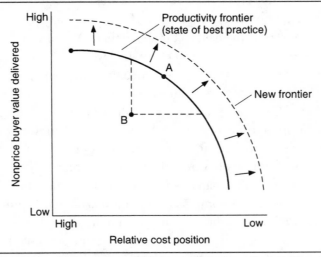

Source: Michael E. Porter, "What is Strategy?," *Harvard Business Review,* November–December 1996, p. 62.

processes, reducing defects, developing better products faster, implementing improved production processes, employing new capital equipment, expanding capacity, improving testing, increasing on-time delivery, streamlining purchasing, outsourcing nonstrategic activities, eliminating waste, employing more advanced technology, motivating employees better, reducing absenteeism, improving workplace health and safety, increasing efficiency, improving customer satisfaction, or empowering organizational learning. Achieving and retaining a position on the frontier of best practice requires vigilant analysis and willingness to change as parts of a continual and relentless effort to improve the firm's processes. It also requires integration with marketing the other functions of the firm so that improvement efforts throughout the firm reinforce each other and so that the functions work together to create and enhance value for customers.

OPERATIONAL EXCELLENCE IS NECESSARY FOR SUSTAINED PROFITABILITY

Operational effectiveness is critical to a firm's competitiveness; it enables a firm to get more from its inputs or to use less of them to produce high-quality output (or to provide better service). A firm that lags behind competitors' operational effectiveness will face higher costs, offer fewer features or lower-quality output (at a given level of costs), or both. For example, in the 1980s many Japanese companies achieved operational effectiveness so far above their Western rivals that the Japanese firms were able to offer customers both lower cost and superior quality. When a firm is on the frontier of best practice, however, competitors will not be able to outperform it on both cost and noncost features simultaneously unless they are able to redefine best practice and push out the entire frontier.

As firms improve their operational effectiveness, they move toward the frontier of best practice or redefine the frontier and push it out ahead of other firms. Indeed, the frontier of productivity continues to shift outward as new technologies, processes, and management methods are developed. During the 1980s and 1990s, concern with improving operations has led to programs in Total Quality Management, continuous improvement, time-based competition, empowering the learning organization, change management, benchmarking, reengineering, and outsourcing. All of this attention has made the development, operation, and improvement of productive processes even more critical for the survival and success of a business. This chapter looks first at measures of process performance and then presents 12 basic principles for achieving process improvement.

MEASURES OF PROCESS PERFORMANCE: WHAT IS IMPROVEMENT?

The goal of process improvement is increasing and sustaining profits. This can be difficult to assess directly, so, for a particular process, managers often use other measures that influence profitability, such as efficiency, quality, capacity, delivery time, and flexibility. These secondary measures can provide important insights about the firm's processes and its opportunities to increase profitability. The trap that often confounds managers is focusing on secondary measures for their own sake and losing sight of the goal of increasing long-term profits.

The secondary measures of profitability are also useful for diagnosing problems and identifying opportunities for improvement. If revenues are rising but profits are falling, measures of process performance can shed critical light on where and why costs are increasing. Thus, even if direct data on profits are available, other measures of operational effectiveness should be monitored and analyzed. (See, for example, Exhibit 8.4.)

The measures that a firm or manager uses are critical. What is measured and how it is measured set very strong incentives for the firm's employees. The old adage that "what you measure will improve" is true. Indeed, many argue that the adage is understated because it may be extremely difficult to affect change on aspects of a process that have not been measured and so are not worked into the practices and culture of the workplace. It is, therefore, important to understand commonly used indicators of operational effectiveness.

Efficiency

Efficiency is sometimes used to mean cost reduction, but it is important to look at costs of a process relative to the value it creates. Efficiency of an *economic system* relates the value of the output to the value of the input. Thus, efficiency should exceed 100%; in a very efficient process, the value of the output (product or service) is much higher than the costs of all inputs used. When value added or profitability is used to indicate efficiency, however, it is important to note that all of the costs or benefits of a process may not be realized in one time period. Benefits may accrue in the future, or if cost reductions are made in ways that hurt quality and reputation over time, then the apparent efficiency indicated by short-term profits may be false. Thus, long-run profitability is a better measure.

EXHIBIT 8.4   Understanding profits by analyzing operational effectiveness.

Profits fell 83% in 1992 for a U.S. producer of plastic pellets. Managers were baffled, because other measures of performance that year were positive. A new marketing strategy aimed at broadening the company's product line and increasing the number of customers had produced record sales for the year. Revenues had increased 20%, production rates had increased 7.4%, and average setup times had decreased 5%. It seemed that the year should have been a success.

The key to understanding the plunge in profits was analyzing operational effectiveness and the fit between operations and marketing efforts. The broader product line had required 10,000 hours of additional setup time for 2,000 additional hours of production. Small batch sizes and large numbers of setups had escalated production costs, causing the drop in profits. Marketing efforts had not taken into account the cost structure of the firm. For the broader-line marketing strategy to be profitable, the firm needed an even more flexible production process. Given the process in place, marketing would add more to profitability by increasing the volume of orders on a smaller number of products.

Source: Leschke and Weiss, "Plastique, Inc.," Darden Graduate Business School Case #UVA-OM-0794, 1995.

Efficiency or utilization of a *physical system* relates the amount of the output created to the amount of the input used, or the percentage of the available (input) resource that is actually used. It cannot exceed 100%. For example, firms measure the percent of time that a machine is actively producing product rather than sitting idle or being serviced. Energy efficiency is another frequently used measure; even the most efficient plant or engine will not deliver more energy than it consumes, so again efficiency cannot exceed 100%. Similarly, firms measure direct labor utilization to determine how many of the hours of paid work were actually used in the manufacture of the product or delivery of the service.

While more efficient physical systems are generally assumed to be better, this is not always the case. For example, a given machine may operate most efficiently with a large batch size, but if the flow of the plant is not balanced, the resulting inventory costs may outweigh the apparent economies on the single machine. The point is that when measures other than profitability are used as surrogates, it is important to keep in mind how these measures affect the profitability of the entire operation.

Quality

Quality can be defined on many dimensions, but it boils down to the following: *Quality* is meeting the customers' requirements. It is what the customer values and pays for. Quality can affect both the cost and the revenue sides of long-run profitability. Poor quality output will immediately or eventually reduce the market value of products or services as well as increase costs of repair, customer service, and handling complaints. These costs may be magnified by reputational spillovers affecting the value of the firm's other products or brands. In addition, poor process quality can increase costs by increasing scrap and rework, reducing utilization and efficiency, increasing downtime, or decreasing customer satisfaction with service processes. The point is that poor quality can create other problems that require time, resources, and managerial effort to resolve. In general, *prevention* of quality problems costs less than inspection and correction.

Output quality can be assessed with internal or external measures. Internal measures generally show how well products or services meet specifications or report the percentage of output that is defective. External measures may compare the product or service to competitive offerings or may assess actual or potential customer satisfaction. In product development, techniques such as Quality Function Deployment or quality architecture focus on identifying customer desires and translating them into engineering specifications for product design to enhance the customer value of the new product.

Process quality affects output quality, and it can be controlled to ensure higher-quality output. Firms may measure such things as missed promises, customer complaints, or on-time deliveries. Service processes and customer interactions may be monitored. Firms may also monitor the settings, temperatures, or force used by machines to ensure proper and consistent operation. Statistical process control measures tend to look at two dimensions of quality: (1) whether the process is "in control" and thus stable and predictable and (2) whether the process is "in compliance" or within the specifications required for the product or by the customer.

Capacity

Capacity is the maximum rate of output generated by a process. It affects the revenue side of long-run profitability by determining how many customers can be served or how many products can be produced. It affects costs in that people must be hired and plant and equipment purchased or rented. These costs may include large capital investments in plants, machines, buildings, or new technologies.

Capacity is measured in units of output (or customers served) per unit of time. In practice, capacity is difficult to measure because it changes over time with changes in the inputs, the mix of outputs, labor, and managerial decisions about the process. In addition, few processes can produce at capacity for long periods or without defects. Effective capacity for the production of nondefective output is much more relevant, but it is also much harder to measure.

The capacity of an integrated or multistep process is determined by the portion of the process with the least capacity, or the bottleneck of the system. Thus, identification and relief of bottlenecks are important issues in process management.

Delivery Time

Speed of delivery may affect the revenue contribution to long-run profitability. The ability of a firm to provide dependable (i.e., on-time) or fast delivery of a product or service may allow it to command a premium price or to sell more units at the standard price. Speed of delivery may also occur in the development cycle, enabling a firm to benefit by offering the first product or the best revision of a product, or to spend less on the upstream product development activities.

Delivery of existing products and services can be measured as the lead time from order to market. Shorter is generally better, but shortening process lead times can adversely affect input costs, quality, or capacity, and thus benefits can be outweighed by new costs. Sometimes, meeting the schedule (providing on-time delivery) is more important than the lead time itself.

Speed of delivery in research and development of new products is trickier to measure because the process involves many contingencies and because the output may not be defined when the research begins. Recent attention focuses on methods for speeding product development, such as concurrent design and engineering.

In service businesses, waiting lines, or queues, may form when customers arrive faster than service is delivered. The length of the queue and the speed at which customers move through it are important measures of the process performance. Long waits may result in lost or disgruntled customers, affecting profitability by reducing the number of current customers, decreasing the rate of repeat customers, and undermining the firm's reputation for quality service.

Flexibility

Flexibility affects profitability through both costs and revenues. A flexible process has a relatively low cost (or short time) for changing inputs used or outputs produced. On the revenue side, the ability to adjust output cheaply or quickly may enable a firm to increase customer satisfaction or to serve additional customers. There is a trade-off, however, because flexible systems may cost more in terms of initial capital investments, operating costs, or both. Managers are keenly aware that flexibility adds value to operations, but they must balance that value with its costs to determine how it affects profitability.

Although the value of flexibility is widely recognized, it is difficult to measure. The value of flexibility is usually discussed in qualitative terms or roughly measured with option value models or decision analysis.

In the context of operations strategy, flexibility refers to opportunities available in the future because of the firm's current capabilities. With superior capabilities, a firm may have opportunities that are not available to competitors or that are available at lower costs than competitors face. Thus, as managers choose among investments or among process improvements, they must highlight in their considerations the capabilities, future flexibility, and options the investments will create. While the value of future options is difficult to measure, it is clear that such options may have significant value and significant effects on long-term profits.

ACHIEVING PROCESS IMPROVEMENT: PRINCIPLES OF OPERATIONS MANAGEMENT

The improvement of processes is a very broad mandate. Much insight can be gained by attacking the issues from a variety of perspectives that offer different principles for process management. Cumulatively, the following five perspectives are extremely powerful in identifying problems, suggesting improvements, and building capabilities:

- Process capacity management.
- Inventory management.
- Continuous improvement.
- Supply chain management.
- Building capabilities.

Process Capacity Management

Principle 1: Capacity is determined by the limiting resource or bottleneck. To increase capacity, increase the limiting resource.

The tendency of managers to be concerned with the efficiency of every machine or person involved in a process is misplaced. The capacity of a system is not determined by the number of idle resource hours. It depends directly on the capacity of the weakest (or least-productive) link in the chain. Once this is recognized, a number of managerial insights follow.

First, since bottlenecks determine capacity, identification and alleviation of bottlenecks is the top priority for increasing capacity. Five ways to identify bottlenecks are shown in Exhibit 8.5. To alleviate bottlenecks, resource allocations should be ranked by the project's contribution to the scarce or limiting resource.

Second, balancing the flow of work through a process will maximize capacity. Maximizing the capacity of individual machines or processes is ineffective since the bottleneck will constrain the system.

EXHIBIT 8.5   How do you identify a bottleneck?

- *Least capacity:* Output of a process is limited by the capacity of the bottleneck.
- *Most utilization:* Activities with the highest rates of use are prime bottleneck suspects. If there is variability in the flow, these areas will sometimes have insufficient capacity.
- *No slack:* Bottlenecks tend to be busy all of the available time.
- *Worker complaints:* There tend to be large numbers of worker complaints about a bottleneck operation.
- *Piled-up inventory:* Inventories (or waiting lines) tend to accumulate upstream of a bottleneck.

Third, downtime on bottlenecks is very expensive because an hour lost on a bottleneck is effectively an hour lost on the entire system. Idle machines or workers in nonbottleneck activities may not have any adverse effect on capacity. Thus, idle time per se need not be viewed as a problem, but idle time at the bottleneck reduces capacity of the entire process.

Fourth, aggregate measures of capacity, utilization, or throughput provide little actionable information. Problem diagnosis and prescriptions for improvement require that analysis be broken down for individual resources. For example, one way to increase capacity is to reduce the time spent on setup of the processes or machines, but this is effective only when setup is reduced on the bottleneck. Reducing setup in other parts of the system will increase the capacity of individual pieces of the system, but not of the process as a whole. Moreover, the bottleneck may be the capacity of machines or of labor, so the analysis should be separated on that dimension as well. For example, a hospital may have plenty of operating rooms for its surgeries, but if there are not enough nurses to staff them, the number of surgeries will be limited by the nursing capacity, not by the physical facilities.

Finally, if there is variability, excess capacity is needed at the bottleneck to keep the flow balanced. If the system has barely adequate capacity on average, then variations above the average will result in shortfalls, creating long waits for output or expensive work-in-process inventory or both. This raises the question of how much excess capacity is reasonable. The answer varies, but in a number of industries, utilization rates much over 80% deserve an extra check to confirm that the capacity is truly adequate.

Principle 2: Capacity also depends on the configuration of processes. Product structure and process structure should be matched appropriately.

Different types of processes are appropriate for different types of services or products, for different types of customer requirements, and for achieving different bases of competitive advantage. Hayes and Wheelwright (1984) identified five process types with corresponding appropriate product types:

- Management of unique projects is generally appropriate for one-of-a-kind products such as a communications satellite or custom-made houses.
- Job shops that produce small batches of a number of different products are appropriate for product lines with high variety and relatively low volume.
- Disconnected line-flow (or batch) processes produce moderate volumes of several products requiring somewhat similar tasks.

- Assembly line (or connected line-flow) processes may be machine-paced or operator-paced, using uniform production paths to produce relatively large volumes of products, usually to inventory.
- Continuous-flow processes involve high-volume, automated, capital-intensive production, usually of commodity-type products.

The basic intuition is that a firm usually will want to operate according to this fit, which is described by the diagonal of the product-process matrix, shown in Exhibit 8.6. Conversely, a firm would not want to be off-diagonal *unintentionally*. Unintentional moves off the diagonal occur, for example, when managers bow to competitive pressures by increasing product variety without adjusting operations to the expanding product line.

There are, however, several good reasons for *intentionally* choosing to be off-diagonal. First, flexible automation techniques enable firms to use connected line-flow processes to produce low-volume products economically, as do cellular manufacturing processes, putting the firm below the diagonal on the matrix. Second, a firm may choose to differentiate its product by handcrafting when competitors use automated processes. Steuben glass is a good

EXHIBIT 8.6   Product process matrix.

	PRODUCT STRUCTURE			
PROCESS STRUCTURE	I Low volume, low standardization, one of a kind	II Multiple products, low volume	III Few major products, higher volume	IV High volume, high standardization, commodity products
I Jumbled flow (job stop)	Commercial printer			
II Disconnected line flow (batch)		Heavy equipment		
III Connected line flow (assembly line)		Flexible manufacturing Cellular manufacturing	Auto assembly	
IV Continuous flow				Sugar refinery

Source: Robert H. Hayes and Steven C. Wheelwright, *Restoring Our Competitive Edge: Competing Through Manufacturing* (New York: John Wiley & Sons, 1984). (Flexible and cellular manufacturing added.)

example of differentiation by handcrafting. Third, a firm may move to automation in anticipation of growth before there is really enough volume to justify the automation.

Inventory Management

In accounting and finance, inventory is often described as raw materials, work-in-process, or finished goods. That categorization tells *what* is in inventory, but not *why*. For operational decisions about how much inventory to hold or how to reduce the amount of inventory, it is more useful to classify inventory by the reasons for which it is held. *Cycle stock* is inventory held to supply the normal production process, to take advantage of economies of scale, and to avoid changing setups too often. *Safety stock* is inventory held in case of a disruption in supply or an unanticipated surge in demand. It is intended to cover variability in supply or demand without stock-outs or service disruptions. *Buffer stock* is held between workstations if the production process is not perfectly balanced. In addition, firms may have *pipeline stock* of goods in transit, *anticipatory* or *seasonal stock* of raw materials or finished goods held in anticipation of changes in availability, or *speculatory stock* of goods held in anticipation of price changes.

All inventory has costs. The costs to firms of holding inventory include warehousing and insurance costs as well as the interest cost of paying for the inputs before they are used. The opportunity cost of capital tied up in inventory is often large. In addition, for firms with global operations, the cost and risk of holding inventory may depend on where the inventory is held. For example, inventory held in Brazil faces greater risk of currency fluctuation than stock held in Canada. On the other hand, if the firm experiences a shortfall, it faces the cost of a shortage or service problem as well as the setup costs or ordering costs for resupply. In addition, inventory enables a firm to fill customer orders faster than the actual production lead time.

Exhibit 8.7 gives some powerful examples of firms increasing profits by improving inventory management.

Principle 3: Inventory decisions hinge on the trade-off between the cost of holding more inventory and the cost of holding less (frequent setups and the risk of shortfalls). Both sides of the trade-off can be managed to reduce inventory costs relative to customer service.

The choice of *how much* cycle stock to hold depends on the trade-off between holding costs and setup or ordering costs. Larger batches require more inventory

EXHIBIT 8.7   The profit impact of inventory reduction.

- Inventory managment is a critical key to Wal-Mart's success. The centerpiece of its operational excellence is a logistics technique known as "cross-docking." Goods are delivered to Wal-Mart warehouses, where they are redispatched to stores, often without ever sitting in inventory. Passing products from one loading dock to another in 48 hours or less has enabled Wal-Mart to avoid inventory and handling costs associated with large orders, and 85% of its goods are handled through this warehouse system, which reduces its costs of sales by 2% to 3% compared with the industry average.

  Source: George Stalk, Philip Evans, and Lawrence E. Shulman, "Competing on Capabilities: The New Rules of Corporate Strategy," *Harvard Business Review,* March–April 1992.

- In 1991, Campbell Soup attempted to change traditional industry dependence on promotional pricing schemes. During promotions, retailers would stock up, purchasing up to three months' inventory to take advantage of the cheap unit prices, which caused huge upswings in volume at manufacturing sites. In an attempt to reform the system to even out inventory fluctuations, Campbell created the Continuous Product Replenishment program, an "everyday low-price strategy," in which Campbell would manage inventories for retail and wholesale customers through a 3090 computer mainframe. Every morning, retailers transmit inventory data electronically to Campbell, which then transmits an electronic purchase order by 2 P.M. each afternoon. Orders are shipped the following day. Inventory analysis and order placement is handled automatically by the computer. As a result, Campbell has been able to ship smaller, more frequent orders, which reduces warehouse space for both Campbell and its retailers and reduces paper-order errors and handling costs. By 1996, the program managed 30% of Campbell's inventory and reduced annual inventory costs by $60 million.

  Source: Mark Halper, "Campbell Soups Up Inventory," *Computerworld Electronic Commerce,* April 29, 1996, and Linda Wilson, "Brand Aid," *Information Week,* October 18, 1993.

- High inventory levels are a costly way to disguise problems. Hewlett-Packard faced the inventory dilemma of high holding costs versus late delivery costs when it realized that only 21% of deliveries to its 50 manufacturing divisions were on time. Early deliveries were expensive to store and hold, but late deliveries wreaked havoc on production lines.

  Defining "on-time delivery" to be three days early to zero days late, Hewlett-Packard began to assess reasons for the breakdown in the delivery process. It found that in 60% of the cases, a lack of clear communication contributed to the delivery problems. Working with suppliers, Hewlett-Packard rewrote its purchase order to diminish misunderstandings and devised an electronic purchase order that flowed directly from its own computers to its suppliers' open-order management systems. The result: on-time deliveries to manufacturing divisions increased by 30%, decreasing bottlenecks and reducing inventory expenses by $9 million.

  Source: David N. Burt, "Managing Suppliers Up to Speed," *Harvard Business Review,* July–August 1989.

to be held, but may enable the firm to take advantage of economies-of-scale purchasing and to reduce setup costs by setting up less often. Shorter setup times enable a firm to produce smaller lots more economically and thus hold less inventory. Indeed, the same basic insight underlies efforts to reduce setup times, size batches economically, and achieve just-in-time production. Decreased batch sizes allow lower inventory, reduced waste, shorter lead time, and faster recognition of quality problems.

Choices about how much safety stock to hold (or when to order cycle stock, which is another way to decide on safety stock) depend on the trade-off between the cost of holding inventory and the cost of a shortage or service problem (as well as economies of scale in purchasing). Pipeline inventory decisions hinge on the cost of holding the inventory compared to the costs of longer lead times or shortages. Anticipatory inventory choices must balance the holding costs with the costs of shortages, substitutions, or subcontracting arrangements. Inventory held for speculatory reasons will depend on the holding costs compared to the cost of price fluctuations or shortfalls.

The management of these trade-offs is often thought of in terms of order quantities, but actually involves that as well as a much richer array of decisions displayed in Exhibit 8.8. For example, management of safety stock is not just a matter of deciding how much inventory to carry. The need for safety stock can be managed by improving quality so that fewer replacement parts are necessary, by reducing variability with long-term contracts, by reducing lead times so that products are made to order (or more nearly made to order), or by improving forecasts so that production can track demand better.

Inventory can also be reduced by holding fewer types of products or parts in reserve. This may be done by reducing product variety, by designing products to share component parts, or by delaying the customization of different products as long as possible and holding inventory only of parts that different products have in common. (See Exhibit 8.9 for a good example of delayed customization.) These reductions in product variety, component variety, or inventory variety essentially pool the risks and require less inventory in total than if individual products or parts were held separately. Centralization of production can facilitate this type of inventory reduction effort.

Principle 4: Don't use inventory to mask production problems. The more production processes and quality are improved, the more inventory can be reduced without increasing the risk of shortfalls.

Inventory provides protection that is needed less and less as processes are streamlined and quality is improved. A useful analogy is to think of inventory as the water in a river and process problems as rocks. As rocks are removed, the

EXHIBIT 8.8   Inventory flow.

Reasons for Inventory	Trade-offs	Decisions
Pipeline (distance)	Cost of inventory versus cost of reducing lead times	Change lead times Change mode of transit Invest in materials-handling equipment Backward-integrate Improve scheduling and loading practices
Cycle (lotsize)	Setup cost versus holding cost	Change lot size Change warehouse procedures Change setup time Invest in technology Affect demand
Safety	Cost of inventory versus cost of downtime or cost of shortfall	Reduce variability Increase quality Change customer service requirements Reduce lead time Reduce forecast errors
Anticipation (seasonal)	Holding cost versus cost of overtime or subcontracting, or cost of shortage	Change amount of inventory Implement quick-response manufacturing Decrease forecast error Smooth out changes in demand Subcontract overtime
Speculation (changing prices)	Holding cost versus price fluctuations, shortages	Change vendors Hedge

Source: Adapted from James Freeland, "Managing Inventories," Darden Graduate Business School Case #UVA-OM-0623.

EXHIBIT 8.9   Delayed customization: Hewlett-Packard.

Hewlett-Packard (HP), in an effort to redesign its products for mass customization, has developed many different solutions to reducing production costs. Because retailers needed DeskJet printers to be delivered on demand, HP produced to stock and faced high inventory costs. To address the problem, the company decided to redesign the product and delay the customization step. For example, instead of customizing the DeskJets for the European market at its factory in Singapore, generic printers (made in Singapore) are sent to its European distribution center in Germany. The distribution center purchases the materials to differentiate the printers (power supplies, packaging, and manuals) and customizes them for the appropriate European market. While manufacturing costs are higher than if the Singapore factory customized the printers, HP is able to hold far less inventory because it now pools risk and holds stock of the generic printer rather than holding stock of each type of customized printer. Total manufacturing, shipping, and inventory costs have decreased by 25%.

Source: Edward Feitzinger and Hau L. Lee, "Mass Customization at Hewlett-Packard: The Power of Postponement," *Harvard Business Review,* January–February 1997.

water runs more freely, but when the water level is lowered, more rocks become apparent. When the process is repeated enough times, the river flows freely with a much lower level of water—that is, much less inventory. The message delivered by this analogy is that the cycle of improving the process and reducing inventory must be *repeated* for continuous improvement and the full benefit of skillful inventory management.

Principle 5: Customer waiting lines may reduce the value of a product or service. Queues need to be managed to balance the (direct and indirect) costs of making customers wait versus idle server time.

In service businesses, "inventory" sometimes takes the form of queues (or waiting lines) of customers waiting to be served or, worse yet, deciding not to wait and going elsewhere for service. Queues involve servers providing a service that varies in time or complexity to customers who arrive at random (unscheduled) times. Managing the length of waiting lines is important because waiting is often costly to customers, reducing the value of the product or service for them and thus the revenues that the firm can earn. The idle time of the server is also costly to the firm since the worker is being paid while idle. Given the uncertainty in both service times and arrival times, waiting time and idle server time cannot be entirely eliminated; the objective is to adjust the "wasted" time to minimize the sum of the costs of poor service and idle servers. (Exhibit 8.10 shows the inverse relationship of service costs and waiting costs.)

Waiting time and idle server time can be managed in a number of ways. The number of servers can be adjusted, using more servers at peak times and fewer at slower times. The rate at which service is provided can be speeded up with training, process analysis and redesign, or investment in technology. The pattern of customer arrivals can sometimes be altered with incentives for customers to arrive at nonpeak times or by extending available service hours to weekends and evenings or with 24-hour telephone services. Arrival rates can also be managed by moving to appointments rather than a first-come, first-served queue. Combining multiple waiting lines helps to ensure that one server is not idle while another has customers waiting. Sometimes this is as simple as forming a snake line at the airport ticket counter. In other situations, cross-training servers and combining service locations may be necessary to combine queues.

As these choices are considered, it is important to keep in mind the relative costs. Idle time is not necessarily bad. It may be preferable to have a clerk idle in the stockroom part of the day than to have a queue of highly paid engineers or mechanics regularly standing idle while they wait for parts at the stockroom window.

EXHIBIT 8.10   **Management of waiting times involves balancing the trade-off between making customers wait and employing more servers. Waiting cost goes down and service cost goes up as more servers are employed.**

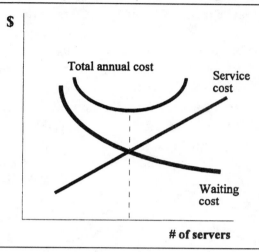

Quality Improvement

The management of product and process quality is critical to meeting customer needs, adding value for customers, and reducing costs. Quality is a multidimensional concept encompassing product quality (e.g., performance, reliability, conformance, features, durability, value, and serviceability), service quality (e.g., atmosphere, comfort, waiting time, value, reliability, and convenience), and process quality (e.g., low cost, low variance, low defects, low waste, control, and predictability). For example, BMW and Toyota both make high-quality cars, but the dimensions of quality that they emphasize are different.

Quality management programs span departmental and even organizational boundaries. Quality programs may include measuring product defects or service problems, establishing systems to prevent quality problems, redefining supplier relationships as partnerships, improving the customer interface to better understand and deliver what the customer values, developing new products to better meet customer needs, changing employee incentives and compensation schemes, and changing business paradigms when necessary to improve processes.

Principle 6: Poor quality is costly. High quality is not free, but it can be a very good investment.

Successful quality management programs pursue quality, not for its own sake, but to enhance the net value delivered to customers by improving efficiency and improving product or service value. Sometimes efforts to improve quality directly reduce costs by lowering the number of defects or by reducing scrap or rework. In these cases, productivity is improved by doing things right the first time around. Sometimes when quality management raises costs, the resulting products or services are differentiated in such a way that customers will pay a premium above the costs of quality management. TQM advocates point out that in both of these instances, quality is free.

Other times, quality management increases costs without an accompanying current price premium. Although quality is not free in that situation, it is a good investment if managers anticipate a *future* payoff in the form of more loyal customers, higher demand, or a future price premium based on the record of high quality. As with other investments, quality process improvement investments may not pay off instantly, but should be undertaken if they provide positive net present value to the firm. The point is not that managers should try to quantify precisely all of the benefits (which may be difficult to measure), but that the value of pursuing quality should be considered relative to its costs, especially since a poorly implemented quality program can add unnecessary costs to the business.

Principle 7: Prevention is less expensive than inspection and correction.

> *"I worry that whoever thought up the term quality control believed that if we didn't control it, quality would get out of hand."*
>
> —Lily Tomlin

Total quality management, or TQM, means different things to different people, but the essence of TQM is using analysis and management of quality to improve profitability. The analysis is critical because it provides the understanding that is the basis of prevention and improvement. The alternative to prevention is inspection followed by correction of problems or selection of which goods to sell and which to scrap. Generally, it is less costly to get it right the first time than to attempt to catch problems and fix or scrap them.

Deming identified two basic sources of problems: *common causes* of quality problems due to management or process design and *special causes* of quality problems due to individual workers or machines. Common causes are systemic and due to deficiencies or oversights in process design or management such as poor product design, machines out of order or in poor repair, inadequate training programs, poor quality or scheduling of incoming materials, improper bills of materials, inappropriate incentives for workers, poor working conditions, or other problems shared by numerous operators, service providers, or machines. Special causes are attributable to particular workers or equipment, such as lack of skill, inattention, one machine operating outside of specification, or one bad lot of incoming material. Deming encouraged the use of statistical process control to distinguish between the two types of problems, followed by action to redesign the system to address common causes and attention to specific workers or activities to correct special causes. Often this action takes the form of continual incremental improvement; however, it may require more radical redesign, or *reengineering*, of systems.

Many companies define *quality* as conformance to requirements. Service or production processes are then considered *capable* if the output meets specifications or customer requirements. If output does not meet specifications, common causes need to be addressed. Service or production processes are considered *in control* if the output is stable and predictable, although it is possible that this output could be outside of acceptable specification limits (and thus need attention to common causes to achieve capability). If a process is capable but not in control (and thus unpredictable or drifting away from acceptable output), attention to special causes is warranted. Clearly, the preferred situation is to have capable processes that are also in control.

Principle 8: Quality requires clear communication and commitment throughout the organization. What you measure and reward will improve.

In contrast to the narrow definition of quality as conformance to specifications, quality is sometimes said to be meeting customer expectations or *what you would want if you were the customer.* From this perspective, continuous improvement requires effective systems and incentives to enhance customer value. This requires managers to identify indicators of customer value that can be measured and effectively tied to compensation. Good indicators of quality are closely tied to attributes of products or services that will command a premium price or will lower the price of a product that is as good as competitors' products.

A relatively short and stable list of clear and timely indicators is most effective. While it is easy to make long lists of possible indicators, it is better to identify a few clear measures that keep the focus on the primary goals of improving customer value. Long, detailed lists of metrics blur the focus. Similarly, focus is blurred by changing the measures too often. The program will be most successful

EXHIBIT 8.11   National Bicycle Industrial: reengineering for mass customization.

In the mid-1980s, the Japanese bicycle industry hit a plateau, threatened by inexpensive imports from Taiwan and Korea and a declining U.S. export industry. National Bicycle Industrial Co., one of the three largest bicycle manufacturers in Japan, needed to rethink how it would be able to compete with these low-cost producers without having to relocate offshore. Bicycle parts were purchased from large component manufacturers and assembled by a labor-intensive assembly production process. National Bicycle had also developed a competitive advantage in the development of a 3-D measurement computer system that measured the dimensional accuracy of each bike frame. The company wanted to position itself for an anticipated boom in sport bicycles, which sold for more than three times the price of transport bicycles. Expensive component parts and the inability to predict demand due to fast-changing trends in sport bicycle fashion, however, made the product extremely risky—a single instance of overproduction could strike a critical blow to the company.

Believing that customization might solve the product differentiation and inventory risk problems, the company set out to *reengineer* its marketing and production processes in order to produce customized bicycles on demand. Like tailored suits, each bicycle would be specially made to fit the exact size, weight, and color, and accessory preference of each customer by using the computerized measurement system already developed by the company. To achieve this, a totally new process for ordering would be required. The Panasonic Order System included a list of specifications to be supplied by the customer and an adjustable "fitting scale" in each retail store, as well as a fax machine at each store to send orders immediately to National Bicycle. Guaranteed delivery within two weeks was made possible by a completely redesigned production process enabling *mass customization* through the use of computer technology and redesigned production processes.

Over the next four years, unit sales for the customized sport bicycle increased by 73%, with over 1,500 international retailers adopting the customized system. While revenues for the Japanese industry decreased 12.1% from 1985 to 1991, revenues for National Bicycle increased 28.5% over the same time period.

Source: Marshall Fisher, "National Bicycle Industrial Co.," The Wharton School Business Case, University of Pennsylvania, 1994.

---

if rewards are tied to measures that employees can improve with effort, not just by chance. Moreover, it is critical that efforts to continually improve these measures are not allowed to block potential big leaps. The most dramatic improvements tend to come from redesigning or reengineering the process to improve value delivered to customers. (Exhibit 8.11 gives an example of dramatic profit improvements from reengineering that could not have been achieved through continuous improvement.)

Quality programs have the additional benefit of being positively focused. Executives explain that after years of programs to improve productivity, they finally achieved their goals by implementing quality programs. While productivity programs sometimes appear technically daunting or threatening to jobs, well-executed quality programs may provide better motivation to achieve the desired results.

Supply Chain Management

Operations management considerations extend beyond the boundaries of the firm to the coordination and configuration of supplier and distributor relationships. As competitive advantage is increasingly achieved by networks of firms, each firm in the network can benefit when the preceding principles of *process capacity management, inventory management,* and *quality improvement* are applied by others in the network. This is why there is such a strong current trend toward cooperation among firms and their suppliers or distributors.

Examples abound. Firms such as Toyota invest substantial time and effort in helping suppliers to improve operations. The Gap works with its suppliers to ensure identical products from multiple sources. Raychem helped suppliers to convert to cellular manufacturing so that its own efforts in cellular manufacturing would not be constrained by suppliers' batch process delivery schedules. Laura Ashley overhauled its information systems and consolidated warehouses, achieving a fivefold increase in inventory turns over three years. National Semiconductor increased sales by over $500 million in two years while reducing distribution costs by moving products from the factory to the customer in four days or less. And on the flip side, Compaq Computer estimated that it lost over $500 million in sales in 1994 because its computers were not available when and where the customers were ready to buy.

Principle 9: Network management requires a mind-set of cooperation among partners rather than competition with suppliers.

Increasingly, it is networks of firms that determine competitive advantage; therefore, counter to the traditional view, suppliers must be thought of as partners, not adversaries along the value chain. In this new context, the development of trust is critical. This can be tricky, especially when firms are competing in some contexts but cooperating in other aspects of the business.

Network relationships should be structured to give each player incentives to make improvements that benefit the whole chain. For example, a network will not lower costs if one firm attempts to lower inventory simply by requiring a supplier to hold the inventory. Overall inventory costs, however, can be reduced by sharing of information among firms so that uncertainty is reduced and less safety stock is needed, or by moving to a just-in-time system throughout the network with smaller production batches and shorter lead times. The point is that the potential gains are greater if the costs are removed from the network, rather than just shifted within it. (Exhibit 8.12 defines Kanban implementation of JIT.)

EXHIBIT 8.12   Kanban: JIT system.

Kanban (a Japanese word meaning "card") is a way of implementing just-in-time (JIT) inventory. It is a simple system that enables suppliers to deliver JIT by signaling with a card, fax, or empty basket when supplies are needed. Thus, demand dictates the flow of inventory, in contrast to a system based on schedule or anticipation.

Principle 10: Improving information flows among network partners reduces costs by reducing variability and uncertainty and improving planning and forecasting.

The old mind-set of competition with suppliers led to practices of rarely, if ever, sharing information. Lower prices from suppliers, however, can be achieved by sharing information that enables suppliers to plan more accurately, lower inventories, and make more accurate delivery decisions.

Toyota, for example, shares its materials requirements planning (MRP) forecasts with suppliers. MRP is a widely used computerized tool that develops schedules for placing orders and performing production tasks based on data about the structure of a manufactured product, its required parts and subassemblies, and the lead times for ordering parts and making subassemblies. This tool was originally developed for firms to improve their own ordering and scheduling decisions. Toyota, however, takes a broader view. It uses MRP to give suppliers forecasts for the schedules of needed parts. This improves suppliers' information and enables reliable deliveries with lower levels of safety stock inventory. Toyota, however, does not place its orders for parts based on the MRP forecasts. Orders are based on Toyota's actual demand; the forecasts just prevent the supplier from experiencing uncertainty that is greater than Toyota's.

MRP has also been extended to Enterprise Requirements Planning. This extends the concept of anticipating requirements beyond manufacturing to include human resources and other functions. Enterprise Requirements Planning methods can be used with the firm or applied to the anticipation of needs among firms in a network.

Better information flows among networks are also often achieved with information technology links such as electronic data interchanges (EDI), which enable suppliers to be notified automatically of product replenishment needs. Campbell's uses this approach to increase accuracy and reduce costs of keeping grocery store shelves stocked with its soups and other products.

Principle 11: Lead time reduction throughout the supply chain is a powerful way for the network to reduce costs and improve customer service.

Long lead times increase uncertainty, increase inventory costs, and decrease responsiveness to customer needs. Reduction in lead times throughout a network enables a just-in-time system that addresses each of these costly problems to some extent. Just-in-time systems operate on the principles of smaller batches, shorter lead times, reduced waste, and faster recognition of quality problems. These systems emphasize the critical nature of supplier relationships, because a firm may not be able to achieve the full benefits of just-in-time production unless its suppliers also operate in a just-in-time delivery (or production and delivery) mode.

Another approach to reducing network lead time is to manage capacity efficiently across product lines so that products with more certain demand are made ahead of time and items with more variable demand are made as close to the purchase date as possible. This improves the market forecasts for the harder-to-predict products. Sport-Obermeyer uses this type of planning logic to work within the capacity constraints of its suppliers and reduce the peak supplier capacity that it needs to meet seasonal demands for its skiing apparel.

Development of Capabilities

A firm's processes of production and service delivery embody its capabilities. For better or worse, these capabilities position the firm for the future. It is therefore critical that decisions about current operations are made with a view to the potential future benefits of the knowledge, experience, and processes that the company develops. The development of key capabilities enables a firm to succeed in its strategy in spite of the uncertainties and changes of a dynamic marketplace.

Principle 12: The development of proprietary capabilities that enable future flexibility requires commitment and investment.

There is much misplaced debate about whether the essence of strategy is making commitments or maintaining flexibility. Strategy critically involves both commitment and flexibility. Commitment is necessary to establish competitive advantage not immediately available to other firms. Flexibility in how to achieve the vision or maintain a firm's strategic position in a changing world is also critical. The irony is that in order to have that future flexibility, firms must make prior commitments. These commitments often take the form of investments in research and development, in plants or capital equipment, or in the development of capabilities. The resulting proprietary knowledge or firm-specific capabilities create an advantaged position for the firm in some possible future conditions. It is not the flexibility per se, but the advantaged position relative to firms without the prior commitment that offers significant value for the firm. The point is that the prior investment enables the firm to react more effectively, more quickly, or at lower cost than those that have to build the capabilities after the need is more certain and apparent.

Managers wanting to create strategic flexibility, therefore, cannot simply wait for opportunities to come along. Investments in flexibility must be carefully chosen to fit within the firm's strategy, not to reverse direction and become what the firm has chosen not to be. For example, Corning Incorporated invests in many technologies not needed for its current products, but its investments are linked to its vision of being the world leader in glass and ceramics. Corning's strategy determines appropriate investments in flexibility and the firm devotes very substantial resources to developing capabilities in those areas.

By investing in capabilities that enable future flexibility, the firm positions itself to prosper *because* of uncertainty, not in spite of it. As the uncertain future unfolds, firms that have developed the necessary capabilities will be in advantaged positions relative to those firms that have not made the prior commitments, and thus the forward-looking firms will have benefited from the uncertainty that disadvantaged others.

OPERATIONS STRATEGY IS THE SELECTION AND BUILDING OF CAPABILITIES

Beginning in the 1980s the critical role of operations in achieving competitive advantage led firms to think strategically about operations management; they began developing and assessing operations strategies. These operations strategies, or patterns of decisions over time, should consistently support and enhance the competitive advantage sought by the firm's business strategy. Indeed, each of the firm's functional strategies (operations, finance, marketing, R&D, etc.) must be aligned with the vision of the business unit strategy for the firm to achieve the full potential of that strategic vision.

Operations strategy must go beyond the pursuit of best practice and meeting the competition in implementation of the latest and greatest improvement programs. Operations give strategic leverage to a firm when efforts are focused on building capabilities in specific processes or activities that the firm does better than competitors. Thus the selection and building of capabilities is the core of operations strategy. These capabilities create opportunities for the firm to succeed in a dynamic, changing, competitive environment.

FOR FURTHER READING

David N. Burt, "Managing Suppliers Up to Speed," *Harvard Business Review*, July–August 1989.

John Colley Jr., "Instructional Note—Planning Labor Requirements in Service Operations," Darden Graduate Business School Note #UVA-OM-0528, 1984.

Edward Feitzinger, and Hau L. Lee, "Mass Customization at Hewlett-Packard: The Power of Postponement," *Harvard Business Review*, January–February 1997.

Marshall L. Fisher, "What Is the Right Supply Chain for Your Product?," *Harvard Business Review*, March–April 1997.

James Freeland, "Managing Inventories," Darden Graduation Business School Case #UVA-OM-0623, 1987.

G.A. Garvin, "Competing on the Eight Dimensions of Quality," *Harvard Business Review*, November 1987.

Eliyahu M. Goldratt and Jeff Cox, *The Goal* (Great Barrington, MA: North River Press, Inc., 1992).

Ann E. Gray, "Process Fundamentals," Harvard Business School Case #N9-696-023, 1995.

Robert H. Hayes and Gary P. Pisano, "Beyond World-Class: The New Manufacturing Strategy," *Harvard Business Review*, January–February 1994, pp. 77–86.

Robert H. Hayes and Steven C. Wheelright, *Restoring Our Competitive Edge: Competing Through Manufacturing* (New York: John Wiley & Sons, 1984), p. 209.

J. L. Heskett et al., "Putting the Service-Profit Chain to Work," *Harvard Business Review*, March 1994.

David H. Maister, "Note on the Management of Queues," Harvard Business School Note #9-680-053, 1979.

John O. McClain, L. Joseph Thomas, and Joseph B. Mazzola, *Operations Management: Production of Goods and Services* (Englewood Cliffs, NJ: Prentice Hall, Inc., 1992).

Peter A. Morris, Elizabeth O. Teisberg, and A. Lawrence Kolbe, "When Choosing R&D Projects, Go with the Long Shots," *Research-Tech Management*, January–February 1991.

Michael E. Porter, "What Is Strategy?," *Harvard Business Review*, November–December 1996, p. 62.

George Stalk, Philip Evans, and Lawrence E. Shulman, "Competing on Capabilities: The New Rules of Corporate Strategy," *Harvard Business Review*, March–April 1992.

9 INNOVATION AND TECHNOLOGY MANAGEMENT

Technology is know-how.[1] Whether it is high-tech or low-tech, technology describes what we know how to do, from the age-old technology for making wine to the state-of-art technology for the newest gene therapy. Technology is embodied in every process a firm performs throughout its value chain,[2] and thus technological change can affect any activity a firm performs as well as the linkages among activities or between firms. Technology not only determines how the firm makes products or serves customers, but also affects what the firm produces and with whom it must compete. The advance of technology, therefore, has profound effects on business. Without the gradual advance of technology, people would be efficiently managing building fires and making stone wheels.[3] Moreover, technology—the know how for doing something—is not an outside force as economists used to think, but an internal one that can be cultivated to increase growth.[4]

Technological change has important strategic implications for companies and for industries. On the industry level, technological advance changes the bases of competitive advantage, creating significant opportunities and threats for competing firms. It may also change industry structure, thereby improving or degrading the average profitability of all firms in the industry. In some instances, technological change completely redefines industries, leading to the decline of some and the emergence of others. Firms can gain advantage by recognizing and exploiting the significance of technological change for the industry.

On the company level, superior management of technology and innovation within the firm can be an important source of competitive advantage. This chapter focuses on the company level and addresses three key issues in innovation and technology management within the firm: (1) developing a *technology strategy* to pursue the right projects at the right times and (2) *managing technological innovation* to achieve commercial success and competitive advantage,[5] and (3) *organizing for innovation*. Each of these issues depends critically on the people involved and on their motivation, incentives, and networks of relationships. In practice, the management of technology and innovation is an intensely social process.

DEVELOPING A TECHNOLOGY STRATEGY

Technology strategy describes the firm's priorities for the development and use of product and process technologies. Like other functional strategies (such as marketing strategy or operations strategy), technology strategy must reinforce the firm's competitive strategy.[6] It should define priorities that enable the firm to achieve the benefit of its competitive position and develop capabilities that enhance the firm's current and future competitive advantage.

But technology strategy is unlike other functional strategies in that technologies are used throughout a firm in all of its activities. Thus, considerations for developing a technology strategy span the firm's functions. Indeed, for a multibusiness firm, corporate technology strategy spans the firm's business units. (Exhibit 9.1 presents examples that illustrate how considerations about new technology-based products, processes, or services span many functions. This chapter focuses on the development of new technology based products rather than on the use of technology throughout the firm.)

EXHIBIT 9.1   Technology strategy is implemented in many functions to enable the success of the firm's competitive strategy.

- The design of digital watches depends on the firm's approach to customer service. Product design and manufacturing will both differ depending on whether the firm intends to service its own watches, have them repaired at any jewelry store, or have them be disposable.
- Crown Cork & Seal makes cans and provides responsive customer service to a select group of customers. It follows a low-cost strategy and does not perform research to pioneer new products. It does, however, do R&D on specific customer problems and on imitation of competitors' product innovations as a fast follower. Its technology strategy supports its competitive strategy of a low-cost position and superb customer service for a select group customers. Other firms competing more broadly in the packaging industry pursue very different technology strategies aimed at developing new packaging products or new materials.

Development of a technology strategy includes a technology assessment developed in conjunction with the business strategy that it supports. The resulting insights are used to prioritize commitments to innovation and technology development. This discussion first describes the five steps in technology assessment and then addresses key principles in choosing priorities for innovation and development projects.

In practice, there should be a great deal of integration between technology considerations and business strategy throughout the process. As with other strategy development processes, much of the value of technology strategy development is in the insights managers gain from the process, so involvement of managers from all key functions is essential. Also like other strategy development processes, an appropriate balance must be struck between thoroughness and simplicity.

Technology Assessment

The five steps of technology assessment include (1) identification of important technologies, (2) analysis of potential change in important current and future technologies, (3) analysis of the competitive impact of important technologies, (4) analysis of the firm's technological strengths and weaknesses, and (5) choice of a tentative set of priorities for research and development projects or for the acquisition of technologies.

1. Identify important technologies.

Technology assessment begins with the identification of all of the current and future technologies important to the business. These include not only product technology and manufacturing process technology, but also technology used in performing activities in other functions such as marketing, information management, customer service, and research. They may include technologies used by competitors as well as technologies used within the firm. Important technologies may also include technologies used by suppliers or buyers with whom the firm works, especially when competition is among networks of firms, rather than among individual firms.[7]

Technologies outside of the current business should be in the set if they may have a competitive impact on the firm or in the industry. In other words, the identification of technologies needs to include consideration of how technologies in development or used in other industries could change the firm's products and processes or change the nature of competition in the business. Such changes can be analyzed by thinking about how each of the activities of the firm might change and by thinking about how new technologies could be used to serve customers differently in the future.

2. Analyze potential change in important current and future technologies.

The next step in technology assessment is forecasting short-term and long-term changes in the identified key technologies. Complex products or processes may involve many subtechnologies. In these instances, forecasting change requires analysis of the subtechnologies.

Forecasts of technological change must be done by people with expertise in the technologies. It also should be constructively challenged by other managers on the team to prevent a forecast based on unquestioned conventional wisdom among the technical community and to encourage thinking about how unexpected changes might occur. It is important to keep in mind that the rate of technological progress varies with the effort applied, so technologies that are key to some competitors' strategies may evolve more quickly than technologies that are necessary but do not provide competitive advantage.

It is also important to realize that mature technologies do not necessarily change slowly. Indeed, the opposite is true if the need for progress leads to the replacement of an old technology with a new one. Rapid change around mature technologies also occurs if the invention of a new technology creates opportunities for new firms to displace industry leaders that prove to be slow adopters of the new processes or products.

3. Analyze competitive impact of technologies.

Analysis of competitive impact identifies technologies or technological changes that can give the firm the greatest competitive advantage, be the greatest threat in a competitor's hands, or change industry structure significantly. For this purpose, technologies can be classified as *base, key,* or *pacing.*[8] Exhibit 9.2 shows the evolution of the competitive impact of technologies.

> *Base technologies* are necessary, but they will not provide a source of competitive advantage. These technologies are usually well understood and widely used throughout the industry. Improving these technologies over time is necessary to remain competitive, but the advances are easily matched by competitors and thus do not confer advantage.
>
> *Key technologies* are critical to competitive advantage. They enable the firm to differentiate its products or services or to compete with lower costs. Often, key technologies are proprietary because of patents, unpatented advances by the firm, or unparalleled expertise in using the technology.

EXHIBIT 9.2 **Competitive impact. Technologies with high potential competitive impact but not yet widely adopted are *pacing* technologies that may change future competition. Critical (often proprietary) technologies for differentiating products or services that are effectively embodied are *key* technologies. *Base* technologies are necessary, but widely understood and thus do not provide competitive advantage.**

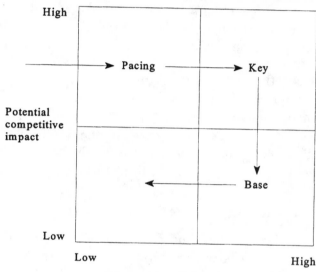

Source: John M. Ketteringham and John R. White, "Making Technology Work for Business," in *Competitive Strategic Management,* edited by Robert Bryden Lamb (Englewood Cliffs, NJ: Prentice Hall, 1984).

Pacing technologies have the potential to change the entire basis of competition or to redefine the industry. They often replace key technologies. When pacing technologies are developed by firms that are not the current leaders, they create opportunities for industry leadership to change. Pacing technologies are sometimes overlooked by established firms because they are very different or because they threaten to cannibalize existing products or replace existing processes that have been key to success. Thus, firms with strong key technologies need to guard against the risk of failing to anticipate pacing technologies.

4. Analyze technical strengths and weaknesses of the firm.

To complete the assessment of competitive impact, managers must assess the firm's strengths and weaknesses in each class of technology as well as the expected cost of advancing each technology. This assessment should be relative to competitors' strengths and weaknesses, and it should take into account not only competitors' current technologies but also their intended positions. By looking at the intended positions and possible future progress of competitors, managers can get more insight about how their own firm's efforts may affect their relative competitive position.

It is often difficult to ensure that this assessment is objective rather than skewed by pride or by unwillingness to acknowledge the competitors' capabilities. It helps to have a team that includes technical specialists who understand the technologies as well as managers who are focused on the markets and keenly aware of competitors' accomplishments and announced directions.

5. Choose a tentative set of priorities.

A tentative set of priorities for the development and use of product and process technologies should then be developed based on the insights from the technology assessment process. This tentative set of priorities evolves into a technology strategy through a process of interaction with the firm's leaders as well as key business managers representing all of the firm's functions.

Choosing a Technology Portfolio

To choose a technology portfolio and develop a technology strategy, the firm's competitive strategy must be analyzed to identify all of the technical achievements throughout the firm that are required to meet the firm's goals for competitive position and competitive advantage. As this analysis proceeds, seven principles should be in the forefront of managers' minds.

Principle 1: Technology strategy must explicitly support the firm's current and future sources of competitive advantage.

Choices of technologies to acquire or develop must be justified by analysis of their link to current or future competitive advantage. Investments in research and development should explicitly aim to help the firm achieve differentiation or achieve a cost advantage. This does not imply a short-term view; it may include developing technologies or capabilities that position the firm for advantage in the future.

Process innovation and product innovation should both be considered as potential keys to achieving competitive advantage. Manufacturing process innovation is often critical to product innovation, shorter time to market, improved customer satisfaction, and proprietary position.

Priorities for investment in technology development should reflect recognition that some technologies can be acquired, licensed, or developed in a follower role, but for other technologies, development of a leadership position is critical. The firm does not need to develop everything in-house, but it should develop and improve technologies that are critical for sustained competitive advantage. This implies that different technologies will be critical to different firms because they have distinct strategic positions and serve different customer needs.

Choices of technologies will also depend on costs and timing. Realistic estimates of costs and timing are important for good decisions about which efforts will contribute most to competitive advantage. Alternatives such as purchasing, licensing, joint ventures, mergers, or acquisitions may make significant differences in costs and timing.[9]

Principle 2: Invention does not always create value.

Technological change is sometimes viewed as good for its own sake, but not all invention creates value. New ideas, new processes, or new products may not be adopted. Some inventions will not meet a need, or they will add value below their cost and thus not be used. People often refer to such innovations as "technologies ahead of their time," but they may more simply be described as too expensive; cost exceeds the value delivered. Other innovations fail to add value because related products or services have yet to be developed. For example, there are now tests that can diagnose genetic diseases for which there is no cure or effective treatment. These tests have value if people can make better decisions about their lives knowing they have the disease, but the value is seriously limited if the diagnosis cannot be followed by a cure.

How do you know if an invention will create value? At early stages of research, you may not know, and some early-stage ideas should be pursued without a clear idea of their eventual applications, especially if they expand the firm's capabilities in areas critical to its strategic vision. But as the innovation process proceeds, the trick is to look beyond the technical elegance of an innovation and ask how it reduces costs or improves the value for customers.

Sometimes managers have trouble envisioning how and for whom an invention creates value even at later stages of development. For example, Bendix envisioned little value creation from its invention of fuel injection for gasoline engines. Fuel injection increases fuel efficiency, reduces emissions, and increases engine performance in almost all weather and driving conditions. But these attributes were not especially valuable to passenger car drivers in the United States in 1967. In Europe, fuel prices were higher and emission standards were tighter, so the market was more obvious. Bendix licensed the technology to a European company, the Robert Bosch Corporation, through an 11-year contract. By the mid-1970s, competitor Bosch had furthered the technology, captured the European market, entered the Japanese market, and begun to sell Bendix injectors in the U.S. market.

Principle 3: All successful innovations serve a market need; for entirely new products or services, carefully identifying the lead customers is more important than detailed estimates of the future market size.

Managers may find it very difficult to think about the use and value of a product that has not yet been introduced. Forecasts of the future market for something entirely new are often wildly inaccurate. The focus of market analysis, therefore, needs to be on how (and to whom) to launch the innovation, rather than just on the size of the potential future market. Innovations tend to have a set of early adopters who value the new product more highly than the broad market and provide early learning opportunities for the producer. Managers need to identify these groups of potential early adopters by analyzing the specific attributes of the new technology or product and asking, "Who values these attributes?" and "Why?" In the process of serving these early customers, products or services are refined and costs are often brought down as learning and experience develop.

The attributes of fuel injection were probably more valuable to commercial drivers than passenger car drivers, especially in the United States. Bendix developers had concentrated on gasoline engines. Trucks and aircraft use diesel engines for which fuel injection was not initially developed. Fuel injection might also have been more valuable to fleets of vehicles, such as taxis or police cars. Had Bendix believed fuel injection was a critical technology in which to develop capabilities, diesel engines or gasoline-powered fleets would have been logical lead markets. Bendix might have launched fuel injection in the United States if it had targeted a commercial market, or created a diesel engine version of its innovation.

Difficulty in identifying the initial market for a new product may also lead to the mistake of attempting to launch a product for which there is no market. Often this mistake can be traced to a lack of contact with potential customers or a lack of understanding of customers' needs and values. Managers may argue that market research is useless because they cannot get good information about customers' preferences for something they have not yet experienced and may not have imagined. But the limits of standard market research are not a good excuse for failing to understand how and for whom a new product adds value. Again, analysis of the value chain of potential customers can reveal the benefits and costs of adopting a new product.[10] Moreover, rather than focusing all attention on estimating the size of the market, managers can get a lot of insight by identifying specific people they know will become customers. If it is difficult to identify 10 actual customers for the new product, it may not serve a need. Beware of excuses when no customers can be identified!

Principle 4: Innovation (or value creation from an invention) is not sufficient to *capture* value.

When invention does create value, the innovator does not necessarily capture the value created. Even spectacular, Nobel-prize-winning advances in technology may not result in profits for the innovator. In the case of the CAT scan, the original invention by Dr. Godfrey Hounsfield of EMI scanned only the brain. The market for brain scans at that time was small; insurance companies rarely reimbursed payments for brain scans, and few effective treatments were available to patients with problems diagnosed by the scans. Widespread adoption and diffusion of the technology occurred only after future generations of the technology were developed to scan the whole body. At that point, the CAT scans could be used to diagnose more conditions for which treatment existed, and insurance companies began to pay for scans of patients. General Electric (GE) profited by leading that generation of innovation in CAT scans, and EMI exited the business entirely within eight years.[11]

The EMI story is dramatic because the innovation won a Nobel prize, but similar stories abound. RC Cola invented diet soda and was first to introduce cola in a can, but Coca-Cola and Pepsi captured much of the value of those innovations. Bowmar introduced the first pocket calculator, but Texas Instruments made the idea succeed. MITS introduced the first personal computer, but never figured among the winners in the industry. In contrast, the IBM PC offered little innovation, but was a stunning success where others had not been.[12]

Principle 5: Familiarity with either the market or the technology (or both) helps the launch of new products and services.

Although innovation is often thought to be the key to success, *familiarity* has a critical role. "Newness" has many dimensions. As Exhibit 9.3 shows, a product, process, or service may be new to a market, or be based on a new technology, or both. One of the keys to success cited by firms is staying on familiar ground on one dimension while pioneering in another. If the technology is new, introduce it in a familiar market, if possible. If the market is new, consider basing the product or service on technology with which the firm has established experience.

Principle 6: The chance of capturing value is increased by proprietary protection, strong and agile R&D, technological complexity, and complementary assets.

Why do innovators often fail to capture value? What enables innovators to succeed in capturing value? The first answer that springs to most people's minds is patent protection. Strong patent protection provides one explanation, but

EXHIBIT 9.3 Successful launch of an innovation is easier when the market or technology are familiar.

How New Is It?

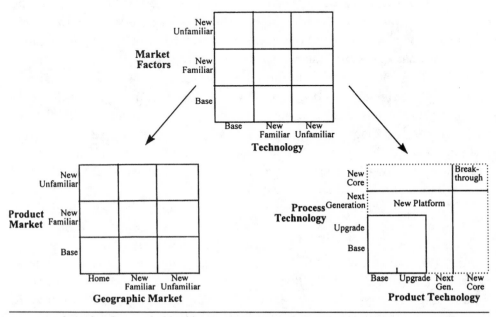

proprietary protection and appropriability are not always defined by patents. Trade secrets, tacit knowledge,[13] and organizational capabilities may protect proprietary know-how without patents. For example, complex, coordinated processes may be difficult to copy, even if competitors can observe them. A firm may understand its processes and know what it is doing, but asking someone to explain it can be like asking Fred Astaire to explain how he dances!

Conversely, patents may not provide proprietary protection if they can easily be invented around or are too difficult to defend in the legal system. In general, patents are more valuable for materials and basic processes than for assembled products and designs because the latter can often be accomplished with different means, making the patent ineffective.

Strong and agile R&D also helps a firm to capture value from an innovation. Often, as in the case of the CAT scan, the first generation of an invention delivers less value to customers than subsequent generations. As the innovation is refined, customer use and value are better understood and costs are reduced, creating more value. The firms that lead those subsequent generations may capture more value than the firms leading the first generation. Moreover, strong and agile R&D capabilities make a firm more likely to see and develop related products or processes after an initial invention.

Technological complexity helps an innovator to capture the value of its invention because a complex innovation is harder to imitate than a simple one. In addition, when the know-how requires a team rather than an individual, it is more difficult for a person to appropriate the know-how for a competing firm. Complexity that aids the capture of value may also take the form of organizational culture or processes that are difficult for another firm to reproduce.

Complementary capabilities or assets also play a major role in determining whether an innovator or a follower captures the value of an innovation. Complementary assets may include manufacturing capabilities, effective sales organizations, appropriate distribution channels, financial strength, reputation, customer relationships, service organizations, or related technology for components, software, or other parts of a system. For example, IBM's success with personal computers is often credited to its corporate sales force, service capabilities, and strong reputation. In the case of the CAT scan, GE's success was partly due to extensions of the technology from scans of the brain to whole-body scans and partly due to GE's expertise in marketing and servicing medical equipment and its ability to finance the capital purchase.

Principle 7: Research results are inherently uncertain. The probability of success and potential impact on revenues are critical considerations for resource allocation.

Given the unavoidable uncertainty about research outcomes, the probability of success must be factored into choices about research priorities. One way to think about which risky projects to undertake is to array the projects according to probability of success and sales impact. Exhibit 9.4 shows an example of such a diagram, with the sizes of the "bubbles" indicating the R&D expense of the project. Note that the probability of success in this kind of analysis includes both technical and commercial success, and thus depends on the firm's technical capabilities as well as on its ability to capture value that is created (discussed in principle 6). The sales impact will be a rough number reflecting the initial market as well as the other markets into which the innovation may expand. In the case of fuel injection, the smaller potential lead market required to launch the technology would not have painted the full picture. Since the question at this point in the analysis is about long-term impact on revenues, the potentially enormous market for fuel injection also needed to be reflected to portray the opportunity.

EXHIBIT 9.4 **R&D resource allocation "bubble chart." By considering sales impact and probability of success, managers can quickly see which projects clearly should be pushed ahead (high sales impact and high probability of success) or terminated (low sales impact and low probability of success). Projects in the upper left corner require more analysis before pushing ahead, unless they are low cost. Projects in the lower right corner have low payoffs, so they must be low cost to pursue.**

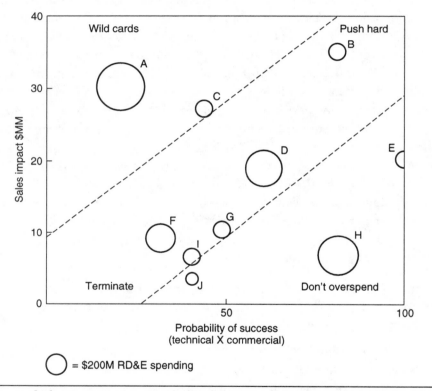

Source: Prof. Thomas C. MacAvoy, Darden Graduate School of Business Administration, University of Virginia.

Once projects are arrayed on this matrix, the insight is that decisions about which projects to pursue are relatively clear.

- If both the probability of success and sales impact are high, it makes sense to push hard.
- Projects with a high probability of success but a low sales impact are low-risk, low-reward projects. Overspending on these would be a mistake.
- Projects with a low probability of success and a low sales impact are high-risk, low-reward projects that should be avoided or terminated.

- If the sales impact is high but the probability of success is low, the project is a long shot, or wild card. Wild card projects may require more analysis before choosing which to pursue. A portfolio of uncorrelated wild cards has a high expected value, but lower risk than the individual projects. A portfolio of correlated wild cards is very high risk, but may have extremely high payoffs. Insight about the value of wild card projects can be developed by analyzing these projects as options, as in Exhibit 9.5.

Choosing the portfolio of innovation and technology projects involves several important balancing acts. Managers must choose a balance between risk and potential gains as well as between support of current products or services and creation of new ones. Keep in mind that the firm has the highest chance of success with a new product or process when it is familiar with both the market and the technology. Incremental changes, however, tend to have lower payoffs. This implies that using familiar technology from one market in a different market with which the firm is also familiar tends to be a good bet as long as there is a real market need for the innovation. Also keep in mind that truly innovative products

EXHIBIT 9.5   The option value of innovation.

Great, technology-based companies thrive on occasional breakthroughs or innovations that serve large market needs, as well as on continual improvement of existing products and processes. The challenge for sustained success is to find the next idea that fits with the firm's capabilities and meets new, large market needs. To do this, the firm has to invest in many fuzzy, early-stage ideas, many of which will fail. These early-stage investments give the firm *options* to pursue later-stage development if research is successful, and to pursue commercialization if development goes well.° If intermediate stages are not successful, the firm can and should abandon the project. Analogously to financial options, such as puts and calls on common stock, an early-stage R&D investment gives the firm the *right* but not the *obligation* to pursue later stages of the innovation process. This recognition of the multistage nature of R&D investments is critical to good decision making about funding projects.

This analogy of R&D to financial options produces a number of insights about the value of innovation projects.°° An R&D option has higher value when the following are true:

- The profit potential from commercialization is high.
- There is high uncertainty about potential future earnings.
- Future commercialization costs are high relative to early R&D investments.
- There is a long window of opportunity, starting soon.
- R&D will resolve significant (but not all) uncertainty before major investments must be made.
- The firm can abandon the project if the future prospects look poor.

°See Peter A. Morris, Elizabeth Olmsted Teisberg, and A. Lawrence Kolbe, "When Choosing R&D Projects, Go for the Long Shots," *Research-Technology Management*, January–February, 1991.
°°See Elizabeth Olmsted Teisberg, "Methods for Evaluating Capital Investment Decisions Under Uncertainty," Lenos Trigeorgis, ed., *Real Options in Capital Investment: Models, Strategies, and Applications* (Westport, CT: Praeger, 1995).

tend to have the highest payoffs, and, contrary to intuition, it is riskier to imitate than to develop a new product. Imitation guarantees competition; for high pay-offs, efforts should aim at big empty spaces in the market.

Analysis of the portfolio of projects needs to be repeated over time as projects progress and understandings of technologies and potential markets change. Over time, some projects will be dropped, others will gain importance, and new projects will be added. Thus, management of the innovation process is, in part, an ongoing review of the firm's technology and innovation priorities, always keeping the firm's strategic positioning clearly in mind. Characteristics of a sound technology strategy are reviewed in Exhibit 9.6.

MANAGING THE INNOVATION PROCESS

Innovation is the process of converting ideas into value.[14] All innovation goes through the stages of conception, gestation, and delivery as ideas are generated, developed, and put into use. Throughout these stages, the management of innovation requires managers to combine discipline with creativity enhancement. This challenge is magnified by the high uncertainty, long time frames, and many people involved. Moreover, the probability of success is best enhanced by coordinating efforts among the functions of technology, marketing, and manufacturing, which adds yet another level of complexity. Because of its nature and requirements, the innovation process is not linear and rational. Managers need to adapt to the breakthroughs and disappointments, implement learning by doing, and set clear milestones by which progress can be judged.

Stages of the Innovation Process

Ideas come from many sources. Innovations build on a treasury of knowledge and skills that enable the ideas to be developed. Often the innovation process is

EXHIBIT 9.6 Characteristics of a sound technology strategy.

- Reinforces the business's competitive strategy
- Enhances the role of technology in the firm's competitive positioning
- Covers both the short and long term
- Identifies major projects with goals and milestones
- Identifies necessary resources and is consistent with the business's financial plan and budget
- Has a method for measuring accomplishment
- Is well understood and communicated
- Has the commitment of key people who must carry it out

Source: Thomas C. MacAvoy, "Developing a Technology Strategy," University of Virginia Darden School Foundation, Instructional Note UVA-OM-0657, 1988.

EXHIBIT 9.7   Stages of innovation. Innovation proceeds through a predictable sequence of stages, however, not in a predictable, linear way. The process often circles back as surprises occur and adjustments are made.

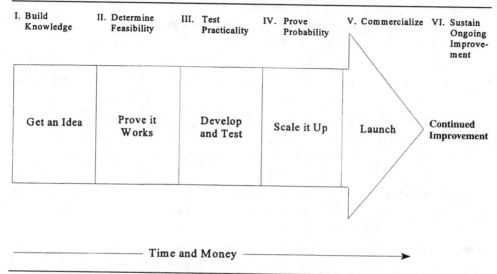

Source: Prof. Thomas C. MacAvoy, Darden Graduate School of Business Administration, University of Virginia.

described by a stage-and-gate model that breaks the innovation process into a series of steps (or stages) with decisions (or gates) between them. Exhibit 9.7 depicts a six-stage model from idea to commercial launch and ongoing improvement. Throughout this process, cumulative investment increases and uncertainty decreases.

Stage I, the knowledge-building stage of innovation, is often referred to as *fuzzy*. Projects at this stage often are not well defined or well linked to markets. The cost of initially exploring ideas tends to be low, but the risk of no payoff is very high. Investing in knowledge building reduces uncertainty, but when time is an important competitive factor there is a trade-off between reducing uncertainty before proceeding and losing the opportunity from too much delay. Given that uncertainty may extend even to how to characterize the uncertainty, managers at this stage face ambiguity. Decisions about resource allocation, therefore, tend to be made heuristically. Milestones that are too specific can be an impediment to progress, so reviews have a more informal nature.

Uncertainty should decrease as projects progress through the stages of determining feasibility and testing practicality, but costs also tend to rise progressively. Clear milestones of technical achievement become increasingly important. The choices of milestones and measures are critical because what is measured will improve, particularly if compensation or recognition is tied to it. For example, firms often measure the output of peer-reviewed papers because that output signals the scientific community's judgment of high-quality research; however, published papers may not be the output the firm most wants to increase.

In stage II, as feasibility is determined, customer input should be incorporated into the idea. At this stage, the process of considering market potential and competition begins and continues henceforth. Also in the feasibility stage, patent disclosures are developed and manufacturing processes should be conceived.

As the process moves to stage III, testing practicality, prototypes are refined and tested on customers, manufacturing and marketing plans are devised, and potential problems with scale-up and commercialization are explored. Estimates of profit potential become much less fuzzy as these considerations are put together with the ongoing market and competitor analysis.

Stage IV, proving profitability, often involves a significant increase in costs as pilot manufacturing begins, full manufacturing and marketing plans are developed, and sales training begins. At this stage, all potential major problems need to be flushed out before the decision is made about whether to go forward with commercial launch. Assessments of the market and competitors must continue; they may change as information improves, uncertainty resolves, and time passes.

At stage V, commercial launch, the firm needs to be prepared to move rapidly down the learning curve and solve problems quickly. Building, running, and debugging production processes can provide important sources of proprietary know-how. Also at this stage, managers must establish programs to enhance and improve the product or process and sustain success. The programs include quality improvement, manufacturing cost reduction, product line extension, and customer support and service functions. Finally, at this stage, revenues begin to come in and profits may be generated.

Stage VI, sustaining success, is often ignored in the stage-and-gate process, but anticipation of this stage provides an important interface between technology managers and managers of other functions. Recognizing ongoing improvement as a stage in the innovation process also helps in balancing pressures to support existing businesses and to develop new products, processes, or lines of business.

It should be recognized that a major innovation project involves many minor innovations along the way. Further, the process rarely runs smoothly and linearly. Problems encountered often require circling back to an earlier stage. It is a merry, if not always predictable, process!

Keys to Success

Throughout the innovation process, the key issues are creating new ideas, improving teamwork, keeping projects on track (project management), reducing risk, speeding up the process, and learning from experience. Success depends on backing the right projects at the right time. This means that managers must identify projects that will create value and structure them so that the firm can capture significant value. To do this, understanding of complementary assets is critical, as is careful analysis of what customers really find valuable and why.

Success also depends on using appropriate decision criteria in the different stages of the process. Early-stage decisions about which ideas to try are often made heuristically. Late-stage decisions, such as building manufacturing facilities, should be based on more sophisticated frameworks and analyses, and commonly are assessed with the net present value of future cash flows. Net present value analysis, however, tends to under-value intermediate stage projects, by failing to recognize the value of future opportunities that may be created, and failing to correctly account for opportunities to abandon projects that are not developing as well as expected. On the other hand, these intermediate stage projects should be analyzed with more sophistication than simple heuristics. Approaches such as option valuation or decision analysis, both of which explicitly recognize the value of future opportunities and decisions, are therefore more appropriate approaches for evaluation of projects in the middle stages of development.

One of the hardest parts of managing the process is terminating weak projects at appropriate times. This requires developing good measures and milestones, using objective criteria, and managing the motivations of people involved so they have other interesting and valuable challenges on which to focus. When projects continue beyond reason, warning signs of overcommitment may be apparent. Managers should recognize these warning signs when enthusiasm has turned to fanaticism, so that good decisions are no longer being made by the project team. Another strong warning sign occurs when no one on the team is willing to try to tell the project's problems to the boss. If those red flags pop up, suspect that project termination may be appropriate, and even overdue.

Of course, judgment about which projects to pursue is critical. On one hand, if decisions are too cautious, the business will shrink over time and opportunities will be lost. On the other hand, if decisions are too bold, poor projects are pursued too long and profitability will decrease.

ORGANIZING FOR INNOVATION

Some firms seem to be better than others at bringing ideas through the innovation process to successful commercialization. Hewlett Packard is known for repeatedly introducing state-of-the-art technology. Corning Incorporated is known for its periodic break though innovations. 3M is renowned for its successful stream of innovations rolled out with the learning by doing philosophy of "make a little, sell a little." These consistent successes are not accidental. Success depends on choosing a good portfolio of projects and managing the innovation process well. It also depends on the organization of the firm and the motivation experienced by employees. Skeptics who argue that organizing for innovation is impossible because creativity cannot be structured are missing a critical point. There are clearly poor organizational structures for innovation; it is widely agreed that some organizations squash creativity or hamper the commercial success of good ideas. In contrast, then, there are better possible structures, and managers must make important decisions in defining the organization to inspire and support innovation.

The creation of a *reservation,* or protected place for innovation, often helps, and there is a wide variety of ways to accomplish the fact or the mind-set of a separate space.[15] The key issues are how to structure a reservation for creativity, how much it should be differentiated from or integrated with ongoing business, how much flexibility the structure should have, and how to integrate ideas and innovations that emerge in the reservation into the company's processes and products.

Structuring a Reservation for Innovation

The idea of a reservation tends to bring to mind extreme examples of ineffective organizational structures. Xerox's PARC labs in California, a continent away from rest of the Xerox's businesses, were not successfully integrated. PARC was very innovative; it created scores of new businesses, but few for Xerox. But there are many less extreme examples in which some separation enables a structure to do things for the first time, rather than doing things consistently well as they have been done many times before. The reservation may have different organizational structures, processes, rewards, or people. While the idea of a reservation may sound old-fashioned if it is interpreted to mean an R&D lab, it can instead be interpreted as a mind-set that can be implemented with cross-functional teams, matrix organizations, concurrent engineering, or other techniques to improve customer contact or speed to market.

There are may ways to create a separate environment for innovation:

- Physical distance (but not so far as to hamper integration of results into the operating organization).
- R&D lab that separates the innovation function from the operating business.
- Temporary dedicated teams for specific innovation projects (but productivity falls as the tenure of team members exceeds four or five years).
- Joint ventures or cooperative R&D (but beware the risks of pursuing innovation with potential competitors).

- Matrix organizations in which people work on both functional teams and product teams focused on an innovation.
- New ventures or spin-offs that financially separate a new business and create entrepreneurial incentives for team members.
- Cooperation with suppliers or distributors that takes the team out of the company to pursue the innovation.

In general, the choice of how much separation to build into the organizational structure depends on how different or radical the desired innovation. More separation of the reservation encourages more distinction between the innovations and existing operations.

Separation versus Integration

Although separation may enhance creativity, it also increases the challenges of integrating the results into the operating business. Thus, the choice about how much separation to create is complex. If the project is very complex and technology-intensive, it may need a separate technical team. If the sources of new ideas tend to be from the lab, separation may enhance the flow. If, on the other hand, ideas for innovation come from manufacturing or marketing, close proximity and regular interaction may be critical.

If the time horizon for a project is very long or the risk very high, separation may facilitate a different reward structure than is appropriate for the operating business. If the project is very unfamiliar or may shift the firm's strategic focus, then separation may help, especially if the innovation threatens existing products or processes. Unless the innovation efforts are separated, firms often have trouble encouraging innovation that may cannibalize existing products.

In contrast, if the pace of change in the business is very fast and new generations of products quickly obsolete previous ones, then more integration may help speed the flow of innovations to commercialization. Also, if employees are owners, especially in a smaller organization, integration of the innovation function may encourage everyone to participate more fully.

Flexibility in Structure

Decisions about how much separation to create are accompanied by decisions about how much flexibility to create. In some organizations, innovation projects are separated in different divisions with separate groups of employees. In others, the scientists and technical specialists are more mobile among projects, creating more flexibility to scale up or scale down individual projects.

This flexibility has two important implications. First, it enables the firm to quickly amass a very large effort behind a project that has unusual potential or a highly competitive race. A firm with smaller, separated innovation teams will not be able to launch such a large endeavor without wrenching effort. Thus, some centralization and flexibility in the R&D function better positions a firm to tackle very large opportunities with potentially very high rewards. Indeed, this type of flexibility enabled Corning to succeed in its large and intensely competitive effort to develop ceramic substrates for catalytic converters. Second, the flip side of the flexibility is that since people can be moved to other projects with relative ease, projects that are not going well can be abandoned with less fanfare and perhaps less damage to morale. People are less concerned about walking away from work on one project if they are moving to participate in an intense, strategic effort for the firm.

Reintegrating Innovations

Innovation can be a destructive process. Integrating innovations into the operating business requires change, which is rarely easy. Companies that succeed in this integration employ a variety of approaches.[16]

Some companies, such as 3M, use a network of R&D labs in each operating division. To ensure that innovations are shaped into potential products, 3M focuses about 80% of its resources on labs tightly tied to applied development efforts. It encourages sharing of technology among the divisions, which is made easier because they are located in close proximity. The motto that conveys 3M's approach is that markets belong to the businesses, but technology belongs to the corporation.

Physical proximity or colocation are effective approaches to encourage informal communication and relationships as well as formal efforts to apply ideas across functions, groups, or divisions. Similarly, training shared simultaneously by multiple divisions or functions, or rotations of personnel through several functions, are sometimes used to increase knowledge of the whole process as well as to improve communication and build relationships. Another approach is the designation of sponsors or champions with emphasis on communication of new visions.

Incentives for commercial success are often employed. Some companies create direct incentives with hefty financial rewards (often stock or options) for big successes. Other firms use competition among teams to increase the speed of new product development or problem solving. Many firms also employ concurrent design and engineering, taking tasks that were traditionally performed sequentially and instead having teams approach the problems cross-functionally.

HOW THE WINNERS HIT HOME RUNS

The experiences of successful companies suggest that big successes in managing innovation and technology development result from efforts that aim at large empty spaces rather than at improvements for markets already being served. Not just any empty market will do, however; the firm needs to be able to develop market access readily. In addition, the innovation for serving that market should build on the firm's technical capabilities, preferably those that are unmatched by most competitors.

Although uncertainty is often viewed in negative terms, in the management of R&D, uncertainty characterizes opportunity. High uncertainty brings with it the chance of high payoff. Managers must recognize that early-stage investments create opportunities, but not obligations, to pursue later stages of development. They must be prepared to abandon projects swiftly when the outcomes look poor, and to accept a high percentage of failures in the search for great opportunities.

As the innovation process unfolds, managers need to explicitly recognize its multistage nature, and not assume that early-stage investment will necessarily be continued.[17] Early abandonment of projects that are not going well is a key to having the resources and vision to aggressively pursue those projects that offer unusually promising returns. This means being realistic and unbiased in assessing the firm's progress, as well as staying alert to market and technical trends. Firms need to organize to enhance innovation and reward creativity, and if they want to win the races to large technical breakthroughs, they will also need an organization that provides the flexibility to expand the innovation team when the race looks tight.

Throughout the innovation process, the role of senior management is critical. Senior management is responsible for the firm's technology, and must set goals, decide what to pursue and, more importantly, what *not* to pursue. Leadership of the innovation process requires the right balance of structure and direction with freedom to create and change. It also requires the creation of incentives and rewards for those who take good risks and offer creative ideas.

In the frenzy to choose a winning portfolio and manage projects through the process to commercial success, managers must not lose sight of the firm's strategic intent and the value that the innovation will create for customers. Successful technology strategy must enable and enhance the firm's current and future sources of competitive advantage. Successful management of innovation must create the technical capabilities necessary for the firm to sustain advantage in the uncertain future.

FOR FURTHER READING

Robert A. Burgelman, Modesto A. Madique, and Steven C. Wheelwright, *Strategic Management of Technology, 2nd Edition* (Chicago: Irwin, Times Mirror Higher Education Group, 1988, 1996).

J. R. Galbraith, "Organizing for Innovation," *Organizational Dynamics,* winter 1982, pp. 5–25.

Thomas C. MacAvoy, "Technology Strategy for a Diversified Corporation," Darden Graduate Business School, Instructional Note UVA-OM-0659, 1989.

Thomas C. MacAvoy, "Developing a Technology Strategy," University of Virginia Darden School Foundation, Instructional Note UVA-OM-0657, 1988.

Peter A. Morris, Elizabeth Olmsted Teisberg, and A. Lawrence Kolbe, "When Choosing R&D Projects, Go For the Long Shots," *Research-Technology Management,* January–February, 1991.

Summe and Uttal Nevens, "Comercializing Technology: What the Best Companies Do," *Harvard Business Review,* May–June 1990, pp. 154–162.

Gary P. Pisano and Steven C. Wheelwright, "The New Logic of High-Tech R&D," *Harvard Business Review,* September–October 1995 pp. 93–105.)

Michael Porter, "Technology and Competitive Advantage," *Journal of Business Strategy,* Winter 1985, vol. 5, no. 3, pp. 60–78.

Philip A. Roussel, Kamal N. Saad, and Tamara J. Erickson, *Third Generation R&D, Managing the Link to Corporate Strategy,* (Boston: Harvard Business School Press, 1991).

David Teece, "Profiting from Technological Innovation: Implications for Integration, Collaboration, Licensing, and Public Policy," *Research Policy,* vol. 15, 1986, pp. 285–305.

Steven C. Wheelwright and Kim B. Clark, *Revolutionizing Product Development Quantum Leaps in Speed, Efficiency, and Quality* (New York: The Free Press, 1992).

10 ACCOUNTING

Accounting is simultaneously a language, a technique, a profession, and an intellectual discipline. Often called "the language of business," accounting provides the structural framework and the quantitative vocabulary with which problems and solutions in all the disciplines of business may be expressed. The late Fischer Black, a partner at Goldman Sachs and academician, said,

> Accounting is a language that people within a firm can use to discuss its projects and progress with one another, and that they can use to tell outsiders what's happening in the firm without giving too many of its secrets to competitors.[1]

The process whereby this quantitative vocabulary is expressed is the technique of double-entry bookkeeping. Accounting is one of the oldest business disciplines, tracing its roots to the invention of double-entry bookkeeping by Venetian merchants in the fifteenth century. Today, the profession is highly developed, with codes, rules, self-governing bodies, and a certification process for its practitioners. Governments, courts of law, and the general public give great credence to the representations of performance given by CPAs.[2] Finally, accounting reports help decision makers target problem areas of the business, thereby beginning the process of implementing change.

This chapter has five objectives:

1. Introduce double-entry bookkeeping and suggest that it embodies the *systemic* nature of the firm.

2. Emphasize that accounting reports are at best approximations of reality.
3. Offer a step-by-step guide to reading financial statements.
4. Illustrate the analysis of financial statements for the purpose of deciding on the financial health of a company.
5. Explore how variance analysis of a project or business unit can yield valuable insights for the operating manager.

DOUBLE-ENTRY BOOKKEEPING CAPTURES THE SYSTEMIC NATURE OF THE FIRM

In studying the financial statements of a firm, the novice often digs no deeper than the results that appear on paper. But the seasoned businessperson sees through these statements to the considerable richness of activity represented by them. Financial statements model the fact that the firm is a *system,* an entity with linkages among its internal parts. To attune your thinking about how financial statements may be used to see into the rich activity of the firm, consider two ideas about how systems behave:

- *Systems resonate under turbulence.* Turbulence does not stay contained. Changes in one part of the firm ripple elsewhere in the firm. The marketing department is affected by what happens in the manufacturing department. A difficult customer can delay payments, return goods to your warehouse, cancel orders, or demand superpremium service—any one of these actions affects two or more areas of your company. A decision to spend cash to buy a machine will result in an increase in the assets found on the plant floor and a decrease in the cash balance of the firm's checking account. Subsequently, the periodic recognition of depreciation expense related to the machine will affect the firm's profits and assets. Accounting provides a means of documenting the resonance within the firm under turbulence.

- *Systems can amplify or dampen turbulence.* A growing firm is a classic example of how turbulence can become *amplified* within the firm. Anticipating that next year's sales will be greater than this year's, managers might invest in more inventory (to prevent stock-outs), beef up the marketing staff, invest in more productive capacity, and expand bank lines of credit. But good management practices might also *dampen* turbulence by tightening inventory controls, asking staff to work longer hours rather than hiring more people, adding a third shift in the plant rather than buying more machinery, and so forth. Accounting cannot change the turbulence, but it can help document how the internal workings of the firm manage turbulence, thus preparing managers to make better decisions.

"Systems thinking" is a management approach oriented to dealing with the unusual turbulence of recent years arising from forces such as deregulation, globalization, rapid technological change, and demographic change. To think systemically is to take into account all direct and indirect effects of a managerial decision—anywhere those effects might hit the firm. In representing the "system" of the firm, accounting facilitates systems thinking.

The fundamental concept of the accounting model of the firm is that the resources of the firm and the claims upon those resources must *balance*. This mirrors economic common sense; claims on the firm should equal the assets standing behind those claims:

$$\text{Assets} = \text{liabilities} + \text{owners' equity}$$

The notion of balance is reflected in the equal sign in this equation. Increases in assets must be financed by increases in liabilities (e.g., a bank loan) or in equity (e.g., a sale of stock). Decreases in assets (such as a debt payment or dividend payment) must be offset with decreases in the corresponding type of capital. Stated in terms of this equation, changes (Δ) must balance out somewhere in the closed system of the firm:

$$\Delta\text{assets} = \Delta\text{liabilities} + \Delta\text{owners' equity}$$

The simplest event in the firm must have at least *two* entries in the firm's accounting books; a minimum of two entries are necessary to capture the nature of balancing. Thus arises the term *double-entry bookkeeping*.

Typically, there are three financial statements in an annual report:

- *Income statement.* This is a measure of the *flows* of business over a period of time expressed in terms of profit and loss. Some of these flows will have been adjusted or "matched" in time to occur with other flows that are economically related. For instance, a unit of goods might have been shipped in 1996, but the cash from this sale was not received until early 1997. Accounting policies would recognize the sales revenues in the 1996 fiscal year since this is when the sale occurred in economic terms. This represents the *accrual basis* of revenue recognition.

- *Balance sheet.* This presents a snapshot of the assets of the firm and the claims upon those assets at a particular point in time (i.e., the end of the fiscal year). In other words, the balance sheet measures the amount of assets, liabilities, and owners' equity.

- *Statement of cash flows.*   Since the income statement and balance sheet result from accruals and allocations made by accountants, it can be difficult to tell what actually happened to the firm in terms of the flows of cash: Did it generate more cash this year than last? The statement of cash flows recasts the performance of the firm into cash-based accounting and helps the reader understand the changes in cash and their causes.

The raw material for developing these statements is a series of *accounts* or "bins" into which the transactions within the firm are recorded. At least one account exists for each line item in a financial statement. For a large corporation, each line item would have many supporting accounts; these accounts run into the thousands. Keeping the books in balance is accomplished by a simple notion of debits and credits, envisioning an account as two columns framed by a "T" (see Exhibit 10.1).

- *Debit* refers to the left side of a T-account and is used to record an increase (if it is an assets T-account) or a decrease (if it is a T-account in liabilities or owners' equity.) Because the results of the income statement flow into the owners' equity account, debits record expenses of the business.
- *Credit* refers to the right side of a T-account and is used to record a decrease in assets or an increase in liabilities or owners' equity. Credits record revenues of the business.

These definitions guide the bookkeeper in deciding how to record a transaction in a firm's system of accounts. Also, at the end of an accounting period, the increases and decreases in an account are summed up to get the closing balance for the period. Much of the artistry in bookkeeping is in correctly identifying the accounts through which the transaction should flow.

To illustrate double-entry bookkeeping, consider these examples. First suppose that Gotham Cinema Company sold $100 million worth of videotapes. Also suppose that the cost of these goods was $25 million.

- To reflect the receipt of the sale proceeds, the bookkeeper would debit (increase) cash $100 million and credit (increase) sales revenues $100 million; the sales revenue causes an increase in owners' equity of an equal amount.

EXHIBIT 10.1   T-account.

T-Account

Debits	Credits

- To reflect the shipment to customers of goods with a cost of $25 million, the bookkeeper would credit (decrease) inventories $25 million and debit (increase) cost of goods $25 million; the cost of goods sold is an expense that causes a decrease in owners' equity of an equal amount.

Consider another example. Suppose Gotham paid its shareholders a dividend of $100 million. To reflect this transaction, the bookkeeper would credit (decrease) cash and debit (decrease) shareholders' equity. Unlike the recognition of cost of goods, however, a dividend represents a distribution of earnings and is not considered to be an expense of the business.

As a final example, suppose Gotham borrowed $300 million in debt and used it to repay debt of $150 million. To reflect the borrowing, the bookkeeper would debit cash $300 million and credit debt $300 million. To reflect the debt repayment, the bookkeeper would credit cash $150 million and debit debt $150 million.

Common to every one of these transactions is this simple but important feature: Every debit (credit) has a balancing credit (debit) somewhere in the system of accounts. At the end of the year, the summation of the credits and debits in each account expresses the *flow* of transactions through that account and the *stock,* or standing, of that account at the end of the period. The total of the debit account balances must equal the total of the credit account balances.

THE TRUTH ABOUT ACCOUNTING: IT PRECISELY GIVES AN "APPROXIMATE" VIEW

Outsiders view accounting as a highly precise, careful specialty, guided by hard rules and professional certification. To novice decision makers, the figures presented in a financial statement carry the aura of certainty. But the truth is that *financial statements are only estimates of reality,* not quantities known with certainty.[3] E. Richard Brownlee II, CPA, has written:

> Accounting is a necessary and useful, but not sufficient, language. Here are some reasons why. Our traditional accounting system was primarily designed for merchandising and manufacturing companies engaged in domestic business activities in an environment characterized by gradual, not rapid, change, and whose *assets* were largely tangible and whose *liabilities* were largely known both in terms of type and amount. Timely financial reporting typically requires extensive estimates and judgments by management. *Two* overriding concepts prevail—*matching* and *conservatism*—yet these can conflict. The financial reporting model attempts to achieve *two* primary qualities—*relevance* and *reliability*—yet these can conflict. The underlying accounting standards are influenced by politics and personalities, special interests, and compromise. The financial reporting model is intended to

present a fair representation of the past, yet also meet the needs of users whose primary interest is in forecasting the future.[4]

In trying to represent the economic reality within a firm, accounting does not recognize revenues and expenses when cash changes hands, but when the goods are delivered (in the case of revenues) or when the goods are used (in the case of expenses). This reflects the belief that performance is best reflected when related revenues and expenses are *matched* in the same period. Because of the time lags between the start and completion of an economic event, it may be necessary to *accrue* financial results so that they can be matched. Accrual accounting is the dominant practice in business. But accrual accounting requires many judgments, as Brownlee acknowledges. The "precisely estimated approximation" nature of financial statements is well illustrated by a careful reading of the financial statements of the firm.

HOW TO READ AN ANNUAL REPORT

Reading financial statements is one of the best ways to gain an understanding of accounting and its significance to business. The Walt Disney Company distributed its *1995 Annual Report* in March 1996. This report covered the activities of the firm in calendar year 1995 and its condition on December 31, 1995. The following guided tour illustrates the nature of Disney's financial statements, how to read them, and how to read the rest of the report. Let us enter Disney's financial "Magic Kingdom."

Step 1: Read the letter from the chair of the board.
This is usually the first item in the annual report and is valuable mainly for understanding at the start the *strategic intent* of the managers of the firm. The letter in the 1995 annual report from Michael D. Eisner, chairman and CEO of Disney, tells us to look for effects in the financial statements from two big events in the company that year: the acquisition of Capital Cities/ABC and the hiring of Michael Ovitz as Disney's president. This letter usually expresses elements of the CEO's goals, values, and vision for the company in the future. A careful reader would get a hint of the issues to look for in the firm's results for 1995, along with insights about next year. For instance, consider the following possible issues and insights:

- Shareholder wealth is important. How profitable has the firm been in the past year? How has shareholders' equity changed? Did the firm share much of its profits with the shareholders in the form of dividends? Were the firm's actions and performance consistent with trying to increase the firm's stock price?

- Eisner values productivity. If productivity of the firm has improved this year, it should have done more business per dollar of assets than in the previous year. Its inventories and receivables should have been managed more closely. Fixed assets should have been worked harder. Did these things happen?

- The Disney brand is a huge asset. Unfortunately under the "historical cost" and conservatism principles of *generally accepted accounting principles* (GAAP), internally developed intangible assets such as patents, brands, and R&D are accorded no value on the balance sheet. Are there other places in the firm's financial performance where the valuable brand might be reflected?

- Eisner values leadership and excellence. This may be an expensive strategy. Has Eisner managed costs and investments carefully while pursuing his strategy?

Critical thinking prompted by a close reading of the chair's letter can lead to better analysis of a firm's financial statements.

Step 2. Look at the auditor's letter.

Investors in companies ordinarily require an annual audit of those companies' financial statements. This is one of the most basic protections intended to ensure compliance with generally accepted accounting and reporting standards. At the end of the financial report, you usually find a letter from the firm's independent auditors that explains what they did and what they concluded. Following the Disney 1995 financial statement as presented in the annual report and in a report filed with the Securities and Exchange Commission, Price Waterhouse wrote:

> In our opinion, the consolidated balance sheet and the related consolidated statements of income and of cash flows present fairly, in all material respects, the financial position . . . in conformity with generally accepted accounting principles.[5]

This is a positive report. A negative opinion by an auditor might cite unfair or unacceptable presentation, nonconformance with GAAP, and material misstatement. In some cases, auditors must explain any material uncertainties affecting the financial statements. These uncertainties depend on the probability of loss due to uncertainty of such things as the "going concern"[6] assumption that underlies the preparation of most financial statements, uncertainty regarding the valuation or realization of assets, or uncertainty due to litigation. *Anything but a positive report (such as Disney's) should, like a flashing red light, signal a major concern to the reader of the report.*

Step 3. Review the income statement.

The income statement is prepared using accrual accounting and is the primary measure of operating performance of the firm. It is organized on the following simple notion:

$$\text{Revenues} - \text{expenses} = \text{profits}$$

This model can help you sort out three concerns in looking at the income statement:

- *The degree of profitability, and why.*   Is the firm making or losing money?
- *The trend of profitability, and why.*   Are profits increasing or declining over time? Are these due to changes in revenues, expenses, or both?
- *The composition of profits.*   Are the size and trend of profits due to ordinary operations, or to odd events that might distort the true profitability of the firm?

To illustrate, consider Disney's 1995 income statement, shown in Exhibit 10.2. Profits for 1995 rose by $270 million compared to 1994; this is good news for investors. Profits for 1994 were up a whopping $810 million. Earnings per share increased from $2.04 in 1994 to $2.60 in 1995. This is a very nice trend. To what can we attribute this?

- *Revenues were up handsomely.*   A 20.5% gain in 1995 is not bad when inflation is running at only 3%
- *Expenses were kept in line.*   Total operating costs and expenses were up only 19.5% in 1995, less than the rate of increase in revenues. Nice going, Mr. Eisner.
- *Unfortunately, the cost of corporate activities almost doubled.*   But this is due mostly to higher interest expense and lower interest income. We will have to look at the balance sheet to see what's happening to the debt balance.
- *Euro Disney lost money . . . again.*   But this was not as bad as in previous years.
- *Income before taxes and accounting changes was up smartly.*   This figure increased by 24%! This is an important line to inspect, because taxes and accounting changes can obscure operating profitability. In Disney's case, this income grew faster than revenues, suggesting that the firm's profit margins were increasing.
- *Accounting changes took a huge bite out of earnings in 1993.*   This showed earnings decreasing by almost $370 million. Nevertheless, these account-

EXHIBIT 10.2   Income statement: The Walt Disney Company.

Year Ended September 30	1995	1994	1993
Revenues			
Filmed entertainment	$6,001.5	$4,793.3	$3,673.4
Theme parks and resorts	3,959.8	3,463.6	3,440.7
Consumer products	2,150.8	1,798.2	1,415.1
	12,112.1	10,055.1	8,529.2
Costs and expenses			
Filmed entertainment	4,927.1	3,937.2	3,051.2
Theme parks and resorts	3,099.0	2,779.5	2,693.8
Consumer products	1,640.3	1,372.7	1,059.7
	9,666.4	8,089.4	6,804.7
Operating income			
Filmed entertainment	1,074.4	856.1	622.2
Theme parks and resorts	860.8	684.1	746.9
Consumer products	510.5	425.5	355.4
	2,445.7	1,965.7	1,724.5
Corporate activities			
General and administrative expenses	183.6	162.2	164.2
Interest expense	178.3	119.9	157.7
Investment and interest income	(68.0)	(129.9)	(186.1)
	293.9	152.2	135.8
Loss from investment in Euro Disney	(35.1)	(110.4)	(514.7)
Income before income taxes and cumulative effect of			
accounting changes	2,116.7	1,703.1	1,074.0
Income taxes	736.6	592.7	402.7
Income before cumulative effect of accounting changes	1,380.1	1,110.4	671.3
Cumulative effect of accounting changes			
Pre-opening costs	—	—	(271.2)
Postretirement benefits	—	—	(130.3)
Income taxes	—	—	30.0
Net income	$1,380.1	$1,110.4	$299.8
Amounts per common share			
Earnings before cumulative effect of accounting changes	$2.60	$2.04	$1.23
Cumulative effect of accounting changes			
Pre-opening costs	—	—	−0.50
Postretirement benefits	—	—	−0.24
Income taxes	—	—	0.06
Earnings per share	$2.60	$2.04	$0.55
Average number of common and common equivalent shares			
outstanding	530.4	545.2	544.50
Pro forma amounts assuming the new accounting method			
for pre-opening costs is applied retroactively			
Net income			$571.00
Earnings per share			$1.05

Source: 1995 Form 10-K filed with the U.S. Securities and Exchange Commission by The Walt Disney Company, p. 33.

ing changes are atypical events: an attempt to bring the statements in line with new policies rather than a reflection of fundamental changes in profitability. Moreover, these accounting changes are probably not *cash events,* so from an investor's standpoint, they may not be material to the recent year's results.

Overall, this is a very positive income statement for investors. Disney's operating profitability is positively robust. Profits grew through an expansion of the business rather than through belt-tightening under static revenues.

Step 4. Review the balance sheet.

The major categories of assets are classified and ranked on the balance sheet according to their liquidity, with cash and other current assets (those that should be converted to cash within one year) at the top and fixed or intangible assets at the bottom.[7] On the other side of the sheet, current liabilities (those due within one year) are listed at the top. Next is debt and other liabilities. At the bottom is shareholders' equity, the residual claim on the firm. Most components of the balance sheet are reported at the lower of *historical cost* or *market value.* The balance sheet does not report all assets and liabilities of the firm, only those that are *measurable, reasonably certain,* and *relatively easy to value;* this is just another manifestation of the conservatism principle in accounting. Contingencies (i.e., potential assets or liabilities arising from past events such as a lawsuit) can be hard to measure and uncertain. The values of brand names, trademarks, and, in Disney's case, proprietary animated characters are hard to measure and uncertain and thus are not reported. In reading the balance sheet, you should aim to satisfy four questions:

- *Is the firm solvent?*   Solvency is the ability to pay liabilities as they come due. The primary test of this is to see whether the value of assets exceeds the value of liabilities.
- *Are the firm's assets sufficiently liquid?*   Liquidity measures the ability to meet near-term cash obligations—these might be liabilities that need to be repaid, or they might be a forthcoming payroll or the need to purchase raw materials in advance of a sudden surge in demand. One test of liquidity is whether current assets exceed current liabilities (whether the current ratio is greater than 1.0). Another test focuses on "quick" current assets such as cash and receivables, and asks whether these are greater than current liabilities (the *quick ratio* is another way to gauge the relative size of these balances).
- *What is the mix of assets?*   You should look for unusual concentrations or categories of assets. Concentration of the firm's resources into a speculative venture would be a cause for concern. Concentration in cash might suggest undue risk aversion or the lack of investment opportunities with attractive

return potential. Also, asset categories that seem to have no relevance to the firm's business purpose should raise a red flag.

- *What is the mix of financing?*   Most mature firms finance their businesses with *some* debt. The absence of debt, or very high proportion of debt, should raise questions about the outlook of senior management, and the "bets" they are making. Again, odd categories of capital (e.g., exchangeable subordinated bonds[8]) may indicate managerial creativity, or it may indicate desperation on the part of management—either way, it should invite the thoughtful investor to dig deeper.

The balance sheet of The Walt Disney Company as of December 31, 1995, is shown in Exhibit 10.3. The firm appears to be solvent in general terms, since the assets ($14.6 billion) handily exceed liabilities of about $8 billion. The firm appears to be liquid, too: Current assets (cash, investments, receivables, and merchandise inventories totaling $4.6 billion) nicely exceed current liabilities (accounts payable, accruals, and taxes payable totaling about $3.0 billion). The mix of assets does not seem unusual; certainly the concentration in theme parks is understandable because of the capital intensity of that business. Finally, the financing mix of the firm shows no sharp departures in 1995 from 1994—half the increase in assets was provided by an increase in shareholders' equity and the other half by an increase in current liabilities. Overall, the balance sheet raises no red flags.

Step 5. Read the statement of cash flows.
This statement reports the cash receipts and outflows classified as operating, investing, and financing activities—this breakdown helps determine where changes in cash emerge. The key questions you should ask include the following:

- Was the firm a net user or generator of cash that year?
- What operational, investing, or financing elements proved to be major drivers of cash flow?
- Are there any major departures in the trends of the cash flow items?

Exhibit 10.4 gives Disney's statement of cash flows from its 1995 annual report and a report filed with the Securities and Exchange Commission. This shows that the firm was a net generator of cash in 1995 ($889.6 million), which was a big change from 1994 and 1993 when Disney was a net user of cash. This swing can be attributed to a very large increase in cash from operations after taxes (about $700 million) and a decline in investing of about $600 million, offset by greater net repayments in financings. Two large departures appear in the line items: (1) The Euro Disney investment turned from absorbing $971 million

EXHIBIT 10.3   Balance Sheet: The Walt Disney Company.

Year Ended September 30	1995	1994
Assets		
Cash and cash equivalents	$1,076.5	$186.9
Investments	866.3	1,323.2
Receivables	1,792.8	1,670.5
Merchandise inventories	824.0	668.3
Film and television costs	2,099.4	1,596.2
Theme parks, resorts and other property, at cost		
Attractions, buildings and equipment	8,339.9	7,450.4
Accumulated depreciation	(3,038.5)	(2,627.1)
	5,301.4	4,823.3
Projects in progress	778.4	879.1
Land	110.5	112.1
	6,190.3	5,814.5
Investment in Euro Disney	532.9	629.9
Other assets	1,223.6	936.8
	$14,605.8	$12,826.3
Liabilities and shareholders' equity		
Accounts payable and other accrued liabilities	$2,842.5	$2,474.8
Income taxes payable	200.2	267.4
Borrowings	2,984.3	2,936.9
Unearned royalty and other advances	860.7	699.9
Deferred income taxes	1,067.3	939.0
Stockholders' equity		
Preferred stock, $.10 par value		
Authorized—100.0 million shares		
Issued—none		
Common stock—$0.25 par value		
Authorized—1.2 billion shares		
Issued—575.4 million shares and 567.0 million shares	1,226.3	945.3
Retained earnings	6,990.4	5,790.3
Cumulative translation and other adjustments	37.3	59.1
	8,254.0	6,794.7
Less treasury stock, at cost—51.0 million shares and 42.9 million shares	(1,603.2)	(1,286.4)
	6,650.8	5,508.3
	$14,605.8	$12,826.3

Source: 1995 Form 10-K filed with the U.S. Securities and Exchange Commission by The Walt Disney Company, p. 34.

in 1994 to throwing off $144.8 million in 1995 (this project has been troubled; the change in flows suggests that a turnaround is under way) and (2) borrowings declined from $1.87 billion in 1994 to $786 million in 1995. You could wonder whether this large swing in borrowing signals a change in how the firm will be financed in the future. Overall, the statement of cash flows tells a positive story.

EXHIBIT 10.4   Statement of cash flows: The Walt Disney Company.

Year Ended September 30	1995	1994	1993
Cash provided by operations before income taxes	$4,067.5	$3,127.7	$2,453.9
Income taxes paid	(557.4)	(320.4)	(308.7)
	3,510.1	2,807.3	2,145.2
Investing activities			
Film and television costs	(1,886.0)	(1,433.9)	(1,264.6)
Investments in theme parks, resorts and other property	(896.5)	(1,026.1)	(813.9)
Euro Disney investment	144.8	(971.1)	(140.1)
Purchases of investments	(1,033.2)	(952.7)	(1,313.5)
Proceeds from sales of investments	1,460.3	1,494.1	841.0
Other	(77.8)	3.0	31.4
	(2,288.4)	(2,886.7)	(2,659.7)
Financing activities			
Borrowings	786.1	1,866.4	1,256.0
Reduction of borrowings	(771.9)	(1,315.3)	(1,119.2)
Repurchases of common stock	(348.7)	(570.7)	(31.6)
Dividends	(180.0)	(153.2)	(128.6)
Other	182.4	76.1	136.1
	(332.1)	(96.7)	112.7
Increase (decrease) in cash and cash equivalents	889.6	(176.1)	(401.8)
Cash and cash equivalents, beginning of year	186.9	363.0	764.8
Cash and cash equivalents, end of year	$1,076.5	$186.9	$363.0

The difference between income before income taxes and cumulative effect of accounting changes as shown on the consolidated statement of income and cash provided by operations before income taxes is detailed as follows:

	1995	1994	1993
Income before income taxes and cumulative effect of accounting changes	$2,116.7	$1,703.1	$1,074.0
Cumulative effect of accounting changes	—	—	(514.2)
Charges to income not requiring cash outlays			
Depreciation	470.2	409.7	364.2
Amortization of film and television costs	1,382.8	1,198.6	664.2
Euro Disney	35.1	110.4	350.0
Other	98.1	121.1	163.5
Changes in			
Investments in trading securities	1.2	—	—
Receivables	(122.3)	(280.2)	(211.0)
Merchandise inventories	(155.7)	(59.4)	(146.1)
Other assets	(287.7)	(81.5)	197.0
Accounts payable and other accrued liabilities	368.3	146.7	544.4
Unearned royalty and other advances	160.8	(140.8)	(32.1)
	1,950.8	1,424.6	1,379.9
Cash provided by operations before income taxes	$1,067.5	$3,127.7	$2,453.9
Supplemental cash flow information			
Interest paid	$122.8	$99.3	$77.3

Source: 1995 Form 10-K filed with the U.S. Securities and Exchange Commission by The Walt Disney Company, p. 35.

Step 6. Read the footnotes to the financial statements.

These can be very technical and difficult for the novice to understand. But aficionados of annual reports say that the footnotes often contain juicy insights. The footnotes to Disney's report offer these tidbits:

- Update on the forthcoming acquisition by Disney of Capital Cities/ABC Inc.
- Report on the turnaround at Euro Disney.
- Reveal that Disney has issued an *extremely long-dated bond*—it matures in 2093.
- Show that Disney has overfunded its employee pension plan.
- Indicate that Disney has ordered two cruise ships at a cost of $700 million.

Individually, such tidbits may not be terribly significant at present, but they can offer insights into the future of the company and can signal management's outlook.

Step 7. Read management's discussion of the year's performance.

An annual report typically contains a detailed discussion of the year just past. The management discussion usually reflects management's efforts to influence the reader's assessment of the company (accounting rules and government regulations limit management's leeway in other areas of the annual report). Disney's annual report is no exception. Accounting for 44 pages out of the 70-page annual report, the management discussion includes 22 pages of photographs and an upbeat review of the year. It helps you to cultivate a critical frame of mind before reading the management's discussion.

ASSESSING THE FINANCIAL HEALTH OF A FIRM

Unfortunately, simply reading the annual report of a firm may not provide the basis to conclude whether the firm is healthy. Further, independent analysis almost always rewards the investor with fresh insights. The key to this added work is *ratio analysis*. Financial ratios show the performance of the firm in four important areas:

- *Profitability* is measured in terms of both *profit or expense margins* and as *investment return*. Investors will focus on the latter measures of profitability.
- *Leverage* ratios measure the use of short-term and long-term debt financing by the firm. In general, higher usage of debt increases the risk of the

firm. Higher ratios of debt to equity and to capital suggest higher financial risk. The ratio of EBIT[9] to interest expense measures the ability of the firm to cover its interest payments; lower levels of this ratio (such as two times or less) suggest high risk.

- *Asset-utilization ratios* measure the efficiency of asset use. For instance, the sales-to-assets ratio shows how many dollars of sales are generated per dollar of assets. A higher figure suggests more efficiency; a lower figure suggests less efficiency. Over the long term, differences in the growth rates of sales and assets can lead to production problems of over- or undercapacity. Days in receivables[10] shows how many days it takes to collect the average credit sale. The longer it takes, the greater the investment in receivables.

- *Liquidity* ratios measure the resources available to meet short-term financial commitments. The *current ratio* is the ratio of all current assets to all current liabilities. The *quick ratio* is the ratio of only cash and receivables (i.e., those assets that can be liquidated quickly) to all current liabilities.

The careful analyst should examine both the *size* and *trend* of these ratios, and, if possible, compare them to the ratios for peer firms (i.e., firms in the same industry).

It can be difficult to assemble a unified view of the firm from these ratios. Fortunately, the *Du Pont System of Ratios* can help analysts integrate their insights. The Du Pont System was developed during World War I when the financial officers of E.I. du Pont de Nemours and Company sought a system to assess the health of their firm and of the segments within the firm. This system decomposes *return on equity* into several constituent pieces: *return on sales,* which measures the profitability of each dollar of revenue; *sales turnover,* which measures the dollars of sales produced by each dollar of assets; and the ratio of *assets to equity,* which measures the financial leverage of the company or the dollars of assets carried by each dollar of equity. Algebraically, the product of these three components is the return on equity:

Return on equity = return on sales × sales turnover × financial leverage[11]

$$\frac{\text{Profit}}{\text{Equity}} = \frac{\text{profit}}{\text{sales}} \times \frac{\text{sales}}{\text{assets}} \times \frac{\text{assets}}{\text{equity}}$$

By examining the Du Pont System for comparative years, it is possible to determine the sources of changes in return on equity.

Exhibit 10.5 presents selected ratios calculated from Disney's 1995 annual report. The profitability ratios present a stable, or upward, trend—we can con-

EXHIBIT 10.5 Ratio analysis of financial statements: The Walt Disney Company

Year Ended September 30	1995	1994	1993
Profitability			
Operating profit margin (%) (operating income/sales)	20.2%	19.5%	20.2%
Pretax profit margin (%) (income before taxes and accounting changes/sales)	17.5%	16.9%	12.6%
Return on sales (%) (net income/sales)	11.4%	11.0%	3.5%
Return on equity (%) (net income/shareholders' equity)	20.8%	20.2%	—
Return on net assets (%) (net income/(assets-payables and accruals))	11.9%	11.0%	—
Return on assets (%) (net income/assets)	9.4%	8.7%	—
Leverage			
Debt/equity ratio (%)	44.9%	53.3%	—
Debt/total capital (%)	31.0%	34.8%	—
EBIT/interest (x)	13.1	16.1	11.1
Asset utilization			
Sales/assets	0.83	0.78	—
Sales growth rate (%)	20.5%	17.9%	—
Assets growth rate (%)	13.9%	—	—
Cash and invest. to sales (%)	8.9%	1.9%	—
Days in receivables	54.0	60.6	—
Payables to sales	23.5%	24.6%	—
Inventories to sales	6.8%	6.6%	—
Annual depreciation/gross P&E	5.6%	5.5%	—
Liquidity			
Current ratio	1.50	1.40	—
Quick ratio	1.23	1.16	—

Source of data underlying the ratios: 1995 Form 10-K filed with the U.S. Securities and Exchange Commission by The Walt Disney Company, pp. 33, 34, and 35.
Source of ratios: Author's analysis.

clude that the firm has been maintaining or slightly improving its profitability over the past three years. The leverage ratios indicate a declining reliance on debt financing—this will reduce the overall riskiness of the firm, though it may also reduce the returns to stockholders if debt is reduced greatly. The asset-utilization ratios have also improved in 1995 over 1994—the firm is using its assets more carefully. Finally, the liquidity ratios of the firm have improved in 1995 from 1994, suggesting an improved ability of the firm to meet its cash demands as they appear. In conclusion, a financial ratio analysis of Disney's statements reveals a very healthy firm.

ASSESSING PERFORMANCE AGAINST A PLAN: MANAGERIAL ACCOUNTING

Financial statements present the performance of the firm to outsiders such as investors, creditors, government regulators, and concerned citizens. However, these statements are too aggregative and backward-looking to help operating managers in their day-to-day work of pushing the firm toward annual performance goals.

Managerial accounting uses many of the tools and concepts of financial accounting to help the operating managers understand their unit's performance against a plan, budget, or standard. A *plan* or *budget* is a target or forecast of performance, expected but uncertain. A *standard,* such as a standard cost, suggests a norm against which actual cost may be compared. You can assess performance of a project or business in terms of *variance* from the benchmark. A *favorable variance* is either actual revenues higher than expected or actual costs lower than expected. An *unfavorable variance* is the reverse.

Variances in revenues and costs can be decomposed into variances due to price or cost changes and variances due to volume changes. Whether a variance arises because of variances in volumes or variances in prices (or costs) is extremely valuable information for the manager. It points the way toward remedying problems and rewarding outstanding performance. Consider this simple hypothetical case study regarding the videocassette release of a new movie by Gotham Cinema Company.

Gotham Cinema Company: Videocassette Release

At the beginning of 1997, videocassette sales for the year of Gotham's 1996 hit movie were expected to realize revenues of $50 million. This was based on an assumed sale of 5 million units, yielding revenues of $10 per unit to Gotham. At the core of the marketing strategy for this video release was a plan to promote aggressively the release through high-volume, mass-market discount retailers. The budgeted $10 unit revenue was a best guess about how substantial would be the concessions demanded by the discount retailers. The cassettes were to be manufactured on contract by a Taiwanese firm for a unit cost of $3. The production contract specified a production volume of 5 million units for 1997. Changes in the production volume or product would entail price increases to Gotham because of substantial job-change and setup costs.

At the end of the year, Gotham's marketing manager beamed with delight as she reported that revenues on the videocassette release would be $54 million, resulting from 6 million units sold at an average price of $9. She pointed out that the submission of cash rebate coupons had been higher than expected, as had the concessions to mass-market discount retailers. Gotham's purchasing manager was not as happy. He reported that the increased volume had prompted the supplier to impose surcharges on the price to Gotham: The average unit cost of the videocassettes was $4. Gotham's CEO grumbled that the project had earned only $30 million instead of the budgeted $35 million. What had gone wrong? Who was to blame, and why?

- *Revenue variance: price or quantity?* The price and volume variances were:

Sales price variance = (actual price − standard price) × (actual units sold)
$$-\$6,000,000 = (\$9 - \$10) \times (6,000,000)$$

The sales price variance was unfavorable to Gotham.

Sales volume variance = (standard price) × (actual volume − expected volume)
$$+\$10,000,000 = \$10 \times (6,000,000 - 5,000,000)$$

The sales volume variance was favorable to Gotham.

Overall, the special price discounts and promotions produced an increase in volume that more than compensated for the lower average price realized. The revenue variance analysis shows that the promotional effort paid off:

Total revenue variance = volume variance + price variance
$$+\$4,000,000 = +\$10,000,000 - \$6,000,000$$

The pickup in volume had been more than enough to compensate for the decline in price.

- *Cost variance: price or quantity?* Regarding the cost to Gotham of buying the cassettes from the manufacturer, we can analyze variances from budget using similar formulas:

Unit cost variance = (actual unit cost − budgeted unit cost) × (actual unit volume)
$$+\$6,000,000 = (\$4 - \$3) \times 6,000,000$$

The unit cost variance was unfavorable to Gotham; it cost Gotham more to have the cassettes made than the company had budgeted. The increase in cost was due to the clause in the supply contract that permitted the supplier to hike the price to Gotham if the production run was higher than expected.

Volume cost variance = (budgeted unit cost) × (actual volume − budgeted volume)
$$+\$3,000,000 = \$3 \times (6,000,000 - 5,000,000)$$

The cost volume variance was also unfavorable to Gotham. This stands to reason, because it had to buy more units than it expected. Overall, the total cost variance was unfavorable:

Total cost variance = unit cost variance + volume cost variance
+$9,000,000 = +$6,000,000 + $3,000,000

The videocassette release project turned out worse for Gotham than expected. Instead of earning $35 million[12] on the release, it earned $30 million.[13] Putting the variance analysis of sales and costs together helps show the sources of Gotham's disappointments. Exhibit 10.6 illustrates that price decreases and cost increases are unhappy outcomes, that sales volume decreases and cost volume increases are unhappy outcomes, and that profits equal sales less costs. The row totals show that the shortfall in budgeted profits was due to the fact that costs rose faster than revenues. However, before we criticize the purchasing manager, consider that part of the rise in costs is due to the fact that Gotham simply ordered more units than it had budgeted. Also, look at the column totals. The columns show that the unhappy news originates in the unit price or cost area, and that culpability is shared equally between the purchasing manager (who negotiates the supply contracts) and the marketing manager (who handles sales policy); half of the unfavorable price/cost variance of $12 million originates in sales and half in costs.

A general manager can use analysis such as this to take thoughtful action. One possibility is that Gotham should stiffen its spine in negotiations with suppliers and customers. Perhaps the managers of purchasing and marketing should be sent to a negotiation skills workshop. Maybe the purchasing manager should be assisted by a skillful lawyer who could draft an agreement limiting the supplier's ability to hike the unit price. Gotham might consider searching for suppliers with more flexible production operations for whom a change order is not an expensive proposition. And finally, Gotham should reconsider the strategy of selling through mass-market discounters; they imposed internal turbulence (in the form of higher-than-expected volume) that rippled backward through the supply chain, causing Gotham to earn $5 million less than it had budgeted.

EXHIBIT 10.6   Gotham Cinema Company videocassette release: analysis of variance against plan.

	Price or Cost Variance	Volume Variance	Total Variance
Sales	$ 6,000,000 ⊗	$10,000,000 ☺	$4,000,000 ☺
Costs	$ 6,000,000 ⊗	$ 3,000,000 ⊗	$9,000,000 ⊗
Total	$12,000,000 ⊗	$ 7,000,000 ☺	$5,000,000 ⊗

Note: ☺ = Favorable variance. ⊗ = Unfavorable variance.

CONCLUSION

A basic mastery of accounting is absolutely essential for the success of the modern manager. Such mastery should include an ability to read financial statements and derive basic insights about the health of the enterprise from them and to assess the performance of a business or project relative to a budget or standard using *variance analysis* of prices, costs, and volume.

Perhaps more important, a basic mastery of accounting will instill in the manager a general sense of irony about performance measurement. On close examination, it becomes apparent that the process of preparing a presentation about the condition of the firm is heavily laden with judgment. Financial accounting is a "precisely approximate" art. Managers need to recognize the many alternatives they face in presenting financial results and make faithful, ethical choices. Investors and creditors need to read financial statements with thoughtful caution, recognizing that accounting reality is an abstraction from true economic reality.

Finally, accounting presents an extremely important framework for thinking about the internal workings of the firm. Assets must equal liabilities and owners' equity; transactions must *balance*, which is preserved through double-entry accounting. This represents the firm as a *system* through which turbulence resonates and whereby the turbulence can be amplified or dampened. The challenge for executives is not to eliminate turbulence, but rather to manage it. To achieve this, managers need to view the firm as a system and to consider the sources of turbulence and its direct and indirect effects throughout the system. This is the thrust of the "systems thinking" approach as developed by Peter Senge and others. Viewed from this standpoint, accounting is not a narrow and technical specialty, but rather an essential tool for corporate renewal and transformation.

FOR FURTHER READING

Mark E. Haskins et al., *Financial Accounting and Reporting* (Homewood: Irwin, 1993).

Peter Senge, *The Fifth Discipline* (New York: Doubleday, 1990).

Roman L. Weil, Clyde P. Stickney, and Sidney Davidson, *Accounting: The Language of Business,* 8th ed. (Sun Lakes: Horton, 1990).

Gerald I. White, Ashwinpaul C. Sondhi, and Dov Fried, *The Analysis and Use of Financial Statements* (New York: Wiley, 1994).

11 FINANCE

Finance is concerned with *raising* and *investing* money. The underlying goal of decision makers in finance should be to *create value*. How to create value (or inadvertently destroy it) through raising and investing money is the gist of all MBA training in finance. The field has an elaborate underpinning of economic theory and empirical research, all of which boils down to this piece of advice: *Buy low, sell high.*

Drawing by Modell; © 1982. Reproduced by permission of New Yorker Magazine, Inc.

While on the surface this advice seems very simplistic, this aphorism has two profound implications for managers. First, it directs them to think about value (what "low" and "high" mean). Second, it directs their gaze outside the firm to the capital markets to test their thinking (i.e., in order to buy or sell.)

The field of finance is devoted to estimating *intrinsic values* as a foundation for taking action. Hence, *valuation analysis* is the core skill used in this field. How you buy low and sell high is guided by the following principles:

1. Think like an investor.
2. Invest when the intrinsic value of an asset equals or exceeds the outlay.
3. Sell securities (raise funds) when the cash received equals or exceeds the value of securities sold.
4. Ignore options at your peril: They are pervasive and tricky to value, and they can strongly influence a decision.
5. If you get confused, see principle 1.

PRINCIPLE 1: THINK LIKE AN INVESTOR

A classic education in finance covers the thinking of three sets of decision makers: investors, intermediaries, and sellers of securities, who are typically corporations. These players are linked inextricably through the *capital markets,* the markets where such financial instruments as stocks, bonds, options, currencies, and futures are traded. Exhibit 11.1 shows that intermediaries stand between issuers and investors in the capital markets.

EXHIBIT 11.1   Major players in capital markets.

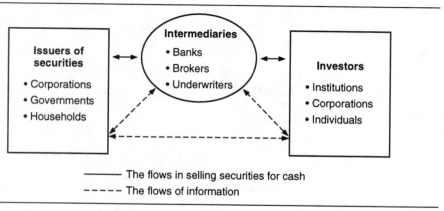

The flows in selling securities for cash
The flows of information

The exhibit also suggests that capital markets embody the flows of not just cash and securities, but in effect they convey *information*. For example, a stock price will reflect information obtained from annual reports and press releases from issuers, recommendations and hot tips from brokers, and in-depth securities analyses from both issuers and investors.

Corporations: Issuers of Securities

Most MBAs choose to concentrate on corporations because these are where most jobs can be found and where most of the interesting dilemmas for intermediaries and investors originate. Corporations are huge investors and raisers of capital, accounting for more than $800 billion in new investment each year.

Even inside a corporation, it is still necessary to think like an investor (see Exhibit 11.2). Corporations are investors themselves—finance argues that corporate managers are *agents* of the owners of the firm. In making investment decisions, managers should take into account the wishes of the owners. Similarly, we can argue that as issuers of securities, corporations need to anticipate the wishes of investors as they design and price those securities.

Intermediaries

As the word *intermediary* suggests, these players stand between issuers and investors and help make the market in securities. To "make the market" means simply to help connect buyers with sellers. Intermediaries earn a fee with the completion of each transaction. Examples of intermediaries are banks, which link depositors (sources of lendable funds) with borrowers (users of lendable funds); investment banks, which link issuers of long-term securities (such as

EXHIBIT 11.2   Examples of areas in which firms should think like investors.

Investing	Raising Capital
Capital budgeting	Bank borrowing
New products	Selling bonds
Cash management	Selling equity
Market expansion	Leasing
New technology	ESOPs
Plant closing	LBOs
Merger/acquisition	Bankruptcy
Divestiture	

corporations) with investors; and insurance companies, which pool or combine the exposures of many risk-averse persons so that risk bearing may be spread.

Intermediaries can be large in absolute terms and in their significance to the national and global economy. For instance, Merrill Lynch, a leading American investment bank, has an asset base of more than $160 billion. Fidelity Management and Research, a mutual fund management company, manages funds that exceed $400 billion. In addition to their size, these firms are opinion leaders or "lead steers" in the valuation of investments—they help frame standards for investment in America and worldwide.

Because intermediaries earn their fees from deals that others make, they have an interest in growth, in the smooth functioning of capital markets, and in liquidity. But most important, intermediaries must act in their clients' interests; issuers need to obtain capital at fair prices, and investors need to earn fair rates of return. For this reason, students of finance tend to proceed directly to an understanding of issuers and investors rather than to dwell very long on intermediaries.

Investors

Even though all eyes are (or should be) turned toward investors, it is stunning to find the conventional thinking that investors are sleepy, ignorant, and indifferent to the performance of corporations. In fact, the reality is quite the opposite. It is true that individual investors are major holders of securities. "Households," as the government calls these investors, account for direct ownership of more than $3 trillion in stocks and bonds. However, individuals tend to buy and hold their securities and to look toward professional analysts and advisors for recommendations. The thought leaders in the pricing of securities are sophisticated institutional investors who today account for over 90% of the trading volume on major securities exchanges. These are major players who spend a great deal of money on obtaining the best analysis and obtaining it sooner than others.

How Do Investors Think?

Principle 1 tells us to think like an investor. (See Exhibit 11.3.) A considerable amount of academic theory and research is devoted to modeling how investors think. Fortunately, however, the behavior of the most successful investors (such as Warren Buffett[1] and Peter Lynch[2]) convey many of the same attributes:

1. Focus on economic reality, not accounting reality.

Financial statements prepared by accountants might not adequately represent the *economic* reality of a business. Accounting reality is conservative, backward-

---

EXHIBIT 11.3   Investor mind-set.

1. Focus on economic reality, not accounting reality.
2. Account for the cost of the lost opportunity.
3. Required return follows risk.
4. Look forward and account for the time value of money.
5. Diversification of portfolios is good.
6. Focus on wealth creation.
7. Invest on the basis of information and analysis, assuming that the market is generally efficient.
8. The alignment of management and owners is beneficial to firm value.

---

looking, and governed by generally accepted accounting principles (GAAP). Investment decisions, on the other hand, should be based on the economic reality of a business. In economic reality, intangible assets such as patents, trademarks, special managerial know-how, and reputation might be very valuable, yet under GAAP these assets would be carried at little or no value. GAAP measures results in terms of net profit; in economic reality, the results of a business are its *flows of cash*. Warren Buffett has written:

> . . . Because of the limitations of conventional accounting, consolidated reported earnings may reveal relatively little about our true economic performance. . . . [We] both as owners and managers, virtually ignore such consolidated numbers. . . . Accounting consequences do not influence our operating or capital-allocation process.[3]

2. Account for the cost of the lost opportunity.

The concept of the *opportunity cost* is one of the most important in finance and marks finance as a sibling of economics. Economics encourages decision makers not to think in terms of simple yes/no decisions, but rather in terms of either/or decisions. In almost all business decisions there is an explicit or implicit *alternative opportunity*—in the case of investing, it is to buy another asset with similar attributes to the one being considered. In investment decisions, for instance, you should compare the attractiveness of a contemplated asset against an alternative investment, which would be forgone (or lost) if you proceed to invest in the first asset. This is nothing more than common sense: *Test any course of action against your next-best alternative.* The concept of the opportunity cost embodies this wisdom in finance. Warren Buffett showed that he accounts for opportunity costs when he stated that an important standard of comparison in testing the attractiveness of an acquisition is the potential rate of return from investing in common stocks of similar companies.

3. Look forward and account for the time value of money.

To look forward means that you should not take into account *sunk costs*, expenses already incurred, or events that have happened in the past. Buffett holds that intrinsic value is the *present value* of future expected performance.

> [All other methods fall short in determining whether] an investor is indeed buying something for what it is worth and is therefore truly operating on the principle of obtaining value for his investments. . . . Irrespective of whether a business grows or doesn't, displays volatility or smoothness in earnings, or carries a high price or low in relation to its current earnings and book value, the investment shown by the discounted-flows-of-cash calculation to be the cheapest is the one that the investor should purchase.[4]

Enlarging on his discussion of intrinsic value, Buffett said:

> We define intrinsic value as the discounted value of the cash that can be taken out of a business during its remaining life. Anyone calculating intrinsic value necessarily comes up with a highly subjective figure that will change both as estimates of future cash flows are revised and as interest rates move. Despite its fuzziness, however, intrinsic value is all-important and is the only logical way to evaluate the relative attractiveness of investments and businesses.[5]

4. Diversification of investments is good.

As the old wisdom says, "don't put all your eggs in one basket." Peter Lynch wrote, "It isn't safe to own just one stock, because in spite of your best efforts, the one you choose might be the victim of unforeseen circumstances."[6] Also, as Buffett said, "Diversification is protection against ignorance."[7] The benefit of diversification is one of the most important ideas in finance and was recognized by the Nobel Prize in 1990. Diversification is good because it spreads (and thus reduces) the risk of loss. This principle is widely illustrated by banks that seek to minimize the impact of credit loss by diversifying their portfolio of loans and by insurance companies who seek to reduce the impact of insurance losses by diversifying their portfolio of insured exposures.

5. Required return follows risk.

Common sense tells us that the more risk you take, the more you should get paid. Thus, the required returns (or discount rates) used in determining intrinsic values should be determined by the risk of the cash flows being valued. This is an extremely important idea in finance and is illustrated daily in the behavior of traders and investors in the capital markets. Consider, for instance, the rates of return available on bonds of different credit risk (*credit risk* refers to risk of default by the borrower).

Exhibit 11.4 shows that the riskier the bond, the higher the rate of return demanded by investors. Indeed, the logic of many investors in determining required rates of return on assets was to add a risk premium to the long-term risk-free rate of return (such as the U.S. Treasury bond yield).

This intuitive relation between risk and return offers additional profound guidance to managers: *Risk is in everything—the point should not be to eliminate it, but rather to price it properly and to manage it carefully.* Walter Wriston[8] has written,

> Our American economic system, like our political system, is untidy—it offends those people who love tidy, predictable societies. We make a lot of mistakes in this country, we have a lot of failures. Some people see only the failures; they cannot seem to grasp the fact that the failures are the price we pay for the successes. It's as though they wanted to have "up" without "down," or "hot" without "cold." We read in our newspapers, and even in our business magazines, solemn words about "risky investments" and "risky loans" from writers who do not seem to realize that these phrases are as redundant as talking about a one-story bungalow. All invest-

EXHIBIT 11.4   Yields by bond ratings (January 31, 1997).

Bond Quality Grade	Annual Yield to Maturity
U.S. Treasuries (commonly regarded as the least-risky bond investment.)	6.41%
AAA "Capacity to pay interest and repay principal is extremely strong."	6.87%
AA "... very strong capacity ..."	6.94%
A "... strong capacity ... somewhat more susceptible to the adverse effects of changes in circumstances and economic conditions"	7.11%
BBB "... adequate capacity ... adverse economic conditions or changing circumstances are more likely to lead to a weakened capacity ..."	7.43%
BB+	7.93%
BB/BB–	9.32%
B "... regarded as predominantly speculative with respect to capacity to pay ... outweighed by large uncertainties or major risk exposures to adverse conditions."	10.90%

Source: Standard & Poor's Current Statistics, January 1997. Rating definitions are quoted from Standard & Poor's *Ratings Guide* (New York: McGraw-Hill, 1979), pp. 327–328.

ments and all loans are risky because they are based on educated guesses about the future, rather than certain knowledge of what will happen.[9]

6. Measure wealth creation by the gain in intrinsic value, not accounting profit.

Buffett wrote:

> Our long-term economic goal . . . is to maximize the average annual rate of gain in intrinsic business value on a per share basis. We do not measure the economic significance or performance of Berkshire by its size; we measure by per-share progress.[10]

The gain in intrinsic value could be modeled as the value added by a business above and beyond a charge for the use of capital in that business. One way to measure this gain is with *economic value added* (EVA™ for short), which is also called *economic profit*.

$$\text{Economic profit} = \text{NOPAT} - \text{charge for capital used}$$

NOPAT is net operating profits after tax. From this is deducted a charge for capital estimated by multiplying the firm's weighted average cost of capital times its capital base. The cost of capital is the blended rate of return required by all investors (creditors and stockholders) in the firm. When economic profit is positive, value has been created. When economic profit is negative, value has been destroyed. Analysts in leading corporations use this yardstick to assess financial performance of corporations and of units within corporations. The appeal of economic profit is that it gives simple and clear guidelines to operating managers about how to create or avoid destroying value:

- *Increase sales.*   Holding other factors (such as costs and capital) constant, an increase in sales will increase NOPAT, which will increase economic profit.
- *Cut costs.*   Holding other factors (sales and capital) constant, a decrease in costs will increase NOPAT and economic profit.
- *Reduce capital employed.*   Holding other factors (such as sales and costs) constant, reducing the capital employed in a business will increase economic profit.
- *Minimize the weighted average cost of capital (WACC).*   It may be possible to lower WACC through sensible management of the firm's capital structure (more is said about this under principle 3). But be careful in the way you think about WACC; the cost of capital is determined by investors, not managers. In competitive markets there is only one reliable way to reduce the cost of capital: Take less risk. But investors want managers to

take sensible risks in the pursuit of premium rates of return. For a manager to try to cut the cost of capital beyond sensibly trying to mix debt and equity capital would be wrongheaded.

7. Invest on the basis of information and analysis, supposing that the market is generally efficient.

Experience shows that it is extremely difficult to beat the market consistently over time. One explanation for this is that the market is very efficient in incorporating news and analysis into current stock prices. If the capital market is efficient in absorbing news into security prices, then securities will be fairly priced on average and over time. Clearly, there are exceptions to market efficiency, and it is to these exceptions that the great investors flock.

Buffett repeatedly emphasized awareness and information as the foundations for investing and was fond of repeating a parable told to him by Benjamin Graham:

> There was a small, private business, and one of the owners was a man named Market. Every day Mr. Market had a new opinion of what the business was worth, and at that price stood ready to buy your interest or sell you his. As excitable as he was opinionated, Mr. Market presented a constant distraction to his fellow owners. "What does he know?" they would wonder, as he bid them an extraordinarily high price or a depressingly low one. Actually, the gentleman knew little or nothing. You may be happy to sell out to him when he quotes you a ridiculously high price, and equally happy to buy from him when his price is low. But the rest of the time you will be wiser to form your own ideas of the value of your holdings, based on full reports from the company about its operations and financial position.[11]

Graham believed that an investor's worst enemy was not the stock market, but oneself. Superior training could not compensate for the absence of the requisite temperament for investing. Over the long term, stock prices should have a strong relationship with the economic progress of the business. Indeed, a reasonably large mass of research suggests that stock prices impound economic news rapidly and without bias—this is the phenomenon of *capital market efficiency*. Efficiency does not suggest that stock prices are the "real" or "correct" intrinsic values, but rather that they impound what is known about the company; investors could still overvalue or undervalue the share of stock as Graham recognized, but it would be difficult to rush in and out of stocks with every new tidbit of news and consistently earn a profitable rate of return.

8. Look for alignment of agents and owners.

When managers think like investors, the goals of managers and investors are said to be "aligned." Usually the point of agreement is on creating value. Explaining his significant ownership interest in Berkshire Hathaway, Buffett said,

I am a better businessman because I am an investor. And I am a better investor because I am a businessman.[12]

As if to illustrate this sentiment, he said,

> A managerial "wish list" will not be filled at shareholder expense. We will not diversify by purchasing entire businesses at control prices that ignore long-term economic consequences to our shareholders. We will only do with your money what we would do with our own, weighing fully the values you can obtain by diversifying your own portfolios through direct purchases in the stock market.[13]

Managers are aligned with the interests of owners through the creation of effective corporate governance systems (beginning with the board of directors) and with the implementation of good incentives. For four of Berkshire's six directors, more than 50% of their family net worth was represented by shares in Berkshire Hathaway. The senior managers of Berkshire Hathaway subsidiaries held shares in the company or were compensated under incentive plans that imitated the potential returns from an equity interest in their business unit.

PRINCIPLE 2: INVEST WHEN THE INTRINSIC VALUE OF AN ASSET EQUALS OR EXCEEDS THE OUTLAY

Thinking like an investor when working inside a corporation can be a challenge, since you are not necessarily managing your own money and since the investment decisions you face generally don't involve stocks and bonds, but physical assets instead. Principle 2 can help focus your thinking like an investor when you face corporate investment decisions.

Here's an example of the kind of investment decisions operating managers face. Suppose that you manage a manufacturing plant. An important machine in your plant has reached the end of its useful life and must be replaced. One of your analysts suggests two alternatives. The first alternative is to put in a new machine that is just like the old one. The second alternative is to put in a new machine that costs $200,000 more to buy, but will save $50,000 per year in labor costs, will free up $25,000 in work-in-process inventory on the plant floor, and can be sold at the end of its life for $30,000. The required rate of return for an investment in either machine is 10%.[14] This is a classic choice between saving on an investment outlay today versus saving on operating expenses in the future. Which should you choose?

First, to think like an investor means to focus on *relevant cash flows,* not on profit or loss. The relevant flows of cash in this decision are the additional investment outlay, the after-tax labor savings each year, the additional depreciation tax shield, the release of inventory, and the salvage cash flow. These are presented in Exhibit 11.5. The discounted cash flow[15] value of the second alternative over the first is $17,626. This figure is called the *net present value* (NPV) because the outlay is netted against the present value of future cash flows. NPV has a very important interpretation—it is the amount by which the value of the firm will increase (or decrease if negative) if the second alternative is chosen over the first. Thinking like an investor, we would choose the second alternative because it creates value: As a rule of thumb, when the NPV is positive, make the investment.

The "Drivers" of Value Creation

The positive NPV in the machine-investment example is a happy surprise and perhaps a mystery. But the source of the value creation need not remain an enigma. Four factors determine the extent to which an investment creates or destroys value:

- The internal rate of return on investment.
- The investors' required rate of return (also called the *cost of capital.*)
- The rate of reinvestment in the project: the percent of cash thrown off that you plow back into the project each year.
- The length of the project's life.

To illustrate how these factors interact to create or destroy value, consider the hypothetical case presented in Exhibit 11.6. Suppose a company has the opportunity to invest $100 million in a business—this is its *cost* or *book value.* This business will throw off cash at the rate of 20% of its investment base each year. Suppose that instead of receiving any dividends, the buyer decides to reinvest all cash flow back into the business—at this rate the book value or investment value of the business will grow at 20% per year. Suppose that the investor plans to sell the business for its accumulated investment value at the end of the fifth year. Does this investment create value for the individual? You can determine this by discounting the future cash flows to the present at the investment's opportunity cost, the required return that could have been earned elsewhere at comparable risk. Suppose that the opportunity cost in this case is 15%. Dividing the present value of future cash flows (i.e., Buffett's "intrinsic value") by the cost of the investment (i.e., Buffett's "book value") indicates that every dollar invested buys securities worth $1.237. Value is created.

Consider an opposing case, summarized in Exhibit 11.7. This example is similar in all respects except for one key difference: The annual return on the investment is 10%. The result is that every dollar invested buys securities worth $0.801. Value is destroyed.

EXHIBIT 11.5 Estimate of the value-added from the new machine, compared to the old.

	Now	Year 1	Year 2	Year 3	Year 4	Year 5
New Machine						
Labor		-$150,000	-$150,000	-$150,000	-$150,000	-$150,000
Depreciation on machine (over 5 years)		-240,000	-240,000	-240,000	-240,000	-240,000
Reduction in tax expense (35% of labor and depreciation)		136,500	136,500	136,500	136,500	136,500
Impact on after-tax profit		-253,500	-253,500	-253,500	-253,500	-253,500
Add back depreciation		240,000	240,000	240,000	240,000	240,000
Reduction in inventory		25,000	—	—	—	—
Salvage value		—	—	—	—	30,000
Investment outlay	-$1,200,000					
Free cash flow	-$1,200,000	11,500	-13,500	-13,500	-13,500	16,500
Old Machine						
Labor		-200,000	-200,000	-200,000	-200,000	-200,000
Depreciation on machine (over 5 years)		-200,000	-200,000	-200,000	-200,000	-200,000
Reduction in tax expense (35% of labor and depreciation)		140,000	140,000	140,000	140,000	140,000
Impact on after-tax profit		-260,000	-260,000	-260,000	-260,000	-260,000
Add back depreciation		200,000	200,000	200,000	200,000	200,000
Reduction in inventory		—	—	—	—	—
Salvage value		—	—	—	—	—
Investment outlay	-1,000,000					
Free cash flow	-1,000,000	-60,000	-60,000	-60,000	-60,000	-60,000
New machine free cash flow	-1,200,000	11,500	-13,500	-13,500	-13,500	16,500
Old machine free cash flow	-1,000,000	-60,000	-60,000	-60,000	-60,000	-60,000
Incremental free cash flow	-$ 200,000	$ 71,500	$ 46,500	$ 46,500	$ 46,500	$ 76,500
Discounted cash flow value of free cash flows, at 10% discount rate	$ 17,626					

Source: Author's analysis.

EXHIBIT 11.6   Hypothetical example of value creation.

Assumptions:

1. Five-year term of investment, at the end of which you liquidate at accumulated investment value.
2. Initial investment is $100 million.
3. No dividends are paid. All cash flows are reinvested. Plowback is 100%.
4. Return on equity = 20%.
5. Required return on equity (discount rate) = 15%.

Year	Now	1	2	3	4	5
Memo: accumulated investment value	$100	$120	$144	$173	$207	$249
Investment	−100	—	—	—	—	—
Returns		20	24	29	35	41
Reinvestment		−20	−24	−29	−35	−41
Liquidation proceeds		—	—	—	—	249
Total cash flow	−$100	$ 0	$ 0	$ 0	$ 0	$249
Net present value =	$ 23.7					
(estimated at required return on equity)						
"Market" or intrinsic value =	$123.7					
book value =	100.0					
market book ratio	1.237					

Value created: $1.00 invested becomes 1.237 in market value.

Source: Author's analysis.

Comparing the two cases in Exhibits 11.6 and 11.7, the difference in value creation and destruction is driven entirely by the relationship between the expected returns and the discount rate (or required return). In the first case, the spread is positive and value is created. In the second case, the spread is negative and value is destroyed. Only in the instance where expected returns equal the discount rate will value be neither created nor destroyed. The capital markets demonstrate this relationship between spreads and value creation each day. Exhibit 11.8 presents the distribution of the 28 companies in the Dow Jones Industrial Index by the spread between their cost of equity and their expected return on equity on the vertical axis and the market-to-book-value ratio (which measures value creation). Immediately, we are struck by the positive slope of the cluster of companies: Positive spreads are generally associated with value creation; negative spreads are generally associated with value destruction.[16]

Exhibit 11.9 varies the reinvestment rate in the project. In Exhibits 11.6 and 11.7, we assumed implicitly that all cash generated was simply plowed back into

EXHIBIT 11.7 Hypothetical example of value destruction.

Assumptions:

1. Five-year term of investment, at the end of which you liquidate at accumulated investment value.
2. Initial investment is $100 million.
3. No dividends are paid. All cash flows are reinvested. Plowback is 100%.
4. Return on equity =10%.
5. Required return on equity (discount rate) =15%.

Year	Now	1	2	3	4	5
Memo: Accumulated investment value	$100	$110	$121	$133	$146	$161
Investment	−100	—	—	—	—	—
Returns		10	11	12	13	15
Reinvestment		−10	−11	−12	−13	−15
Liquidation proceeds		—	—	—	—	161
Total cash flow	−$100	$ 0	$ 0	$ 0	$ 0	$161

Net present value =	($ 19.9)
(estimated at required return on equity)	
"Market" or intrinsic value =	$ 80.1
book value =	100.0
market/book ratio	0.801

Value destroyed: $1.00 invested becomes $0.801 in market value.

Source: Author's analysis.

the project (i.e., 100% reinvestment). If the reinvestment assumption is scaled back, investors get some cash earlier, but the lump sum at the end is smaller. Exhibit 11.9 shows what happens to the NPV and market-to-book ratio if reinvestment varies between 100% and 0%. With positive-spread projects, the investor is worse off with lower reinvestment rates. This is because the cash coming out of the project is implicitly assumed to be reinvested at the discount rate, which is lower than the rate of return being earned on the project. With negative-spread projects, the investor is *better* off with lower reinvestment rates. This is because investors can earn a higher rate of return by redeploying their cash in the capital markets (and earning the 10% opportunity rate) than by plowing it back into the project. The conclusion is that *higher reinvestment amplifies the creation or destruction of value; lower reinvestment dampens it.*

Exhibit 11.10 varies the lifetime of the project. In Exhibits 11.6, 11.7, and 11.9, we assumed a five-year life of the project. But what if managers can take actions to extend or shorten the life of the project? The life of machinery can be

EXHIBIT 11.8   VBM evidence. Market-to-book vs. forecasted spread.

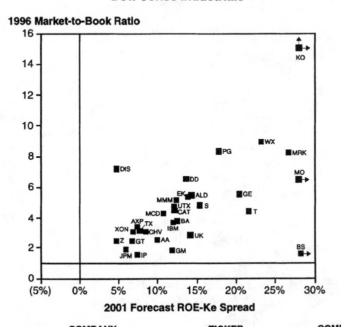

Dow Jones Industrials

1996 Market-to-Book Ratio

2001 Forecast ROE-Ke Spread

TICKER	COMPANY	TICKER	COMPANY
ALD	Allied Signal Inc	GT	Goodyear Tire & Rubber Co
AA	Aluminum Co of America	IBM	International Business Machines
AXP	American Express Co	IP	International Paper Co
T	AT&T Corp	MCD	McDonalds Corp
BS	Bethlehem Steel Corp	MRK	Merck & Co Inc
BA	Boeing Co	MMM	Minnesota Mining & Mfg Co
CAT	Caterpillar Inc	JPM	J P Morgan & Co Inc
CHV	Chevron Corp	MO	Philip Morris Cos Inc
KO	Coca Cola Co	PG	Procter & Gamble Co
DIS	Walt Disney Co	TX	Texaco Inc
DD	Du Pont E I De Nemours & Co	UK	Union Carbide Corp
XON	Exxon Corp	UTX	United Technologies Corp
GE	General Electric Co	WX	Westinghouse Electric Corp
GM	General Motors Corp	Z	Woolworth Corp

Note: Ke = Tech Ke.
Source: Reproduced with permission from Marakon Associates © 1997.

extended by quality maintenance, careful use, and tinkering. The life of profitable consumer products can be extended by reformulations, repackagings, and repositionings in the markets. Alternatively, money-losing plants can be shut down. Value-destroying product lines can be discontinued. Exhibit 11.10 shows that *longer life amplifies the creation or destruction of value; shorter life dampens it.*

In summary, value is created by positive spreads and destroyed by negative spreads. Lengthening the project life and increasing the reinvestment in the

EXHIBIT 11.9 Illustration of value creation and destruction as reinvestment in the project varies.*

		Reinvestment Rate				
		0%	**25%**	**50%**	**75%**	**100%**
Return on equity	20%	1.168	1.183	1.199	1.217	1.237
	15%	1.000	1.000	1.000	1.000	1.000
	10%	0.832	0.825	0.817	0.809	0.801

*This table presents the market/book ratios associated with projects offering three different returns and five different reinvestment rates. The cost of equity is constant across all cases: 15%. Therefore, where return on equity is 20%, the project offers a *positive spread* over the required rate of return. Note that all of these positive spread projects create value (i.e., their market/book value ratios are greater than 1.000). Where the return is only 10%, the spread over the required return is negative—these projects destroy value (i.e., their market/book value ratios are less than 1.000). Where the return is 15%, the spread is zero, and the project neither creates nor destroys value (the ratios are equal to 1.000).

The table shows that as the reinvestment rate increases, the creation or destruction of value is amplified; as the reinvestment rate decreases, the creation or destruction of value is dampened.
Source: Author's analysis.

project amplifies the creation or destruction of value. Shortening the life and disinvesting dampens the value effect. Understanding the value drivers of an investment and their managerial implications is an enormously important contribution of finance to the work of general managers. With the help of this framework, you can not only think, but also act, like an investor.

EXHIBIT 11.10 Illustration of value creation and destruction as the lifetime of the project varies.*

		Lifetime in Years		
		5	**10**	**15**
Return on equity	20%	1.237	1.531	1.893
	15%	1.000	1.000	1.000
	10%	0.801	0.641	0.513

*This table presents the market/book ratios associated with projects offering three different returns and three different lives. The cost of equity is constant across all cases: 15%. Therefore, where return on equity is 20%, the project offers a *positive spread* over the required rate of return. Note that all of these positive spread projects create value (i.e., their market/book value ratios are greater than 1.000). Where the return is only 10%, the spread over the required return is negative—these projects destroy value (i.e., their market/book value ratios are less than 1.000). Where the return is 15%, the spread is zero, and the project neither creates nor destroys value (the ratios are equal to 1.000).

The table shows that as the lifetime lengthens, the creation or destruction of value is amplified; as it is shortened, the creation or destruction of value is dampened.
Source: Author's analysis.

PRINCIPLE 3: SELL SECURITIES[17] (RAISE FUNDS) WHEN THE CASH RECEIVED EQUALS OR EXCEEDS THE VALUE OF SECURITIES SOLD

The field of finance also sheds light on how the firm should raise its capital. The orientation to thinking like an investor and to the value-creation framework is relevant here, too. The main difference encountered here is that the firm *takes the perspective of a seller* rather than of a buyer, because in financing itself the firm is selling securities and receiving cash. Principle 3 invites us to compare the "gives" and "gets" (similar to principle 2) and to proceed with the financing if the "gets" are greater than or equal to the "gives." This decision can be reduced to a problem of valuation.

An Example: Valuing an Issue of Debt

Suppose that you manage a hospital that needs $1 million to build a new wing. You hire a financial advisor and underwriter who recommends that your hospital issue bonds with repayment in a lump sum at the end of five years. The bond-rating agencies[18] give this issue a single-A rating. Your financial advisor tells you that an 8% coupon[19] should be offered. But your underwriter thinks she can place the bond issue with some investors who believe that the bond and your hospital are really worth a double-A rating. The yield on other single-A-rated hospital issues is currently 8.5%; on other double-A issues it is 7.75%. Should you proceed to issue this debt?

Exhibit 11.11 gives the net present value calculation of this bond. The proceeds of the issue are $1 million, which represents a positive inflow. Outflows are the annual interest payments and the principal payment at the end. Because you agree with the single-A rating, you discount these cash flows at 8.5% and estimate the net present value to be $19,703. This financing creates value for the hospital because the proceeds (+$1,000,000) exceed the present value of the liability incurred ($980,297). In this example, the source of value is the underwriter's ability to place the securities with investors who disagree with you about the risk (and required return) of the issue.

But the net present value calculation ignores one other potential effect: tax savings on interest payments. A for-profit hospital's interest payments are a deductible expense in the calculation of tax payments. By permitting this deduction, the government in effect subsidizes the cost to your hospital of this bond issue. The benefit of this subsidy should also be reflected in your decision.

EXHIBIT 11.11   **Simple NPV calculation of a bond's cash flows (from the standpoint of the issuer).**

Assumptions

1. Coupon rate = 8%
2. Term = 5 years
3. Principal repaid at maturity

	Now	Year 1	Year 2	Year 3	Year 4	Year 5
Principal	$1,000,000					$(1,000,000)
Interest	—	$(80,000)	$(80,000)	$(80,000)	$(80,000)	(80,000)
Cash flow	1,000,000	(80,000)	(80,000)	(80,000)	(80,000)	(1,080,000)
NPV @ 8.5%	$ 19,703					

Source: Author's analysis.

Exhibit 11.12 recomputes the NPV of the bond issue, reflecting the tax shield of the interest expense. This reduces the cost of the issue dramatically. The NPV now is $130,041.

Finding the Optimal Mix of Debt and Equity

As the bond valuation example shows, the tax deductibility of interest payments creates an enormous incentive to borrow. Shareholders reap the gain of the government subsidy of debt costs. The naive conclusion under the "Think like an

EXHIBIT 11.12   **Simple NPV valuation of a bond's cash flows, reflecting corporate tax deduction of interest expense (from the standpoint of the issuer).**

Assumptions

1. Coupon rate = 8%
2. Term = 5 years
3. Principal repaid at maturity
4. Corporate tax rate = .35

	Now	Year 1	Year 2	Year 3	Year 4	Year 5
Principal	$1,000,000					$(1,000,000)
Interest	—	$(80,000)	$(80,000)	$(80,000)	$(80,000)	(80,000)
Tax shield	—	28,000	28,000	28,000	28,000	28,000
Cash flow	1,000,000	(52,000)	(52,000)	(52,000)	(52,000)	(1,052,000)
NPV @ 8.5%	$ 130,041					

Source: Author's analysis.

investor" principle would be that the firm should borrow to the hilt, since more borrowing means more positive NPV.

The problem with this naive conclusion is that more borrowing increases the risk that the firm will default on its debt payments (to *default* means to be unable to pay interest or principal on schedule). The operating earnings of almost all firms are uncertain. They expand and contract with the regular cycle of the national economy, with changes in technology, with the entrance or exit of competitors in the industry, with changes in consumer sentiment, and so on. Unfortunately, debt payments are fixed by legal contract; they do not increase or decrease as the firm's capacity to pay increases or decreases. Lenders and investors in firms are quite conscious of this risk of default and set their required returns in reference to that risk. Beyond some "reasonable" level of indebtedness, lenders and investors will sense that the firm is assuming more and more default risk, and will raise the required returns (the interest rate) on their loans and on their equity investments.

For instance, bond investors make an assessment of the firm's creditworthiness through a process of credit analysis. Credit analysis could be as simple as making qualitative judgments on a set of standard criteria such as the "five Cs of credit" (see Exhibit 11.13) or as complicated as a highly technical computer simulation of the probability of default. For many long-term bonds, creditworthiness is summarized in a bond rating. As the firm borrows more, the rating will decline. As the rating declines, the return that investors require will rise.

As required returns are increased, the NPVs of the bonds will fall. This is the simple result of time value of money: The higher the discount rate, the lower the present value. As the borrowing of the firm increases, the effect of default risk will *reduce* the value created by borrowing. At some point in the range between all equity and debt financing of the firm, the impact of default risk will begin to more than offset the benefits of debt tax shields. That point is the optimum mix of debt and equity financing for the firm. Cast in graphical terms, Exhibit 11.14 illustrates this effect. The value of the firm rises as the firm goes from no debt to a moderate amount—this is because of the beneficial effects of

EXHIBIT 11.13   The five Cs of credit.

Cash flow: Is the firm's expected cash flow large enough to meet the debt payments?
Collateral: If we have to foreclose on the loan, are there sufficient assets in the firm that we could sell to repay the loan?
Conditions: Do the current economic conditions favor timely debt payments?
Course: Is the use to which these funds will be put appropriate? Is the general strategy of this firm "on course"?
Character: Are the people involved not only sufficiently intelligent and skilled, but are they also *morally inclined* to honor the repayment commitment?

the debt tax shields. Then the effect of default risk begins to be felt: As leverage increases beyond the optimum, the value of the firm begins to decline. Increasing the mix of debt beyond the optimum destroys value—it is equivalent to accepting financing whose cash received is less than the present value of future debt payments. Destroying value is the opposite of principle 3. To "think like an investor" in financing the firm is to choose the mix of debt and equity that maximizes the value of the firm.

PRINCIPLE 4: IGNORE OPTIONS AT YOUR PERIL: THEY ARE PERVASIVE, TRICKY TO VALUE, AND CAN STRONGLY INFLUENCE A DECISION

Principles 2 and 3 are presented in terms of discounted cash-flow valuation; but DCF does not tell the whole story of finance. DCF is based on fixed, "point estimate" forecasts, which may ignore contingent choices that the firm may have today or in the future. Contingent choices are rights to take actions that are sensible only if other things happen, such as in the following examples:

- The right to abandon a plant *if* it loses money.
- The right to hand over the reconstruction cost of a burned-out plant *if* you have a fire.
- The right to exploit a mineral deposit *if* exploration proves the existence of the deposit.
- The right to call a loan (demand immediate repayment) *if* the borrower defaults.

EXHIBIT 11.14   Finding the optimal mix of debt and equity.

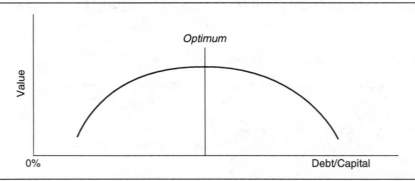

Options are rights (not obligations) to take action. Options permeate the business economy. For instance, all insurance policies are options. Any time managers say "I have the flexibility to . . ." they are expressing the fact that they have a right or an option.

All options are valuable, even if it seems unlikely that they would ever be exercised. In the financial pages of the newspaper you can find traded options that are deeply "out of the money" (i.e., to exercise the option would not be profitable)—yet these options trade at a positive price. The reason why all options are valuable is that there remains some chance (however small) that the option would be "in the money" (i.e., profitable to exercise) in the future.

A great deal of research in universities and in the financial community has modeled how options should be valued. The modeling is highly mathematical, but it boils down to the provocative insight (among others) that *options are more valuable the greater the uncertainty and the longer the life of the option.* This is because more uncertainty and longer life increase the chance that it will be profitable to exercise the option at some time in the future.

DCF, with its foundation in fixed forecasts, does not embrace the uncertainty and thus does not value the options that managers have. To think like an investor means to incorporate the value of options into your estimate of the intrinsic value of an asset.

Decisions by managers and firms frequently demonstrate the significant hidden value of options, as the following examples show:

- A manager approves an investment proposal in R&D to reengineer an aging product. The proposal has a negative NPV, but the manager believes that the R&D may lead to profitable product extensions or entirely new products. This investment consists of an unattractive fixed portion and a valuable call option on new discoveries.

- XYZ Company must choose between two communities, Sparta and Corinth, in locating a new plant. The communities are equally attractive on all counts, except that Sparta has higher taxes but grants companies more flexibility in cleanup of toxic waste spills than Corinth. XYZ chooses Sparta: Even though the DCF value is worse, the option value there is sufficiently greater to overcome the comparatively negative DCF.

In summary, options are pervasive and potentially highly valuable. The standard valuation approach (DCF) ignores option value. On the other hand, investors do not ignore potentially valuable options. To think like an investor, you must incorporate options into your assessment of business opportunities and problems.

PRINCIPLE 5: IF YOU GET CONFUSED, RETURN TO PRINCIPLE 1

No one ever said finance was easy. Business problems are rich and complex. The use of economic models and advanced quantitative methods appears to deepen the complexity. It is easy to become confused. Finance argues that thinking like an investor is an excellent point of departure for sorting out financial problems. Of course, investors themselves rarely agree precisely.[20] No fields in business, however, offer strictly "right" answers—they merely help us avoid the wrong ones. Making financial decisions when you are ignorant of the demands and perspective of investors is a formula for calamity. By thinking like an investor, you increase the likelihood for success.

FOR FURTHER READING

Peter L. Bernstein, *Capital Ideas: The Improbable Origins of Modern Wall Street* (New York: Macmillan, 1992).

Peter L. Bernstein, *Against the Gods* (New York: Wiley, 1996).

Harold Bierman and Seymour Smidt, *The Capital Budgeting Decision,* 8th ed. (New York: Macmillan, 1993).

Thomas Copeland, Michael Koller, and Timothy Murrin, *Valuation* (New York: Wiley, 1994).

William E. Fruhan Jr., *Financial Strategy: Studies in the Creation, Transfer, and Destruction of Shareholder Value* (Homewood: Richard D. Irwin, Inc., 1979).

Sidney Homer and Martin L. Liebowitz, *Inside the Yield Book* (Englewood Cliffs, NJ: Prentice Hall, 1972).

Michael Lewis, *Liar's Poker* (New York: Penguin Books, 1989).

Peter Lynch, *One Up on Wall Street* (New York: Simon & Schuster, 1989).

Burton G. Malkiel, *A Random Walk Down Wall Street,* 4th ed. (New York: Norton, 1985).

Thomas R. Piper and William E. Fruhan Jr., "Is Your Stock Worth its Its Market Price?," *Harvard Business Review,* May–June 1981, pp. 124–132.

G. Bennett Stewart, *The Quest for Value* (New York: HarperCollins Publishers, 1991).

12 HUMAN RESOURCE MANAGEMENT

INTRODUCTION

The classroom looks like any college classroom. The "professor" is talking and showing overhead slides. The "students" are taking notes and raising hands to ask questions. The subject matter "Total Quality Management" indicates a graduate course in business. The university: Motorola University. Motorola requires at least two weeks per year of training and education for all of its employees, from the chief executive officer down through the entire organization. Motorola has decided that its competitive advantage in its businesses can only be maintained through a massive investment in people.

Human resource management (HRM) is the set of philosophies, processes, and procedures that a company uses to manage (1) the entry and exit processes in the firm, (2) the growth and development of employees, (3) the reward and recognition systems, and (4) the total organizational climate for how people are treated.

The purpose of this chapter is to explain how the concept of HRM has evolved from a set of administrative tasks to a set of strategic imperatives and to examine several of these new strategic imperatives that most companies today are dealing with in the competitive global business environment.

In the next section we explain how HRM has evolved from the personnel function to play an important role in managing the affairs of the corporation.

Then we'll discuss the basics of the HRM function in an organization and suggest how these four basic tasks are connected to the traditional ones of personnel. After that we'll show how these four basic tasks are connected to the strategic thrusts of the corporation in light of the new competitive realities. And finally, we'll analyze how HRM can be evaluated in its new strategic role.

HRM: FROM ADMINISTRATION TO STRATEGY

Pick up any textbook on management and turn to the chapter on HRM, or *personnel* as it was called until very recently. You'll find headings such as Manpower Planning, Recruitment, Selection, Socialization, Training and Development, Performance Appraisal, Benefits Administration. The traditional role of the human resources manager was to forecast how many people the company was going to need, to recruit those people, train them, administer their benefits, and keep records of the appraisal processes, promotions, transfers, and so forth. In short, personnel was seen as a purely staff function that performed the necessary tasks of finding and keeping up with the employees. The actual management of the employees was left up to the particular division or function where the employee had direct responsibility. Personnel was strictly an advisory role, though such advice was more often than not codified in thick manuals of "personnel policies." One of the main jobs of personnel managers was to be sure that the company was in compliance with the law, and the surest way to have legal compliance was to issue a set of internal laws in the form of policies.

In many firms, the additional task of labor relations often fell to the personnel department. Here, the jobs of administering the union contract, negotiating new contracts, managing any grievance procedures, and so on required expertise that cut across the traditional operations functions of the firm. While supervisors in the plants managed or directed the work of the employees, the personnel manager was called upon to adjudicate disputes, to interpret the contractual obligations, and to give advice about how to handle situations where conflict was sure to arise.

The paradigm or set of assumptions that underlies this view of HRM as a set of administrative tasks is the idea that a company is a hierarchy, rationally defined by a set of positions or job descriptions. Given that certain jobs need to be performed, then people must be selected and molded to fit those jobs. As long as the external environment is stable, as long as there is little change, then this bureaucratic understanding of the corporation and this administrative view of personnel works very well.

However, as we have argued in earlier chapters, we no longer live in such a world. Today's business world is one of turbulence and change, of decreasing hierarchy and rules, and of people who want to express a large part of themselves through their work. Consequently, personnel has evolved from a largely administrative role to one that seeks to increase the competitive success of the corporation through people-management systems. In the words of James Burke, former CEO of Johnson and Johnson, "The only competitive advantage that we have is what's in the minds of employees."[1]

In today's world, delivering world-class products and services, outstanding customer service, and providing challenging work environments for employees means more than administering the traditional personnel functions. Human resources plans, policies, and systems must support the overall strategic thrusts of the business.

First of all, HRM tasks must be set in the context of the current business environment. HR managers must understand the impact of multiple-country sourcing, the variety of legal environments that companies face in a global business, and the strategic imperatives surrounding costs and quality. Each of the traditional HR tasks must be reinterpreted in light of the new competitive realities. For instance, work today is increasingly being done by teams. It is easy to see that if the compensation system does not recognize the necessity of teams and working in teams, then the human resources function is not supporting the business strategy.

Second, HRM tasks today must reflect the changing nature of the workforce. Today's workforce is more diverse than in the past, and this means new and changing needs. It is probably true that the very idea of a personnel policy to fix everyone's problems is an anathema.

HR managers today must adopt the strategic tasks of aligning the organization's culture with its external environment in general and competitive reality in particular in everything that they do, from training and development to compensation and benefits administration.

THE BASIC TASKS OF HUMAN RESOURCE MANAGEMENT

We've suggested that HRM has four important roles to play in an organization: (1) managing the entry and exit process, (2) managing the growth and development process, (3) managing the reward and recognition process, and (4) managing the overall climate of the organization.

Managing the Entry and Exit Process

Traditionally, the HR function was responsible for forecasting how many and what kinds of people the organization would need in the future, and it went out to recruit the people. Suppose that plant A is going to need 3 new managers and 25 new production workers in the next two years. Typically, such forecasts would be collected for the company as a whole, and a recruiting plan would be developed.

Today, a great deal of college and MBA recruiting is handled by the HR departments in most organizations. Recruiters are dispatched to campuses, and the process eventually ends with the potential recruit being screened by the HR people and the actual unit for which the recruit would work. At lower levels in the organization, each department or division may have an HR person who coordinates the hiring for that division or department.

In addition to the tasks of planning and hiring people, HR managers have also been involved in the exit or separation process. Exit can occur in many different forms, all of which have a different HR role. The normal exit, for most companies, was traditionally retirement. At the end of a career or a number of years of service, the employee retired if he or she had reached an appropriate retirement age. The HR role was really the management of benefits, so that at retirement the employee could enjoy the fruits of years of service and work. HR typically managed the pension process and guided the employee through the maze of regulations that retirement entails, from company retirement plans to health care benefits to Social Security.

A second mode of exit is for the employee to be fired. Traditionally, HR has played a heavy role in the firing process. Typically, a manager about to fire an employee would involve the HR people in the firing process. The HR manager would have knowledge of legal issues regarding the firing, use proper protocols and procedures, and in many cases help the fired employee adjust to the news.

Managing the Growth and Development Process

Managing the growth and development process in an organization includes a number of traditional HR tasks, such as socialization, training and development, and performance appraisal. The growth and development process in an organization should ideally begin the first day on the job. All employees enter an organization with a set of expectations, and the effective human resources manager tries to shape these expectations around opportunities the organization offers to the new employee. Processes must be designed so that the employee understands the overall scope and direction of the organization. Merely doing your job in a narrowly defined way is not good enough in today's business environment.

At Donaldson, Lufkin and Jenrette (DLJ), a New York–based investment bank, new employees hired fresh from college and MBA programs come together for several days to meet each other, to listen to senior executives in the bank talk about their areas of expertise, and to hear outside speakers on a variety of topics such as business ethics. The obvious purpose of such a training program is, of course, the training and education that goes on during the program. A less obvious but equally important objective is that participants learn the DLJ culture—from corporate procedures to the language and dress of the executives. The program serves to begin a complex process of socialization.

At Disney, each new employee goes through a program called "Traditions." The purpose of Traditions is to relate the history of Disney to the employee, to talk about the vision of Walt Disney, and to show how this vision is alive in the company today. When Michael Eisner and Frank Wells took over Disney in the mid-1980s, they went through Traditions along with every other new employee, from executives to street cleaners. The course creates a common experience, a common understanding, and hopefully a common bond among all employees.

Most successful organizations spend a great deal of time and energy on training and development, and this continues to be one of the key tasks of the HR manager. Many HR managers adopt a process in which they conduct a formal needs assessment in an area where the organization needs more skills. After specific needs are identified and analyzed, a training program can be designed and implemented to address these specific needs. Training programs are usually oriented around the acquisition of specific skills, and usually these skills are related to improved work performance. For instance, a company might design a new order entry system that requires that salespeople be trained in the use of the system.

Many companies go beyond training for specific skills—they design education programs or participate in university-run education programs. These programs are meant to increase the overall ability of the participants by giving some business skills, but also by broadening their thinking. Over the past 20 years, thousands of managers and executives have attended education programs at the Darden School at the University of Virginia that are aimed at increasing the ability of participants to make sound business judgments.

Often, training and education are used to address individual development needs of an employee. It is here that the traditional task of performance appraisal is important. Of course, informal appraisal is a daily activity in most organizations. However, no matter how good a particular manager may be in giving informal appraisal and advice to an employee, most organizations have a formal process, resulting in a written document, often signed by the manager and the employee, that serves as an assessment of how well that employee is performing and identifying areas of needed development.

The HR manager does not perform the appraisal, but he or she is responsible for administering the process of performance appraisal. Since appraisals result in written documents, the HR manager is also the keeper of the personnel files that contain important documents such as performance appraisals.

Effective performance appraisals are not just ratings along a set of dimensions that are related to how well an employee does his or her job. They may include a set of critical incidents, specific behaviors, regarding how well an employee performed. By linking specific behaviors to evaluation, employees get a more concrete idea of a manager's expectations.

Managing the Reward and Recognition Process

One of the most critical tasks that HR managers perform is the overall management of how people in the organization are rewarded and recognized. Rewards come through the administration of compensation and benefits, and recognition comes in the form of promotions, job assignments, and rotations. In addition, the process of rewards and recognition includes the countermeasures of demotions and disciplinary action.

There has been a great deal written about the administration of compensation and benefits. Consulting firms such as Hay Associates have elaborate models designed to take into account the existence of market factors in designing compensation systems. The basic idea is that an employee's worth to the firm is roughly the value of the employee's skills in the labor market. To this value is added the degree to which an employee has specialized his or her skills to fit the particular organization and its technology. An employee who has learned to operate a special machine or to use a particular service process may not be able to readily transfer this value to other firms.

Performance appraisal is a critical input into the reward and recognition systems in a company. It is oftentimes during the formal performance appraisal that trouble spots are addressed in employee behavior, and it is a time for development plans that lead to promotions or job transfer. During performance appraisal, employees often take the opportunity to think through their careers and to make known the kinds of challenges they are seeking in the firm.

Managing the Overall Climate

An important element of human resource management is an analysis of the overall organizational climate. Is the company seen by employees as a good place to work? If so, then it will make selection and recruitment a much easier process. Does the organization pay attention to the needs of the employees? What is the climate between management and nonmanagement? Is there a union, and, if so, are labor relations friendly or hostile?

Many companies conduct annual employee surveys. The surveys are conducted anonymously, usually by an outside firm such as the consulting firm of Mercer Associates. The purpose of the survey is to get an overall measure of the organizational work climate, to determine employee satisfaction, and to identify areas of strength and needed improvements.

Most business organizations have a unique corporate culture, a way of doing things that sometimes may be unconscious. Corporate culture is the way that the company has evolved to deal with a complex set of external relationships in its history. For instance, at Du Pont many meetings begin with a discussion of safety. In the words of Du Pont chairman Edgar Woolard, "If you're in the business of making gunpowder, you make it safely, or you don't make it for very long." Du Pont is in many businesses other than gunpowder, but this concern with safety has pervaded these other businesses as well. Employee surveys, climate surveys, and the like are designed to keep a finger on the pulse of the company culture.

HRM IN THE NEW COMPETITIVE REALITY

The four roles of HRM have become enormously more complicated in the changing business environment of the 1990s. As the administrative tasks of personnel have evolved into strategic roles of the new competitiveness, HRM has increasingly become recognized as an important source of competitive advantage. In this section we shall discuss some of the new HRM challenges that managers currently face and are likely to face in the next century.

Entry and Exit Processes

Managing the entry and exit process continues to be an important part of the HR task. Under the set of business assumptions that produced relatively stable hierarchies as the main form of organizational design, there was an implicit (oftentimes made explicit) *psychological contract* (see Chapter 3 for a definition) that assured employees that they would be taken care of in return for their loyalty. The paradigm case was depicted in the novel *The Man in the Gray Flannel Suit.* Employees who excelled at their jobs could expect upward promotion. Those who were average could expect continued employment and gradual increases in pay. Nonmanagement employees could expect few layoffs and a job for life through adequate performance.

In today's world that contract has changed. Almost all large firms have undergone difficult processes of restructuring. Massive layoffs at General Motors, IBM, AT&T, Xerox, Eastman Kodak, to name but a few, have affected managers and nonmanagement employees. According to one survey, middle managers have suffered 19% of the cuts while making up only 8% of the work-force.[2] In an attempt to make organizations more customer-market-focused, many organizations have taken out whole layers of middle managers and drastically curtailed the scope of opportunities for others.

At the same time that middle managers are being restructured, downsized, rightsized, and smartsized (to use a few of the current buzzwords), HR managers are trying to find entry-level employees who have the knowledge and skills to work in the new information technology–rich world of global business. While the effects of downsizing are difficult to determine, we have observed that it can easily lead to a culture of "doom and gloom" as employees anticipate the next restructuring. Some organizations, such as Eastman Kodak, have found that they cut too many people and that such cuts don't always improve performance. Professor W. Warner Burke concludes, "The point about restructuring is that much of what is known shows more negative than positive outcomes."[3]

The HR role in downsizing and restructuring is crucial both for the employees who remain after a large layoff and for those who exit the firm. AT&T won major praise from its employees for taking out an advertisement in newspapers offering its "good people" to other companies. Companies who set up outplacement counseling, give help in finding jobs to those who are displaced, and in general create a "soft landing" for downsized employees have a better chance to manage the normal feelings of anger and guilt felt by those employees who stay as well as those who leave.

A second issue in managing the process of entry and exit of employees is related to the restructuring of firms, and this is *outsourcing:* By taking a hard look at the business processes, a corporation may contract out those processes that can be done more efficiently and effectively by a third party. Employees are replaced by contracts with vendors. For example, many corporations have long outsourced their cafeterias, reasoning that ARA, Marriott, and Guest Services are in the food service business and will provide the service more cost-effectively. The recent wave of outsourcing has included the management of computer and telecommunications systems, legal work, public relations, even the design and manufacture of non-core-technology components.

One standard method for outsourcing is to take workers who were employees and turn them into suppliers. The company reduces its head count and reduces its liability for medical and pension benefits, and the employee becomes a contractor rather than an employee.

Yet another related entry and exit issue is the emergence of temporary workers. Companies may be hesitant to hire more full-time employees and are increasingly opting to hire contract employees on a temporary basis. Once again, the pluses to the company are clear, since there are few benefits to be paid, and temporary workers can more easily be moved around or laid off.

Restructuring, outsourcing, and contracting with temporary workers—all change the methods for entry and exit. The HR manager's job in riding herd on the entry and exit process becomes enormously more complicated. No longer is there one set of policies and procedures that works for all employees, for the simple reason that there are different levels and types of employees. A particular difficulty revolves around the legal tasks of the HR executive: being sure that the company is in compliance with all legal requirements. If temporary workers are treated exactly the same in terms of work assignments, then the company may well be liable for pension benefits, medical benefits, and so forth. When a company is restructured and when work is outsourced, companies must be very careful to be in compliance with laws preventing discrimination by age, gender, or race. Some have argued that restructuring has led to hiring younger, more temporary workers and getting rid of older workers.

Indeed, one of the most talked about HR issues of the 1990s is that of *diversity*. Diversity refers in part to how employees differ with regard to age, gender, race, sexual orientation, physical abilities, and ethnicity. While there are many definitions and dimensions, the basic idea is that in the United States, the workplace has traditionally been seen as the space of the white male. For the past 20-plus years, there has been a growing presence of nonwhite males in the workforce, especially in the managerial workforce.

Traditionally, work has been organized along the lines that suited the one-wage-earner (typically male) family. With the rise of different lifestyles many companies have been forced to rethink the very definitions of work. For example, with two-career managerial couples increasingly the norm, companies have had to rethink their policies about transferring fast-track employees from assignment to assignment. Many companies have opened or begun to sponsor day-care and elder-care centers. There has been a dramatic increase in the use of technology to encourage telecommuting. All of these issues represent an incredible set of changes for the HR manager, but diversity cuts across each of them.

A number of people have asked why the top tiers of most large corporations are heavily weighted with white males. Are the selection processes for senior managers biased? Are the entry processes for employees biased? Increasingly, HR managers have tried to be sure that their hiring and firing processes are free from bias. Now some have argued that such an attempt to "manage diversity" is the correct thing to do from an ethical perspective and that in today's world companies must get the best people in the right positions. There are a number of legal requirements that HR people must be sure the firm follows. In the interviewing process many companies have strict guidelines about questions that are legally off limits, such as "Do you plan to start a family?" (asked of a woman), or culturally insensitive comments like "Some of my best friends are African-American" (said by a white person to an African-American). Diversity training is a growing industry, as companies try to create a climate where everyone can thrive.

The Growth and Development Process

As you might imagine, with shifting processes for entry and exit, there are enormous new challenges in managing the growth and development process for employees. Of course, restructuring, contracting out, and diversity all raise challenges to growth and development.

For starters, if there are increasingly fewer middle-management positions, then the normal way of thinking about careers as a continual stream of promotions is no longer valid. There are more people and fewer managerial positions. Some companies have experimented with lateral career moves whereby an employee is "promoted" based on technical expertise but not necessarily given more managerial authority.

In addition, many organizations today are adopting team-based organization structures in which a team leader emerges or else the team is self-led, meaning there is no formal leader. Training people in effective teamwork and helping them to be good team members is an important HR challenge. In our individualist culture, creating an atmosphere of teamwork and effective teams is not easy.

Performance appraisal has also changed in the new business environment. A number of companies are moving from the traditional boss-subordinate models of performance appraisal to *360 feedback,* which is a process whereby employees receive input from a sample of the people with whom they work and whom they affect. Customer satisfaction data, employees in other departments, peers, teammates, and bosses all provide input into a comprehensive assessment of performance. At AT&T and other companies, many employees participate in the performance appraisal of their boss. If this new idea of management as coaching (see Chapter 3) is to be effective, then the hierarchy must be reversed carefully to provide candor and honesty for performance improvement. With the new emphasis on competitiveness, many companies have tried to turn their performance appraisal processes into more effective tools for performance improvement.

To meet the challenges that we have discussed, some companies like Motorola have taken their traditional concern with training and development to a new level. Indeed, as we said at the start of this chapter, Motorola has its own "university." Motorola claims that for every dollar it spends on education, it receives a $30 return. Motorola has used education as a strategic tool to manage both the entry and exit processes as well as the growth and development processes. For example, rather than laying off an employee, Motorola offers retraining. It figures that the resulting loyalty far outweighs the cost of training, and the company retains an employee who is oriented, socialized, and knows the Motorola culture. Such a human resources policy directly supports Motorola's strategy of dominating its core markets through expertise and technology. When those markets change, the company uses the ability of its employees to learn new skills, thus entering new markets by redirecting its substantial capabilities.

While Motorola is an example of a large company that uses training and education to manage the HR challenges, the much smaller Johnsonville Sausage Company in Wisconsin has a similar approach. At Johnsonville, the purpose of the company, as articulated by owner Ralph Stayer, is to serve as a means for personal growth for its members. At Johnsonville, employees are rewarded for learning, and they receive raises when they learn to do budgeting or production planning or when they are team leader for a while. They learn basic economics and study competitive conditions in the industry. The atmosphere is one of constant improvement, both in the sausages that they make and in the people who make them.

At Lockheed Martin, Freddie Mac, Bell Atlantic, Bethlehem Steel, and a few other companies, there is an emphasis on action learning. Teams of executives are sent to a university-run consortium program at the University of Virginia's Darden School. Executives study the latest management techniques and theories, but also are responsible for applying these ideas to projects that have some strategic significance in their companies. HR's traditional executive development role has thus been put into a new light: exposing executives to new thinking while they are actively engaged in a process that combines learning and work.

Managing the Reward and Recognition Process

Traditionally, the processes that affect compensation have been internally driven by a perceived need for consistency in job descriptions and job scope. Professor Edward Lawler has suggested that companies are beginning more and more to tie compensation to performance and competitive conditions. He calls this trend "the new pay" or "strategic pay."[4]

Strategic pay distinguishes between *base pay*, which is tied to the particular labor market conditions that are relevant, and *incentive pay*, which is tied to individual or organizational performance. By distinguishing between these kinds of rewards, managers can use the compensation system to encourage corporate or subunit goals like teamwork and customer satisfaction. All employees—not just a few top executives with large stock option packages—become engaged in the success of the organization.

In addition to meeting the demands of a changing workforce, more companies are moving to *flexible benefits* or *cafeteria benefits.* Under these arrangements, employees can design their own package of benefits to meet their individual needs. For example, one employee may well need a benefits package with child care and medical care paid for in pretax dollars, whereas another employee may prefer more catastrophic coverage or life insurance. The basic idea behind strategic pay is to design a compensation system that best meets both the employees' and companies' needs for success.

At GE, senior management has used stock options as a form of variable or incentive pay. Managers throughout the GE hierarchy are offered options if their performance and their unit's performance warrants them. GE chairman Jack Welch believes that this is a healthy process even for those who don't get options, because they should have a conversation with their bosses about why they didn't get options. Such candor is conducive to GE's success, according to Welch.[5]

Wal-Mart takes a different approach. After a brief initial period, all employees are encouraged to become actual owners of the company. Everyone, from managers to cashiers, is offered opportunities to buy stock. In addition, profit sharing, incentive compensation, and other techniques all link Wal-Mart "associates" to the success of the firm. Wal-Mart executives are always available to associates. "Mr. Sam" Walton began the practice of visiting stores and listening to employees, and his successors have continued this practice. The compensation system is aligned with the other Wal-Mart values to foster the sense of ownership that makes Wal-Mart a special company with high-performing people.

Managing the Overall Organization Climate

In summary, human resources management in the turbulent business environment of today must foster a climate that challenges employees to better levels of performance. Of course, the organizational climate is not a variable to be managed or even designed. The key notion here is that all of the organization's processes and procedures, from its compliance with the law to its new strategic initiatives, must be aligned. Together, these processes must foster the high-performance atmosphere.

Professors James Heskett and Leonard Schlesinger have studied so-called high-performance or high-capability organizations for a number of years.[6] Leading such high-performance organizations as Wal-Mart, Taco Bell, Southwest Airlines, and ServiceMaster means that the senior managers, including the CEO, are intimately involved in the human resources management process. High-performance cultures are usually based on values and vision that are shared throughout all levels of the organization. Since the values are important in their own right, employees will go to great lengths to realize those values, especially when they are given the latitude and permission to do what it takes to get the job done. High-performance leaders are involved in the entry and exit decisions because they believe that these are some of the most crucial decisions that the organization makes. In these strong-culture companies, people almost "self-select" into and out of the organization. The growth and development of people is based in part on instilling a sense of pride in employees and pride in what they do—without the arrogance that usually accompanies it. To instill this pride, executives must constantly articulate, communicate, and embody the corporate values while setting the performance bar at a very high level.

High-performance organizations reward and recognize people for their contributions great and small. CEOs pay a great deal of attention to being sure that employee contributions are publicized throughout the company and valued.

In addition HR managers in these companies spend time and resources benchmarking "best HR practices" in terms of all of the functions of HR. Exhibit 12.1 lists the results of a survey of best practices across a sample of 110 companies. These practices are roughly equivalent to some of the findings in *Built to Last*. The bottom line is that good HR practices are extremely relevant to financial success.

A number of organizations, such as Legent under former CEO Jere Stead, have taken this idea even further and adopted a model of high performance known as the "employee delight" model. The model distinguishes *delight* from *satisfaction*. Employees find not only satisfaction but joy in what they do—they are delighted. The idea is that employee delight leads to customer delight leads to shareholder returns and reinvestment in employee delight. Pumped-up and engaged employees will go the extra mile to satisfy customers, so they return again and again to buy products and services from the firm. In these workplaces, employee delight is seen as the key driver of financial success.

In all of these high-performance workplaces we find the idea that employees are not there merely to put in time and do a job. Rather, work is engaging to them; their teams and tasks matter because the organization plays an important role in their lives. Work has the connotation of joy and imagination and fun rather than drudgery and something to be sharply distinguished from play. The

EXHIBIT 12.1 Eight best human asset management practices.

Values: A constant focus on adding value in everything rather than simply doing something. In addition, there is a conscious, ongoing, and largely successful attempt to balance human and financial values.

Commitment: Dedication to a long-term core strategy. They seek to build an enduring institution while changing methods but avoiding the temptation to chase management fads.

Culture: Proactive application of the corporate culture. Management is aware of how culture and systems can be linked together for consistency and efficiency.

Communication: An extraordinary concern for communicating with all stakeholders. Constant and extensive two-way communication using all media and sharing all types of vital information is the rule.

Partnering: New markets demand new forms of operation. They involve people within and outside the company in many decisions. This includes the design and implementation of new programs.

Collaboration: A high level of cooperation and involvement of all sections *within* functions. They study, redesign, launch, and follow up new programs in a collective manner, enhancing efficiency and cohesiveness.

Innovation and risk: Innovation is recognized as a necessity. There is a willingness to risk shutting down present systems and structure and restarting in a totally different manner while learning from failure.

Competitive passion: A constant search for improvement. They set up systems and processes to actively seek feedback and incorporate ideas from all sources.

Source: Jac Fitz-enz, "The Truth about Best Practices," *Human Resource Management*, spring 1997, vol. 36, no. 1, p. 100.

human resource challenges of the next century will involve more attention to the processes of innovation, creativity, and fun, while continuing to find creative ways to do the administrative tasks that are a vital part of a firm's success.

EVALUATING HRM EFFECTIVENESS

How are we to evaluate whether human resources has adopted this new strategic role that we have argued is so important? While there are no magic formulas to use, we can look to a number of experiences. First of all, we turn to business practice. Exhibit 12.2 gives a set of principles articulated by Clifford Ehrlich, senior vice president of human resources at Marriott International, for effective human resources management.

Second, we look to the academic world, where many companies and many practices have been studied over time. In particular, we turn to Professor Michael Beer and his colleagues at the Harvard Business School, who have suggested four criteria for evaluating the success of the new human resources function in an organization.

EXHIBIT 12.2   Principles for building the future.

1. Human resource strategy must be anchored in the business strategy.
2. Human resource management is not about programs; it's about relationships.
3. The human resource department must be known as an organization that anticipates change and understands what is necessary to implement it.
4. Human resources should be an outspoken advocate of employee interests, yet it must understand that business decisions have to balance a range of factors that often conflict with one another.
5. The effectiveness of HR depends on staying focused on issues rather than personalities.
6. Human resource executives must accept that constant learning and skill enhancement are essential to their being contributors to the business.

Source: Clifford J. Ehrlich, "Human Resource Management: A Changing Script for a Changing World," *Human Resource Management,* spring 1997, vol. 36, no. 1, p. 87.

The first criterion is *competence.* HRM is effective if there are people performing their tasks in an effective matter. We would suggest that in today's world a large part of the idea of competence is the employee's ability to work in a changing world. Hence, adaptability and flexibility must be built into competence.

The second and third criteria are *commitment* and *congruence.* HRM is effective if the employees are committed to the company and what it stands for. Commitment happens when there is a congruence between the company goals and employee goals. Commitment and congruence are more easily garnered when the company has a core set of purposes or values that resonate with those of the employees at all levels.

Finally, HRM must be *cost-effective.* In today's world, simply paying more is not the answer. Effectiveness means low turnover, few absentees, very few strikes, and a long line of people at the door who can't wait to sign up to work for the company.

Human resources management is an exciting and vibrant field of inquiry and practice. The current business environment dictates that people really are central to a corporation's success. And it is only with aligned human resource systems and creative human resource managers that corporations can create the kinds of cultures that allow companies to thrive across the globe.

FOR FURTHER READING

P. B. Beaumont, *Human Resource Management: Key Concepts and Skills* (London: Sage Publishers, 1993). This is a non-U.S.-oriented text with a comprehensive overview of HR issues.

M. Beer, B. Spector, P. Lawrence, D. Mills, and R. Walton, *Human Resource Management: A General Manager's Perspective*, 1st ed. (New York: Free Press, 1985). This classic statement of how HR should be every manager's job has been written by a team of professors from the Harvard Business School.

A. Harzing and J. Van Ruysseveldt, *International Human Resource Management* (London: Sage Publishers, 1995). This is a sourcebook of essays by leading thinkers and practitioners in the HR field, especially dealing with issues of globalization of HR.

Human Resources Management, The Society of Human Resource Management and John Wiley & Sons. This journal represents the best new thinking in the field of HR.

R. Noe, J. Hollenbeck, B. Gerhart, and P. Wright, *Human Resources Management: Gaining a Competitive Advantage* (Chicago: Irwin, 1997). This is an encyclopedic textbook that combines the traditional personnel administrative tasks with the new strategic tasks of HR.

13 STRATEGY: DEFINING AND DEVELOPING COMPETITIVE ADVANTAGE

The central goal of a firm is sustained, superior return on investment. *Superior* returns, relative to other competitors in the industry, require a sustainable competitive advantage (that is, a way of providing value to customers that is unmatched by competitors). *Sustained* profits require investment in capabilities that enable the advantage to be improved and renewed in the future. *Strategy*, therefore, is concerned with the definition of competitive advantage and the development of activities, resources, and capabilities that enable the firm to sustain advantage in a changing world.[1]

Essentially, strategy is the definition of how a firm competes (see Exhibit 13.1). Strategy defines the firm's competitive position in an industry and develops consistency of purpose among the firm's activities to achieve that position. Strategy is not a detailed plan describing what the firm will do; instead, it provides direction for making significant choices and strong guidance about what the firm will *not* do.

The strategy development process creates insight about how to position the firm for sustainable competitive advantage. The challenge of strategic planning is to open the minds of managers, provide new perspectives on threats and opportunities, challenge conventional wisdom, and develop a vision of the firm's competitive advantage. Exhibit 13.2 defines the three levels of strategy.

EXHIBIT 13.1   What is strategy?

Michael E. Porter defines strategy as creating a company's position, making trade-offs, and forging fit among activities:

> "Strategy is the creation of a unique and valuable position, involving a different set of activities."
> "Strategy is making trade-offs in competing. The essence of strategy is deciding what not to do."
> "Strategy is creating fit among a company's activities."

Source: Michael E. Porter, "What Is Strategy?," *Harvard Business Review,* November–December 1996, p. 62.

THE STRATEGY DEVELOPMENT PROCESS

"Plans are worthless; planning is priceless."
—Dwight David Eisenhower

A variety of strategy development approaches are used in practice, such as frameworks for analyzing industry profitability, competitive positioning, core competencies, capabilities, resources, strategic intent, and future scenarios.[2] Each of these frameworks provides a guide for thinking through critical questions; none provide answers. The "answers" come in the form of the insights generated by the process. Using any of the frameworks well is an art, so different managers may find they are more effective in developing insights with different frameworks.

Think of a framework as a box. The box limits vision if you step into it and close the lid, but it expands vision if you stand on top for a better view of the horizon. Thus, the value of a strategy framework can be seriously limited by the person using it. Be skeptical when someone says that a given framework is useless; the statement may simply mean that the person has other frameworks in mind for the same purpose, or it may mean that person does not know how to use the framework to develop insight. Frameworks used only to validate old views are useless. Frameworks must be used to gain insight and inspire vision, to see new perspectives and develop new ideas.

Also be alert to the allure of the latest and greatest frameworks and buzzwords. Although new approaches for thinking about strategy can help managers to perceive new opportunities, the danger is that popular strategy fads encourage rivals to compete in similar ways and thus undermine the firm's attention to competing differently from other firms. Competing *differently*—with unique positioning, special target customers, or innovative ways of performing activities—is the essence of competitive advantage.

EXHIBIT 13.2   Three levels of strategy: corporate, competitive, functional.

A firm's strategy is often discussed at three levels: corporate or multibusiness strategy, competitive or business unit strategy, and functional strategy within a business. This chapter focuses on competitive strategy. Functional strategies are discussed in Chapters 7, 8, and 9.

Corporate strategy is the definition of the firm's values as expressed in financial and nonfinancial goals. It centers on the identification and building or acquisition of key resources and capabilities and entails the decisions of which industries the firm will compete in and how the businesses will be linked. Corporate strategy determines how resources will be allocated among the businesses of the firm, and thus the constraints on what the firm will do and will not do.

Competitive strategy defines how a firm competes in a given industry. A firm's competitive strategy is how the firm creates a valuable position in the industry. This involves a vision (explicit or implicit) of what customers the firm serves and how it delivers value for them. But competitive strategy is more than vision; it is the combination of specific activities and processes throughout the firm's operations that enable a firm to create unique value for customers. Thus, strategy also entails the fit among the firm's activities so that efforts throughout the firm consistently reinforce the potential advantage in the firm's competitive positioning.

Functional strategies, such as marketing strategy, financial strategy, research and technology strategy, and operations strategy, reinforce the firm's competitive strategy and define activities and processes to enable the firm to achieve the benefit of its competitive position. Articulating and analyzing functional strategies clarify whether and how the firm's functions fit with the competitive strategy and focus explicit attention on the coordination among functions.

A complete strategy development process includes using several frameworks and doing a lot of creative thinking about the implications of the analysis. The seven-step process outlined in Exhibit 13.3 covers the critical strategy questions from a variety of perspectives.

STEP 1: INDUSTRY ANALYSIS—INDUSTRY PROFITABILITY TODAY AND TOMORROW

One of the fundamental insights of competitive strategy is that average profitability varies among industries. Average return on investment in the pharma-

EXHIBIT 13.3   The seven steps of the strategy development process.

1. Industry analysis—industry profitability today and tomorrow.
2. Positioning—sources of competitive advantage.
3. Competitor analysis—past and predicted.
4. Audit of position—assessment of relative position and sustainability.
5. Option generation—a creative look at new customers and positions.
6. Assessment of capabilities—positioning for future opportunities.
7. Choose a strategy—position, trade-offs, fit.

ceutical industry in the late 1980s and early 1990s was about 25%, whereas the trucking industry achieved only about 5% on average. Those differences in averages are due to structural differences in the industries; the key for a firm in either industry is to outperform the average and achieve superior return relative to its competitors.[2]

Industry analysis is critical for several reasons.

- First, the success of the firm is indicated by its *return relative to other firms in the industry.* A 15% rate of return in trucking in the early 1990s was impressive, but a 15% rate of return in pharmaceuticals indicated serious underperformance.

- Second, industry analysis allows managers to *understand the drivers of industry profitability* and thus how it may change in the future. A common mistake is to analyze only the current profitability, but much of the power of the analysis is in using it to consider potential future changes and their implications for the firm's strategy.

- Third, different segments of the industry may have different profit potential. Industry analysis can help to identify the *attractive and unattractive segments.*

- Fourth, the current level of industry average profitability should not be taken for granted. Firms may have significant opportunities to *improve industry structure* or to prevent its deterioration. These opportunities may apply throughout the industry or in a specific industry segment.

- Fifth, industry analysis provides a good first *test on the rigor of new strategy frameworks and approaches.* Frequently, the examples claimed to prove the validity of the latest strategy fad can be entirely explained by differences in industry average profitability, leaving the additional insight of the new model in question.

Determinants of Industry Profitability

Industry profitability (or "attractiveness") can be analyzed by considering five forces: buyer power, supplier power, rivalry, the threat of substitutes and the threat of new entry.[3] Exhibit 13.4 displays these five forces and the drivers of their power. By assessing the strength of each of these forces, one can understand and predict industry average profitability. So, for example, the high average profitability of the pharmaceutical industry in the 1980s and early 1990s was explained by industry structure. Buyer power was low because patients did not shop based on price. Doctors chose products with little reason to consider price;

patients paid. The threat of substitution was low because substitutes of other types of therapy or doing without treatment usually offered little value compared to effective pharmaceuticals. Supplier power was low because the inputs tended to be available from multiple sources. Rivalry was limited by firms competing in different niches with patent protection. The threat of new entry was blocked not only by patents, but also by the complicated regulatory process for new drug

EXHIBIT 13.4   The five competitive forces that determine industry profitability.

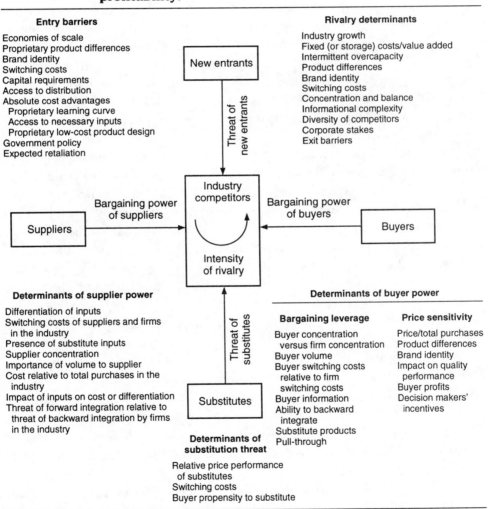

Entry barriers

Economies of scale
Proprietary product differences
Brand identity
Switching costs
Capital requirements
Access to distribution
Absolute cost advantages
  Proprietary learning curve
  Access to necessary inputs
  Proprietary low-cost product design
Government policy
Expected retaliation

Rivalry determinants

Industry growth
Fixed (or storage) costs/value added
Intermittent overcapacity
Product differences
Brand identity
Switching costs
Concentration and balance
Informational complexity
Diversity of competitors
Corporate stakes
Exit barriers

Determinants of supplier power

Differentiation of inputs
Switching costs of suppliers and firms
  in the industry
Presence of substitute inputs
Supplier concentration
Importance of volume to supplier
Cost relative to total purchases in the
  industry
Impact of inputs on cost or differentiation
Threat of forward integration relative to
  threat of backward integration by firms
  in the industry

Determinants of buyer power

Bargaining leverage

Buyer concentration
  versus firm concentration
Buyer volume
Buyer switching costs
  relative to firm
  switching costs
Buyer information
Ability to backward
  integrate
Substitute products
Pull-through

Price sensitivity

Price/total purchases
Product differences
Brand identity
Impact on quality
  performance
Buyer profits
Decision makers'
  incentives

Determinants of substitution threat

Relative price performance
  of substitutes
Switching costs
Buyer propensity to substitute

New entrants

Threat of new entrants

Industry competitors

Bargaining power of suppliers

Suppliers

Bargaining power of buyers

Buyers

Intensity of rivalry

Threat of substitutes

Substitutes

Source: Reprinted with the permission of The Free Press, a division of Simon & Schuster, from *Competitive Advantage: Creating and Sustaining Superior Performance* by Michael E. Porter. Copyright © 1985 by Michael E. Porter.

approval and the difficulty of establishing sales forces and distribution systems. Even a firm with a new biotech drug might need to ally with a major drug company to produce, market, and distribute its product.

Conversely, the trucking industry faced large, powerful, price-sensitive buyers that could easily switch to other truckers. Suppliers included large automakers as well as powerful unionized labor. Substitutes such as rail and airfreight provided real alternatives. Rivalry was intense because many competitors were vying for the same business without distinct strategic positions. Entry was as easy as leasing a truck, although given the other industry forces, one would not expect to make much money doing that.

In general, to do an industry analysis one must gather data and make observations about the considerations listed in Exhibit 13.4. Although the examples of pharmaceuticals and trucking are unambiguous, the picture is often less clear. Frequently, some forces are positive and others negative, so one must assess the strength of the forces and qualitatively weigh the overall picture. Often, one can also gather profitability data about some firms in the industry and use that to help calibrate current profitability.

It is critical, however, not to stop the analysis with a judgment about current industry average profitability. Much of the power of the analysis is in the view of the future that it can provide. The next step is to consider trends and possible changes in the industry and then analyze how these changes would affect profitability. For example, if current buyer power is moderate and supplier power is low but both are increasing, the industry can be expected to be less profitable in the future. As a result, rivalry is likely to become more intense unless the firm can position itself to compete in an industry segment where competitors are unlikely to venture or succeed.

The pharmaceutical industry provides an example of industry structural change under way. Buyer power is increasing as buyers consolidate. Large government payers and HMOs are covering drugs and becoming price-sensitive to a degree that individual patients never were. Rivalry is increasing as generics become increasingly common and as price pressure fuels competition. The threat of substitute products is increasing in markets where over-the-counter alternatives are available. And the threat of new entry by biotech companies is increasing. A few biotech firms have even managed to develop their own marketing and distribution channels.

Industry analysis of separate industry segments can be used to consider which segments are most profitable or are likely to be more profitable in the future. For example, proprietary drugs have a much more profitable industry structure than generics. Similarly, future industry analysis can sound a critical warning about industry segments that are likely to experience a serious decline in profits.

Analysis of future industry structure is a tough step to perform because change is difficult to predict. Established firms often get trapped in conventional wisdom and lulled by widely shared forecasts, making them less able to see the problems and opportunities presented by possible future change. Thus, free-ranging brainstorming about the future and challenges to conventional wisdom about the industry should be encouraged in this process. It is often useful to ask what the competitors might predict, which technologies might leapfrog those currently used, and how a seemingly very unlikely future might be explained if it came to pass. Used in this manner, industry analysis is a powerful tool for developing insights about strategy for future success.

STEP 2: POSITIONING—SOURCES OF COMPETITIVE ADVANTAGE

Positioning analysis addresses the question of why some firms outperform industry average profitability and others fail to achieve it. Superior performance demands that a firm have a sustainable competitive advantage and invest in the development of capabilities that will enable it to renew that advantage as the future unfolds.

Fundamentally, competitive advantage stems from superior value creation for customers. *Value* in this context is the way a consumer thinks when shopping; it is enhanced either by a lower price for the same good or by qualities or features that are superior for a given customer. As in the common usage, an inferior product may not be a good value, even at a low price. Conversely, a superior product at too high a price is not a good value.

In strategy, the two sources of superior value creation for customers are known as *lower cost* and *differentiation*. (See Exhibit 13.5.) In both cases, competitive advantage stems from offering more value to customers than competitors offer. This additional value is delivered by performing activities and processes differently from competitors in ways that reinforce or accentuate the value.

Analysis of positioning is often facilitated with a diagram such as a "value chain" (see Exhibit 13.6) or "business system map." These diagrams picture all of the firm's activities and processes from procurement to after-sales service, including also research and development and overhead activities. They are used to enable or encourage a thorough analysis of how each activity throughout the firm affects costs and differentiation. They may also be used to identify impor-

EXHIBIT 13.5   Types of competitive advantage.

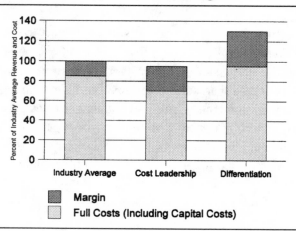

tant processes or linkages among activities that span several functions or are performed through alliances or by suppliers.

Increasingly, competition takes the form of a network (a loose alliance of a firm with its suppliers and distributors) competing with other firms or other networks.[4] A firm may perform activities differently and increase value for its customers by the way it manages the linkages among its own activities or by the way it manages the linkages with other firms in its network. This underscores the potential benefit of coordination among firms in a network to lower the overall

EXHIBIT 13.6   The value chain.

Firm infrastructure				
Human resource management				
Technology development				
Procurement				
Inbound logistics	Operations	Outbound logistics	Marketing and sales	Service

cost for customers or enhance the noncost elements of value delivered, such as shorter lead times or better service. Rather than focus on appropriating value from buyers and suppliers in the firm's network, the cooperative mind-set of network management needs to consider how the network as a whole can create the most value. Relationships need to be built and managed so that each player in the network profits by advancing the network's strategic position. These relationships can be complicated because firms may cooperate in some activities and compete in others.

Cost Leadership: Equal Quality at Lower Costs

Cost leadership stems from performing activities and processes (or groups of activities) in less expensive ways than competitors. It is not a matter of providing inferior products or services; indeed, matching (or exceeding) the quality of competing products or services is critical for providing greater value to customers. Above-average returns result from being able to earn a higher margin than competitors earn for equal-quality products without charging a higher price (as pictured in Exhibit 13.5) or from selling an equal-quality product with the same margins as competitors, but at a lower price and thus commanding a bigger market share. Sometimes the firm can achieve cost advantage by offering a lower price to a focused group of customers that is happy to forego certain product features or service attributes. Because these customers do not care about the additional features, they view an inherently less costly product as having equal quality, and they benefit from its lower price.

Brilliant examples of cost leadership, such as Crown Cork & Seal (metal containers), have strong consistency of purpose throughout the firm's functions. Crown Cork & Seal's "no-waste, no-nonsense" approach to cost saving included relentless attention to detail. Its tile floors and metal desks left no doubt about its attention to cost reduction. R&D did not focus on innovation, since the fast-follower approach was cheaper. But not all R&D expenses were pruned. R&D expertise was available to customers with problems on their canning lines. Superior customer service built loyalty, reduced marketing costs, and increased economies of scale; thus it was not a "frill" but a savvy approach to implementing the low-cost strategy.

Gallo Wines' successful cost leadership includes economical purchasing of grapes, specially developed blending technology, low-cost bottling operations, and distribution through supermarkets. National advertising may sound like an expensive practice for a cost leader, but it reinforces the cost advantages of volume production and supermarket distribution.

Differentiation: Value above and beyond the Premium Price

Differentiation is a matter of delivering value for which customers are willing to pay a premium. Thus, differentiation is much more than simply offering a different or better product. The key to success is making additional (costly) expenditures only on activities or features that cost the firm less than the value they add for customers. Diligent cost cutting remains important in all areas that do not affect the differentiation for which customers will pay a premium price. The result is usually a premium-priced product or service, but it is still a good value (or even a "bargain") to customers who desire the additional benefit of convenience, customization, special service, durability, or some other dimension of nonprice value. As this suggests, differentiation often involves choosing a defined customer base and not trying to serve other customers who value different attributes than the company's target market.

As in a well-executed low-cost strategy, well-executed differentiation shows up in many processes or activities performed differently from those of competitors. For example, Sony achieves differentiation in high-quality consumer electronics with extensive R&D into new consumer applications, minimal defects in manufacturing, an authorized sales and service network, and responsive after-sales service. Many of these activities entail extra expense to achieve the quality that differentiates Sony. On the other hand, Sony reduces costs with efficient-scale facilities and tight cost control.

Drivers of Competitive Advantage

While discussions of competitive advantage often focus on the value perceived by customers, the firm must understand the sources of advantage in terms of specific activities or processes that it performs throughout the firm to reduce costs or increase nonprice value. This is where the functional strategies within the firm come into play. Excellence in the implementation of each function is critical to achieving advantage, but the functions must be well coordinated or they may undermine each others' efforts. The role of strategy is to guide the fit among the various functions and coordinate efforts toward a common, clearly communicated vision.

Failure to understand actual costs is a common pitfall for both low-cost and differentiation strategies. It helps to consider each function of the firm (including support activities as well as line operations) and attempt to compare costs of that function with competitors' costs. This analysis should then be followed by a hard look at possible ways to reduce costs further or enhance the nonprice value added for customers. Careful thinking through how, why, and when the product

EXHIBIT 13.7   Cost drivers and differentiation drivers.

Cost Drivers	Differentiation Drivers
Scale	*Intrinsic*
Learning	Product quality
Capacity utilization	Product variety
Linkages within the value chain	Bundled services
Interrelationships across business	Timing and delivery
Levels of integration	*Signals of Value*
Timing	Reputation or image
Location	Cumulative advertising
Institutional factors	Product appearance
	Installed base
	Price

Source: Reprinted with the permission of The Free Press, a division of Simon & Schuster, from *Competitive Advantage: Creating and Sustaining Superior Performance* by Michael E. Porter. Copyright © 1985 by Michael E. Porter.

or service is used often adds ideas for ways to accentuate value that were not initially obvious. In addition, the "drivers" of low cost and differentiation listed in Exhibit 13.7 may spark other ideas for sources of improvement.

STEP 3: COMPETITOR ANALYSIS—PAST AND PREDICTED

Although common sense points to the importance of analyzing competitors before deciding how to compete, ignoring competitors is a frequent mistake.

- Clorox should have predicted that a new product combining bleach and detergent would be swiftly matched by Procter & Gamble, but it did not anticipate that response when it entered the detergent market in 1988. Clorox might even have predicted that the marketing muscle of P&G and the strength of the Tide brand would have the net effect of reducing the bleach market, yet Clorox faced that outcome as an unpleasant surprise.

- Epson may have predicted that offering a low-priced laser printer in 1989 would hasten the decline of the dot-matrix printer market. But it appears to have assumed that the decline would not matter because loyal Epson customers would buy Epson laser printers. Epson failed to foresee that Hewlett-Packard, the leader in laser printers, would notice the competitive entry and could lower prices. The unfortunate result for Epson was the accelerated decline of its dot-matrix market combined with rapid growth in HP's laser printer sales, rather than Epson's.

The moral of these all too common stories is that a vital step in strategy development is viewing the issues and opportunities from the perspective of specific competitors. You should consider not only how competitors may react, but also what strategic initiatives competitors may pursue. Although managers often mistakenly assume that competitors are caught in a state of inertia, they should instead assume that competitors are pushing ahead at full speed. Ongoing analysis of the competitors' perspective is important for avoiding unpleasant surprises that you later realize were predictable.

Beyond improving prediction of competitors' moves, competitor analysis may enable a firm to influence those moves. Again, rather than stopping with an improved understanding of the situation a firm faces, managers can use strategic analysis to spur thinking about ways to reshape the future. In addition, competitor analysis provides a new perspective on an individual's own business and on relative sources of competitive advantage.

Considerations for Competitor Analysis

Competitors' moves and reactions are often consistent with their stated goals, their past assumptions, their known strengths and weaknesses, and their leaders' public statements. Thus, to do a competitor analysis, you should assess the following for each competitor:

- Current strategy (market position and source of advantage).
- Leadership (recent or anticipated changes).
- Capabilities (cost position, value provided to customers, exclusive relationships, proprietary skills or processes, intangible assets, etc.).
- Future goals (what, when, and why).
- Assumptions (their view of the future market and of competitors).
- Stakes (economic, strategic, and emotional).
- Signals they have sent to other firms.

A surprisingly clear picture of competitors' future intents can be developed from public sources and customer and supplier comments. The trick is to develop the competitor's profile rather than to get caught in the trap of just collecting data that validate current assumptions about the competitor. Then, as competitive moves are chosen, managers must also keep in mind the general characteristics of good moves and poor tactics displayed in Exhibit 13.8.

EXHIBIT 13.8   Competitive dynamics: good moves and poor tactics.

Good Moves . . .	Poor Tactics . . .
Hard for your competitor to match —Would cost their firm more	Simply raising advertising —Easy to match —Little commitment value
Fit with the firm's capabilities	Price cuts by a higher-cost firm —Give lower-cost competitors an advantage —Intensify rivalry; provoke price wars
Help (or at least do not damage) industry structure	Damage industry structure
Aim at blind spots or empty positions	Copy competitors
Anticipate the competition	Try to influence competitor *after* it has made commitments
Respond with appropriate force (tit for tat)	Provoke competitors
Are clear (or well signaled)	Cause emotional reactions
Have commitment value	
—Are costly to reverse	
—Intentions will be believed	

STEP 4: AUDIT OF POSITION—ASSESSMENT OF RELATIVE POSITION AND SUSTAINABILITY

Assessment of the firm's competitive position in the industry integrates the insights from analysis of the industry, the firm's position, and the competitors. At this point it is critical to clearly identify the firm's current position in the industry, in terms of both its financial results and its strategy. The insights from the previous stages of the strategy process may provide a new perspective on the firm's strengths and weaknesses relative to others in the industry.

The trend toward networks of alliances among firms means that a firm may need to assess the position of its network relative to other networks. A cooperative mind-set is then required to consider how the weaknesses in a network can be corrected by combined efforts, such as working more closely together, sharing information, or changing processes to improve coordination or reduce costs.

It is also critical at this stage to go beyond the analysis of the present to consider the sustainability of the firm's (or network's) competitive advantage in the future. Even stunning current success does not guarantee the future. Examples abound of leaders assailed, such as Fairchild in semiconductors, Kodak in film, or Caterpillar in earth-moving equipment. Over time, new products and services become more commonplace, easier to copy, or less valuable relative to more recent innovations. Without investment and improvement, a firm's profitability will fall as other firms invest and improve.

Generally, threats to sustainability fall into four categories: imitation, substitution, appropriation of value by firms upstream or downstream (termed *holdup*), and shrinkage in profits due to rising costs of salaries, discretionary expenditures, or changes in the division of revenues among partners (termed *slack*).[5]

STEP 5: OPTION GENERATION—A CREATIVE LOOK AT NEW CUSTOMERS AND POSITIONS

Change, often viewed as a threat to profitability, is the most powerful source of new opportunities. The insights from strategic analysis can help firms to identify new needs, new customers, new distribution channels, promising new technologies, and, generally, new competitive positions.

To generate options, you want to think in an entrepreneurial mind-set, adopt the perspective of industry outsiders, and challenge conventional wisdom about how to compete. The goal is to generate a broad, creative list of truly different strategies. New strategic positions are not obvious; they rely on inspiration, vision, and insight. On the other hand, the quality of the brainstorming of future strategic possibilities can be greatly enhanced by a solid understanding of the industry, customers, competitors, and firm's own strengths. The trick is to avoid narrow thinking about traditional ways of competing.

Remember that a strategic position defines how a firm creates value for its customers. Fundamentally, a firm needs to focus on its customers' goals and values. New positions will stem from new ways of creating value or from serving new sets of customers. This means that following competitors and copying their positioning is a mistake. Copying increases competition without adding new value. It also means that unserved customer groups or empty strategic positions may present important opportunities. New strategic positions stem from finding better ways to provide the value the customer seeks. When the customer is a business, insight is gained by looking for ways to improve how that business serves its customers.

STEP 6: ASSESSMENT OF CAPABILITIES—POSITIONING FOR FUTURE OPPORTUNITIES

Future success of the firm depends critically on the capabilities the firm develops. New strategic positions usually require additional capabilities that cannot be acquired or built overnight and that are costly to reverse, so the investment is at least partly irretrievable. Thus the options under consideration must be analyzed from the perspective of required future capabilities. Developing those capabilities will involve a series of investments and changes in activities or processes. The direction and vision can be specified, but the precise steps cannot. The point is that each of the strategic options under consideration may have different implications for development of capabilities, because different capabilities support different sources of competitive advantage. The difficulty of developing the required capabilities and the potential payoffs from the capabilities should be explored.

Komatsu's strategy in earth-moving equipment shows a progression of capability development. Threatened by Caterpillar in Japan in the 1960s, Komatsu first developed improved quality, then undertook serious cost reduction. Komatsu next developed export markets, and then in the 1970s launched significant efforts in new product development. In the 1960s, critical capabilities were product and process excellence to defend its home market. In the 1970s, future success required more; it required innovation to shape the new product offerings and lead the market.

Although some argue that developing capabilities is an implementation issue, it is important to consider future capabilities and the investments they require in the strategy development process for three reasons. First, a strategic position is a path, not a point. The dynamic development of the path should not be taken for granted. Analyzing required capabilities focuses the decision makers on the future. Second, the development of future capabilities may require significant current investments that are costly to reverse, either in terms of money or in terms of reputation or relationships that affect future returns. Analysis of these investments is an important aspect of choosing a strategy. Third, some capabilities can be gained effectively through network relationships among firms, but others will be less expensive or more effective if the firm develops them itself.

Investing in development capabilities is risky in the usual (financial) sense of investing capital for uncertain returns. *Not* investing, however, is at least as risky, but in the strategic sense of falling behind or failing to sustain profits. Compromised capabilities lead to lost opportunities. And lost opportunities lead to failing to improve capabilities. A vicious cycle of failure may result.

STEP 7: CHOOSE A STRATEGY—POSITION, TRADE-OFFS, FIT

Competitive advantage stems from difference: serving different needs, different customers, or different geographic locations or providing different access, different products, or different dimensions of value. The point is to find a way of creating value that customers will not get from other sources. The most common error in choosing strategy is *imitation*. Successful strategy requires choices *not* to follow competitors.

Another common error is to try to eliminate the trade-offs between firms' different competitive positions. Superficially, it may seem advantageous to be able to match the competitor, but you must remember that eliminating trade-offs makes both firms' positions more vulnerable. Strategy should aim to sharpen the trade-offs between positions, not to eliminate the trade-offs. In addition to making competitive advantage more sustainable, very distinct positions can improve industry structure.

Strong leadership is necessary to define the firm's different, unique position and delineate directions in which the firm will not go. Strong leadership is also necessary to communicate the strategy clearly so that choices made by managers throughout the firm will be consistent with the firm's positioning. That consistency is critical to the successful implementation of strategy; without it, decisions made at the functional level (i.e., in marketing, operations, or finance) may work against each other, or even against the source of competitive advantage that the firm seeks.[6]

With increasingly global competition, part of the challenge of creating fit among activities and consistency with strategic goals is deciding where to configure activities around the globe and how to coordinate dispersed activities.[7] Generally, large economies of scale, steep learning curves, and tough coordination issues push toward the decision to concentrate activities rather than disperse them around the globe. Dispersion is increasingly attractive when local market needs or governments require local presence, transportation costs are high, learning is country-specific, or a single site has significant risks that can be hedged with multiple locations.

When activities are dispersed, the challenge of creating fit and consistency among activities is accentuated. Information, knowledge, and technology from diverse locations must be effectively integrated. Strategic goals and choices must be clearly communicated throughout the worldwide functions of the firm. Because these challenges make an effective global configuration difficult to copy, well-executed coordination can make appropriately dispersed activities a significant source of competitive advantage.

Evaluating a strategy is not a simple matter of looking at results. Because the goal is sustained, superior return on investment, short-term profits are not a sufficient indicator of success. Indeed, some firms that achieved brilliant success began with five or more years of negative cash flows. So how do you know if a strategy is good?

- A good strategy reflects and reinforces the values of the firm's leaders.

- A good strategy has at its center a specific understanding of competitive advantage. This understanding should be clear enough to state its essence in a single sentence.

- A good strategy is consistent. It is pursued consistently throughout the firm's functions, creating a whole that is strongly reinforced and greater than the sum of its parts.

- A good strategy does not flip-flop over time. It defines a dynamic path that clearly bounds the firm's choices but does not constrain the firm from adjusting to the uncertain future.

STRATEGY: COMMITMENT OR FLEXIBILITY?

There is a long-standing debate about whether the essence of strategy is commitment or flexibility. One side argues that strategy requires commitment, so place your bets wisely. Strategy does require commitment, but this advice is about as useful as "buy low, sell high." It doesn't provide insight about *how* to choose wise bets. The other side argues that in a changing world, strategy requires flexibility, so keep your options open. Strategy does require flexibility given the world's uncertainty, but this advice is about as useful as "do nothing risky." You cannot keep all options open, and this advice does not tell *which* options to foreclose.

Strategy actually requires *both* commitment and flexibility. The two are not in conflict when you recognize that a firm must make investments now (commitments) in order to develop the capabilities (flexibility) that will enable it to succeed in the changing and uncertain future. Strategy defines the types of capabilities in which to invest and the types of investments to forego. Commitment to a vision of the essence of the firm's competitive advantage is critical. That vision points to a path of strategic positioning that is not fully defined or planned in advance. Choices along the way are guided by consistency with the vision. This means that the vision has to be explicit about how the firm differs from competitors, rather than simply stressing high quality, leadership, or other laudable but vague goals.

Flexibility is developed through investments in building capabilities that other firms will not have without similar advance investments.[8] For example, prior investments in a product line create the option to expand the line. Prior investments in new technologies enable the firm to use these technologies or to apply them better (or less expensively) than competitors as the future unfolds. Prior investments in processes and organizational knowledge enable the firm to perform its activities in ways that competitors cannot easily match.

In short, flexibility is not a strategic position, but investments in developing capabilities provide flexibility to implement a strategy in a changing world. These investments define the firm's future opportunities that sustain competitive advantage. The capabilities and resulting future options that a firm creates through its strategic investments enable critical flexibility to achieve a *dynamic* strategic vision. Thus, while it is not reasonable or even desirable to keep *all* options open, successful strategy must develop the capabilities required to create value for customers in a changing world.

FOR FURTHER READING

Pankaj Ghemawat, *Commitment: The Dynamic of Strategy* (New York: The Free Press, 1991).

Pankaj Ghemawat, "Sustainable Advantage," *Harvard Business Review*, September–October 1986.

G. Hamel, and C. K. Prahalad, "Strategic Intent," *Harvard Business Review*, May 1989.

Henry Mintzberg, "Crafting Strategy," *Harvard Business Review*, July–August 1987.

Kenichi Ohmae, "Getting Back to Strategy," *Harvard Business Review*, November–December 1988.

Michael E. Porter, *Competitive Advantage* (New York: The Free Press, 1985).

Michael E. Porter, "The Competitive Advantage of Nations," *Harvard Business Review*, March–April 1990.

Michael E. Porter, *Competitive Strategy* (New York: The Free Press, 1980).

Michael E. Porter, "What Is Strategy?," *Harvard Business Review*, November–December 1996.

C. K. Prahalad and G. Hamel, "The Core Competence of the Corporation," *Harvard Business Review*, May–June 1990.

George Stalk, Philip Evans, and Lawrence E. Shulman, "Competing on Capabilities: The New Rules of Corporate Strategy," *Harvard Business Review*, March–April 1992.

Elizabeth Teisberg, "Strategic Response to Uncertainty," Harvard Business School Note #9-391-192, 1991.

Elizabeth Teisberg, "Methods for Evaluating Capital Investment Decisions under Uncertainty," Lenos Trigeorgis, ed., *Real Options in Capital Investment: Models, Strategies, and Applications* (Westport, CT: Praeger, 1995).

PART III
New Horizons

Part III addresses topics that raise challenges for businesses entering the new century. Chapter 14, "Leading from the Middle," captures the essence of this new edition of *The Portable MBA*. It is our contention that the old command-and-control paradigm is a bankrupt concept and that the future of tomorrow's enterprise lies in the hands of middle mangers who must lead the enterprise into the twenty-first century. Chapter 15, "Strategic Alliances," further extends the leading-from-the-middle metaphor and posits that firms no longer can afford to act in isolation. Constellations of firms, in cooperation with each other, determine ultimate competitive success. These constellations, or alliances, compete on a global basis for market share, low-cost supply, and access to resources. Chapter 16, "International Business," places the entire book in perspective and emphasizes the truly global nature of business. Capital knows no boundaries; the Internet makes information available to millions with a keystroke; and human assets are not restricted to a single location based on the availability of natural resources. Simply put, businesses compete locally but must think globally. And Chapter 17, "Some Final Thoughts," brings the book to a close with some brief reflections about value creation.

14 LEADING FROM THE MIDDLE: A NEW LEADERSHIP PARADIGM

INTRODUCTION

Fundamental changes have occurred in the business environment during the last 20 years, yet our understanding and response to these changes have been at best partial and at worst woefully inadequate and harmful. We must rethink the very idea of management as a hierarchical and directive activity concerned primarily with efficiency. Middle management as we know it and as we teach it in MBA programs and executive development seminars around the world is bankrupt. We begin this rethinking by examining the most important management role of all: leadership. We need to replace our idea of leadership as a top management task directed downward toward middle managers and workers with the idea that managers lead from the middle. While "leading from the middle" at first blush may appear to be ambiguous, it is the core concept necessary for reinventing corporate life.

Leading from the middle has three different yet connected meanings, each of which is relevant to understanding business today. First, managers must lead from the middle of the hierarchy. The traditional role of middle managers—to carry out the directives of senior managers and then supervise the implementation of these orders by lower managers and workers—is irrelevant. Second, managers must lead from the middle of an organization's core competencies, values, and purpose. In short, leading from the middle in this sense is about leading from commitment. Third, managers must lead from the middle of a network of relationships, some of which include not only organizational members, but also customers, suppliers, and others. Exhibit 14.1 is a depiction of these three modes of leading from the middle. The rest of this chapter sets the stage for understanding these three meanings.

In the following section we will discuss two basic changes that have profoundly affected the management of today's corporation. The first is the liberalization of markets, particularly the freeing of capital markets from geopolitical constraints. The second change, which is connected to the first, is a liberalization of the political institutions in society, from the Helsinki Agreement on Human Rights to the more recent fall of totalitarian regimes. We speculate about the role of technology as the underlying cause of these two changes, and we postulate that the effects of technology on managerial and corporate behavior have been and will continue to be profound. In essence, these changes require a new framework and a rethinking of the entire process of management.

After that, we'll examine some partial solutions to the managerial problems raised by the shifts in the economic and political institutions in the world. In particular, we focus on Total Quality Management, reengineering, mass customization, and strategic alliances. We outline how such solutions have achieved mixed results at best, allowing a managerial practice that ignores the fundamental shifts that have occurred.

Next we'll explore the three meanings of "leading from the middle." We explain the new mind-set that is needed to lead from the middle, and we propose some of the activities and skills that are necessary to achieve this goal. We begin such a task here. And finally, we'll offer some advice to senior managers and some tentative conclusions. It is important to note at the outset that many scholars and practitioners are writing about the issues that we address here, broadly under the rubric of "business transformation." While our approach does not purport to view leading from the middle as a panacea, it nevertheless opens the door to our reinventing the very terms and concepts of business life. If we are correct about the profound changes affecting business, no less than a revolution is in fact afoot.[1]

FUNDAMENTAL SHIFTS

The Liberalization of Markets

The first fundamental shift that has occurred in the past 20 years and has given rise to the need for restructuring organizations and rethinking the practice of

EXHIBIT 14.1   Leading from the middle: three views.

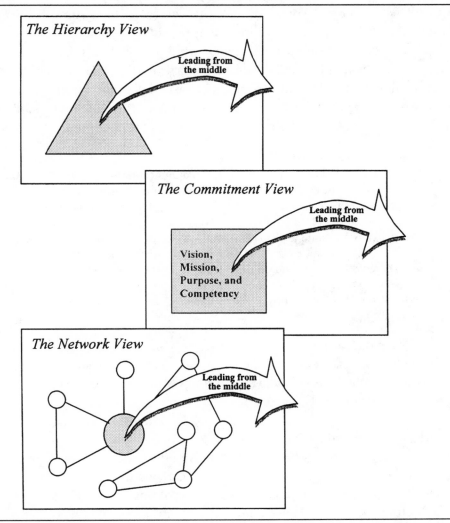

management is the liberalization of markets. Liberalization of international markets has occurred through freer trade and capital flows, liberalization of domestic markets through deregulation and privatization, and liberalization of government through the demise of communism and a resurgence of democracy (which we will address later). In this broad liberalizing process we see the strong arm of technology. It has been a catalyst, facilitator, and motivator for change.

Although change of this type cannot be precisely dated, we believe 1973 was the turning point, with the breakup of the Bretton Woods era as the epochal event. The Bretton Woods Conference of 1944 established the basic set of assumptions that would apply to international trade and investment and created the institutions that would govern these activities. Coming after the Great Depression and World War II, the design of the system that Bretton Woods established was largely directed at providing stability for international commerce. The postwar economic policy within and between nations was pursued in such a way as to avoid the destabilizing events of the interwar era. Without returning to the gold standard that established the rules for the period from 1870 to 1914, economists and government officials hoped to reestablish the business environment that Keynes so piquantly described in an often-quoted paragraph[2]:

> What an extraordinary episode in the economic progress of man was that age which came to an end in August 1914. The inhabitant of London could order by telephone, sipping his morning tea in bed, the various products of the whole earth, in such quantity as he might see fit, and reasonably expect their early delivery on his doorstep; he could at the same moment and by the same means adventure his wealth in the natural resources and new enterprises of any quarter of the world, and share without exertion or event trouble in their prospective fruits and advantages; or he could decide to couple the security of his fortunes with the good faith of townspeople of any substantial municipality in any continent that fancy or information might recommend.

It is not our purpose to debate the success or failure of Bretton Woods, but we do believe that the environment it created was a major factor contributing to the dominance of American industry in the postwar era, giving rise to the hierarchical, command-and-control corporation that characterized it. The United States emerged from the war with the overwhelmingly largest market in the world and an industrial base that was intact, although it was in need of transition from its wartime footing. From that base, American industry prospered, taking advantage of the economies of scale that its market size supported.

The successful, prototypical corporations of this era were U.S. Steel, General Motors, and IBM. The model of corporate governance and control was described by Alfred Sloan in *My Life at General Motors* and generalized by business historian Alfred Chandler in *Strategy and Structure*. This success, however, was not without its systemic problems. The very seeds of these great companies' success also contained the virus that would later cause a form of institutional rot. While Sloan wrote of GM as an enormous and efficiently running machine, others such as Peter Drucker believed it was a machine without a heart or a soul.

Economist Joseph Schumpeter predicted the problem long before the current wave of restructuring, rightsizing, and other ways of revitalizing large corporations were ever conceived. In *Capitalism, Socialism and Democracy*, published in 1942, he stated that large, rigid organizational forms would eventually dominate industry and government. Governments would enact policies for providing stability. Firms would respond by developing structures to benefit from that stability. Corporations would become hierarchical and bureaucratic, with rules and strategies that deterred innovation. These nonentrepreneurial firms would seek to maximize the return on investment by prolonging product lives rather than introducing new products. They would extend the lives of capital equipment rather than develop new processes. Management in these firms would emphasize cost containment and predictable efficiencies related to growth rather than entrepreneurial reinvention. In a world where competition was restricted by regulation and protectionism, there was no competitive threat to this kind of complacency.

There was no place in this corporate world for what Schumpeter called "creative destruction," which was the essence of entrepreneurial spirit and activity that he felt contributed to innovation and dynamic, rather than static, economies. The entrepreneur discovered a better product or process, which was the creative side of the equation. The entrepreneur could then put together a deal that brought suppliers of material, labor, and capital together with customer needs and desires. The creation of new products and processes would naturally lead to the destruction of the old way. Capitalism, in Schumpeter's view, contained its own seeds of reinvention through the process of creative destruction. However, the bureaucratic world of the postwar era dampened the process of creative destruction, ushering in an era of declining real growth rates, first in the United States, then in Europe, and finally even in Japan.

Schumpeter's gloomy prophecy for the West seemed all too real as Bretton Woods began to break down, the first oil crisis occurred, and socialism was the system of choice for most of the world's developing countries. However, in hindsight, the early 1970s began to look like an inflection point when the policies of governments and the structural imperatives for corporations began to change. It is difficult to pinpoint a single cause for this phenomenon, although George Gilder's view of technology in his book, *The Microcosm,* offers an intriguing premise. Gilder argues that the application of quantum physics to the development and production of electronics altered the forces that determine economic success. The silicon revolution has disengaged corporate institutions from specific physical locations. Economic success in the Industrial Age depended upon access to physical or material resources. The great steel industry of the United States had to develop in Pennsylvania where there was a confluence of water for transportation and power, iron ore, and coal. But Silicon Valley, with its vast electronics industry, could be located anywhere. It was far less dependent on physical resources than on human resources.

The microcosmic pursuit has been global. According to Gilder,

The United States has led only because the United States has been most open to global forces, immigrants and ideas. There are no separate destinies in the microcosm. There is just the difference between being free and in tune with the deeper disciplines and possibilities of the time, and being entangled and stultified by the materialist superstitions of a grim past of nationalist bondage and poverty.

The liberalization of capital markets caused enormous upheavals in the way today's corporations are run, but few have understood that these changes are fundamental, as Schumpeter, Gilder, and others have pointed out. During times of relative stability, hierarchical organizations with command-and-control systems can thrive. Today, with capital and resources flowing more freely than ever across geopolitical boundaries, hierarchies simply cannot anticipate change fast enough. In addition, the pace of change is accelerated because these very geopolitical boundaries that serve as forces of stability are themselves under siege.

The Liberalization of Political Institutions

Once physical resources became less important, the regulatory systems and organizational structures put in place to protect them could no longer ensure commercial success for the enterprises that owned these resources. Societies that continued to adhere to the old rules fell behind and, in the extreme, like the communist countries of Eastern Europe, imploded. Ultimately, these societies began to dismantle the rules and regulations that have restrained the market and opened both old and new industries to competition, along with the resurgence of creative destruction.

The last decade has seen an unprecedented fragmentation of political regimes. While it is difficult to delineate what is cause and effect, suffice it to say the early 1970s was an inflection point. In the United States and other Western countries, we began to see a large-scale decline in the trust citizens afforded to their governments. Some of the factors that contributed to this lack or trust were the social and political crusades that started in the turbulent 1960s, the emergence of worldwide agendas around the rights of women and minorities, the environmental crisis, and the so-called human rights movements in repressive regimes from China to South Africa. In short, government was identified as part of the problem.

With the signing of the Helsinki agreement on human rights, governments around the world acknowledged, at least on paper, that every human being has value, with certain rights that government could not take away. Of course this agreement was understood as a diplomatic parlor trick in many repressive regimes, but it served to put the issue of human rights on the agenda and became a catalyst for change around the world.

The development of information technology, from Minicams to satellites, from fax machines to personal computers, put the human rights issues into the living rooms of millions of people around the world via CNN. This clearly illustrates the shake-up of postwar era political regimes, such as seen in the disaster of Tienanmen Square.

Like it or not, human rights and economic activity are now inextricably tied together. (It is, of course, ironic to come to such a realization almost 200 years after Adam Smith told us the very same thing.)[3] In many ways, technology itself contains the elements of this linkage. First and most obviously, it is increasingly difficult for political regimes to hide their repression. There are too many ways to be found out. Tienanmen Square is only one dramatic example. Second, the information technology that does information processing at the local level (at the nodes, rather than at the central network processor) encourages a kind of local control of information. Again, the emergence of the Internet is but one dramatic example. (Could the Internet be shut down or repressed? How? Does this question even make sense?) Finally, technology itself inherently connects ethics and economics around such issues as intellectual property and copyright. While the Chinese government may have rejoiced at the failure of the Clinton administration to revoke its most-favored-nation status as a result of the suppression of human rights, in reality it is business that will continue to put reform pressure on China as it seeks a solution to the copyright protection issue.

The connection between the liberalization of markets and the liberalization of political regimes is easy to see. Success for the firm depends on how well it can harness its human resources and its mental capacity. In the old structure, a CEO or strategic planner set the direction for the firm. In the new model, however, direction must come from throughout the organization. As scholars Hamel and Prahalad claim, "It is an amalgamation of the collective intelligence and imagination of managers and employees throughout the company who must possess an enlarged view of what it means to be 'strategic.' "[4] At the center of any new mind-set must be the creative potential of the human beings that make up the corporation.

The Implications for the Practice of Management

Corporations and their managers face a fundamental revolution in structure, conduct, and performance. This revolution has been brought on by a gale of creative destruction induced by the inadequacies of large corporations to respond with agility to changes in demographics, technology, regulation, and lifestyles— forces that have liberated capital markets, political regimes, and the people who make up these institutions. The agents of these simultaneously creative and destructive processes are invariably outsiders: foreigners, entrepreneurs, inventors, managerial iconoclasts, visionaries, and academicians.[5]

The response of corporations has been dramatic: extensive downsizing (the loss of 1.4 million managers, executives, and administrative professionals between 1987 and 1993, double the rate of the previous five years), process reengineering, alliances, and so on. In the next section, we observe that each of these efforts represents at best a partial solution to an underlying need created by this wave of creative destruction. Before exploring this topic, let us briefly investigate the current managerial mind-set that is in need of change. Exhibit 14.2 represents some characteristics of the dominant mental model.[6]

Obsession with Command and Control

The largest component of the old mind-set is the obsession with command and control. From human resource systems to production planning, the old mind-set makes the avoidance of surprise a number one priority. And small wonder, if Schumpeter is correct. As institutions emerged to make the world more stable, organizations that thrived on that stability invented systems to take advantage of it. Firms are slow to give up control, which often leads to an inability to respond to changing environmental conditions.

Vision of a Stable Future

A second attribute of the old corporate mind-set lies in the expectations of senior management about the future: predictability, steady growth, and the absence of discontinuous changes due to technology, regulation, demographics, or lifestyle attitudes. The planning activities of the old corporate mind-set are oriented toward extrapolating the past and present into the future rather than toward questioning fundamental assumptions or exploring radically different scenarios.

EXHIBIT 14.2   The dominant model of managerial practice in the old mind-set.

Obsession with command and control
Vision of a stable or predictable future
Competitive advantage through economies of scale/expertise
Specialization of labor
Hierarchical structure: centralization of power
Control by technical rationality
Separation of personal and professional life

Competitive Advantage Based on Economies of Scale and Expertise

The old corporate mind-set seeks profitability and competitive security through sheer size and domination of markets and through the commitment of massive investments in relatively fixed and inflexible plants, equipment, information systems, and organizations. Commitment to a strategy of scale and inflexibility is a tangible manifestation of a relatively certain future—a future that looks not unlike the present or the past.

Specialization of Labor: The Emergence of Narrow and Repetitive Work

The push for scale economies transforms factory and service work by focusing on specific tasks that the worker could learn to do quickly. The worker *becomes* part of the machinery or service process as employee discretion declines. Work protocols are designed to maximize the throughput of materials and the output of standardized products.

Hierarchical Structure: The Centralization of Power

The structure of these organizations is a high and steeply sloped pyramid. Reporting relationships and career progression are *vertical* and typically *tracked along functional lines.* Power in the form of information, money, expertise, and decision authority were concentrated at the apex of the pyramid. Executives manage by *command,* from the top down. Silo mentality breeds "turfism."

Control by Technical Rationality: The Rule by Rules

Upward-oriented planning and reporting are major administrative activities for middle and senior managers. The corporate policies and procedures manual blossomed in the post–World War II world as a way to institutionalize rational decision processes (e.g., discounted cash flow investment decisions). This has had the effect of homogenizing and slowing the evaluation of business opportunities and the flow of innovation. Somewhat analogous to factory workers, managers and administrative professionals have become part of the administrative machinery.

Separation of Personal and Professional Life

An individual's contribution to the success of the enterprise is on the corporation's terms. Employees conform in order to advance in the hierarchy. Chester Barnard believed that the executive who functioned well in the bureaucracy would have a public persona that may well differ from that of his or her private life. The past 40 years is replete with stories from literature, such as *The Man in the Gray Flannel Suit* and *Something Happened,* which explore the psychic pain of this separation.

So What?

The old mind-set is no longer appropriate due to the fundamental shifts in the liberation of markets, political institutions, and people. The advent of information technology, distributed computing, and network communications release information and expertise quickly and widely. Intensifying competition in product markets demands a sense of urgency, which is inconsistent with the sedateness of the command-and-control decision-making processes. The same competition demands higher performance in quality and lower cost, both of which are achieved through cross-functional teamwork. The more extensive freedom of people requires a relaxation in the process rules that dictate who may be heard, how, and when. Experimentation with teamwork clashes with functional turfism, suggesting sideways reporting relationships and career progression. Finally, the fuller engagement of people challenges the separation of personal and professional life.

It is only free people who will exercise and improve their mental capacities for the common good of those affected. The command-and-control view of telling people what to do and watching them do it is simply made obsolete by the free flow of capital and ideas across nations. Invention and creation, the driving force of capitalism, cannot be commanded and controlled; it can only be enabled and activated. How companies can harness or unleash this force is the major challenge in rethinking current managerial practice.

PARTIAL SOLUTIONS

Unfortunately, the responses of many who are concerned with the changes that are affecting the practice of management miss the fundamental nature of the transformations that have occurred. Many corporations have resorted to a modest amount of strategic and operational introspection, oriented around competitive advantage rather than addressing the fundamental shifts described in the previous section. The question for many companies has been how to adjust and refine ongoing activity to respond to these changes in the surrounding environment. In short, corporations have responded by trying to adapt to these shifts under the old mind-set. Not surprisingly, the vehicles companies have chosen to accommodate the new and more turbulent competitive conditions are rolled out with much celebration, only to founder on the shoals of time in two to three years. We are treated monthly to the popular press accounts of how the latest fads repeatedly fail.

We know the litany of familiar terms: Total Quality Management (TQM), reengineering, mass customization, and strategic partnering. Corporations have heartily embraced these programs to enhance innovation and quality, streamline operations, and forge partnerships to match or exceed similar initiatives by competitors. Undeniably, each of these programs has promised benefits, and many have delivered on some of these benefits. However, these efforts often have proven to be time- and resource-intensive, with few clear deliverables. These programs have been implemented in a workforce that has considerable skepticism generated from weariness of this month's new transformative program.

Strategic reasoning regarding the selection and cultivation of alliances or committed reengineering efforts is inappropriate or a waste of corporate resources. There will always be a cutting-edge-like mass customization or TQM, as groups of very bright people craft improvements in ongoing operations. These initiatives, in combination, have indeed defined the new competitive status quo. To play the game in international markets today, companies must restructure and be more innovative. Through the implementation of such programs, companies have attempted to reach a best-practices standard, thereby improving quality, building in new product and process efficiencies, and becoming more flexible and innovative through mass customization and alliance building. Today, all tough competitors are asking how to become more market- and customer-driven. Companies are examining and changing their internal systems whereby product and service quality is maintained at the highest level. They are searching kindred industries for strategic partners who can significantly leverage their firm's resources. These efforts are to be commended. However, these efforts should be seen as the minimum requirements to compete at the top of an industry. These programs are the new basic standard to which anyone wishing to remain competitive must aspire. They are the new entry hurdles.

Total Quality Management (TQM)

Total Quality Management certainly is an important process. We do not deny that such programs have become essential for competition in today's market. Yet, as alluded to previously, taken in isolation, TQM is not a panacea for the firm struggling against formidable competitors. TQM may have become a "right of entry," a necessary attribute for the firm to compete. The question becomes—what other processes and skills must be incorporated for the firm to be a viable competitor? Undoubtedly, TQM lies at the core of many espoused solutions for corporate transformation. Used in isolation, however, it is not enough. Quality processes, products, and services not based on market realities are fundamentally flawed.

For example, when American Express worked on new quality processes to ensure phones were answered by the second ring, management initially neglected to ask what happens after the call is answered. To respond quickly and not be prepared to address the customers' questions or concerns is an indication that TQM is merely a partial solution to a more fundamental problem. In short, we can say that (1) quality management processes are essential, but must be defined by the customer and not by the company's internal technical definitions of quality, and (2) quality processes must lie along the value chain and extend backward to suppliers and forward to customers.

Business Reengineering

A second partial solution has been the use of business reengineering, which refers to a process or view that discards all the old rules, resulting in managers looking for new ways to manage the business. Reengineering gurus Hammer and Champy believe that business reengineering is intended to help the firm manage uncertainty while simultaneously questioning not only how to do things faster, cheaper, and better, but also whether certain functions or processes should be done at all—and whether other functions can be done better by others. In some organizations, business reengineering is being used as a code word for downsizing or rightsizing. In other organizations, reengineering exercises have stripped certain functions from the firm and have outsourced other activities. The question often not asked is whether such skills are critical to the firm and whether future success depends on the development of certain capabilities. In a more recent book, Champy redefines and clarifies what business reengineering is and, equally important, what it is not.

One problem with business process reengineering is that cost reduction alone is not the goal. Reengineering should entail a fundamental assessment of the firm and its capabilities and an analysis of what skills, human capital, and resources are critical for future success. A second problem is that business reengineering should not be confused with benchmarking. Reengineering acknowledges that being "world class" at a particular activity is a laudable and worthy pursuit; however, we should not seek such a goal blindly. Instead, we should question the basic underlying activity and fundamental processes, first deciding whether, in fact, they are useful or necessary. However, caution must be exercised in this situation. A third problem is that business reengineering should not be attempted without full recognition of what the firm's strategic intent and goals are. A fourth problem is that business reengineering cannot be effectively applied unless the firm includes its suppliers and customers in the process. We must calculate the impact of shedding certain activities and determine if there are others who are willing and able to assume these tasks.

Mass Customization

A third partial solution in this discussion of current management practices is mass customization, which is linked inextricably to the two previously mentioned programs. The concept of mass customization grows from a failure inherent in the mass-production paradigm espoused by bureaucratic organizations.[7] While low costs are important and are an essential component of the mass-production paradigm, the premise upon which such a model is built is no longer valid across a number of industries. Markets are not homogeneous; they are fragmented. Product life cycles are shorter, and cycle time has become a critical element of competitive response. Customers are demanding products and services that are tailored specifically for them. Mass customization demands processes, systems, and structures that are responsive to changes in the marketplace and can be implemented with little change in the cost and structure of the product and service.

Management scholars Boynton, Victor, and Pine caution that a company cannot move directly from mass production to mass customization. There are interim stages, such as continuous improvement, that must precede this evolutionary change. Such changes affect both organizational structure and information technology; these changes are not trivial. Cross-functional teams become central to the process, functional silos must fall, and firms must acknowledge that R&D, manufacturing, procurement, and marketing must be linked if the firm is to meet the customer as one segment. Such dynamic processes require a very sizable investment in information technology, which is the central nervous system of these processes. It is not enough to manage inventories and production processes to reduce setup times and production scheduling; you must link customers, suppliers, R&D, production, and logistics in order for the entire process to operate seamlessly across functional and occasionally across organizational boundaries. Clearly, it is not enough for a company to convey that each one of its customers is treated as a unique market segment. You must begin to question where along the value chain customization occurs and how information is shared among all the functions and firms that deliver value to the customer. Flexible manufacturing or service delivery is a small part of the process.

Alliances and Partnerships

A fourth partial solution is the use of alliances and partnerships. There is no question that these organizational forms (e.g., joint ventures, technology agreements, long-term purchasing arrangements, and horizontal marketing relationships) are on the rise. The numbers of alliances and partners have increased exponentially in recent years. For example, you cannot pick up the *Wall Street Journal* without seeing an announcement of a new alliance or partnership in the biotech, computer, telecommunications, pharmaceutical, or airlines industries. Despite the increase in alliance activity, the results of these activities are not that encouraging. A majority of alliances fail, according to work by Harrigan, Bleeke and Ernst, and others.[8] Failure can be attributed to a number of factors, ranging from how firms conceive of alliances as part of their strategy to the implementation and management of the alliance over time.

Alliances must be seen as strategic in nature and must be tied intimately to the strategic goals of the firm. Managers must be able to articulate how the alliance fits within the larger strategic framework of the firm's objectives.[9] All too often, managers become enamored with the thought of a partnership and fail to develop a comprehensive business case for the alliance or to understand why one form of alliance is better than another. It not unusual to find that managers spend more effort building a case for the internal request for funds than they do for the rationale for an alliance. In addition, firms fail to conduct adequate research in their selection of an alliance partner. For instance, how do you determine if the potential partner is really a pirate whose sole intent is to expropriate expertise or knowledge? In some industries (most noticeable today is the multimedia industry), firms get caught up in the feeding frenzy, attempting to partner so as not to be left without an alliance. In these high-stakes games in which billions of dollars are at risk, fundamental questions are often ignored regarding the alliance health (as opposed to the financial health) of the potential partner. In the heat of the deal, it's easy to ignore the more behavioral, qualitative aspects of the partner. Companies fail to address questions that affect the development of personal relationships that must grow concurrently with the building of the business. Key issues to resolve prior to consummating the partnership agreement include management style, corporate culture, compatibility of goals, and an ability to share decision making.

Problems arise also as the alliance grows and moves forward. Questions of equity (i.e., reward in return for effort and resources), interdependence, quality of personnel assigned to the alliance, conflict management techniques, and so forth can all affect the tone and health of the alliance. So long as the business prospers, you can easily ignore the personal and interpersonal dimensions of the alliance. If the business begins to falter, these alliance management processes and skills become essential to weathering the economic turbulence facing the partners.

In summary, alliances are not the answer to business success, although they do offer a number of opportunities. If viewed as a singular solution to competitive problems, alliances are bound to fail. There are a number of management challenges to overcome. It is probably better to focus less on the alliance per se, recognizing instead that the effort (and the ultimate reward) lies in the alliance management process itself.

Partial Conclusions about Partial Solutions

Although improvement can be achieved through these efforts, these programs represent incremental improvements when seen against the backdrop of corporations as a whole in the context of the last decade of this century. Specifically, in areas such as manufacturing or R&D and product design, these programs have offered sufficient incremental improvements so as to be deemed justifiable by those responsible for budgeting the monies. From the longer-term viewpoint of the corporation and its critical outside linkages to customers and suppliers, however, these programs have been only partial solutions. They are palliatives that have eased the pain without curing the disease. Unfortunately, the partial successes of these programs have deflected attention from more fundamental questions about the challenges facing leaders. In reality, these programs rarely alter the core assumptions and mind-sets of the companies within which they are introduced; therein lies the problem.

This outcome is not surprising. Short-term, verifiable improvements in competitive positioning can disguise the predictable and ever present inertia of corporate hierarchies that hold on tightly to the mind-sets and operating assumptions that have guided them for the last 25 years. While change to the status quo may be recognized as desirable and even essential, the power and comfort of things as they have always been done, defined, and implemented has a quiet stranglehold over most companies, even as the tremendous effort and commitment of resources to reengineering and TQM efforts reassured participants that something significant was happening.

Another way to view these proposed solutions as partial is to go back to Exhibit 14.1. While each "solution" proposes some rethinking that could be called "leading from the middle," none goes far enough. Total Quality Management encourages middle managers to lead from the middle of the hierarchy and to lead from commitment, but it is difficult to see how TQM is applicable in the network arena. Similarly, strategic alliances are a method for leading from the middle of a network, but do little to redefine the hierarchy or focus on core commitments or values. Business process reengineering can break up the hierarchy and put companies in control of their key processes, but again it does not address purpose and commitment.

While the latest, fashionable programs represent new, higher standards for operating, these programs have distracted managers from the new paradoxes that represent a more fundamental competitive challenge. Leaders at every level of the organization, particularly at upper levels, must make a leap of vision to see this equally important arena for strategic thinking. This leap of conceptualization takes corporate leaders from their often implicit and unconscious focus on hierarchy to a cognizance of the power and potential of networks. It shifts the lens through which we define leadership responsibility from a preoccupation with things (capital, equipment, budgets, information technology) to a radically different understanding of people. What we need is a new framework, a new mind-set that revitalizes the practice of management.

REINVENTING THE PRACTICE OF MANAGEMENT

The command-and-control framework is in the process of being displaced by a new managerial mind-set that stands in stark contrast to this mentality. This new mind-set puts the liberalization of markets and people at its very center, causing us to revolutionize our concept of how organizations work in the next century. In what follows, we set forth some of the elements of this new managerial mind-set and how it turns the concept of leadership on its hierarchical head.

We have called this new mind-set *leading from the middle.*

Leading from the middle may appear to be ambiguous, because it has at least three related meanings. First, leading from the middle signals that the traditional role of the middle manager must be transformed. This is the hierarchical sense of leading from the middle. The fundamental changes that have occurred have made the job of the middle manager superfluous in many instances, replaced by information technologies deployed in flatter organizations with processes that have been reengineered across organizational functions. The middle manager as functional expert is simply no longer needed in a transfunctional world. Therefore, if there are any middle managers left (and we know that there are plenty), they must lead rather than manage. They must begin to adapt the mind-set that redefines who they are and what they do.

The second view of leading from the middle is the commitment view. In this case, leading from the middle means that we lead from the middle of a set of core values, a core competency or capability, or from a purpose. Porras and Collins, Drucker, and other management thinkers have reinforced the idea of answering the question "What do you stand for?" as an anchor in times of uncertainty and great change. The changes that have affected business are too fundamental for allowing organizations just to drift. Only a core purpose that is well understood and agreed upon can serve as a cornerstone for action. James Burke, former CEO at Johnson & Johnson, remarked about the use of such a purpose, called the Credo at J&J, during the Tylenol crisis: "We had lots of people making decisions on the fly, and we made very few mistakes."[10] Burke attributes the successful handling of the crisis to the fact that all of the employees involved were working from the same basic page: the J&J Credo. While credos and values statements are not for everyone, leading from the middle requires that there be a sense of purpose that drives the business. When this purpose includes a shared vision, then managers can lead from the middle of the hierarchy or from the middle of a network.

The third sense of leading from the middle is the network view. In this case, the hierarchy of power and the pyramid of organizational control has been replaced by a network of relationships. Some of these relationships are within the organization, some are outside, and some cross the boundary. Leading from the middle implies leading from the middle of a network of people, products, and relationships. Such a vantage point does not confer positional power, expert power, or even referent power. Rather, it offers an opportunity for creative destruction: the marshaling of resources, people, and ideas to create value that others in the network find worthwhile. The manager becomes the facilitator and the catalyst for action and creative change. Such a networked view of capitalism is increasingly the model for both large and small firms.[11]

Exhibit 14.3 summarizes some of the elements of this new framework. Many authors and business leaders have discussed these ideas in a piecemeal fashion. However, when you compare these two managerial models, the new mind-set stands out in stark contrast to the old.

EXHIBIT 14.3 Elements of the new managerial mind-set: leading from the middle.

Owning the whole enterprise
Boundarylessness
Customer orientation
Dynamic engagement
Invention of the future
Role of learning
Integration of the personal with the professional

Owning the Whole Enterprise

The new mind-set requires that every employee feel some ownership of the whole enterprise. To *own* is to feel accountable for, and not simply to participate in. To focus on the *whole* rather than the part (or even the sum of the parts) is to challenge the employee and manager to think broadly about *outcomes* rather than narrow tasks.

Boundarylessness

Equally important is the fact that the new mind-set requires managers to think outside of traditional boundaries. Boundarylessness stands for an end to functional stovepipes and an openness to alliances, partnerships, and new ideas without regard to who commands and controls the resulting activity. Outcome orientation demands access to information, expertise (or critical judgment), and tangible resources. The new mind-set eliminates walls around functions and encourages lateral interaction.

When boundarylessness is combined with owning the whole enterprise, managers must see themselves amidst a network of relationships. The boundary between customer, supplier, employee, and traditional stakeholder roles is becoming hopelessly blurred. For example, in the telecommunications industry, prior to trivestiture, AT&T at once was a large supplier of switching equipment, a customer of the local telephone company via access charges, and a fierce competitor of the regional Bell companies. Alternatively, global alliances that provide a firm with partners all along the value chain make it difficult to say which employee belongs to which company. Many firms are contracting out work to former employees. The Brazilian firm SEMCO is the most radical example of this phenomenon. At SEMCO, these independent contractors work on company facilities in teams with customers and suppliers.

Customer Orientation

Rather than aiming to dominate or exploit markets, the new mind-set encourages firms to delight customers. It is important to note that *customer delight* is different from *customer satisfaction*. Just doing the job for customers and satisfying them is no longer enough in a world of global capital markets. Instead, today's companies have to be distinctive. They want customers to think of them when they think of service. In the airline industry, legends are being created at SAS, Singapore Air, and British Air as they have left the pack behind. Likewise, everyone is familiar with success stories such as Nordstrom, Wal-Mart, Honda, Sony, and Toyota—or upstarts like Saturn.

The difference between the old and new mind-sets is in an attitude of *caring* about the customer and focusing on specific relationships rather than on aggregate demographics. Selling as a corporate activity is frequently being replaced by relationship management as the dominant mode of dealing with customers. Information is readily accessible in many markets because markets are global, companies from around the world have raised service standards, and political regimes have gone through a liberalization process. There are increasingly fewer places for companies to hide if they exploit customers or treat them as if they are in a one-shot negotiation, never to be seen again.

Dynamic Engagement

Desired outcomes and the challenges to achieving them shift constantly. No rigid organizational structure in place today will be appropriate for tomorrow. The new framework aims to construct an organization that reconstitutes itself as the situation requires. The result is an *agile* organization, one where time and relationships change constantly, and yet the level of engagement remains high. We have called that element of the mind-set "dynamic engagement."[12] This element says that, above all, values are important. People can achieve extraordinary things if they believe their achievements are important, and these achievements resonate with their sense of self and what they want to accomplish in life. In short, these factors point to values. Dynamic engagement means that organizations must be value-driven. This usually requires a sense of urgency. Values are not trifles. They are urgent, to be acted on precisely because they are values.

In a recent book about what distinguishes truly great companies from those that are better than average, Jim Collins and Jerry Pouras remarked that being driven by values (their own notion of ideology equals values plus purpose) distinguishes the likes of GE, Motorola, Merck, Hewlett-Packard, and others. These values have been fairly constant over the long histories of these companies. It is no coincidence that Collins and Pouras's list of visionary companies includes precisely those that are in a position to respond to the fundamental changes we have seen. Many have had to dismantle the bureaucracy or literally blow up the command-and-control systems and procedures they have placed on top of the values. However, these cutting-edge companies have been and still are engaged in this very task with a sense of urgency that has enabled them to leapfrog their competitors.

Invention of the Future

The fundamental assumption of the leading-from-the-middle mind-set is that the future will vary significantly from the past. This implies that simple extrapolation of the present into the future is doomed to failure. Instead, managers need to develop out-of-the-box skills in thinking, questioning, and learning. Additionally, the current fashionability of business process reengineering is recognized as a remedy for past and present problems rather than a proactive effort to build for the future. In the world that we see, the future is there to be invented—not predicted and responded to.

Role of Learning

As with dynamic engagement, *a zest for ideas and information is essential*, both at the personal and organizational level. Learning becomes an end in itself and is recognized as having many dimensions: the acquisition of new information, the mastery of new techniques and technologies, and the growth in expertise and judgment. It is only through learning that the new mind-set becomes sustainable and produces a renewing corporation. Learning is more than job training; it is *attitude and value.* In a recent book, Peter Senge has set forth the disciplines of learning: *mental models, shared vision, team learning, personal mastery,* and the fifth discipline, *systems thinking,* which ties the others together. Competitive advantage goes to the organization that can learn the best and that practices these disciplines as a routine matter of course. Whether it is at Motorola University or a skills training class at Johnsonville Sausage Company, leading from the middle requires continuous attention to learning and to improving your ability to learn. The role of the manager is to model that learning and to foster others' desires to learn in the workplace.

Integration of the Personal and the Professional

All of the other elements of the mind-set mentioned so far require that people both show up to work and show up with their hearts. The new mind-set asks managers and workers to be whole people. In the old mind-set, employees were willing to trade some of their individuality for a promise from the company to take care of them. Such loyalty is the exception in today's new world. Continuous improvement and transformation work only if corporations can embrace the differences of many kinds of employees. Differences provide diverse and rich knowledge. Greater knowledge fosters competitive advantage as well as meaningful work. Employees today must make critical judgments in addition to performing what used to be normal, unthinking jobs. Thinking and doing, separated at birth in the old mind-set, are inextricably joined together in leading from the middle. People are treated as ends in themselves, who have projects and values of their own that they are going to accomplish by working together in the corporation. Differences are respected and celebrated. Companies who are shortsightedly restructuring by slash-and-burn management are destroying any hope of a great future.

Leading from the Middle: Managerial Skills

Michael Hammer remarked that "A successful career will no longer be about promotion. It'll be about mastery."[13] But mastery of what? We offer four essential elements for the tool kit of those who will lead from the middle:

1. *Learning, and learning how to learn.* The competitive environment is currently so fluid and fast-paced that learning set-piece concepts and skills dooms the learner to obsolescence in the short term. You don't go to school to "get fixed" just once; today you must constantly "be getting fixed." We must emphasize three dimensions about learning. First, learning must be *in real time* (i.e., it must be occurring constantly). Second, you must learn *from actual experience.* From this standpoint, mistakes and defeats are hugely important, more so than merely absorbing information from secondary sources. Third, to learn in real time and from actual experience requires a *mastery of the art of reflection.* Donald Schön[14] has studied accomplished professionals in a variety of fields and remarked that the central intellectual attribute in all fields was an ability to reflect and learn. In other words, professional work is a process of reflection. Chris Argyris[15] has warned that "single-loop" kinds of communication such as surveys, focus groups, and management-by-walking-around can block the ability of an organization and its middle managers to learn at a more fundamental level. "Double-loop learning," as Argyris calls it, springs from asking why, challenging assumptions, disclosing potentially embarrassing information, and taking personal responsibility. Numerous examples of effective and ineffective learning appear in the history of technological innovation. James Utterback[16] believes that the displacement of dominant product designs by newer, more effective designs is usually effected by outsiders to the industry. Utterback speculates that owners of the dominant designs become so invested in their positions that they fail to see (i.e., learn) the threat posed by radical new alternative designs.

2. *Teaching, coaching, acculturating.* The skills of learning and the learning mind-set are virtually useless to a firm if held in isolation. Their powerful

impact on the firm increases exponentially to the extent that they spread. Thus, essential skills for the manager include *direct teaching* (conveying lessons to others), *coaching* (motivating and guiding others to learn), and *building the learning culture* (legitimizing, cheerleading, and rewarding learning efforts). The need to acquire and practice these skills has not been obvious to middle managers; until recently, business school curricula and the practitioner press have had virtually nothing to say about them. *Challenging and motivating* the inquisitive natures of employees become essential foundations of the learning environment. Chris Argyris has remarked that ". . . for companies to change, employees must take an active role not only in describing the faults of others, but also in drawing out the truth about their own behavior and motivation. . . . Leaders and subordinates alike—those who ask and those who answer—must all begin struggling with a new level of self-awareness, candor, and responsibility."[17]

3. *Developing and involving others in creating local visions.*   Active learning without a compelling vision to motivate it is like deploying a weapon without aiming. The emphasis of the new framework is on both the *process* (developing and involving) and *scope* (e.g., local) of the visioning effort. To create the new corporation, middle- and junior-level managers have a responsibility to facilitate the development of *meanings, concepts,* and *insight* about the business or desired outcome at hand. In some sense, developing a vision for the large-scale business is easier than a local vision. Large-scale visions are abstract and not easily linked to the day-to-day lives of employees; local visions are much more immediate and graspable. To develop a local vision requires an ability to manage downward and sideways (rather than upward) and to grapple with fears and aspirations of the people who must try to deliver the vision. Moreover, the visioning process should be ongoing. As Gary Hamel and C. K. Pralahad have stated:

> Developing a point of view about the future should be an ongoing project sustained by continuous debate within a company, not a massive one-time effort. Unfortunately, most companies consider the need to regenerate their strategies and reinvent their industries only when restructuring and re-engineering fail to halt the process of corporate decline. To get ahead of the industry change curve, to have the chance of conducting a bloodless revolution, top managers must recognize that the real focus for their companies is the opportunity to compete for the future.[18]

4. *Using and inventing technologies to involve others.*   Employment of new information technologies can enable and accelerate the foregoing skills. Many middle managers, however, find themselves to be followers rather than leaders in the use of information technology. The realization that their

junior (and younger) employees have information system skills that exceed theirs is threatening to many middle managers—and at the same time presents a fresh opportunity to improve a manager's engagement with the team or organization on behalf of learning and visioning. Given the relatively nascent status of systems hardware and software, it may be desirable to design or customize systems that meet the needs of the team. The rise of virtual teams illustrates the power of information technology to help achieve crucial new-framework objectives. Boeing designed its new 777 airframe entirely on computer in a networked system that connected engineers and specialists throughout the company as well as customers and suppliers. The virtual design process slashed development costs and shortened cycle time. Similar stories are told throughout the automotive industry. At Kodak, a new, single-use 35mm camera was developed in half the usual time, with a reduction of engineering and tooling costs by 25% and 15%, respectively.

LEADING FROM THE MIDDLE: SOME CONCLUSIONS

First of all, leading from the middle recasts the role of senior managers. In fact, leading from the middle makes no great distinction between senior and other managers—or even other employees. Leading from the middle is about fluidly marshaling resources to create value and doing it with a sense of purpose and engagement. In place of command-and-control, corporate executives must substitute a style of "release and guidance." Managers need to be chosen less for their ability to kowtow to the prevailing philosophy in the executive suite and more for their ability to make decisions and to implement proficiently for their businesses and teams. *Letting go* is a radical departure for senior managers whose careers may have been shaped in the old command-and-control crucible. To let go is not merely to release others from their immediate tight control, it also means *blowing up* the hierarchy that imposes its own stultifying force on the forward ranks of the organization.

When Asea and Brown Boveri merged on January 1, 1988, they became formally engaged in a transformation process, using many elements of leading from the middle. This process enabled two small-country firms to unite as a potent global competitor. Like any successful business transformation, the ABB story doesn't have an ending. (Only failed transformations end.) However, like almost all successful transformations, it began with a vision. Percy Barnevik, former CEO of ABB, believes that world-class global competitors need to simultaneously manage three contradictions: being global and local, being small and large, and being decentralized and centralized.

Barnevik's solution for ABB was to organize the merged companies into a federation of 4,500 companies and profit centers, each with its own governing board and bottom line. This allowed at least 4,500 people to lead from the middle. Residing in a cell of ABB's matrix, companies such as ABB-Germany and a business area affiliation provide each country with a national locus and a local perspective. Its business area affiliation places the company within a global business and as part of a network of firms contributing marketing, production, or technology to achieve worldwide success. Because it is one of thousands of such companies, it is necessarily small and relatively independent. Yet because of ABB's control system, named ABACUS, each firm is monitored by ABB's small headquarters staff. Managers at ABB have to lead from the middle, marshaling people, resources, and ideas to create value, while being coached and helped by ABB's senior managers.

Second, according to Bartlett and Ghoshal, senior managers must create an environment in which an *entrepreneurial process* exists: "A bottom-up entrepreneurial process can occur only when frontline management's role is transformed from implementer to initiator, and when senior management's role is to provide a context in which entrepreneurship can happen. At the foundation of an institutionalized entrepreneurial process is a culture that sets great store by the ability of the individual."[19]

Finally, a challenge for senior managers is to *create a learning culture.* Contrary to the assertions of business reengineering consultants, this must be more than just investing in job training. A learning culture springs from basic attitudes about intellectual honesty, the virtue of debate and challenge, and a zest for new ideas.

Where this leaves senior management, and indeed all managers, is with a different task and learning challenge. In the leading-from-the-middle mind-set, control (such as it is) is imposed through the second sense of the phrase: articulation of *vision and core values* of the firm. Recruiting and setting compensation remain crucial responsibilities. However, in the new mind-set, these factors are deployed for change rather than for stasis. Attending to high-level relations with suppliers, customers, creditors, stockholders, and governments is a critical task for all who lead from the middle, not just so-called senior management. In the new framework, these relationships are developed not with a view toward dominance and exploitation, but rather toward partnering for mutual benefit. These relationships provide the very foundation for learning that is so vital.

Simple yet profound changes have occurred in the underlying conditions that modern corporations face. The liberalization of markets and of political regimes have worked hand in glove to intensify the scope and pace of business around the world. Many companies have responded to some of the effects of these changes by restructuring their processes, by involving their people in broader and deeper decision making, and by attempting to change their cultures to become more focused on the external world, especially on shareholders and customers.

However, such restructuring, as difficult as it has been, is not enough. The changes require a dismantling of the hierarchy and a reinvention of what constitutes good practice. Such tasks are not easily accomplished, and we have no pretensions to having done so in this chapter. However, we are convinced that something similar to leading from the middle will have to emerge if Schumpeter's prediction of the demise of capitalism is to be proved wrong. We look at the profound changes that have occurred with a sense of optimism and a sense of drama that the real story of capitalism is being rewritten before our very eyes—by those people who see the opportunity to create value in the very turbulence that drives today's world.[20]

FOR FURTHER READING

Michael Best, *The New Competition* (Cambridge, MA: Harvard Press, 1991).

Howard Gardner, *Leading Minds* (New York: Basic Books, 1995).

Frances Gouillart and James Kelly, *Transforming the Organization* (New York: MacGraw-Hill, 1995).

M. Hammer and J. Champy, *Reengineering the Corporation* (New York: Harper Business, 1993).

Charles Heckscher, *White Collar Blues* (New York: Basic Books, 1995).

John Kotter, *Leading Change* (Cambridge, MA: Harvard Business School Press, 1996).

John Kotter, *The General Managers* (New York: Free Press, 1982).

J. Pine, *Mass Customization* (Cambridge, MA: HBS Press, 1993).

J. B. Quinn, *The Intelligent Enterprise* (New York: Free Press, 1992).

Peter Senge, *The Fifth Discipline* (New York: Doubleday, 1990).

J. Womack, D. Jones, and D. Roos, *The Machine That Changed the World* (New York: Harper, 1991).

15 STRATEGIC ALLIANCES

In recent years the face of the airline industry has changed dramatically. The industry has witnessed a growth of alliances among carriers worldwide so that you can fly on United from Washington to Sydney, transfer to Thai Airlines, and fly on to Bangkok. In Bangkok you can transfer to Lufthansa for the flight to Frankfurt and then on to Washington. Mileage is booked on United and counts toward United's frequent flyer program, flight codes may be shared across the three airlines, and all information is stored with United, who maintains a single point of contact with the traveler. This alliance competes with British Air and its alliance partners as well as with Northwest and KLM for market share in the global air-travel marketplace.

There is no doubt that the nature of competition in virtually all global businesses has changed over the last decade. The preceding example could easily have used the telecommunications industry to demonstrate how AT&T, British Telecom and MCI, and Global One (Sprint and its European partners) compete for the global voice and data requirements of major corporations that deal with customers and suppliers on a worldwide basis. The reality of business today is that alliances are on the rise. Firms from each corner of the world and across all sectors of the economy find that global competitive advantage is partially a function of a firm's ability to successfully find and manage a range of alliances.

Despite the rise of alliance activity, the data are less encouraging because the failure rate associated with alliances is quite high; in some instances, it is estimated to exceed 60%. On the surface, this figure appears to be high. However, if we use as a comparison point the rate of failure associated with the introduction of new products, alliance-related activities share a similar profile. Alliances are often a response to an uncertain world or set of market conditions. As a consequence, alliances inherently have a high degree of risk built into the process. When seen in this light, the failure rate should not be that surprising. Although alliance formations are increasing and spreading across a number of business sectors, the rate of alliance failures has not diminished. For instance, the number of alliances in the banking industry has increased almost tenfold since 1990. While some of this alliance activity can be attributed to the need for reducing backroom expenses by combining operations, the bulk of this activity is linked to new delivery mechanisms such as smart-card technology and PC and Internet banking. A simple explanation for this alliance activity is that banks have formed alliances in response to the threat that Microsoft and other nonfinancial companies pose to the retail banking industry.

This chapter will investigate the rise of alliances and will specifically explore alliance-related behavior—from the formation of alliances to the management of those alliances over time. Additionally, we will examine the role of the alliance manager. Finally, we'll will explore the rise of short-term kinds of alliances.

WHAT IS A STRATEGIC ALLIANCE?

Alliances tend to be a reaction to uncertainties that are either market- or technology-based. A small biotech firm might have developed an expertise in certain immunological research and be looking to partner with Glaxo Wellcome, which can maneuver the FDA requirements and clinical trial process and which has access to the market through its sales force. In this scenario, both companies gain from the alliance because each brings complementary strengths to the partnership. The Chinese government requires that all foreign companies who wish to do business in China work with a Chinese joint-venture partner. In some instances, the venture has a finite life. Once the Chinese partner gains the requisite skills or expertise, the foreign partner is required to sell its interest in the joint venture. In this example, the alliance becomes the only mechanism for gaining a market presence in China. In other examples, many corporate buyers are finding they can leverage the competence of their partners by single-sourcing with a supplier who provides knowledge and expertise in addition to products and services. Ford Motor Company shares its new-vehicle plans with Johnson Controls, which provides seats and related components that fit with

Ford's performance requirements. Thus, through this buyer-supplier alliance, Ford provides only performance specifications and Johnson Controls invests its own resources to ensure that these requirements are met. In the past, Ford would play one supplier against the other in search of lower costs, issuing an RFP containing lengthy design requirements.

From the preceding examples, you can see that the term *strategic alliances* includes a wide array of organizational forms, ranging from long-term purchasing agreements to comarketing and licensing agreements, R&D collaboration teams, and joint ventures. Despite the differences in organizational form, each of the definitions of these alliances converge on several salient themes. Each alliance has goals that are both compatible and directly related to the partners' strategic thrust. Each alliance also has access to the resources as well as the commitment of its partner. Alliances additionally represent an opportunity for organizational learning.[1] A *strategic alliance* is a close, long-term, mutually beneficial agreement between two or more partners, whereby resources, knowledge, and capabilities are shared, with the objective of enhancing the competitive position of each partner.

THE RATIONALE FOR ALLIANCES

Alliances should be positioned within the strategic efforts and goals of the firm. Alliances are driven by both offensive and defensive factors. *Offensive alliances* include focusing on accessing or creating markets, defining or setting industry standards, anticipating and preparing for new political developments, and preempting market access from competition. *Defensive alliances* concentrate on protecting or solidifying an existing market position, sharing the financial risk of an expensive technology, or gaining economies of scale. These activities of defensive alliances are often accomplished by combining processes and production capabilities.

Alliances are formed also to facilitate learning. For example, learning may involve gaining access to innovative new technology or to financial, marketing, and production expertise. One outcome of this approach is to speed time-to-market or access to technology. However, a darker side exists to such learning. Firms might use alliances as a means to expropriate proprietary technology at the expense of a willing, albeit naive, partner. In addition, alliances can be formed as a precursor to a merger or an acquisition. Recent work by McKinsey[2] examines the pros and cons of progressing from an alliance to a merger. On one level, an alliance allows partners to establish a level of comfort and rapport before engaging in an expensive merger. On another level, these alliances also allow firms to proceed slowly, thereby reducing some of the costly mistakes often associated with a rapid acquisition. Time, however, is a two-edged sword: On the one hand, time encourages rapport building; on the other hand, a need for consensus can slow the process, thus allowing resistance to the alliance to build. This was the case with the failed merger between Volvo and Renault in 1993.

Exhibit 15.1 demonstrates a range of trade-offs that a firm must consider when engaging in the decision whether or not to form an alliance. Questions arise regarding how to manage expectations pertaining to the gains and costs associated with the outcome of the alliance. In a conversation with one senior executive from a company engaging in many alliances and whose alliance management is acknowledged to be a core competence, I was told ". . . try to avoid forming alliances if you have a choice—the amount of management energy and attention needed to keep the relationship on track is enormous." Despite this warning, this particular firm had no choice but to form alliances because its skills were in basic science and technology. Many downstream ventures and opportunities became available to this company only through alliances with market-facing partners.

Interestingly, little is known about which kind of alliance is better for a set of partners and how to evaluate the risk or reward profiles of one form versus another. For example, if partners wish to share technology, it is difficult to determine whether a joint venture is better than a less complex, technology-sharing agreement. That is, different alliance forms can achieve the same results. However, under conditions of high uncertainty, where the consequences of failure are costly, less structured forms of alliances are apparently preferred. Similarly, when control is important in order to minimize the loss of proprietary information, highly structured alliances (e.g., joint ventures) are more advantageous. Even within the same industry, different alliance forms often emerge. AT&T and its world partners are best described as a network form of alliance in which members are loosely tied, while the BT-MCI concert alliance looks more like a joint venture. (This latter alliance, incidentally, is presently transitioning to a

EXHIBIT 15.1   Balancing alliance trade-offs.

Acquire Capability	Yield Control
Access to markets	Market overlap
Access to technology	Use of technology
Access to networks of firms	Entanglements
Knowledge	Loss of some control
Risk sharing	Sharing of profits
	Access to proprietary skills/expertise

purchase/merger of MCI by BT.) Both alliances, however, are focused on gaining a share of the global telecommunications market. Exhibit 15.2 describes a continuum of alliance types, comparing them on three critical criteria: cost, control, and flexibility. While the alliance rationale may appear to be the same, different alliance forms can emerge, depending on other organizational demands or constraints.

CORE DIMENSIONS OF ALLIANCES

Despite the different form alliances might take, each alliance must share certain key dimensions to be considered an alliance. Such clarification is important, because the term *strategic alliance* is overused and little understood. In addition, companies tend to talk in code, using the term to mean something else. For example, many sellers hear the term *alliance* and become concerned that the buyer is interested only in price concessions, playing one seller against the other in search of these concessions. We need only be reminded of the GM Lopez Affair[3] to understand a seller's worse nightmare of an alliance. Certain key dimensions must exist if a relationship between firms is a true alliance. To the extent that these dimensions exist, an alliance can be considered more stable. Stability is important, since alliances by their very nature are unstable and require an entirely different managerial mind-set. Hierarchy and command and control are no longer meaningful concepts. Alliances are governed by a loose set of rules and norms that emerge between firms, which maintain their autonomy and work together in support of mutual gain. Influence and cooperation replace administrative fiat. Discussion of key dimensions follows.

Goal Compatibility

Both parties have agreed that their goals, while not necessarily similar, are compatible, so that each party can achieve its own objectives as well as the objec-

EXHIBIT 15.2   Different alliance forms.

	Networks of firms	Buyer-Seller Alliances	Horizontal Marketing Programs	Value Added Distribution	Joint Ventures
Low Cost to Implement	< --- >				High Cost
High Flexibility	< --- >				Low Flexibility
Low Control	< --- >				High Control

tives upon which the alliance might be built. Part of the dilemma facing the partners is whether their individual goals and independence will be sacrificed for the good of the alliance. The loss of autonomy is often viewed as a potentially serious detriment to the formation of such close ties, and this is held in check when the parties acknowledge that both sets of goals do not need to run counter to each other. With the development of MS-DOS, IBM and Microsoft shared similar goals. As the OS-2 development process was tied to the Intel 286 chip, the two firms began to focus on different goals.[4] Bill Gates envisioned the need to move beyond the 286 because he was in the process of developing the Windows platform, while IBM was tied to the 286. This divergence in goals eventually caused the two firms to move in separate directions. Ironically, since that time, IBM has been plagued by the emergence of the de facto Wintel (Windows-Intel) standard.

Strategic Advantage

The perceived benefit that will be gained from the alliance is often the raison d'être for the relationship. A strategic advantage for the partners includes the pooling of resources, the ability to gain access to markets and technical information, complementary strengths to be leveraged, and the ability to lower the total cost of production. As a screening device, each party must assess what the other potential partner brings to the alliance. Furthermore, companies must determine whether a strategic alliance is the most appropriate vehicle for achieving relative competitive advantage. While the data suggest[5] that the ROI of alliances is higher than for mergers and acquisitions, it still remains a complex problem to determine the best vehicle for achieving long-term competitive advantage. In fact, much of the decision to engage in outsourcing alliances revolves around a set of decisions regarding what is core to the firm and what can be managed by an external partner who has more expertise or experience. Many firms, for example, have made the decision to outsource their logistics and their information technology functions.

Interdependence

Broadly speaking, to engage in any exchange is to become dependent on your trading partner. Part of the purchase decision process entails an evaluation of the benefits and risks involved in becoming dependent on the exchange partner. While interdependence is an antecedent to cooperation, it is also a precursor to conflict and is endemic to any relationship. The key is to manage the relationship in such a way that the cooperative and cohesive aspects of interdependence emerge and the dysfunctional aspects of conflict are minimized. Prior to the announcement that Bell Atlantic would merge with NYNEX, the two firms formed a joint venture to combine their cellular operations. Given that both companies together controlled the mid-Atlantic and Northeast corridors, a large percentage of cellular phone traffic flowed through their respective territories. Each firm became strong because of the other; it would be difficult to untangle the contributions made by one versus the other. When considering the amount of traffic that flowed just between New York and Washington, the degree of interdependence between the two companies is readily apparent.

Commitment

The handmaiden of interdependence is the threat of opportunism. As firms begin to share resources and decision making, opportunistic behavior can have a devastating effect on the partnership's longevity. In fact, Hamel and colleagues[6] urge potential collaborators to proceed with caution. Despite the opportunity for deceit and guile, implicit in all strategic alliances is trust, which serves as the counterbalance to such threats. Trust, or the belief that a party's word or promise is reliable and will fulfill its obligation in an exchange, is highly related to a firm's desire to coordinate activities closely with another firm. Commitment builds from trust and connotes solidarity and cohesion. A challenge for many alliances in the area of distribution is for both the manufacturer and the distributor to show commitment. Manufacturers are reluctant to provide exclusive territories and must look for other ways to demonstrate commitment. Manufacturers demonstrate commitment by education, distributor support programs, lead-generation programs, and cooperative advertising dollars. Distributors often show commitment by agreeing not to carry competing lines or by dedicating personnel to the manufacturer's products.

Communication and Conflict Resolution

Conflict resolution can take two paths: constructive and destructive. The direction taken by the firms involved depends upon whether the relationship is cooperative or competitive. Although partners in an alliance are, by definition, joined in a cooperative venture, some aspects of the exchange are likely to be competitive. Managing the situation in order for cooperation and constructive conflict resolution to prevail becomes the problem. Open and honest communication of relevant information leads to the constructive resolution of conflict. Mohr and Spekman[7] show that open channels of communication not only reduce conflict but also lead to higher levels of satisfaction between alliance members.

Conflicts are likely to be resolved through problem solving and persuasion when there is agreement about goals. Given the contingent and uncertain nature of many alliances, it would be virtually impossible to establish a priori a set of rules for resolving problems and conflicts in the future. A legal contract would not be able to address each and every future exigency. Certainly, legal regulation is less tenable. Many successful strategic alliances are based instead on self-regulation, whereby alliance partners establish mechanisms and processes for resolving future conflicts. To the extent that the alliance is perceived as being fair and providing equitable resolution of future conflicts, the alliance will rest on a stronger foundation.

Researchers[8] at the Darden School have developed the concept of the "blameless review," whereby alliance managers attempt to reduce conflict by working together and utilizing facts rather than by determining which party is at fault. This is done in order to better understand how to create mechanisms to gain mutually beneficial resolutions to problems affecting the alliance. The primary goal of the Blameless Review is for firms to work jointly to address obstacles facing the alliance. If resolution cannot be attained, it is hoped that dissolution will occur, following a spirit of fair dealing.

Coordination of Work

As mentioned, interdependence is tied closely to the specialization of work. With recognition of their interdependence, strategic partners exchange valued resources, and, in many cases, specialization is viewed as an extension of the work flow. Clearly, one advantage of collaboration is that the coordination of activities such as production scheduling, delivery, inventory management, and research and development can be approached at the level of functional integration without the bureaucracy and costs of ownership. Just-in-time (JIT) systems, electronic data interchange, joint marketing programs, shared R&D, and dedicated production facilities are examples of the types of strategic alliances in which the linkages between two companies must be flawless if the entire system is to run effectively. Programs whereby suppliers provide technical assistance or predesign expertise are often less obviously linked, but are no less important to the value chain and the efficiency of the production process.

Planning

The substance of planning in market exchanges is limited to the scope of what is being exchanged. To a large degree, planning (probably a misnomer) equates to the form and substance of the contract under negotiation. Strategic alliances are built on a belief that planning the substance of the exchange is secondary to planning the structure and processes of exchange. Parties recognize that the future planning of substantive issues will occur naturally as a function of the structure and processes established at the beginning of the relationship. These processes must also be flexible to accommodate future change. Partners must openly share future plans and take each other's concerns into consideration when planning. By sharing information and being knowledgeable about each other's business, partners are able to set compatible goals that help maintain the relationship over time. Jointly forecasting the impact of technological advances or market developments enhances the alliance's ability to evaluate its joint outcomes. In other cases, the investments required to meet projected changes in technology and markets raise switching costs and exit barriers. To protect a firm's investment in an alliance, it is crucial that planning not be done in isolation.

An evaluation of these dimensions provides a greater understanding of the preconditions for alliances, providing us with a greater appreciation for the issues germane to launching an alliance. Yet such a discussion tends to ignore questions of process. A concern for process adds a temporal dimension that affects how managers negotiate, execute, and modify alliances over time. A focus on process suggests that significant gaps remain when considering the following kinds of questions: How do alliances appear to evolve over time? What are the managerial skills and perspectives required to manage an evolving alliance? What kinds of problems can alliance managers expect to address over the life of an alliance?

A LIFE-CYCLE APPROACH TO STRATEGIC ALLIANCES

Studying an alliance's evolution over its life cycle helps us understand the process view of alliances.[9] Life-cycle analysis is a widely accepted approach in the marketing, management, and organizational literature. It is applied to products and markets, research and development, organizational growth and evolution, production processes, and personal relationships.[10]

Exhibit 15.3 illustrates the different stages of the alliance life cycle. Each stage is built upon a changing alliance landscape as the vision becomes reality and the reality grows into a mature business. *Anticipating* is the preliminary stage whereby an organization envisions the possibilities, ideas, and dreams of an alliance. A firm begins to articulate its strategic intent for the alliance as well as forming the requisite criteria for a potential partner. Prework is performed at this stage to determine why an alliance is the preferred strategic option. *Engaging* is the next stage, which is characterized by the partners beginning to sort or

EXHIBIT 15.3 Differences can be found over alliance life-cycle stages.

	Anticipation	Engagement	Valuation	Coordination	Investment	Stabilization	Decision
Characteristics of life cycle stage	Pre-alliance Competitive needs & motivation emerge	High energy Complementarity Congruence Strategic potential	Financial focus Business cases Analysis Internal selling	Operational focus Task orientation Division of labor Parallel activity	Hard choices Committing Resource reallocation Broadening scope	High interdependence Maintenance Assessment of relative worth and contribution	Where now?
Key business activity	Partner Search	Partner identification	Valuation Negotiation	Coordination Integration	Expansion Growth	Adjustment	Reevaluation
Key relationship activity	"Dating"	Imaging	Initiating	Interfacing	Committing	Fine-tuning	"Reassessing" "Dialoging"
Role of alliance manager	Visionary	Strategic sponsor	Advocate	Networker	Facilitator	Manager	Mediator

286

shape their mutual expectations for the alliance. Key managers begin to take ownership of the proposed partnership. *Valuing* is that period during which the terms of the business exchange are finalized. It is at this time that the business case is fully and completely made. Terms and conditions are negotiated, relative contribution of each firm is assessed, and resultant benefits are determined. *Coordinating* describes the stage in which joint work formally begins and more permanent governance structures begin to emerge. Firms at this stage focus on the integration and coordination of complementary business activities so that the alliance partners can leverage the anticipated gains derived from the alliance. *Investing* captures the hard realities of the alliance, at which point partners must invest in (i.e., commit to) the future course of the alliance. Now the vision is translated into an economic reality as key resources are dedicated to the alliance. Finally, *stabilizing* defines the stage in which the alliance has become an ongoing, viable entity. Homeostasis exists, and efforts by each partner are dedicated to managing the alliance with the adjustments and fine-tuning needed to keep it on course.

Simply enumerating a set of stages, however, fails to impart the full impact of examining an alliance through the lens of the life-cycle perspective. There is also a dynamic interplay of activities, people, and processes. By examining this interplay, a more robust picture emerges.

From Exhibit 15.3, it is also clear that an alliance is a complex interaction of business and interpersonal activities whose purpose is to achieve mutually beneficial goals. Both of these activities are at work in an alliance's development; both work simultaneously with each other. An examination of the business cycle helps us understand the evolution of the commercial side of the alliance, while a study of relationship activities provides insight for understanding the interaction between partner organizations and individuals. These business and interpersonal activities support each other. The full strength of the alliance is dissipated when attention is diverted from either of these components.

The *business life cycle* relates to the economic purpose of the alliance (its raison d'être) and can be best appreciated from a traditional product-life-cycle perspective. Each phase is characterized by a set of questions and can be recognized by a series of activities that revolve around the alliance's business-related issues. Concerns of the business life cycle relate to issues such as business processes, environmental changes, potential or actual competitive responses, financial projections, market access, customer acceptance, and mechanisms for sharing risks and rewards.

The *interpersonal life cycle* describes the interactions between the alliance partners over time. Each phase is characterized by a set of relationship development questions or issues that impact the alliance's relevant interpersonal or organizational relationship issues. Concerns regarding these interpersonal interactions relate to getting to know your partner, developing commitment and trust, managing conflict, and learning to manage in an ambiguous authority structure.

Business and relationship activities work together. A company cannot focus exclusively on the commercial logic of the deal. Interpersonal relationships are key to working relationships, and they are more important when they occur across organizational hierarchies. The interpersonal relationship provides a cushion of trust that braces the alliance, especially when the business is under stress. It is the safety net that protects the alliance from self-destruction when the business is underperforming or when expectations are not being realized. It would be naive to contend, however, that a strong relationship is sufficient for an alliance to succeed; there must first exist a strong business proposition. A number of alliances initially evolve because senior managers look for reasons to work together; however, a strong business rationale must prevail if the alliance is to succeed. A cushion of trust can prevent partners from acting rashly in an attempt to fix the business quickly and salvage the investment. There is a tendency for partners in the alliance to take a more measured approach to business problems.

Ironically, when the business is strong, partners are very willing to ignore problems facing the interpersonal side of the relationship. It is natural to ignore problems when there are slack resources and goals are being reached. However, if attention is diverted from the interpersonal relationship, a false sense of security can easily develop in the good times. As a result, strength of conviction disappears in the face of adversity. Conversely, a company must also guard against the possibility that the relationship might exhibit greater value than the alliance itself. If the business proposition is truly bankrupt, the strength of interpersonal ties must not cloud sound business judgment.

Alliance management is a complex effort that changes over the life of the alliance. The complexity and difficulty of alliance management stem from its very nature. An alliance brings together two or more independent companies, each with its own objectives, agenda, and culture. Culture, for example, is not limited to national differences; there are corporate cultures that affect firms' abilities to work together. When the Regional Bell Operating Companies (RBOCs) started to form alliances with the cable companies, the press suggested that problems were due, in part, to the cultural differences. In one article, these differences were summarized by making reference to a merger between the Roman legions and the Huns. To complicate matters further, a temporal dimension exists: Objectives change as the alliance develops and matures. The discussion here regarding the alliance life cycle takes the topic of alliance management well beyond partner selection and other concerns that are typically the focus of research, which is limited to issues germane to alliance formation.

THE ALLIANCE MANAGER

Exhibit 15.3 also highlights the role of the alliance manager. We have previously made reference to the importance of trust and commitment. These dimensions exist at the individual level and are fundamental to the role of alliance managers who provide coordination and integration between the alliance partners. Yoshino and Rangan[11] state that firms that make the best use of alliances tend to assign responsibility for their management to a specific manager. Simply put, an effective alliance manager is essential to alliance success.

Exhibit 15.3 further suggests that different alliance management roles follow different stages of the alliance life cycle. In the early stages of the alliance, alliance management is concerned with *visioning* and *sponsoring*. Alliance management first requires the formulation of the alliance idea, followed by internal selling, which helps the firm recognize the potential benefits of the alliance. As the alliance begins to take shape, alliance management concentrates on being an advocate for the alliance to important stakeholders and *networking* within and across companies to secure the commitment and participation of key organizational players. As the business solidifies, alliance management becomes concerned with *managing* and overseeing the operation of the ongoing alliance, in addition to *mediating* conflicts between partners, which can occur through the alliance's normal maturity and decline. What is important here is that the management focus shifts in concert with the temporal evolution of the alliance.

With all of the changing priorities and evolving focus in management, it is not surprising that managers are ill prepared to deal with the complexities of managing alliances. This problem raises the following question, which is critical to understanding how successful alliances are built and managed: What makes a good alliance manager at a given stage in an alliance's evolution?

Successful alliance management must operate simultaneously on three levels. These levels are interorganizational, intraorganizational, and interpersonal. On the *interorganizational level,* the alliance manager must balance the needs, resources, and desires of each of the partner companies. On the *intraorganizational level,* alliance managers must manage the needs, resources, and desires of their own company. On the *interpersonal level,* the alliance managers must manage relationships with superiors, peers, and subordinates, not only in their own firm, but also across boundaries of their various partner organizations.

Alliance management poses a unique set of challenges that set it apart from hierarchical management. Alliance management spans the boundaries of independent firms who agree to collaborate. Compromise, influence, trust, and so forth emerge as key operative terms; one company cannot dictate or issue directives. The partners' agreement must be obtained on mutually achievable goals, and processes must be enacted to achieve these goals. Research on alliances between entrepreneurial firms[12] demonstrates that formal contracts have little effect in maintaining the relationship between trading partners. It appears that social bonds between alliance managers are important and play a critical role in alliance development and continuity.

In order to accomplish this managerial challenge successfully, alliance managers must possess skills and competencies in three areas: functional skill sets, interpersonal skill sets, and alliance mind-sets. *Functional skill sets* can be considered the tools that a manager calls upon to accomplish specific objectives throughout the business cycle. These skill sets are similar to the range of skills learned in an MBA program. *Interpersonal skill sets* can be considered the tools an alliance manager uses to initiate, cultivate, and maintain relationships throughout the relationship cycle. For instance, social skills and communications skills are important; however, credibility is a critical skill, and it can only be earned over time. *Alliance mind-sets* are overarching perspectives that frame how a manager approaches alliance problems and creates order from ambiguity and chaos.

In Search of an Ideal Managerial Profile

There are a host of alliance management challenges that interplay regarding relationship ambiguity, a shift in managerial mind-sets, and the complex linkages among strategies, structure, and systems of both the partner firms and the alliance. These factors work in tandem with each other and are best illustrated by the different role requirements of the alliance managers. At this point, let's take a normative perspective and attempt to craft a profile of an effective alliance manager.[13]

Given the skill sets and mind-set constructs, we suggest that alliance managers will exhibit varying degrees of skill-set capabilities and different mind-sets; the optimal blend of skill sets and mind-set will vary across alliance stages. For example, in the very early stages of an alliance, the ideal alliance manager would be expected to display strong business and interpersonal skill sets, framed in the interpretive perspective of a learning mind-set. This combination would form an optimal fit between the alliance environment and the manager. The strong business skill set takes advantage of the breadth of industry knowledge required to formulate sound strategy. The strong interpersonal skill set addresses the need to rapidly develop and cultivate strong relationships. The learning mind-set draws on a variety of experiences to interpret and manage the uncertainty of the early alliance environment. As this environment becomes more complex, a learning mind-set becomes more critical.

Conversely, in the late stages of an alliance, the ideal manager might display strong functional skill sets and moderate interpersonal skill sets, framed in the interpretive perspective of an incremental mind-set. The strong functional skill set allows the manager to squeeze every bit of remaining value out of the venture. The moderate interpersonal skill set addresses the need to maintain, rather than grow, the alliance relationship. This incremental mind-set is able to work confidently within the managerial parameters laid down by the alliance partners.

Clearly, the particular managerial needs of any given alliance will vary in response to a wide variety of influences. Nevertheless, the skill sets and mind-set framework offers a perspective for identifying the most appropriate manager for a given set of situational circumstances. This framework also encompasses an appreciation for the different roles played by the alliance manager over the various stages of the alliance's life cycle. As stated previously, in the early stages of the alliance, the alliance manager might be a strategic sponsor—a combination of visionary and emissary. As the alliance grows, the manager takes on the role of networker and facilitator who is responsible for linking key people, functions, and business areas in the pursuit of the alliance's goals. In addition to being a manager who shoulders responsibility for the business of the alliance, the alliance manager must also be an adept mediator.

Although our focus here has been on alliance-building skills and competencies, one can argue that such capabilities also apply to managing within an organization, across either functional areas or business units. The role of project leader, team leader, and parallel team leader encompasses many of the competencies previously enumerated. Kotter's[14] view of a prototype for a twenty-first-century executive is also similar to our vision of a successful alliance manager. The commitment to learning, seeking challenges, and reflecting honestly on success and failure is consistent with our profile. The successful alliance manager is the symbol of the learning organization. Kotter describes this lifelong learner as someone who is a risk taker and a careful listener, reflective and open to new ideas.

Our entire previous discussion assumes that all alliances are expected to have an anticipated life that spans a number of years. In fact, alliance longevity is often used as a surrogate measure of alliance success. Interestingly, these more sustainable alliances are often described through the marriage metaphor, which itself implies a relationship that is expected to last a long time. While many alliances do in fact last decades, managers cannot afford this luxury under conditions of rapidly changing markets and technologies. Therefore, in a number of newly developed industries, we are witnessing a class of alliances whose life expectancies are quite short.

INTERIMISTIC ALLIANCES

Interimistic alliances represent fast-developing, often short-lived alliances in which partners combine their skills and resources to address a transient, albeit important, business opportunity. This opportunity may involve market access, technology development, or new product development. Interimistic alliances are typically found in swiftly evolving industries and markets marked by rapid technological change and uncertainty. Examples of these alliances abound, appearing in nascent industries such as biotechnology or electronic commerce. These alliances often are spawned by new technological developments, such as recombinant DNA or the Internet.

These alliances appear to challenge conventional academic wisdom with respect to how partners develop relationship attributes necessary for the creation of alliance value, at what levels these attributes must exist, and the definition of alliance success. As stated previously, it is natural to take a long-term view of alliance creation. Conventional wisdom suggests that the relationship characteristics (for example, trust and norms) are necessary for effective operation and value creation and are developed over a considerable length of time. In fact, the life-cycle research referred to previously suggests that it can take alliances three to five years to work through their start-up problems. Such a time frame can often exceed the entire life of an interimistic alliance, given the rapidly evolving environment in which it operates and the fact that competitive requirements often change in turbulent markets. Because of the need for immediate strategic impact and the fact that their objectives are typically short term in nature, interimistic alliance partners must hit the ground running. The partnership characteristics required for the effective operation of the interimistic alliance have to be either in place or developed in a highly compressed period of time.

In addition, questions about such issues as trust, opportunistic behavior, and commitment arise. Academic literature often uses the analogy of marriage to describe alliances, assuming long-term relations as the norm. Because of the shorter-term nature of interimistic alliances, relationship attributes necessary for a functional alliance, such as commitment and trust, exist—but in modified form. For example, commitment in interimistic alliances appears to be more project-bound than broad-based. Norms tend to be tied more to expectations derived from the industry rather than established through the relationship. Moreover, these relationships tend to be less proprietary in nature and are often nonexclusive. This is particularly true if the goal of the alliance is to set standards or to gain wider acceptance of a singular operating system.

Finally, it appears that interimistic and sustainable alliances have different measures of success. Interimistic alliances appear to be more focused on achieving success that is narrower in scope and not as results-oriented as the strategies pursued by sustainable alliances. Interimistic alliances help firms achieve milestone objectives on the path to greater final measures of success, such as market share or profitability. These alliances accomplish goals that, if not reached, make it very difficult for the final objectives to be attained. Companies involved in sustainable alliances often define success with a metric that more closely monitors the initial business proposition upon which the alliance was formed. Conversely, interimistic alliances focus on intermediate measures of success that, hopefully, at some future time, will result in financial gain for each partner. For instance, many of these interimistic alliances merely position firms so that they can participate in a future market or avail themselves of a new technological opportunity. These types of alliances allow firms to hedge their bets and, in effect, purchase options on future market and technological developments. These alliances provide an opportunity for firms to experiment with the future, learn from that experience, and continue to move forward wiser and better informed. For example, CyberCash has formed a number of alliances with the intent to promote its encryption protocol as the standard for Internet commerce. If its technology does not emerge as the dominant standard, CyberCash is likely to have difficulty participating as a full player as Internet commerce grows.

With respect to scope, traditional alliances are often broadly defined, encompassing sets of interrelated activities or functions. For example, alliances in the airline industry are often quite complex and far-reaching, involving the need for coordination at the operations level with flight crews, kitchens, and baggage handlers and at the administrative level with joint procurement of fuel, integrated frequent-flyer programs, scheduling, and mechanisms for revenue sharing. Interimistic alliances, on the other hand, are often designed to achieve more narrowly defined objectives such as acquiring know-how, producing a new product, or influencing industry standards.

A Metaphor

To illustrate the differences in the relationship development process between sustainable and interimistic alliances, a biological metaphor is used, comparing the life cycles of fruit flies and elephants.[15]

A life cycle consists of a series of stages or changes in form or function through which an organism passes. Generally speaking, fruit flies and elephants have an equal number and similar types of life-cycle stages. Each of their life cycles progress through birth, growth, maturity, and decline. There are differences, however, in the duration of each stage. The fruit fly's developmental stages are considerably shorter than the elephant's. A fruit fly reaches adulthood much sooner than does an elephant (approximately 22 days after birth compared to 12 years for the elephant), and its life ends much earlier than the elephant's (70 days versus 60 years). Although both elephants and fruit flies pass through roughly the same developmental milestones, fruit flies develop in a highly compressed period of time.

Similarly, while sustainable and interimistic alliances have the same life-cycle stages and developmental milestones, interimistic alliances develop and end much more quickly than sustainable alliances. As mentioned previously, the growth stage alone in a sustainable alliance can take years and can last for decades; interimistic alliances may last for a year or less. For example, SIECOR, the fiber-optic joint venture between Siemens and Corning, will soon enter its third decade of operation, whereas the alliance between IBM/Lotus and AT&T to develop Network Notes, a high-profile effort to connect users of IBM's Notes program over AT&T's network, lasted less than one year. Interimistic alliances have a narrow window of opportunity for maturation, given the rapid environmental turbulence and uncertainty they face.

Differences in the environmental drivers of these alliances account for differences in how relationship variables develop and at what levels these variables are present in both types of alliances. Sustainable alliances appear to occur in an environment of relatively low to moderate market and technology turbulence, which allows for a longer time horizon and the deliberate development of the necessary relationship attributes. Interimistic alliances, on the other hand, appear to be motivated during times of very high market and technological instability. Because the market and technology underlying the alliance's product and services are rapidly changing, and speed to market is often critical, partners are forced to proceed to the value-creation stage of relationship development very quickly. Also, rapidly changing competitive requirements such as changes in product or process technology needed to compete or changes in the marketplace (e.g., when the proprietary on-line market was replaced by the Web) compel partners' perspectives to be much more transient in nature. The speed of relationship development necessary and the partners' realistic projection that the alliance will be short-lived force the firms to either find ways to truncate the relationship development process or to modify the form of the relationship attributes achieved. Moreover, success in an interimistic alliance often allows participation in later alliances. This progression is analogous to the new product development process and the use of gates—a company cannot pass further through the development process until the requirements for a previous gate have been met. Imagine situations (for example, Internet commerce, digital cellular, EDI) in which there must first emerge a widely accepted standard before a new market or technology can be developed.

A Comparison of the Development of Relationship Attributes

Relationship attributes, such as trust and commitment, are dimensions that have been utilized as predictors of relationship performance, and they are necessary for an alliance to mature to a value-creation stage.[16] The manner in which these attributes evolve and at what level they exist in interimistic alliances is often different from the traditional model of alliance development. These attributes include trust, mutual goals, norms, interdependence, social bonds, commitment, and performance satisfaction. Our conclusions are summarized in Exhibit 15.4.

Trust is a precondition for alliance formation and is not an attribute that emerges over the life of the alliance; there is often insufficient time for this attribute to develop. Two important points arise here: (1) Trust is assumed to exist at a threshold level *before* the alliance partners consummate an interimistic alliance, because there is little time to let trust emerge. The alliance decision becomes binary: there *is* sufficient trust or there *is not* sufficient trust. Thus, past behavior as a partner becomes the predictor of future expectations about behavior and trustworthiness. (2) Trust is more context-specific and is limited to the scope of the interimistic alliance and the parts of the partners' business affected by it. Since many interimistic alliances tend to be nonexclusive, trust must be framed within that context. In traditional alliances, trust is viewed almost as an emergent core value of the alliance, built through the interactions of the partners.

Similarly, commitment, social bonds, and norms are tied more closely to the context of the alliance and are less embedded in a web of strong social ties between alliance partners. Dependence is linked to the goal of the alliance, and partners are motivated to cooperate so long as each views the other as essential to accomplishing each firm's longer-term goals and the alliance's mutual goal. While seemingly opportunistic, such self-serving behavior is held in check by the fact that partners are likely to meet again in the future; opportunistic behavior would be self-destructive in the long term. One partner's enlightened self-interest is modified by a set of norms that exist in the industry, which serve to guide interfirm behavior, thereby shaping expectations. This is in contrast to research[17] that shows how social norms emerge over time as part of the alliance partners' continued interaction. Interimistic alliances are driven by the moment, and the mutual goals become part of the "contract." In this sense, goal compatibility is seen as conditional on the changes in environmental events that can drastically alter industry demands. Both partners recognize that influences beyond their control, such as changing technology or a set of unexpected competitors, can make initial motivations for the alliance irrelevant, thereby eliminating goal congruence. At that moment, partners may decide to go their separate ways. Or

EXHIBIT 15.4 A comparison of sustainable and interimistic alliance.

Relationship Attribute	Sustainable Alliances	Interimistic Alliances
Evolution to value creation stage	Deliberate and lengthy.	Quick and short.
Expected life span	Long.	Short.
Environmental/industry conditions	Stable technological change. Reasonably predictable market and technology trajectory, increasing competition forces cost reduction and/or increasing valued-added.	Rapid technological change. High level of uncertainty regarding market and technology. Importance of speed to market.
Trust	Evolves over time.	Based on previous experience with partner, and/or on reputation, and/or a pragmatic view of the partners' "mutual hostage" position.
Mutual goals	Critical, often broad-based.	Critical, although it is project- or conditionally oriented.
Norms	Relational exchange norms; based on the expectation of mutuality of interest. Prescribing stewardship behavior. Enhance the well-being of the relationship as a whole.	Shared "enlightened" self-interest; norms based on the mutual understanding that the firms will work together as long as the alliance makes good business sense.
Interdependence	High and self-renewing.	Recognized but specific to the alliance task at hand.
Social bonds	Strong and pervasive.	Some level is essential. Broad reach is limited by virtue of the narrow scope of project. Some preexisting relationship sometimes exists.
Commitment	Strong.	Strong, but conditional, and/or bounded by scope of project.
Performance satisfaction	The usual measures of corporate success: development of long-term cost and/or differentiation advantages, and achieving a certain threshold level of profitability/market share.	Less tangible measures of success: influencing standard setting, part of achieving a portfolio of technology options, strategically positioning for the future, acquiring know-how, signaling partners/competitors/the market.

they might agree to refocus their energy and jointly pursue a new opportunity. Nimbleness clearly is a virtue.

The nature and development of norms in interimistic alliances differ from those of sustainable alliances. When environmental influences dictate otherwise, it is understood that the alliance could end quickly and that the partners might well become competitors. In this context, parties have expectations about potential individualistic or competitive actions by the partners and harbor less of a sense of continuity about the relationship. There is a mutually expressed or tacit understanding that the firms will work together as partners as long as the alliance makes good business sense. One key difference between sustainable and interimistic alliances is the emphasis placed on competitive considerations. For example, VISA and MasterCard International cooperate in such areas as standards setting, encryption, and basic smart-card technology. However, they knowingly and vigorously compete against each other once agreement has been reached.[18] These companies know that without agreement on fundamental strategic points facing the whole of the bank credit-card industry, both will face limited opportunities. In this context, it might be more appropriate to refer to the emerging literature on "co-opetition,"[19] which attempts to combine the best elements from research on cooperation and competition. The notion of complementors might become salient as parties ally to reap certain mutual gains so that they might both later compete in an expanded marketplace.

Interimistic alliances are partial solutions to business problems that exist in a turbulent environment. Therefore, performance metrics should be pegged to the goals associated with the reason for the alliance. In addition, it is best to view interimistic alliances as providing a set of options for partners to pursue future, or a series of future, alliances. Failure in an early alliance may preclude access to a later alliance. As such, it is very likely that firms will engage a series of alliance partners as they attempt to achieve competitive advantage.

Performance satisfaction is the degree to which the business transaction meets the business performance expectations of the partners. Defining appropriate measures of success and performance have been debated without resolution in the literature.[20] In interimistic alliances, in addition to social outcomes having a reduced priority, more project-oriented measures of success are utilized. These might include influencing standards setting, developing a strategic portfolio of technology options for the future, strategically positioning for the future, acquiring know-how, signaling to partners, competitors, and customers, or simply taking the only avenue open to the firm if it wants to be a player in an emerging arena. Success might better be viewed as a staging point or intermediate position on the way to a future competitive gain. Parties might successfully partner now so that each can successfully compete later in what is expected to be a larger market. If this alliance fails, neither partner might have acquired the requisite skills, knowledge, or influence over the market to compete later. Success in the interimistic alliance is necessary, but not sufficient, for the individual firm's future profitability.

Importance of Reputation

Because partners have different temporal expectations about interimistic alliances, these alliances require that partners play by a set of rules that is somewhat different from those applicable to sustainable alliances. While these interimistic alliances might often be as close and collaborative as any sustainable alliance, they tend to exhibit a higher degree of self-interest and bounded commitment. To a greater degree, partners in this type of alliance must adopt a stance of duality tinged with a sense of opportunism: How can the partners manage the existence of such seemingly diametrically opposed postures without jeopardizing the collaborative spirit that must exist between the partners in order for them to quickly create value? In part, expectations must be shaped to tolerate a certain level of self-interest. However, it seems that a more significant factor affecting the ability of the partners to balance self and alliance interests and quickly bring the alliance up to speed is the pivotal role of each partner's *reputation* in interimistic alliances.

The partners' reputation as a fair-dealing and competent alliance partner is critical to short-cutting the relationship development process. This reputation can be based on prior direct experience with the firm or general business community consensus. Without strong positive mutual reputational effects, firms in alliance cannot quickly progress to the value-creation stage, as is often necessary in rapidly evolving markets. A reputation for *fair-dealing* is the platform whereby partners can take the leap of faith necessary to quickly achieve a state of close collaboration. This gives the partners reassurance that, within delineated bounds, they will be dealt with in a spirit of good faith. The existence of a short-lived opportunity must not result in opportunistic behavior.

The second important reputational component is *competence*. Competence has two dimensions. One dimension deals with a partner's skills, know-how, and core competencies. Partners are desirable by virtue of their technical or market acumen. For example, because of their recognized expertise, both Sun Microsystems and Netscape participate in a number of nonexclusive, nonproprietary, potentially competitive alliances. Both of these firms are acknowledged as technology leaders in their respective fields. The second dimension captures the notion of alliance competence, which is a more nebulous construct. A reputation for an alliance competence assures potential partners that the firm is managerially well versed in structuring and implementing alliances. This makes the firm more attractive to potential partners, because it will enhance the ability of the alliance to quickly get up to speed and it improves the probability of alliance success. In this case, the partner is an enabler or a facilitator who is able to achieve heightened alliance results by minimizing the nonproductive energy associated with alliance formation and value creation. In addition, firms with high alliance competence have a wider choice of potential partners and have more discretion in selecting the best partners. Better partners are taken first, while less competent partners have fewer choices available to them.

Perhaps the best way to develop both alliance competence and, simultaneously, a reputation for competence is to develop a deep base of alliance experience. However, learning how to manage successful alliances is an evolutionary process. Firms can only truly learn by doing. For example, not only does Hewlett-Packard spend a considerable amount of money and effort training its managers on the art of alliance management, but Hewlett-Packard also uses alliances to learn about alliances. A business development manager at Hewlett-Packard commented that "after each alliance is formed, we hold a postmortem with all the involved (HP) parties. We look at the original objectives, the implementation, what went right, what went wrong." This information goes into a written management briefing, which later goes into an alliance database. By building a systematic approach to learning from alliance experiences, HP improves, throughout the corporation, its future alliance management capabilities on a real-time basis. It is no surprise that HP enjoys positive reputational effects as an alliance partner. Corning, as well, seems to have a positive alliance culture as a core strength. Managers are tested early in alliance situations and, over time, gain escalating alliance responsibilities.

SUMMARY

In this chapter we have described the alliance phenomenon as a major corporate activity. As conglomerates were to the 1960s and 1970s, alliances have emerged as an important organizational form in the 1990s. We have defined what alliances are and have established precise criteria, partly in response to the observation that the term *alliance* is overused and little understood. Moreover, alliances and alliance management have been described as a dynamic process that appears to follow a life cycle in which objectives, demands, and managerial processes vary over time. Finally, we introduced the concept of interimistic alliances, more fast-paced, transient relationships that appear to capture the nature of alliances in more embryonic industries. These shorter-term alliances capture the notion of networks of firms competing with other networks. These alliance forms have been compared to more traditional, stable alliances, which are often described through the use of marriage analogies.

FOR FURTHER READING

Joel Bleeke and David Ernst, *Collaborating to Compete* (New York: Wiley, 1993).

Jorden Lewis, *Partnerships for Profits* (New York: Free Press, 1990).

Jorden Lewis, *The Connected Corporation* (New York: Free Press, 1994).

Robert Lynch, *Business Alliance Guide* (New York: Wiley 1993).

James Moore, *The Death of Competition* (New York: Harper Collins, 1996).

Robert E. Spekman, Lynn Isabella, Thomas MacAvoy, and Theodore Forbes III, *Alliance and Partnership Strategies* (Lexington, MA: ICEDR Monograph, 1997).

16 INTERNATIONAL BUSINESS

In a provocative article written in 1990, Robert B. Reich, secretary of labor in the first Clinton term, asked the question, "Who is Us?" Mr. Reich made the point that identifying companies as American, German, or Japanese because they originated or were headquartered in these countries was a distorted view of business and a poor basis for policymaking. Because of the growing importance of international business, companies have expanded their manufacturing, research and development, and sales activities across borders. Many companies have more foreign employees than domestic workers, greater global sales than local sales, and a higher proportion of profits generated overseas than at home. Exhibit 16.1 shows prominent American firms that are substantially global. This being the case, in what sense are such companies designated as a particular nationality? Reich argues that these companies are not of a particular nationality, hence government policies should recognize this fact and, in turn, encourage companies to invest in the human capital of the nation, regardless of its nationality.

Although Reich makes this important point, it tends to obscure an equally important one—namely, the difficulty of conducting international business and balancing the often conflicting cultures and objectives of different participants. Conducting international business brings with it extraordinary opportunities, but also new challenges and risks for the corporation and the manager. Some of the challenges are broad: how to organize the firm and how to understand the economics and policies of the host country. Other challenges are narrower but quite

EXHIBIT 16.1 The globalization of American firms.

	Sales	Profits	Assets
Xerox	51%	64%	53%
Bankers Trust	41%	31%	50%
Chevron	33%	78%	55%
Exxon	53%	60%	56%
Mobil	75%	70%	63%
Gillette (1994)	70%	60%	66%
Manpower Inc.	72%	78%	72%

Note: 1995 data unless otherwise noted.
Source: Company annual reports.

crucial: What should the compensation system be, and how do we manage exchange risk?

In this chapter, we are going to focus on four aspects of doing business globally: (1) making the foreign investment decision, (2) managing political risk, (3) understanding foreign exchange, and (4) organizing the transnational firm.

MOTIVES FOR INTERNATIONAL INVESTMENT

Operations in distant and culturally different places are inherently more difficult than domestic operations. Conversely, domestic companies have a competitive advantage. Consequently, firms must have a variety of positive reasons to invest overseas.

Possible Competitive Advantages of Foreign Firms

There are several possible compensations for incurring the risk and problems of foreign investment. Some industries are characterized by economies of scale, because firms with larger market shares globally are able to operate more efficiently, with lower cost structures. A large multinational corporation (MNC), therefore, has an advantage over smaller, local firms because of its lower unit costs of production. Moreover, local production might be the only way to capture or maintain market share. Many firms shift from an export orientation to overseas production because trade barriers restrict or threaten their access to current or potential markets. If competitors establish production facilities inside the trade barriers, they might be able to expand their market share, reduce costs, and compete more effectively in all other markets. This is one example of defensive foreign investment (i.e., overseas expansion motivated by a desire to protect market position). As regional trading agreements have grown in importance, companies from outside those areas have sought to establish insider positions by investing in a member country. An important example of this is Japanese firms that have invested in England and Mexico so they can be inside the European Economic Community and NAFTA.

Another advantage that firms can exploit is superior knowledge or technical expertise. This might be the result of research and development activities or skills related to the marketing of products. Knowledge-intensive industries, such as the chemical, pharmaceutical, and electronics industries, have been major sources of foreign investment activity. Consumer products industries, where brand identification and promotion skills are important, have also been a major source of foreign investment activity. Both types of knowledge—production and marketing—can be exploited by companies in order to compensate for the additional difficulties of overseas investment. These companies might provide reduced operating costs or product differentiation that would allow them to compete with even a higher cost structure.

Although the advantages of superior knowledge explain how firms can successfully compete overseas, these advantages do not necessarily explain why a company invests overseas. These advantages can be utilized to expand export sales. However, when export sales are threatened by restrictions or competition, overseas production becomes desirable. Once a foreign firm has established a market for a product or service through exports, domestic competitors enter that market. With protection through quotas or tariffs, the domestic firms are able to compete with and, in some cases, totally displace foreign producers.

In the current economic environment, debt-burdened, less-developed countries are pursuing aggressive trade policies. These policies frequently include import substitution. Encouraging local production causes imports to be reduced and incentives to be created for foreign investment.

Many countries are engaging in extensive privatization programs. Formerly state-owned enterprises are being converted to private firms, often with substantial foreign ownership. Within the telecommunications industry, privatization frequently entails the continuation of a protected market in order to attract the foreign investment.

Another primary motive for overseas expansion is directly related to cost reductions. Foreign investment is often necessary in order to secure low-cost raw materials such as petroleum, bauxite, or rubber. Without access to these materials, firms find themselves at a competitive disadvantage in comparison to vertically integrated competitors. Labor can be viewed in this context as a raw material, so establishing foreign operations to take advantage of lower overseas labor costs fits into this category.

Related to cost reductions is the need to establish overseas offices and facilities to serve customers located abroad. Even companies that market primarily through export channels have found that after-purchase relationships with customers require in-country operations. This is true even for service companies such as banks, which have followed the flag as their domestic customers have expanded overseas.

Another motive for overseas investment is for companies to take advantage of subsidies offered by foreign governments. In order to attract technology, jobs, and foreign exchange, many countries offer foreign firms special tax treatment, tariff protection, or below-market financing. These subsidies frequently represent crucial considerations when a firm is evaluating an overseas location. Without the added inducement, the project would not be justified; however, with the proper inducement, the project is acceptable.

A final motive for direct foreign investment is the desire by a firm to diversify its wealth position. Modern financial theory has shown the advantages of holding a diversified portfolio of assets. Just as there are potential gains from diversification across industries, there are also gains from diversification across national borders. Unfortunately, a number of factors exist that make it difficult for individual investors to own securities in other countries.

These factors include the following: (1) Many nations have restrictions on capital flows that disallow portfolio investment; (2) capital markets in most less-developed countries, and even many developed nations, lack depth and breadth; and (3) there are relatively few traded securities, and they are held by a small number of investors, making it almost impossible for foreign investors to acquire assets in these countries even when formal restrictions are absent.

Even in developed countries, investment is difficult to accomplish. Tax rules are different from nation to nation, and information about securities is not as available in other countries as in the United States. Consequently, although investors believe that there are benefits to international diversification, they are unable to diversify their own portfolios.

An alternative to individual diversification is to invest in MNCs. With their legal staffs and industry knowledge, these companies are able to engage in direct investment despite the information barriers that thwart individuals. The logical extension of this argument is that shareholders may desire management to diversify in order to substitute for individual diversification, which is blocked by formal and informal barriers. However, there is no direct evidence that firms are in fact motivated by the diversification issue.

Disadvantages Related to Foreign Operations

As stated previously, firms face added difficulties relating to overseas operations. It is worthwhile to keep the following potential difficulties in mind when cash-flow forecasts and risk adjustments are discussed in subsequent sections:

- The firm is perceived as being foreign, which causes resentment among consumer groups, domestic competition, and government officials. Often, these interest groups or stakeholders mistrust the foreign parent. The local interest groups perceive these firms as having a different loyalty. It is this attitude that Reich suggests is inaccurate.

- Foreign operations are physically located very far from headquarters. Information is more difficult to gather and disseminate, making managerial control more difficult.

- Cultural differences exist that need to be considered in determining organizational design and personnel policies.

- A new set of tax and legal rules must be learned and incorporated into financial planning and firm policy.

- Transactions occur in a foreign currency, which adds to the uncertainty of cash flows and becomes a significant new element of risk.

- The firm must operate in a different political environment. A failure to understand that environment and its laws can lead to severe penalties, including placing a firm in conflict with the laws of its home country.

In addition, if the political atmosphere is less stable than in the home country, the firm must deal with a rapidly changing environment. Keeping up with events requires resources that must be expended on information gathering.

Assessment of Foreign Cash Flows

A frequent shortcoming of cash-flow forecasts is that they fail to identify all of the potential benefits and problems related to an overseas investment. It is likely that fewer errors will be made if the motivation for the project is kept in mind at the time the cash flows are estimated.

The major difficulty faced by analysts evaluating foreign investment cash flows is the divergence between the cash flows generated by the investment project as a freestanding local project and the cash flows accruing to the parent company. Several factors contribute to these divergences; some are controlled by the investor, and others are determined by the firm's operating environment, including the government. The factors leading to these divergences are elaborated later on, but regardless of the source of the discrepancy, it is important for investors to recognize that cash flows that affect their position are the relevant ones to include. Estimation of these cash flows involves a three-stage process. The first stage is a forecast of the total or freestanding project; the second stage is the estimation of corporate, systemwide benefits and costs; the third stage takes into account all of the tax and exchange rate effects but leads to an estimation of investor cash flows. This three-stage process requires an identification of the factors that cause the two cash flows to diverge and a procedure for converting estimated foreign currency flows into the home currency of the investor.

SOURCES OF DIVERGENCE

Interdependencies

As indicated in the preceding section, overseas investment is often prompted by defensive motives. This is a reaction to trade restrictions or competitive pressures. In these cases of overseas investment, some of the sales generated by the project are cannibalized from export sales formerly made by existing divisions of the firm. Sales that are taken away from other units but would have been maintained without the overseas expansion should not be included among the project's revenues. At the same time, if these sales are lost owing to trade restrictions or competition, they are correctly attributed to the project.

An example can help clarify this point. A firm is contemplating an overseas investment that will have sales of 6,000 units per month at a price of $50 per unit. The firm currently services that market with export sales of 4,000 units at a price of $60 per unit. A major competitor is establishing a facility in the same region in order to avoid import quotas that will be in place the next year. If the firm does not follow suit and make the investment, its estimated export sales will be 1,500 units at $50 per unit. If it does make the investment, export sales will fall to 1,000 units. What is the amount of sales revenue that should be credited to the foreign investment?

The correct answer is the amount that is incremental to the project compared with what would be generated if the project were not undertaken. That amount is $275,000 per month, the difference between the $350,000 total sales with the expansion and the $75,000 that would be realized without it. The $275,000 represents the $300,000 in sales that the investment generates less the $25,000 that is cannibalized from existing sales. The remaining decline in export sales ($165,000) is not deducted from the project because those sales would be lost even if the investment were not made.

Changes in sales revenues are utilized in the example to illustrate interdependencies, but they are only one side of the cash-flow equation. In a more complete analysis, costs are also considered. If costs were higher at the foreign operation, the increase would have to be taken into account when cash outflows were estimated. The net impact on total cash flows is the relevant issue here.

Interdependencies also show up through transfer pricing. Once foreign operations are established, it is likely that intracompany transactions will cross international borders. Firms establish transfer prices when these transactions clear between the operating entities. These transfer prices are not always set at market levels because of tax effects and currency restrictions. Transfer pricing might be used to shift earnings from a high-tax jurisdiction to a low-tax jurisdiction. An internal effect of this pricing policy is to reduce stated cash flows in the high-tax country and increase them in the lower-tax country. From a corporate viewpoint, the tax reduction increases total cash flows, but without careful analysis the source of the cash flows might be identified incorrectly. The following problem exemplifies interdependency in transfer pricing.

A firm is considering investing in an overseas assembly plant that will buy components from the parent. The market price of the component is set at $30, at which price the contribution margin for the parent is $8. After assembly, which adds $10 to the cost, the subsidiary will sell the finished product for $50. The effective tax rates in the parent's and subsidiary's countries are 30% and 40%, respectively. At the existing transfer price, the after-tax cash flows for the corporation are $11.60: $5.60 at the parent level and $6.00 at the subsidiary level. Because of the differences in tax rates, a higher transfer price would lead to higher after-tax cash flows for the corporation as a whole. At a transfer price of $40, the subsidiary's profits are eliminated entirely, whereas the parent's after-tax earnings rise to $12.60. If the $40 transfer price is used in evaluating the overseas project and the subsidiary is not credited with its share of the final cash flows, the investment will be turned down. As an extreme case, suppose all of the sales are dependent on building the assembly plant (because of trade restrictions). The correct cash flows to the project then would be the full $12.60, even though none of these cash flows show up on the subsidiary's books. Because of the presence of interdependencies, it is important to identify accurately the amount and source of all relevant cash flows.

Remittance Restrictions

Countries frequently impose limits on the amount of funds that subsidiaries can pay to their overseas parents in the form of dividends. These policies are generally part of a more comprehensive program to reduce a balance-of-payments deficit. Descriptions of restrictions in force and changes in policies can be found in *Exchange Arrangements & Exchange Restrictions,* published annually by the International Monetary Fund. At the time that an investment decision is being made, it is important that current restrictions are understood and that some estimate is made of the probability of continuing restrictions or of restrictions being imposed in the future. The latter necessarily involves an evaluation of the host country's balance-of-payments position.

Restrictions come in a variety of forms, usually allowing only a maximum percentage of annual earnings, retained earnings, or sales to be paid. Whatever their form, restrictions have the effect of deferring the receipt of cash flows, thereby reducing the value of these cash flows. The amount of loss is determined by the severity of the restriction, the length of time that receipt of the flows is delayed, and the opportunity available for investing the blocked funds before repatriation. For example, assume that an investment with a 10-year life generates annual net cash flows of $1 million. Restrictions on dividends limit payments to $400,000 each year for the first nine years but allow payment equal to accumulated retained earnings at the end of the tenth year. The appropriate cash flows to consider in this case are then $400,000 per year for the first nine years and $6 million in the last year. If the funds can be reinvested during the interim, the additional interest income should be included. If the $400,000 can be invested at 10% and these earnings are also available for dividends at the end of the tenth year, the final cash flow will be $6,400,000 plus $2,303,600 in interest.

In the example, cash flows and earnings are considered to be the same. That is usually not the case because of the presence of noncash expenses such as depreciation. The disparity between earnings and cash flows creates some ambiguity about which cash flows are available for repatriation. If the dividend restriction establishes a limit on payments that is based on earnings, the positive cash flow related to depreciation will not be available to the firm for repatriation. Unless these funds can be used beneficially elsewhere in the country, it will usually be in the parent corporation's interest to keep depreciation expenses low in order to maximize after-tax income available for foreign dividends. There is no general rule to follow that fits all cases, but it is necessary to understand fully whatever restrictions exist and their implications.

Taxation

Differences in tax rates have already been shown to enter the cash-flow calculations. Effective tax rates in different countries vary a great deal. From the standpoint of a U.S. investor, the tax rate that applies is usually the higher of the two effective rates. The United States gives credit for foreign taxes, but only up to the maximum U.S. rate. Therefore, any taxes beyond that rate reduce the return to the investor.

Subsidies

Decisions to invest in particular projects are often influenced by inducements offered by the host country. As indicated in the preceding section on motives for foreign investment, these can take a variety of forms. Given sufficient subsidies, projects that otherwise would not be acceptable become viable investments. For potential investors, a key question is whether the subsidies can be taken away if the host country has a change of policy. The current government may offer a tax benefit that is of substantial value if it stays in effect for the life of the project. This tax benefit serves as the necessary incentive to attract capital or technological knowledge. Once the investment has been made, the government may alter the tax laws or impose a new restriction that offsets the original subsidy.

Potential investors need to evaluate the subsidy and the probability that it will be eliminated. A very conservative approach is to accept only projects that would be viable without the subsidy. A more reasonable method is to adjust the cash flows in order to take account of the risk or probability of losing the subsidy at some future time; being aware of the importance of the subsidy also allows the investor to take steps to reduce the impact of its loss.

POLITICAL AND OPERATING RISK

Definitions of political risk vary, but some general characteristics and examples may be readily identified. First, however, it is important to distinguish between the closely related concepts of country, economic, and political risks and to note their relationship to each other.

Country risk refers to elements of risk inherent in doing business in the economic, social, and political environment of another country. In international lending decisions, for example, bankers typically examine the economic conditions of the country in question, including the country's balance of payments, its central bank policies and their effectiveness, principal economic sectors (imports and exports, trends and prospects, flow of funds, and financial intermediation), social conditions, international relations, and the impact of world events on the domestic economy.

Generally speaking, *economic risks* are not politically generated, and they include those risks resulting from technological changes, the actions of competitors, and/or shifts in consumer preferences. In many cases, however, there is a close link between political events in a country and economic risk. For example, the disintegration of the market structure in Lebanon during its civil war, the banning of certain Western products by the Khomeini regime after the success of the Iranian revolution, and the uncertainties posed by the breakup of the Soviet Union are clear instances where economic risks were exacerbated by political events.

Similarly, while most labor strikes are limited in scope and economic in origin (e.g., disputes over wages, benefits, or other work-related issues), many general strikes, such as those in Nicaragua in 1978 and Poland in 1980, are clearly political in nature and have wide-ranging economic repercussions. Even events with clear economic purposes, such as price controls designed to control inflation, often carry political overtones. Thus, it is sometimes very difficult to distinguish between economic and political risks, and there are few events that are purely one or the other.

While definitions of political risk vary, for the purposes of this discussion political risk should be regarded as a subset of country risk. *Political risk* may generally be defined as the exposure to a change in the value of an investment or cash position because of government actions or other nonmarket events that are political in nature. Whereas country risk focuses generally on the overall investment environment of a country, political risk arises from the political environment. The following are examples of political risk events that may negatively affect the magnitude and distribution of cash flows from an overseas investment:

- Changes in tax regulations and exchange controls, especially those that are discriminatory or arbitrary.
- Host-country stipulations about local production, sourcing, or hiring practices.
- Commercial discrimination against foreign-owned businesses.
- Restrictions on access to local borrowings.
- Governmental interference with privately negotiated contracts.
- Expropriation without adequate compensation.
- Damage or destruction of facilities or harm to personnel, resulting from political riots or civil war.

Because the effects of political risk events may be varied, managers should be aware of the full range or types of political risk events that may affect the host country as well as their particular industries, companies, or projects.

Among the most dramatic losses stemming from political risk events are those resulting from revolutionary upheaval and terrorism. For example, in December 1977, GTE signed a telecommunications contract worth more than $500 million with the Iranian government. In accordance with the contract, GTE advanced Iran $94 million in open letters of credit, commonly used in the Middle East in lieu of performance bonds. Given its longtime experience and confidence in Iran, the company did not specify the grounds on which Iran could call the letters of credit, and no insurance was taken to cover the risks. After the revolution, work on the project proved impossible, and the company stood to lose over $50 million, not including the letters of credit. If those are included, GTE's potential after-tax losses could have exceeded $60 million, possibly the largest single-firm loss in Iran.

In addition to revolutions, coups, and violent acts of terrorism, political risk can also take the form of legislative or regulatory changes. In Iran, for example, B.F. Goodrich had built the largest tire plant between Europe and the Far East, with assurances of trade and investment protection from the government. Such protection was prematurely lifted, however, in favor of two competitors in the mid 1970s, forcing the U.S. firm to go from three shifts to a single eight-hour production schedule. Changes in the law or in regulations can also be directed at companies collectively, as when the shah decided to mandate public stock offerings on the part of Iranian-based corporations so as to increase worker ownership and participation. The action was expensive and very disruptive to foreign businesses.

Changes in government, whether the result of an election, coup, or revolution, may be partly determined by economic events, and thus may bring about changes in policy toward foreign investors. For example, shifts in political-economic ideology may lead to the expropriation of most, if not all, foreign-owned firms.

While dramatic events such as revolutions or expropriations attract a great deal of attention and might cause a company to shy away from more turbulent parts of the world, a political event in itself does not necessarily constitute a risk to business. In fact, political instability can present opportunities as well as risks. For example, Gulf Oil Corporation in 1975 was able to negotiate a very favorable relationship with the Marxist governing party during the Angolan civil war, and Dow Chemical was able to reenter Chile after the overthrow of Salvador Allende in 1973.

Such dramatic events are the exception rather than the rule, however. Although the Cuban and Iranian revolutions undeniably created major problems for U.S. firms, most politically generated contingencies present macro- rather than microrisk, and, increasingly, affect operations rather than ownership. Rather than full or partial expropriation, such changes in government or ideology more typically entail price controls, restrictions on expatriate employment, local content regulation, or other regulatory constraints. For example, when

Venezuela ran short of foreign exchange in 1983, it ordered domestic companies to extend payments on their foreign debts for several years. Recognizing that money has time value, many creditors negotiated immediate settlements at steep discounts and suffered heavy losses.

Indeed, political instability and conflict are not necessary or even frequent prerequisites to constraints on foreign firms as a result of changes in the political environment. Price controls and other regulatory constraints may result from the regular functioning of the political process owing to losses or gains in the regime's power or to changes in the character and power of the opposition or of interest groups. The privatization program in the United Kingdom under Prime Minister Thatcher in the 1980s and, in contrast, the nationalization policy pursued by President Mitterand in France during the same years are examples of how different political philosophies are manifested in economic terms, with important financial consequences for managers and investors.

Another example of how the normally functioning political process affects international investment is the European Community (EC) 1992 single-market movement, which carries with it enormous political risks as well as opportunities for global companies. As Europe proceeds with its economic and political unification, companies may find themselves shut out of certain markets, owing to regulatory changes. For example, Spain and Portugal, which are currently enjoying a great deal of foreign investment because of their cheap labor relative to the rest of Europe, may not be as attractive in the future as they increase wages to comply with the EC 1992 single-market program. Companies that have made significant investments in Western Europe based on pre-1992 economics may thus find their investments turning sour in the post-1992 world. The importance of keeping up-to-date with political and regulatory changes can hardly be overstated.

Turning to Eastern Europe, the relatively stable economic and political climate that accompanied the Cold War has become turbulent and unsettled as the former Communist countries attempt the transition to a market economy. A glance at the former Eastern bloc reveals the full panoply of political risk. In the former Yugoslavia, once prosperous towns and productive factories have been devastated by ethnic fighting and civil war. In Czechoslovakia, the split between the Czechs and Slovaks over the pace of economic reform has led to the breakup of the country, which could have adverse effects for the foreign companies that have invested in the Slovak republic. General Electric's much vaunted $150 million investment in the Tungsram lighting plant in Hungary has lost money because the government has not devalued the forint in line with Hungary's soaring inflation. Chevron, which entered into a joint venture agreement with the former Soviet government, now finds itself in the position of having to negotiate with several independent republics. Moreover, Russia is chronically short of hard currency, and its vacillating monetary policy and price reforms cast a long shadow of uncertainty over any prospective investments.

Russia offers an example of another type of political or country risk. The economic transformation taking place there has moved more quickly than the transformation of the legal system. Investors in Russia have to contend with nonexistent or rapidly changing rules and laws affecting private property, making it difficult to protect investments and establish the rights of investors.

The tangled and often contentious U.S./China trade relations offer another interesting example of political risks. American companies have invested billions of dollars in China in order to have access to the enormous Chinese market and to manufacture for exportation to the United States. A critical requirement of using China as an overseas manufacturing base for products sold in the United States is that China must maintain its most-favored-nation (MFN) status. This allows Chinese goods into the United States at the lowest prevailing tariff. Revocation of MFN would lead to prohibitive tariffs that would offset any cost advantage gained by manufacturing in China.

Continuation of China's MFN status has been questioned on several grounds: China's human rights policy, its sale of nuclear materials, and its failure to uphold trade agreements on copyright protection for intellectual property. Each of these issues has provoked an outcry from human rights organizations, firms hurt by the pirating of intellectual property, and members of Congress who want to revoke China's MFN status. Thus far, efforts to revoke MFN status have been rebuffed, but the threat of such action jeopardizes the value of investing in China and must be considered as part of any investment decision.

Another example of political risk and the odd twists that it might take involves the executive of a Canadian firm, Sherritt Inc. Executives from this firm and their families have been banned from the United States because their company operates mining properties in Cuba that were nationalized by the Castro regime. The United States passed the Helms-Burton Act in 1996, which established sanctions on non-U.S. companies operating in Cuba. Sherritt does not do business in the United States, has not broken any Canadian laws, and yet the children of its executives are not allowed to go to Disney World or anyplace else in the United States.

As these examples indicate, the global marketplace is by its very nature uncertain and turbulent. The question of whether particular aspects of this turbulence and uncertainty constitute a risk to business is problematic, and its answer depends on industry, firm, or project characteristics and managerial actions. Thus, the elements of political risk will vary widely among different countries and companies. Even within a country, political risk is usually industry-specific, and in many cases, project-specific as well. Rural insurgency, for example, may pose serious problems to a commercial farming operation, but its impact on a company specializing in financial services or insurance might be minimal. Assessing the political risks of direct foreign investment, therefore, involves the analysis of elements of aggregate or countrywide risk as well as of elements of political risk specific to the company or to its project.

Monitoring Developments

Monitoring involves establishing an intelligence network that provides political, social, and economic information with which to understand events in the host country. For large firms with extensive worldwide investments, such as the major petroleum companies, the intelligence-gathering process can be almost entirely in-house. The same is true for multinational banks with extensive branch systems. Area or divisional personnel can be assigned the primary responsibility for collecting information and forwarding it to headquarters for evaluation.

Many large companies now have staff economists and political scientists who provide country risk assessments. Although these staff people play an important role in the monitoring process, their analyses should be used in conjunction with evaluations of line personnel who are stationed in the country. Relying solely on either staff or line personnel can provide biased analysis. Staff evaluations tend to be more objective, but because these evaluations are done at a distance from a country, they often ignore insights that can be gained only by living in an area. Line personnel have this living-in-the-area experience, but are often unwilling to recognize or admit negative aspects of their own nation or the country for which they have managerial responsibility, in part because negative information might adversely affect their own activities. For example, bank-calling officers or branch managers would be the appropriate line personnel to provide country information, but their personal interest is in expanding loans or the sale of other bank services. This basic conflict often introduces a bias into the information-gathering process.

Smaller firms generally do not have the resources to develop their own information networks. Instead, they rely on information purchased from firms organized for that purpose. Even if the company's primary information sources are external, the company should still establish an internal monitoring system as a secondary source. Area personnel should file informal country evaluations, and the headquarters' staff should visit the country on a regular basis. The assessments of area personnel and headquarters' staff should be matched against those of the external source to check for consistency and accuracy. A firm should not become too dependent on a single source or too complacent to change to another advisory service if its current one is missing too many trends or changes.

Anticipating Policy

All information should be evaluated with the objective of anticipating policy changes of the government or in the attitudes of other stakeholders in the host country. Some changes affect the general operating environment of the firm, whereas other changes have a direct impact on the operating or ownership structure of the firm.

Environment changes can be both general and specific. Among the former are macroeconomic policies that attempt to stimulate or restrict economic activity. Countries that have accelerating inflation or difficulty in servicing external obligations are likely to pursue contractionary monetary or fiscal policies. For a firm with largely domestic sales, this would reduce revenues. Other changes related to macroeconomic policy are the imposition of price and wage controls and currency restrictions. From the earlier discussion of cash-flow forecasts, it should be clear how these changes would affect the firm and the value of the investment. The point is that if management can anticipate these policies, it can take steps to reduce their impact: Prices might be raised prior to controls being enacted; foreign currency payments might be made before the local currency becomes inconvertible; or arrangements for parallel loans might be made to reduce the amount of local currency blocked in the country.

There are other longer-term policies that a firm might pursue to reduce risk. Labor unrest in the form of strikes varies in severity from country to country. In nations where strikes are frequent, the firm might choose less labor-intensive technology or adopt employment policies that reduce the threat of strikes.

A large U.S. electronics firm with major manufacturing facilities in the United Kingdom has a totally nonunion labor force in a highly unionized country. This firm has been able to maintain this status by having generous benefits and an open employee-management relationship. These policies entail some added costs, but reduce the risk of labor strife. The company has not lost manufacturing time owing to strikes, and it has added flexibility in establishing its seniority and compensation system.

More specific policies that arise from concerns about the economic environment can directly affect the operating structure of the firm. Requirements concerning local content in manufacturing and domestic nationals in management positions, pricing to subsidize local consumption, or requirements that firms provide investment in infrastructure are examples. In general, so are regulations that affect transfer pricing or establish restrictions on licensing arrangements and royalty payments.

The final type of political risk comes in the form of government interference with the ownership of the assets or investment of a company. There are many ways in which governments can garner the wealth of foreign investors, ranging from punitive taxes and fees to outright expropriation. In between these two extremes are requirements for local participation in ownership and nationalization with some form of compensation. Regardless of the form it takes, it is unlikely that any involuntary change in ownership structure will benefit the original investors. If it would, then the original investors would have brought it about without coercion. Generally, increased interference and changes in attitudes toward foreign investment are preceded by significant economic or political events. That is what makes the monitoring and anticipation activities worthwhile; these activities allow a firm to reduce its exposure while there is still room to maneuver.

Adapting to Conditions

Adjustments and alterations in policies that firms make in response to changes in policies in host countries are signs of their adaptability. Doing business overseas requires a willingness and ability to respond to different legal, political, social, and economic environments. Sometimes these adjustments are undesirable on other grounds but necessary in order to reduce risk related to investing overseas. Entering into a joint venture is an important example.

Joint ventures represent shared ownership and control of operating entities by two or more independent firms or groups of investors. A requirement of local joint ownership is often mandatory for foreign investors. It arises from a sense of nationalism and a desire that some of the returns on capital investment be retained in the host country. At other times, firms voluntarily seek out joint venture relationships because of synergy. For example, one firm may have capital or an established distribution network and its partner may have special technological skills or a brand name.

Despite some major exceptions, survey research has indicated that the majority of U.S. firms are hesitant to form joint ventures, especially those involving local partners. There seems to be a variety of grounds for the opposition, most focusing on the control aspects. The partner company acquires access to technology and pricing information that might make it a formidable competitor at some future date. Differences in objectives might lead to disputes over dividend policies, transfer pricing, financial structure decisions, licensing agreements, and efforts by the foreign partner to rationalize production among its worldwide subsidiaries.

The trade-offs in favor of joint ventures include access to markets that might otherwise be unavailable and a reduction in the probability of government interference directed toward foreign investors. By having local nationals involved in ownership and management, the subsidiary loses some of its foreign character. This helps deflect criticisms related to exploitation, capital flight, and external control. The local partners have a stake in the company, which leads them to lobby on its behalf. Any restrictions imposed by the government might adversely affect local interests.

It is important to be careful in choosing a local partner. Under the best of circumstances, the local partner brings to the enterprise skills or attributes other than a convenient nationality. If nationality is in fact the only contribution, the foreign investor should try to find a partner that is reliable and in the mainstream of local politics. Having a local partner that is in the opposition party might lead to harsher treatment than would otherwise be the case.

A final course that might be followed to reduce risk exposure is the purchase of insurance. A number of developed nations, including the United States, have governmental or quasi-governmental programs for insuring foreign investment against the risk of war, expropriation, or currency inconvertibility. There is also a private insurance market organized through the auspices of Lloyd's. In the United States, the Overseas Private Investment Corporation (OPIC) provides insurance as well as project financing for U.S. private investments in less-developed countries. OPIC's fees vary depending on the type of coverage and, to some extent, on the risk related to the investment. OPIC has been very successful at marketing its programs, and the majority of nonpetroleum investments in less-developed countries have some form of OPIC coverage.

The decision to buy OPIC insurance must be made along the lines of risk management decisions in general. Firms need to weigh the costs against expected losses and their willingness and ability to bear those losses. Buying OPIC coverage might create a moral hazard for firms. Having protection could lead firms to ignore other risk-reduction policies and contribute to a higher incidence of loss. Ultimately, this would show up in higher premiums or a lessened availability of insurance. Since settlements under OPIC are usually the result of a long negotiating process, firms should avoid the attitude of "why worry, we're insured."

As a final caveat, investors should not associate political risk only with investments in less-developed countries. Each of the types of risk discussed in this section are, or have been, present in almost every nation. Certainly, the environmental factors are omnipresent; however, even in Western democracies, nationalization and changing attitudes toward foreign investment are prevalent. The investor might have better recourse under the law in Western democracies, but the interference in business operations and the loss of wealth are real possibilities that must be considered in making investment decisions even in these countries.

FOREIGN EXCHANGE RATES

A big part of what makes international business different is money. It is not that global firms are any more or less interested in making money, but that the value of the money they pay and receive changes constantly. For at least one party to every international transaction, the monetary unit used in the deal is not their own currency. This adds an element of uncertainty that does not exist in purely domestic transactions. Companies involved in international business need to understand the factors that influence exchange rates, the amount of risk involved, and ways to manage or mitigate that risk.

A foreign exchange rate is the price of one currency in terms of another. If the exchange rate between U.S. dollars and British pounds is $1.62, it means every pound someone wants to buy costs $1.62. Sometimes the relationship is expressed as the reciprocal, in which case $1 could be bought for .6173 pounds. The two prices, $1.62 per pound and £.6173 per dollar, are identical.

Exchange rates are quoted for different delivery dates. If the transaction is to take place immediately (actually one or two days later because of the bank clearing process), it is referred to as a *spot exchange rate;* for transactions that will take place sometime in the future, the exchange rate is referred to as a *forward rate.*

Forward rates are quoted for a number of delivery dates. In the financial press, they are seldom given for more than 90 days or 180 days, but financial institutions might be willing to give a quote for a several-year period. Exhibit 16.2 provides both spot and forward rates for several different maturities and currencies. The relationship between the spot and forward rates is determined by the relative interest rates in the two countries. A country with the higher interest rate will have a currency that will cost less for forward delivery than for spot delivery. According to Exhibit 16.2 the British pound costs $1.6262 for spot delivery and only $1.6226 for 90-day forward delivery. The pound is said to be trading at a forward discount to the dollar. On the other hand, the yen is at a premium to the dollar. It costs more to buy a yen for delivery in 90 days than it does for spot delivery. Interest rates in Japan are lower than those in the United States, which are lower than interest rates in Britain.

EXHIBIT 16.2   Spot and forward exchange rates ($, dollar per foreign currency unit).

	Pound	Yen	Deutsche Marks
Spot	$1.6262	$.008288	$.5925
30-day	$1.6253	$.008324	$.5935
90-day	$1.6226	$.008396	$.5958
180-day	$1.6209	$.008508	$.5996

Source: The Wall Street Journal.

It is important to understand how a forward contract works. The price or exchange rate is established today, although the transaction will not take place until the future delivery date. A buyer of forward pounds agrees to pay $1.60 in 90 days. At that time, the buyer is obligated to take delivery and pay the agreed-upon rate regardless of the prevailing spot rate of the pound. If, in 90 days, the spot pound is at $1.70, the buyer will then make a profit of $.10 per pound. A $1.55 spot rate will lead to a $.05 per pound loss. Forward contracts can be used to speculate on the value of a currency but, as shown in the next section, they are the primary means by which exchange risk is managed or hedged.

Firms that engage in cross-border business generally bear some amount of exchange risk. That risk comes from the variability of exchange rates and, therefore, the uncertain value of future cash flows. An American company that imports German machine tools that are priced in deutsche marks (DM) cannot be certain of the dollar value of the DM obligation when the payment is due. If the machine tools cost DM 3 million and payment is due in six months, the dollar value will be determined by the spot exchange rate in six months. If the deutsche mark is worth $.60, the dollar cost will be $1.8 million, and if it is $.70, $2.1 million. It is not unusual for the exchange rates of developed, major economies to change by 10% to 15% over 6- to 12-month periods; therefore, the amount of uncertainty is significant.

Companies that invest overseas have a continuous challenge in managing exchange risk. Budgets, compensation, the cost of financing, and the value of repatriating profits all vary as exchange rates fluctuate. There is also the added complication of preparing consolidated financial statements when operations are conducted in a variety of currencies. The Financial Accounting Standards Board has issued a series of statements to address a very complex and controversial set of issues around the translation of foreign-currency-denominated accounts.

Another way that companies are significantly affected by exchange risk is in their ability to compete against foreign competitors. When a currency strengthens or rises in value, it becomes more expensive to buy goods priced in that currency. Therefore, a strong dollar works to the disadvantage of U.S. companies trying to export or compete with non-U.S. companies that sell goods in the United States. The competition between Caterpillar and Komatsu provides a notable example, in part because the head-to-head struggle between these two companies has been thoroughly documented in the press and in a series of case studies. In the 1960s, Komatsu launched a long-term plan, first to catch up with and then to surpass Caterpillar, the then market leader in heavy machinery. This plan was very successful until Caterpillar began an aggressive effort to overhaul its operations.

Caterpillar made an intense commitment to improve its U.S. manufacturing operations. Rather than join the stampede of U.S. manufacturers that set up low-cost operations in Mexico and around the Pacific Rim, Caterpillar sought to make its domestic plants competitive on a world scale. To do so, it launched its so-called Plant with a Future (PWAF) program. The program called for overhauling virtually all the company's U.S. factories, installing fancy new robotics, streamlining assembly systems, and so forth.

However, Caterpillar officials now worry that the slumping yen threatens years of work at their factories. "How long do you think it takes a company to take 20% out of its cost structure?" asks D. G. Paris, a company economist. (The answer for Caterpillar's PWAF program: seven years.) In recent months, Mr. Paris has frequently telephoned Federal Reserve officials to make this point.[1]

The seven years of painstaking and painful change, undertaken at a cost of over $2 billion, was more than offset by the 30% depreciation of the yen that took place over a 16-month period in 1989 and 1990.

Hedging Exchange Risk

Exchange-related risk such as that faced by Caterpillar is very difficult to manage. Caterpillar's attempt to make its manufacturing efficient and flexible represents a long-range commitment to inoculate itself against the competitive impact of currency appreciation. Within a moderate range it is effective, but when currencies change dramatically, such efforts can be overwhelmed.

Other types of exchange risk can be managed more directly and effectively by using forward contracts. Recall the example of the American importer of German machine tools. The importer incurred an obligation to pay DM 3 million in six months. Because the importing company has a liability (a short position) in DM, it could lock in the dollar cost of the debt by acquiring an equal but offsetting position in the forward market. To do so, the importer would buy a DM 3 million forward contract at the prevailing rate. Using the rates in Exhibit 16.2, the six-month DM is selling for $.5996. If the importer buys forward, it will lock in a dollar cost of $1,798,800, regardless of the $/DM exchange rate in six months. The importer will acquire the necessary deutsche marks at the forward rate and use them to pay off the liability. The action of locking in the exchange rate and reducing or eliminating the uncertainty is referred to as *hedging*.

Importers, exporters, and investors in financial assets, as well as multinational companies, utilize forward contracts to hedge. Other methods of hedging include borrowing or depositing money in foreign currency and the use of swaps or options. These alternative hedging techniques have different costs and risk profiles related to them. Managers must decide what level of risk they are able to bear and how much they are willing to pay to eliminate risk.

Purchasing Power Parity

It is very hard to predict future exchange rates. Many forecasting services exist, and there is vast academic literature discussing various models of exchange-rate determination. Some of these models are very simple, and some are complex. One of the simplest models is to use today's forward rate to predict the future spot rate. Other models utilize sophisticated statistical relationships. Unfortunately, there is little evidence that these models work particularly well. However, one empirical relationship does seem to hold over relatively long periods of time: A country that experiences a higher rate of inflation than another country will see its currency decline relative to the other country's currency. This observation, and the theory underlying it, have led to the *purchasing power parity* (PPP) relationship.

The basis for PPP is the relationship between the prices of goods in two countries. The law of one price states that the same good should sell for the same price, regardless of the currency used to denominate the price. Suppose that the price of an automobile is $30,000 in Dallas and that same car sells for 150,000 francs in Paris. For the cars to have the same price, the dollar must equal Fr 5. If the dollar were worth Fr 6, then someone could take $25,000, buy Fr 150,000, and get the car cheaper in Paris. This would violate the law of one price.

In fact, we know that the law of one price generally does not hold under all circumstances. Transaction costs such as transportation, tariffs, taxes, and different distribution systems lead to different prices. However, as a tendency, the law of one price does seem to be valid. Moreover, as prices in the two countries change, we observe that the exchange rate changes to reflect the different rates of inflation. Returning to the example, if car prices in the United States rose 10% to $33,000 and in France, they rose 20% to Fr 180,000, then the value of the franc should decline relative to the dollar: PPP says that the depreciation should produce Fr 5.45 = $1.00.

Although by no means perfect, PPP is a very useful way of determining whether a country's currency is over- or undervalued. If a country's currency has not depreciated at a rate roughly consistent with the inflation differential of another country, then it is overvalued.

ORGANIZING THE MULTINATIONAL FIRM

Managing a multinational corporation has many additional challenges. Percy Barnevik, CEO of ABB and one of the most highly regarded international executives, summed up these challenges as the need to reconcile three contradictions:

Be global and local.
Be big and small.
Be centralized and decentralized.

The essence of Barnevik's views is that, although business decisions are made at a local level, a company must be willing and able to respond anywhere in the world. To do so requires large size and the economies of scale that large size makes possible. Customers want the efficiencies that only scale economies can provide. To get those economies, certain functions need to be centralized and best practices must be identified and put in place throughout the organization. Yet, because business is local, it is important that the multinational be responsive and agile, which in turn requires a delegation of authority that is only present in a decentralized organization.

When Barnevik created ABB from the merger of a Swedish and a Swiss company, he sought to create a company capable of competing globally in the twenty-first century. To manage the contradictions, he established a broad-matrix organization along business and geographic lines. Individual managers within the matrix are given a great deal of autonomy. At the same time, they are part of global business segments and regional or country organizations.

Two academics, Christopher Bartlett and Sumantra Ghosal, have examined ABB and numerous other multinational firms in order to determine effective organizational design. One of the most important conclusions they reached is that there is a need for four different types of managers, each with a different set of attributes and different roles within the organization. The management taxonomy is:

Business manager: strategist + architect + coordinator
Country manager: sensor + builder + contributor
Functional manager: scanner + cross-pollinator + champion
Corporate manager: leader + talent scout + developer

It is interesting to see how the four roles or types span the management of Barnevik's contradictions. Barnevik himself is the corporate manager. He is the leader who developed the organization and selected the right people to manage it. Along one dimension of his matrix, he has country managers. They do business locally, build organizations, and contribute to strategic analysis. Along the other dimensions are the global business managers, who have overall strategic responsibility and coordinate the activities of a business worldwide. Finally, within the countries and businesses are functional managers, who determine best practice and ensure that these best practices are adopted across business and geographic lines.

FOR FURTHER READING

Mark Eaker, Frank Fabozzi, and Dwight Grant, *International Corporate Finance* (Hinsdale, IL: Dryden, 1996).

Ricky Griffin and Michael Pustay, *International Business: A Managerial Perspective* (Reading, MA: Addison-Wesley Publishing Co., 1995).

Alan Rugman and Richard Hodgetts, *International Business: A Strategic Management Approach* (New York: McGraw-Hill, 1994).

Anant Sundaram and J. Stewart Black, *The International Business Environment: Text and Cases* (Englewood Cliffs, NJ: Prentice Hall, 1994).

17 SOME FINAL THOUGHTS

A former colleague of one of the authors used to say, "All you need to know about business is buy low, sell high; pay late and collect early." He was speaking tongue in cheek, but there is a certain appealing wisdom and historic truth to that advice. Clearly, if you don't sell your goods and services for more than they cost you, it will be impossible to earn a profit and stay in business. Paying late and collecting early captures both the time value of money and the distinction between cash and accrued earnings.

Historically, buying low and selling high was the essence of business enterprise until the Industrial Revolution. Business was about trading, primarily commodities, and businesspeople were merchants who bought commodities at one price, transported them, possibly stored them, and hoped to sell them at a higher price—straightforward, although certainly not easy or risk-free.

Today's successful firms must also buy low and sell high, but the tasks of management are far more complex than just trading successfully. In the various chapters of this book we have tried to introduce the primary themes and techniques that today's MBAs master in their programs of study. Those topics range from a basic discussion of financial statements to describing the steps involved in establishing a strategic alliance. How should we think about the lessons if not in terms of the simple concept of buying low and selling high?

Instead of focusing on profit generation, much of what we have written about is value creation. Managers utilize resources in a manner that creates value for customers. Buying low and selling high have been replaced by the notion of creating value through the transformation of resources. Operations, finance, marketing and other topics are about the utilization and allocation of resources to create value for customers. As value is created, some of it is retained by the firm in the form of higher profits, some goes to employees in the form of higher wages, and some to shareholders in the form of greater wealth. Value gets created through the efficient use of resources. Companies that invest in technology, engage in successful research and development, manage resources well, and focus on the needs of their customers create value. Competition and the economics of the industry determine how much goes to workers, managers, and owners.

In a book that examines the characteristics of companies with outstanding records of long-term success, Jim Collins and Jerry Porras make the distinction between clock builders and time tellers.[1] The latter focus on short-term profitability, whereas the former attend to building a business. Collins and Porras compare the financial performance of their outstanding companies and a set of firms in the same industries. The firms that were oriented toward value creation and not just profit maximization wound up creating more wealth for their shareholders and employees. The moral is clear: We measure profits by the difference in buying high and selling low, but the size of the profits is determined by what the firm does to create value.

Success at creating value does not come from the application of specific rules or formulas. The application of the techniques that are developed in this book and in MBA programs throughout the world is not a guarantee of success. If following a set of rules were a guarantee of success, then the value of managerial excellence and leadership would be low. Almost everyone can follow a set of mechanistic decision rules. All of the calculations involved in a net present value analysis are now performed by computers and handheld calculators. The techniques cannot be the answer to the question of what distinguishes outstanding firms. In fact, we have observed that the compensation of executives and senior managers has risen. We believe that has occurred because as business has become more complex, the market has had to increase the rewards to managerial excellence. Individuals who demonstrate an ability to use their judgment to make decisions and to manage resources have become a more valuable resource.

Throughout this book and especially in Chapter 14, "Leading from the Middle," we have pointed out the characteristics of successful firms. The quality of the people within a firm and their commitment to excellence and value creation are what distinguish successful firms from others. That leadership must come from throughout the organization, not just from one or two senior executives. Organizations that have managerial and leadership depth are able to be flexible and responsive. They can meet the needs of customers, anticipate new requirements of doing business, adapt to changing conditions, and respond to crises without sacrificing core beliefs.

Flexibility and responsiveness are crucial because decisions are made in an environment of uncertainty. The models, techniques, and theories discussed in this book cannot be followed blindly. They are not a substitute for judgment. They enhance judgment. The concepts give us frameworks with which to analyze outcomes, develop solutions, and monitor progress as we implement those solutions. As we discussed in Chapter 2 on managing the future, the future is never what we predicted, so we need to adapt as we go.

We hope that this book will be a guide to those who are making business decisions in an uncertain world. It is one of many steps to successfully navigating through turbulent and often uncharted waters. The book and its lessons do not ensure a safe journey, but they increase the chances of one. For those who strive to lead and those who seek to work with others in order to create value, improving the odds of success is an important point of departure.

CHAPTER NOTES

CHAPTER 1: WHAT IS BUSINESS?

[1] Peter Drucker, *The New Realities* (New York: Harper Business, 1989).

[2] Michael Piore and Charles Sabel, *The Second Industrial Divide* (New York: Basic Books, 1984).

[3] This term is attributed to James Brian Quinn, *The Intelligent Enterprise* (New York: The Free Press, 1992). The section on the intelligent enterprise is based on this book.

[4] This term is taken from James Moore, *The Death of Competition* (New York: Harper Business, 1996).

[5] This section is based on work by Michael Best, *The New Competition* (Cambridge, MA: Harvard University Press, 1990).

[6] Alfred Chandler Jr., *The Visible Hand* (Cambridge, MA: Harvard University Press, 1977).

[7] Peter Drucker, *Post-Capitalist Society* (New York: HarperCollins, 1993).

[8] This section is based on James Moore, *The Death of Competition* (New York: Harper Business, 1996).

[9] Andrew Grove, *Only the Paranoid Survive,* 1996.

CHAPTER 2: THE FUTURE

[1] David Einstein, "Think Tank Helps Prevent Future Shock," *The San Francisco Chronicle,* June 10, 1995.

[2] Gary Hamel and CK Prahalad, "Seeing the Future First," *Executive Excellence,* November 1995.

[3] Ibid.

[4] Carol Kennedy, "Future Shock or Future Success?," *Director,* July 1995.

[5] Ibid.

[6] Barbara Ettore, "2020: What's the World Coming To?," *Management Review,* September 1996.

[7] Peter Swartz, *The Art of the Long View* (New York: Doubleday Currency, 1991).

CHAPTER 3: MANAGING PEOPLE

[1] There are many good introductions to the history of management. We have relied on the textbook, *Management,* 6th edition, by James F. Stoner, R. Edward Freeman, and Daniel R. Gilbert Jr. (Englewood Cliffs, NJ: Prentice Hall, 1995) especially chapter 2; Peter F. Drucker, *Concept of the Corporation* (New York: Times Mirror, 1946) especially chapters 1 and 2; Harvard Business Review, *Classic Advice on Aspects of Organizational Life,* (New York: Harper, 1985); and James Bowditch and Anthony Buono, *A Primer on Organizational Behavior,* 4th edition (New York: John Wiley and Sons, 1993).

[2] Douglas MacGregor, *The Human Side of Enterprise* (New York: McGraw-Hill, 1960).

[3] For a wonderful discussion of the history of Deming's ideas, see Lloyd Dobyns and Clare Crawford-Mason, *Quality or Else: The Revolution in World Business* (Boston: Houghton Miflin, 1991). Of course, Deming precedes MacGregor historically, but it is only since MacGregor isolated theory X and theory Y that Deming's ideas and those of others regarding theory Y began to have an impact.

[4] For a discussion of needs theory, see Richard Steers and Lyman Porter, *Motivation and Work Behavior* (New York: McGraw-Hill, 2d edition, 1979).

[5] Ibid., p. 104.

[6] Stanley Milgram, *Obedience to Authority* (New York: Harper, 1974).

[7] Deborah Tannen, *You Just Don't Understand* (New York: Morrow, 1990); and Tannen, *Talking from 9 to 5* (New York: Morrow, 1994).

[8] Tannen, 1990, infranote 6, p. 26.

[9] Ibid.

[10] Judith B. Rossener, "Ways Women Lead", *Harvard Business Review,* November–December 1990, pp. 119–125.

[11] Chris Argyris, *Understanding Organizational Behavior* (Homewood, IL: Dorsey, 1960); see Peter Herriot, "Psychological Contract" in Nigel Nicholson (ed.) *Organizational Behavior,* volume VI, *The Blackwell Encyclopedia of Management* (Oxford: Basil Blackwell, 1997), pp. 455–456.

[12] D. Rousseau and R. Anton "Fairness and Implied Contract Obligations in Job Terminations: The Role of Contributions, Promises and Performance," *Journal of Organizational Behavior,* volume 12, pp. 287–299, 1991.

[13] Charles Heckscher, *White Collar Blues* (New York: Basic Books, 1995).

[14] This idea is attributed to Tuckman by Stoner et al., infranote 1, p. 505.

[15] Stoner et al., infranote 1, p. 501.

[16] See F. E. Emery and E. L. Trist, *Towards a Social Ecology* (London: Plenum Press, 1973) for a statement of Trist's view on participatory management and autonomous work groups. The general ideas in this book are even today, 25 years later, just beginning to be understood by management theorists.

[17] Jon Katzenbach and Douglas Smith, *The Wisdom of Teams: Creating the High Performance Organization* (Boston: Harvard Business School Press, 1993).

[18] Ibid., p. 12.

[19] Ibid., p. 13.

[20] Ibid., p. 13.

[21] Ibid., p. 14.

[22] These paragraphs on group conflict are based on James Bowditch and Anthony Buono's excellent book, *A Primer on Organizational Behavior*, 4th edition (New York: John Wiley and Sons, 1993).

[23] This section is based on the rich set of ideas contained in Peter Senge and Associates, *The Fifth Discipline Fieldbook* (New York: Doubleday, 1994).

[24] John Wisdom, *Philosophy and Psychoanalysis* (Berkeley: University of California Press, 1969).

CHAPTER 4: BUSINESS ETHICS

[1] This case has been around the business ethics field for quite some time. Thanks to Michael Josephson, Thomas Donaldson, and Joan Dubinsky for pointing it out to us. We have no idea who originally designed it, but it has been validated as real by hundreds of executives.

[2] For a more complete view of relativism and its problems, see R. Edward Freeman and Daniel R. Gilbert Jr., *Corporate Strategy and the Search for Ethics* (Englewood Cliffs, NJ: Prentice Hall, 1987).

[3] For a more careful statement of "the separation thesis," see R. Edward Freeman, "The Politics of Stakeholder Theory," *Business Ethics Quarterly*, vol. 4, no. 4, 1994.

[4] For a clear statement of Smith's view, see Patricia H. Werhane, *Adam Smith's Legacy for Modern Capitalism* (New York: Oxford University Press, 1991).

[5] These paragraphs are based on R. Edward Freeman, "A Note on Ethics and Business," The Darden School, Charlottesville, VA, UVA-E-0071. Also see William C. Frederick, "Corporate Social Responsibility and Business Ethics," in S. Prakash Sethi and Cecilia M. Falbe, *Business and Society* (Lexington, MA: Lexington Books, 1987), pp. 142–161.

[6] The quote from George Merck is from "Merck & Co., Inc. (A)," The Business Enterprise Trust, Stanford, California, 1991.

[7] We are glossing over the philosophical point that values are about "the good" and rights are about "the right." Any introductory textbook on ethics can provide more detail for those interested.

[8] We make no distinction between rules and principles here. Some see principles as higher-order rules—indeed, as the justification for rules. For more, see Tom Beauchamp

and James Childress, *Principles of Biomedical Ethics,* 3d edition (New York: Oxford University Press, 1989).

[9] Stephen Covey, *The Seven Habits of Highly Successful People: Restoring the Character Ethic* (New York: Simon and Schuster, 1989).

[10] See Norman Bowie and Stephanie Lenway, "H.B. Fuller in Honduras" in T. Donaldson and P. Werhane (eds.) *Ethical Issues in Business,* 5th edition (Englewood Cliffs, NJ: Prentice Hall, 1996) pp. 78–90.

[11] This section is based on R. Edward Freeman, "Understanding Stakeholder Capitalism," *The Financial Times,* 19 July 1996, and R. Edward Freeman and Jeanne M. Liedtka, "Stakeholder Capitalism and the Value Chain," *European Journal of Management,* volume 16, no. 3, in press, June 1997. The authors of the present volume are grateful to the editors of both publications for permission to reprint selected paragraphs. Defining *stakeholder capitalism* is an ongoing project. For some preliminary statements see R. Edward Freeman, "Managing for Stakeholders," in N. Bowie and T. Beauchamp, *Ethical Theory and Business,* 5th edition, (Englewood Cliffs: Prentice Hall, 1997) and R. Edward Freeman, "The Politics of Stakeholder Theory," *Business Ethics Quarterly,* volume 4, number 4, 1994, pp. 409–422.

[12] For a more careful history see R. Edward Freeman, *Strategic Management: A Stakeholder Approach* (Boston: Pitman Inc., 1984), and Thomas Donaldson and Lee Preston, "The Stakeholder Theory of the Corporation: Concepts, Evidence, and Implications," *Academy of Management Review,* volume 20, 1995, pp. 65–91, and more recently still, Ronald K. Mitchell, Bradley R. Agle, and Donna J. Wood, "Toward a Theory of Stakeholder Identification: Defining the Principle of Who and What Really Counts," University of Victoria, Faculty of Business, manuscript.

[13] Thomas Donaldson, *The Ethics of International Business* (New York: Oxford University Press, 1989).

CHAPTER 5: MAKING DECISIONS RIGOROUSLY: THE USE OF QUANTITATIVE METHODS

[1] Howard Raiffa, *Decision Analysis: Introductory Lectures on Choices under Uncertainty* (Reading, MA: Addison-Wesley, 1970), footnoted on p. 264.

[2] The range of returns on small stocks is calculated by adding or subtracting the standard deviation of the small stocks' returns (34.6%) from the arithmetic mean return (17.4%).

[3] With computer spreadsheets programs such as Excel, you can ask the computer to look up the value for you.

[4] The discount rate should be a percentage rate of return equal to the rate of return available to investors on investment projects of similar risk. Chapter 11, "Finance," discusses the discount rate concept in more detail.

[5] Raiffa, ibid., pp. 268–272, offers an excellent and more extensive discussion of the pros and cons of decision analysis. The discussion in this section draws from Raiffa's insights.

[6] Be careful. Lazy thinkers the world over have used this hoary old saying to dismiss any attempt at rigorous decision analysis. The fact is that for most of the interesting future outcomes in business, there exists no true underlying probability distribution. Unlike

drawing cards from a deck, the true probability distribution is not known. Thus, how can a wildcatter's assessment of a 10% chance of striking oil be described as "garbage"? Uncertainty about a future distribution should not necessarily disqualify the estimate.

[7] These defenses included a $300 million termination fee to CSX if the acquisition did not go through, a dead-hand poison pill guaranteeing that even if Conrail's directors were removed by Norfolk they could still decide to leave the poison pill in place, and a promise by Conrail's directors not to entertain any other offers for several months.

[8] The net present values and probabilities are estimates by the author, based only on public information. They may not reflect the actual perspectives of CSX, Norfolk Southern, or Conrail.

CHAPTER 7: MARKETING MANAGEMENT: LEVERAGING CUSTOMER VALUE

[1] This discussion draws from P. Kotler, *Marketing Management*, 9th ed. (Upper Saddle River, NJ: Prentice Hall, 1996).

[2] Jack Welch's "Encore," *Business Week*, October 28, 1996, p. 155.

[3] This position is consistent with discussions in Frederick F. Reichheld, *The Loyalty Effect* (Cambridge, MA: Harvard Business Press, 1996).

[4] See, Peter Drucker (New York, NY: Harper & Row *The Practice of Management*, 1954).

[5] The notion of cultlike cultures is developed in James Collins and Jerry Porras, *Built to Last* (New York: Harper Business, 1994).

[6] See, Gary Hamel and P. K. Prahalad, *Competing for the Future*, Harvard Business School Press, 1994.

[7] This term is borrowed from Nicholas Imparato and Oren Harari, *Jumping the Curve* (San Francisco: Jossey Bass, 1994).

[8] See A. Kohli and B. Jaworski, "Market Orientation: The Construct, Research Propositions, and Managerial Implications," *Journal of Marketing*, vol. 54, April 1990, pp. 1–18. John Narver and Stan Slater, "The Effects of Market Orientation on Business Profitability," *Journal of Marketing*, vol. 54, April 1990, pp. 20–35.

[9] R. Buzzell and B. Gale, *The PIMS Principle* (New York: Free Press, 1987).

[10] Buzzell and Gale, op cit.

[11] For a more complete presentation of antitrust issues in marketing, see L. W. Stern and T. Evaldi, *Legal Aspects of Marketing Strategy* (Upper Saddle River, NJ: Prentice Hall, 1984).

[12] For a complete discussion of mass customization, see Joseph Pine, *Mass Customization* (Cambridge, MA: Harvard Business School Press, 1993).

[13] Booz Allen & Hamilton, "New Product Development for the 1980s," in-house report, 1982; Eric von Hipple, "New Ideas from Lead Users," *Research-Technology Management*, May/June 1989, pp. 82–96.

[14] See M. Leenders and D. Blenkhorn, *Reverse Marketing* (New York: Free Press, 1988).

[15] Parts of this discussion are based on Reichheld, op cit.

[16] See F. Webster, *Market-Driven Management* (New York: Wiley 1994).

CHAPTER 8: OPERATIONS MANAGEMENT: IMPLEMENTING AND ENABLING STRATEGY

[1] I want to thank Thomas C. MacAvoy, Kamalini Ramdas, and Elliott Weiss for helpful comments on this chapter, and Katarina Paddack for research assistance.

CHAPTER 9: INNOVATION AND TECHNOLOGY MANAGEMENT

[1] This chapter has benefited enormously form my opportunity to work with Thomas. C. MacAvoy, the Paul M. Hammaker Professor of Business Administration at the Darden Graduate School of Business Administration, University of Virginia and retired President and Vice Chairman of the Board of Corning Incorporated. The chapter draws on instructional notes written by Prof. MacAvoy, as well as other sources. MacAvoy's instructional notes are listed in the Further Reading section.

[2] The value chain is discussed in Chapter 13.

[3] This point is made by Prof. Thomas C. MacAvoy, Darden Graduate School of Business Administration, University of Virginia.

[4] Stanford economist Paul Romer argues this view in his work on growth theory.

[5] For a good discussion of the effects of technological change on industry structure and the implications for strategy, see Michael Porter, "Chapter 5: Technology and Competitive Strategy," *Competitive Advantage* (New York: The Free Press, 1985).

[6] See Chapter 13, "Strategy," for a discussion of competitive strategy and competitive advantage. See Chapter 8, "Operations Management," for a discussion of functional operations strategy.

[7] See Chapter 8, for a discussion of the trend toward competition among networks with cooperating firms in each network.

[8] See John M. Ketteringham and John R. White, "Making Technology Work for Business," in *Competitive Strategic Management,* edited by Robert Bryden Lamb (Englewood Cliffs, NJ: Prentice Hall, 1984) or Philip A. Roussel, Kamal N. Saad, and Tamara J. Erickson, *Third Generation R&D, Managing the Link to Corporate Strategy* (Boston: Harvard Business School Press, 1991).

[9] Alliances are discussed in Chapter 15, "Strategic Alliances."

[10] For further discussion of understanding user needs for very new products, see Dorothy Leonard-Barton, Edith Wilson, and John Doyle, "Commercializing Technology: Imaginative Understanding of User Needs," Harvard Business School Instructional Note 9-694-102, 1994.

[11] GE's success is also attributable to complementary assets, discussed in Principle 6.

[12] David Teece discusses these and other examples in "Profiting from Technological Innovation: Implications for Integration, Collaboration, Licensing, and Public Policy," *Research Policy,* vol. 15, 1986, pp. 285–305.

[13] Tacit knowledge is something understood but not easy to communicate, as opposed to codified knowledge, which can be written down or explained and thus more easily transferred or copied.

[14] This discussion focuses on technology-intensive innovation, although innovation occurs in all of a firm's activities and in many low-tech settings.

[15] The term *reservation* is used by Jay R. Galbraith in "Organizing for Innovation," *Organizational Dynamics,* winter 1982, pp. 5–25.

[16] See David A. Garvin, "Building a Learning Organization," *Harvard Business Review,* July–August 1993, and Steven C. Wheelwright and Kim B. Clark, *Revolutionizing Product Development, Quantum Leaps in Speed, Efficiency, and Quality,* New York: The Free Press, 1992.

[17] This multistage analysis is the essence of option pricing and decision analysis approaches to valuation of R&D projects.

CHAPTER 10: ACCOUNTING

[1] Quoted in E. Richard Brownlee II, "Communicating Corporate Value in a Global Economy," presented at Conference on Finding Reality in Reported Earnings, Association for Investment Management and Research, December 4, 1996, p. 3.

[2] CPA stands for Certified Public Accountant, a credential awarded after successful completion of a challenging examination and other professional requirements.

[3] Auditors are very careful not to promise Absolute Truth and Precision in their work. Disney's auditor, Price Waterhouse, wrote in its report on the 1995 financial statements: "We conducted our audits of these statements in accordance with *generally accepted* auditing standards which require that we plan and perform the audits to obtain *reasonable* assurance about whether the financial statements are free of *material* misstatement. . . . We believe that our audits provide a *reasonable* basis for the opinion expressed above." (Italics are the author's.)

[4] Brownlee, op. cit., pp. 9 and 10.

[5] The Walt Disney Company *1995 Annual Report,* p. 69.

[6] The "going concern" assumption holds that the firm will operate for the foreseeable future and that its assets will not be liquidated hastily in a fire sale. For instance, hasty liquidation of inventory ordinarily realizes lower values than will the regular conduct of business.

[7] On the balance sheet of many companies headquartered outside the United States, the order of priority differs greatly. Don't let the differences confuse you. Just remember that assets = liabilities + equity.

[8] Exchangeable bonds may be exchanged at the firm's option into another type of security, such as preferred stock. Subordinated bonds rank behind senior bonds in payment if the firm is liquidated. Exchangeable subordinated bonds were issued by Revco Drug Stores in 1986 in its leveraged buyout. Revco went bankrupt 19 months later. The issuance of these bonds was both creative and imprudent.

[9] EBIT stands for *earnings before interest and taxes.*

[10] Days in receivables is also called *days' sales outstanding* and is calculated as the ratio of accounts receivable divided by annual sales multiplied by 365 days.

[11] *Financial leverage* generally refers to the use of debt financing. A highly levered firm has a high proportion of debt in its capital structure. There are numerous ratios that measure leverage, but one of the most graphic is the ratio of assets to equity. High leverage would be associated with a high ratio.

[12] Under the budget for the videocassette release, sales were to be $50 million and costs $15 million.

[13] The actual results for the project were sales of $54 million and costs of $24 million.

CHAPTER 11: FINANCE

[1] Warren Buffett is one of the most successful investors in history. Through his public holding company, Berkshire Hathaway, he has managed a portfolio of public and private securities that grew in value at 38% per year from 1977 to 1994, compared to an average return on the market of 14.3% for the same period. In 1996 Buffett was said to be worth about $7 billion.

[2] Peter Lynch was the legendary manager of the Fidelity Magellan Fund. During his 13 years of fund management (from 1977 to 1990) the average annual return on the Magellan Fund significantly beat the average market returns. "Around Fidelity, Peter Lynch was God," remarked one observer.

[3] Berkshire Hathaway Inc. *Annual Report,* 1994, p. 2.

[4] Berkshire Hathaway Inc. *Annual Report,* 1992, p. 14.

[5] Berkshire Hathaway Inc. *Annual Report,* 1994, p. 7.

[6] Peter Lynch, *One Up on Wall Street* (New York: Simon & Schuster, 1989), p. 242.

[7] Quoted in *Forbes,* October 19, 1993, and republished in Andrew Kilpatrick, *Of Permanent Value: The Story of Warren Buffett* (Birmingham: AKPE, 1994), p. 574.

[8] Walter Wriston was the CEO of Citicorp, one of the premier banks and financial services institutions in the United States, during its era of rapid expansion in the 1970s and early 1980s.

[9] Walter B. Wriston, *Risk and Other Four-Letter Words* (New York: Harper & Row, 1986), pp. 222–223.

[10] Berkshire Hathaway Inc. *Annual Report,* 1994, p. 2.

[11] Originally published in Berkshire Hathaway *Annual Report,* 1987. This quotation was paraphrased from James Grant, *Minding Mr. Market* (New York: Times Books, 1993), p. xxi.

[12] Quoted in *Forbes,* October 19, 1993, and republished in Andrew Kilpatrick, *Of Permanent Value; The Story of Warren Buffett* (Birmingham: AKPE, 1994), p. 574.

[13] "Owner-Related Business Principles" in Berkshire Hathaway *Annual Report,* 1994, p. 3.

[14] This is like saying that the investors expect you, the manager, to earn per year an annual cash flow of 10¢ on every dollar invested in the machine.

[15] For a discussion of the purpose and methodology of discounted cash flow, see Chapter 5, "Quantitative Methods in Decision-Making."

[16] Perfectionists may wonder why the figure does not show a straight line of dots to indicate a perfect correlation. The expected returns and capital costs are drawn from *Value Line Investment Survey*, which may estimate them imperfectly (as do most analysts). Alternatively, perhaps the market pricing is inefficient in certain stocks. But the fact is that the degree of association observed in Exhibit 11.8 is pretty good for economics and the social sciences.

[17] The injunction to "sell securities" applies most readily to corporations. But when you think about it, it is equally applicable to individuals. For instance, any homeowner who has borrowed to finance the purchase of a house has "sold" a mortgage.

[18] Bonds are rated for their likelihood of default by independent rating agencies. The bond ratings can run from high quality (AAA) to low quality (B). See Exhibit 11.4 for a listing of rating definitions.

[19] A coupon is a chit that the investor literally snips off the bond certificate and sends in to the company to receive interest payment. In common business parlance, the *coupon* of a bond is the annual interest payment of the bond, expressed usually as a percentage rate of return. With the advent of an electronic business economy, actual paper coupons will become a rarity.

[20] If they did, there would be no trading of stocks and bonds and no market. On every trade there is a pessimistic seller and an optimistic buyer.

CHAPTER 12: HUMAN RESOURCE MANAGEMENT

[1] James Burke, "Business Ethics: The Roundtable," produced by Public Broadcasting System 1993.

[2] Annual Survey by the American Management Association, 1988–1993, quoted in Charles Heckscher, *White Collar Blues* (New York: Basic Books, 1995), p. 3.

[3] W. Warner Burke, "What Human Resource Practitioners Need to Know for the Twenty-first Century," *Human Resource Management*, spring 1997, vol. 36, no. 1, pp. 71–79.

[4] Edward Lawler, *Strategic Pay* (San Francisco: Jossey-Bass, 1990).

[5] "Jack Welch, GE's Revolutionary," case study and video materials available from Harvard Business School.

[6] This paragraph is based on James L. Heskett and Leonard A. Schlesinger, "Leading the High-Capability Organization: Challenges for the Twenty-first Century," *Human Resource Management*, spring 1997, vol. 36, no. 1, pp. 105–113.

CHAPTER 13: STRATEGY: DEFINING AND DEVELOPING COMPETITIVE ADVANTAGE

[1] This chapter has benefited enormously from the eight years I spent working with and teaching with Michael E. Porter at the Harvard Business School. I also want to thank Michael Rukstad for helpful comments and Katarina Paddack for her assistance.

[2] Michael E. Porter developed the 5 forces framework for analyzing industry attractiveness in his book *Competitive Strategy,* New York, The Free Press, 1980.

[3] For more on profitability and competitive positioning, see Michael E. Porter, *Competitive Advantage* (New York: The Free Press, 1985). For more on core competencies, see C. K. Prahalad and G. Hamel, "The Core Competence of the Corporation," *Harvard Business Review,* May–June 1990. For more on capabilities, see George Stalk, Philip Evans, and Lawrence E. Shulman, "Competing on Capabilities: The New Rules of Corporate Strategy," *Harvard Business Review,* March–April 1992. For more on strategic intent, see G. Hamel and C. K. Prahalad, "Strategic Intent," *Harvard Business Review,* May 1989. For more on future scenarios, see Elizabeth Teisberg, "Strategic Response to Uncertainty," Harvard Business School Note #9-391-192, 1991.

[4] See the related discussion of Supply Chain Management in Chapter 8, "Operations Management."

[5] Ghemawat, Pankaj, *Commitment: The Dynamic of Strategy* (New York: The Free Press, 1991).

[6] Discussion of this point, with examples, can be found in Chapter 8.

[7] For detailed discussion of these challenges, see Michael E. Porter, "The Competitive Advantage of Nations," *Harvard Business Review,* March–April 1990.

[8] Such investments are known in economics as *real options.*

CHAPTER 14: LEADING FROM THE MIDDLE: A NEW LEADERSHIP PARADIGM

[1] The literature on business transformation grows daily. For a sample see N. Imparato and O. Harain, *Jumping the Curve* (San Francisco: Jossey-Bass, 1995); F. Gouillant and J. Kelly, *Transforming the Organization* (New York: McGraw-Hill, 1995).

[2] J. M. Keynes, *The Economic Consequences of Peace.*

[3] Patricia H. Werhane, *Adam Smith and the Legacy of Modern Capitalism* (New York: Oxford University Press, 1992).

[4] G. Hamel and C. K. Prahalad, *Competing for the Future* (Cambridge, MA: Harvard Business School Press, 1994).

[5] As Mark Twain wrote in *A Connecticut Yankee in King Arthur's Court,* "The best swordsman in the world doesn't need to fear the second best swordsman in the world; no, the person for him to be afraid of is some ignorant antagonist who has never had a sword in his hand before, he doesn't do the thing he ought to do, and so the expert isn't prepared for him; he simply does the thing he ought not to do; and it often catches the expert out and ends him on the spot."

[6] For more on the idea of how mental models work and the difficulty of changing them, see Peter Senge's *The Fifth Discipline.*

[7] See J. Pine, *Mass Customization* (Cambridge, MA: Harvard Business School Press).

[8] Harrigan, *Strategies for Joint Ventures;* Bleeke and Ernst, *Collaborating to Compete.*

[9] R. Spekman, L. Isabella, T. MacAvoy, and T. Forbes, "Creating Strategic Alliances that Endure," *Long Range Planning,* vol. 29, 1996, pp. 346–357.

[10] "James Burke: A Career in American Business," Harvard Business School videotape.

[11] A. Larson, "Dyads in Entrepreneurial Settings: A Study of the Governance of Exchange Relationships," *Administrative Sciences Quarterly,* March 1992.

[12] See J. Stoner, R. E. Freeman, and D. Gilbert Jr., *Management,* 6th ed. (Englewood Cliffs, NJ: Prentice Hall, Inc., 1995).

[13] Quoted in Hal Lancaster, "Managers Beware: You're Not Ready for Tomorrow's Jobs," *The Wall Street Journal,* January 24, 1995, p. B1.

[14] See Donald Schön, *The Reflective Practitioner.*

[15] Chris Argyris, "Good Communication That Blocks Learning," *Harvard Business Review,* July–August 1994, p. 77.

[16] James Utterback, *Managing the R&D Innovation Process* (Cambridge, MA: Harvard Business Press, 1994).

[17] Chris Argyris, "Good Communication That Blocks Learning," *Harvard Business Review,* July–August 1994, p. 85.

[18] Gary Hamel and C. K. Pralahad, "Competing for the Future," *Harvard Business Review,* July–August 1994, p. 128.

[19] Sumantra Ghoshal and Christopher A. Bartlett, "Changing the Role of Top Management: Beyond Structure to Processes," *Harvard Business Review,* January–February 1995, p. 89.

[20] The authors gratefully acknowledge the contribution made by their colleague, Professor Andrea Larson.

CHAPTER 15: STRATEGIC ALLIANCES

[1] J. D. Lewis, *Partnerships for Profit: Structuring and Managing Strategic Alliances* (New York: Free Press, 1990). Yves Doz, "The Role of Partnerships and Alliances in the European Industrial Restructuring," in K. Cool, D. Neven, and I. Walter, eds., *European Industrial Restructuring in the 1990s* (London: MacMillan, 1992), pp. 294–327.

[2] Joel Bleeke and David Ernst, *Collaborate to Compete* (New York: John Wiley & Sons, 1995).

[3] Frederick E. Webster Jr., *The Lopez Affair* (Hanover, NH: Amos Tuck School of Business, Dartmouth College, 1993).

[4] IBM and Microsoft: A Partnership UVA-M-0429.

[5] Bleeke and Ernst, op. cit.

[6] Gary Hamel, Yves L. Doz, and C. K. Prahalad, "Collaborate with Your Competitors—and Win," *Harvard Business Review,* January/February 1989, pp. 133–139.

[7] Jakki Mohr and Robert E. Spekman, "Characteristics of Partner Success," *Strategic Management Journal,* vol. 5 (1994), pp. 135–152.

[8] Robert E. Spekman, Lynn Isabella, Thomas MacAvoy, Theodore Forbes III, *Alliance and Partnership Strategies,* monograph published by the International Consortium for Executive Development Research, 1997.

[9] Much of this discussion is taken from R. Spekman, L. Isabella, T. MacAvoy, and T. Forbes, "Creating Strategic Alliances That Endure," *Long Range Planning,* vol. 29, # 3 1996, pp. 340–357.

[10] See, for example, P. Kotler, (1991), *Marketing Management: Analysis. Planning, Implementation, Control,* 7th ed. (Englewood Cliffs, NJ: Prentice Hall, 1991).

[11] M. Yoshino and U. S. Rangan, *Strategic Alliances* (Cambridge, MA: Harvard Business School Press, 1995).

[12] A. Larson, "Network Dyads in Entrepreneurial Settings: A Study of the Governance of Exchange Relationships," *Administrative Science Quarterly,* 37:76104, 1992.

[13] This section is derived from a series of case studies (BA-USAir (A) & (B), UVA-OB-0584 & 0585; Shell Italia (A) & (B), UVA-OB-0586 & 0587, Christie-Reid, Inc., UVA-OB-0597, Renault-Volvo Strategic Alliance (A), (B), (C), & (D), UVA-G-0480, 0481, 0482, 0483) based on very extensive field research of existing alliances in different stages of their development.

[14] J. P. Kotter, *Leading Change* (Cambridge, MA: Harvard Business Press, 1996).

[15] We also thought this imagery fit well, given a similar analogy used by Kanter (1989) in *When Elephants Learn to Dance.* In her book, she discusses how large, entrenched firms use alliances to improve their nimbleness and ability to adapt during times of change. We have tried not to reify the example by giving humanlike emotions to the elephants simply to further our position.

[16] D. T. Wilson, "An Integrated Model of Buyer-Seller Relationships," *Journal of the Academy of Marketing Sciences,* vol. 23, no. 4, 1995, pp. 335–345.

[17] Robert E. Spekman, Deborah J. Salmond, and C. Jay Lambe, "Consensus and Collaboration: Norm-Regulated Behavior in Industrial Marketing Relationships," *European Journal of Marketing,* forthcoming, 1997.

[18] Although VISA and MasterCard share many of the same bank members (e.g., Citibank, Chase), the example is still quite valid. However, it is interesting to note that Doz (1988) suggests that firms that cooperate upstream and compete downstream are more likely to have more conflict-ridden alliances.

[19] Adam M. Brandenburger, and Barry J. Nalebuff, *Co-opetition* (New York, New York: Doubleday, 1996).

[20] Jakki Mohr and Robert Spekman, "Characteristics of Partnership Success: Partnership Attributes, Communication Behavior and Conflict Resolution Techniques," *Strategic Management Journal,* vol. 15, 1994, pp. 135–152.

CHAPTER 16: INTERNATIONAL BUSINESS

[1] Robert L. Rod, "Currency Squeeze: Caterpillar Sees Gains in Efficiency Impeded by Strength of Dollar," *The Wall Street Journal,* April 6, 1990.

CHAPTER 17: SOME FINAL THOUGHTS

[1] James Collins and Jerry Porras, *Built to Last* (New York: Harper Business, 1994).

ABOUT THE AUTHORS

Robert F. Bruner is The Distinguished Professor of Business Administration at the Darden Graduate School of Business, University of Virginia. The author of numerous published articles and case studies and a casebook in corporate finance, his research has dealt mainly with capital structure management and the effects of various forms of corporate restructuring. He has received numerous awards for excellence in case teaching and case writing. *Business Week* cited him as one of the "masters of the MBA classroom" in 1994. He has consulted for various industrial corporations and financial institutions, and formerly was a loan officer and investment analyst for First Chicago Corporation. He received his B.A. from Yale University, and his M.B.A. and D.B.A. from Harvard University.

Mark R. Eaker is a Professor of Business Administration at the Darden Graduate School of Business at the University of Virginia. Mr. Eaker has a B.S. from Washington and Lee University and A.M., M.B.A., and Ph.D. from Stanford University. Prior to joining the faculty at Darden, he taught at Duke, SMU, and the University of North Carolina. He has been an adjunct Professor at Institute Theseus in France.

Mr. Eaker has coauthored four books in the areas of macroeconomics, international finance, and international business. He has numerous publications with an emphasis on international finance, foreign exchange, and risk management. He has consulted extensively and taught corporate seminars throughout the world.

Mr. Eaker is also a founding partner of Sire Management Corporation, an investment management firm in New York City.

R. Edward Freeman joined the Darden Graduate School of Business Administration in 1987 as Elis and Signe Olsson Professor of Business Administration and Director of the Olsson Center for Applied Ethics. Freeman is also Professor of Religious Studies. Prior to coming to The Darden School, Mr. Freeman taught at the University of Minnesota and The Wharton School, University of Pennsylvania.

Freeman's areas of interest are business ethics, strategy and leadership, and organizational studies. His most recent books are *Ethics and Agency Theory* (with N. Bowie), *Business Ethics: The State of the Art*, *The Logic of Strategic* (with D. Gilbert Jr., E. Hartman, and J. Mauriel), *Management*, 6th edition (with J. Stoner and D. Gilbert), and *Corporate Strategy and the Search for Ethics* (with D. Gilbert Jr.). He published *Strategic Management: A Stakeholder Approach* with Pitman Publishing in 1984. He has written more than 40 articles in a wide variety of publications. He is on the editorial boards of *Business Ethics Quarterly* and *Research in Corporate Social Performance and Policy*. He is the editor of the Ruffin Series in Business Ethics published by Oxford University Press. And he is currently editing (with P. Werhane) *The Dictionary of Business Ethics* and a volume in Blackwell's *Encyclopedia of Management*.

Mr. Freeman has a Ph.D. in Philosophy from Washington University and a B.A. in Mathematics and Philosophy from Duke University.

Robert E. Spekman is the Tayloe Murphy Professor of Business Administration at The Darden School. He was formerly Professor of Marketing and Associate Director of the Center for Telecommunications at the University of Southern California. He is an internationally recognized authority on business-to-business marketing and organizational buying behavior. His consulting experiences range from marketing research and competitive analysis, to strategic market planning, supply chain management, strategic procurement planning, and strategic partnering. Professor Spekman has taught in a number of executive programs in the U.S., Canada, Asia, and Europe. He has edited five books and has authored (coauthored) over 70 articles and papers. Professor Spekman also serves as a reviewer for several marketing and management journals as well as for the National Science Foundation. Prior to joining the faculty at USC, Professor Spekman taught in the College of Business at the University of Maryland, College Park. During his tenure at Maryland, he was granted the Most Distinguished Faculty Award by the MBA students on three separate occasions.

Elizabeth Olmsted Teisberg is the Associate Professor of Business Administration, The Darden School, University of Virginia. She is an economist with expertise in management of innovation, real option valuation, and strategy in the face of uncertainty. Much of her research and consulting focuses on the value of innovation and analysis of strategic opportunities in high-technology and health care industries. She is the author of numerous articles in professional publications such as the *Harvard Business Review*, *Rand Journal of Economics*, *Management Science*, the *Energy Journal*, *Research-Technology Management*, and *Science*. Prior to joining Darden, she was an Associate Professor at the Harvard Business School. She holds an A.B., summa cum laude, from Washington University in St. Louis; M.Eng. from University of Virginia; and an M.S. and Ph.D. from Stanford University.

INDEX

ABB, 322
Accounting:
  double-entry bookkeeping, technique of, 173–177
  financial ratios, and assessment of firm's financial health, 186–188
  financial statements:
    balance sheet, 175
    income statement, 175
    statement of cash flows, 176
  managerial, 189–191
  reading/analysis of annual report:
    auditor's letter, 179
    balance sheet, 182–183, 184 (exhibit)
    footnotes to financial statements, 186
    income statement, 180, 181 (exhibit)
    letter from board chair, 178–179
    management's discussion of year's performance, 186
    statement of cash flows, 183–184, 185 (exhibit)
  reports, as approximations of reality, 174, 177–178
  role of, as "language of business," 173
Aggregate demand, 90, 93
  fiscal policy influence on level of, 94
  monetary policy influence on level of, 95
Aggregate supply, 90
AirBus, 7
Alderfer, Clay, ERG theory of, 29–30
American Airlines, 112
American Express, 262

American Management Association, survey of, on anticipated managerial concerns of twenty-first century, 12
Anderson Consulting, 112
Anticipatory stock, 136, 139 (exhibit)
Antitrust behavior, new interpretation of, 6
Argyris, Chris, on "single-loop" versus "double-loop" learning, 271
Asset-utilization ratios, 187
AT&T, 5, 16, 87–89, 113, 123, 222, 224, 268, 277
Auditor's letter, 179
Authority relationship, role in management of people, 30–32
Automatic stabilizers, 94

Bain and Company, 121
Balance of payments, 97–98
Balance sheet, 175, 182–183, 184 (exhibit)
Bandag, 104–105
Barnevik, Percy, 322–323
Base technologies, 154
Beer, Michael, on criteria for evaluating HRM effectiveness, 228–229
Bell Atlantic, 225
Bendix, 157, 158
Benetton, as example of new competition, 4
Berkshire Hathaway, 201–202
Bethlehem Steel, 9, 225
B.F. Goodrich, 311
"Blameless review," 284
"Blueberry organization" (Peters), 13–14